COPING IN SPORT

THEORY, METHODS, AND RELATED CONSTRUCTS

COPING IN SPORT

THEORY, METHODS, AND RELATED CONSTRUCTS

ADAM R. NICHOLLS
EDITOR

Nova Science Publishers, Inc.
New York

LIBRARY OF CONGRESS CATALOGING-IN-PUBLICATION DATA

Coping in sport : theory, methods, and related constructs / editor, Adam R. Nicholls.
p. cm.
Includes index.
ISBN 978-1-60876-488-4 (hardcover)
1. Sports--Psychological aspects. 2. Athletes--Psychology. 3. Stress (Psychology) I.
Nicholls, Adam R.
GV706.4.C686 2009
796.01--dc22
                        2009038993

Published by Nova Science Publishers, Inc. † New York

CONTENTS

PREFACE

'Coping in Sport: Theory, Methods, and Related Constructs' is the first book dedicated exclusively to coping in sporting contexts. Edited by Adam R. Nicholls, a scholar whom has published extensively in the coping literatures, this book includes contributions from 26 leading international researchers including Yuri Hanin, Robert Grove, Peter Crocker, Deborah Feltz, and Patrick Gaudreau. This book covers information on a range of topics in relation to coping such as:

- Conceptualizing Coping
- Methodological Issues
- Coping and Moderating Variables such as Gender, Age, and Ethnicity
- Coping Effectiveness
- Future Orientated Aspects of Coping

Coping is related to a variety of other psychological constructs, which can be very diverse in nature. As such, a number of constructs that are related to coping are also discussed in this book:

- Personality and Mental Toughness
- Anxiety
- Self-Determination
- Achievement Goals
- Self-Concept and Self-Esteem
- Choking

Chapter 1 - The sport psychology coping literature is growing by the year, but there is still confusion regarding what coping is and the criterion required for a thought or behavior to be classified as a coping strategy. This is partly due to vast number of coping classifications and a general misunderstanding of coping. This chapter will attempt to clarify this problem and summarize the vast number of coping classifications that are used within in the coping literature in order to make these understandable for the reader. Finally, the chapter will conclude by evaluating the usefulness of categorizing coping strategies within dimensions.

Chapter 2 - Coping has been qualified as "constantly changing" and the process-oriented approach has been the dominant paradigm in the sport-related coping literature. Yet, the constantly changing properties of the coping construct remain under-specified in current definition, theory, and research on coping, both in the sport domain and in general psychology. What does it mean to assume that coping constantly changes? This chapter formulates a useful distinction between stability and consistency in coping utilization. Also, it proposes that coping can be studied across four levels of analysis (i.e., time, situation, context, or life in general) using both a state-like and a trait-like scope of analysis. This chapter delineates some of the many meanings attached to the notion of variability and stability/consistency by drawing on recent advances in personality theory. Empirical evidence from the sport literature are reviewed to demonstrate the normative/absolute, differential/relative, idiographic, idiographic/nomothetic, and structural stability/consistency and variability of the coping construct. It is argued that coping can combine intricate characteristics of stability, consistency, and change. Not all athletes change their coping across time and even the "changers" vary in both the magnitude and direction of their change in coping utilization and psychological adjustment. Such multinomial patterns of change highlights the need of moving beyond the sole reliance on traditional analyses of change and the need to abandon the dogmatic and nomothetic debate about the trait-like versus state-like nature of coping. This chapter concludes by presenting sophisticated quantitative approaches with potential of shedding new lights regarding the antecedents and consequences of individual differences in longitudinal coping utilization.

Chapter 3 - Over recent years, a variety of different methods have been employed in sport to measure coping among athletes. A large volume of research has used traditional methods such as questionnaires and interviews. However, more recently researchers have adapted different techniques from the mainstream psychology literature such as concept maps, diaries, think aloud protocols. One method that has not been used in sport, but has potential is Ecological Momentary Assessment. The purpose of this chapter is to describe the various methods used to assess coping, illustrate how each method can be used, and discuss its strengths and limitations.

Chapter 4 - This chapter reviews the various quantitative and qualitative research questions and methods that have been asked and used within coping in sport literature to date. The authors also discuss quantitative and qualitative research methods that could be used, but are generally not used or underrepresented, to better understand coping in sport. To this end, the authors discuss quantitative research designs predominantly focusing on mediation, moderator models, and multilevel and multilevel longitudinal modeling of coping. The authors also discuss various issues relevant to qualitative research including the need for prolonged time in the field, consideration of the number of participants, bracketing, and methods of data collection, analysis, and representation.

Chapter 5 - The aim of this chapter was to systematically review the recent literature on gender and coping in sport. In particular the authors examined gender differences in coping, whether males and females differed in the appraisal of stressors (e.g., stress intensity and perceived control of stress), and examined evidence for the situational and dispositional hypothesis among athletes. A detailed literature search of SPORTdiscus, Medline, PSYCHinfo, PSYCHarticles, yielded 16 studies spanning 19 years. Thirteen of these studies found gender differences in coping among athletes. However, the findings of these studies are equivocal and questionable, because important constructs such as type of the stressors and stressor appraisals were not controlled for in these studies. It is suggested that poor methodologies are preventing researchers from addressing the issue of whether male and female athletes cope differently and the underlying reasons for any such differences.

Chapter 6 - The past twenty-five years of sport psychology research has witnessed a burgeoning amount of attention to the study of coping. However, there have been few attempts to understand how athletes' coping changes across the lifespan. This chapter provides knowledge about the development of coping as it is studied in sport psychology. Specifically, three lines of research are reviewed: (a) the direct study of age-related differences in athletes' coping, (b) the indirect study of age-related differences in athletes' coping, and (c) maturation differences in athletes' coping. A developmental agenda for the study of coping in sport is offered. The authors conclude the chapter by addressing future directions for sport research.

Chapter 7 - This chapter addresses an area of coping with sport stress that has been relatively neglected; the influence of culture in the coping process. Culture reflects the customary practices and language associated with a particular racial or ethnic group, and influences a person's view of the world based on shared social beliefs and values. In competitive sport, culture reflects the athlete's values, psychological needs, expectations, habits, thought patterns, behavioral tendencies, and identity of a group that promote certain goal-directed actions that are accepted as "right" (i.e., appropriate) or "wrong" (i.e., inappropriate). Why should the authors be surprised when athletes from different cultures differ in their respective ways of coping with stress? Why, also, should be expect athletes of all cultures to experience and respond to stressful events in a similar manner? This chapter reviews selected studies on coping with sport stress. Far more studies have examined athletes from various countries, but relatively few studies in the sport coping literature have examined differences between cultures. It is concluded that culture serves as both a moderator and a mediator variable in various studies in attempting to improve the authors' understanding of the factors that affect the coping process in sport.

Chapter 8 - The role of personality on coping has received scant attention in the domain of sport. However, there are a number of ways how personality might influence coping either directly or indirectly among athletes. Evidence from other life domains is provided suggesting that personality can affect the type and frequency of stressors encountered, the appraisal of the stressor (including stress reactivity), coping, and coping effectiveness. These mechanisms are not independent from each other and suggest that certain personalities are more vulnerable or resistant to stress. In particular, individuals high in neuroticism might experience mood spill-overs and the so called neurotic cascade. Based on the general psychological literature, specific evidence is provided regarding how The Big Five personality dimensions extraversion, neuroticism, agreeableness, conscientiousness, and openness to experiences are related to stressor exposure, appraisal, and coping. The authors also discuss the role of the sport specific personality construct mental toughness in the stress-coping process. In particular, the different approaches to mental toughness are briefly discussed. A number of studies are discussed that support the notion that more mentally tough athletes are more like to appraise stressful situations as less severe and more under control. Also, mentally tough athletes are more likely to use problem-focused coping strategies to tackle the problem at hand rather than emotion-focused or avoidance coping strategies.

Chapter 9 - This chapter describes an individualized and evidence-based approach to coping with anxiety in high-achievement sport. The Individual Zones of Optimal Functioning (IZOF) model as applied to pre-competition anxiety and performance-related emotions is used as a framework to examine the relationship between *anxiety* and *emotion-focused* and *action-focused coping*. Anxiety is emotional experience (state-like, trait-like and meta-experience) and a component of *psychobiosocial* state which can be described along five basic dimensions: form, content, intensity, context and time. Individually optimal intensity of anxiety is used as criterion to evaluate if the current and anticipated anxiety should be reduced, increased, or maintained at a level that is optimal for the individual. Guidelines for *anxiety-centered* coping are proposed with the emphasis on emotion- and action-focused strategies that affect situational emotional experiences accompanying performance. The Identification-Control-Correction (ICC) program provides the step-wise procedures to optimize the process of task execution. Successful action-focused coping is reflected in emotion dynamics signaling a shift from the dysfunctional to functionally optimal person-environment (P-E) interactions. Both *reactive* and *anticipatory* coping strategies are relevant to achieve an optimal balance between current (or anticipated) task demands and personal resources. Future research should focus on coping with trait-like emotional experiences, meta-experiences, anticipatory coping, and the role of change and change management in coping.

Chapter 10 - Research on coping has traditionally focused on the situational, cognitive, and personality antecedents of coping utilization. However, Lazarus argued that coping is also influenced by motivational processes as goals and motives provide meaning to the person-situation transaction. This chapter explores the relationship between motivation and coping within the confines of self-determination theory. To this end, the underlying tenets of self-determination theory are presented to distinguish between self-determined and nonself-determined types of motivational orientations. Empirical evidences showing the cognitive, emotional, and behavioral advantages of self-determined motivation are briefly reviewed before delineating the adaptive processes through which coping and self-determination are linked. Then, sport and social psychology studies that investigated the associations between self-determination and coping are described. Researchers have recently questioned the directionality of this association as motivation and coping could influence each other in a complex reciprocal manner. Longitudinal studies are reviewed to explore the possibility that motivation influences coping which, in turn, produces meaningful changes in one's level of self-determined motivation. The chapter concludes by presenting future research directions aimed at further investigating the associations between coping and self-determination.

Chapter 11 - The purpose of this chapter is to discuss the role that achievement motivation plays in the authors' understanding of coping responses and strategies in sport. First, the authors outline the tenets of achievement goal theory by focusing on the original approaches championed by Nicholls and Dweck, as well as the role of motivational climate as a key situational factor. The body of academic knowledge illustrating the potential relationships between task and ego goals and coping is then reviewed. As an antecedent of coping-related behavior, a high task goal has been consistently associated with adaptive forms of coping, whereas an ego goal has been related to less adaptive coping responses. However, the methodological sophistication of past studies, the lack of understanding of the combined effects of task/ego goals, and the scarcity of studies at a situational level leaves many questions unanswered. A number of relevant future directions for this research area are therefore presented.

Chapter 12 - Relationships among appraisal, coping responses, and identity-related constructs such as self-concept and self-esteem are examined. Emphasis is placed on the way in which selected coping strategies may invoke affect regulation, self-protection, and self-enhancement mechanisms to help athletes maintain a positive sense of self in threatening circumstances. The specific threatening circumstances considered are impending competition, performance slumps, injury, and transitional experiences. A conceptual model of identity-maintenance coping at the individual level is presented, and a parallel model is proposed for identity-maintenance at the group-level.

Chapter 13 - This chapter discusses choking under pressure, which is presented as a case of self-destructive behavior that involves: ego threat, emotional distress, and self-regulation failure. When high levels of egotism are threatened, emotional distress often occurs. Athletes choke when they self-regulate to escape these unpleasant emotions (tradeoffs) or when they engage in mis-guided self-regulation strategies, which are also referred to as counterproductive strategies. The attempts to cope may backfire and cause performance failure (self-destruction). Empirical evidence, primarily from real-world research, is presented for each of these steps. Recommendations to prevent choking (reduce ego threat, normalize emotional distress, and optimize self-regulation) are based on this model and inspired by lessons learned from high-reliability organizations such as airlines and hospitals.

Chapter 14 - It is essential that athletes cope effectively with stress in order to maintain emotional well-being during competitive sports events. This chapter identifies which coping effectiveness model/theory/approach/explanation is the most appropriate for researchers and applied practitioners in sport settings. The outcome model, goodness-of-fit approach, the automaticity explanation of coping effectiveness, choice of coping strategy explanation of coping effectiveness, the path analysis of coping effectiveness model, and the research associated with these models is critically evaluated. Based on the current literature, it appears that the choice of coping strategy explanation is the most accurate and practical theory of coping effectiveness, as coping strategies appear to be predominantly effective or ineffective. Assessment issues, applied implications, and future research directions in the area of coping effectiveness are also considered.

Chapter 15 - An athlete's ability to cope with the environmental demands of stress in competition is important to successful performance. Coping self-efficacy (CSE), defined as the belief regarding one's ability to cope with diverse threats (e.g., stress, unwanted thoughts, difficult situations, or pain), is regarded as an important variable affecting an athlete's coping effectiveness. This chapter provides an overview of self-efficacy, the concept of CSE and its measurement, and a review of relevant research. The chapter ends with recommendations for researchers and practitioners on future directions in this area to prompt further research and inquiry.

Chapter 16 - Future-oriented coping describes how individuals respond to stressors as well as ways in which they may learn from these experiences and plan to deal with future stressors. Although some aspects of future-oriented coping have been reported in studies of competitive athletes, little research to date has adopted a future-oriented approach to studying coping. The authors suggest that future-oriented models of coping may offer a fresh perspective for thinking about the ways in which athletes cope with stressors in sport. Using models of coping which captures athletes' preparation, planning, and anticipation of stressors could reveal important insights into coping with stressors before their occurrence. In this chapter the authors describe two models of future-oriented coping which may be useful within a sport context. By considering coping from a future-oriented perspective, athletes may also learn how to cope more effectively with stressors and achieve better performances.

PART I: CONCEPTUALIZING COPING

In: Coping in Sport: Theory, Methods, and Related Constructs   ISBN: 978-1-60876-488-4
Editor: Adam R. Nicholls   © 2010 Nova Science Publishers, Inc.

Chapter 1

COPING CONCEPTUALIZED AND UNRAVELED

Adam R. Nicholls[1] and Richard C. Thelwell[2]
[1]University of Hull, UK
[2]University of Portsmouth, UK

ABSTRACT

The sport psychology coping literature is growing by the year, but there is still confusion regarding what coping is and the criterion required for a thought or behavior to be classified as a coping strategy. This is partly due to vast number of coping classifications and a general misunderstanding of coping. This chapter will attempt to clarify this problem and summarize the vast number of coping classifications that are used within in the coping literature in order to make these understandable for the reader. Finally, the chapter will conclude by evaluating the usefulness of categorizing coping strategies within dimensions.

INTRODUCTION

Research suggests that participating in competitive sport can be a stressful experience. Stress has recently been defined as "the quality of experience, produced through a person-environment transaction, that, through either over arousal or under-arousal results in psychological or physiological distress." The study of stress in sport has received considerable attention in recent years, due to the negative consequences that are associated with stress among athletes. For instance, failing to manage stress may result decreased performance (e.g., Haney and Long, 1995; Lazarus, 2000a), decreased satisfaction (e.g., Scanlan and Lewthwaite, 1984), increased risk of injury (e.g., Smith, Ptacek, and Smoll, 1992), decreased well-being (e.g., Nicholls, Backhouse, Polman, and McKenna, 2009), and the failure to pursue a career in professional sport (e.g., Holt and Hogg, 2004).

However, stress affects people differently (Aldwin, 2007). Not everybody suffers with problems in their performance when experiencing stress during sport, nor does every stressful experience result in performance decrements. Certain athletes seem to adapt or adjust to stressful conditions better and are subsequently able to operate more effectively. According to Lazarus and Folkman (1984) adaptation refers to the capacity of a person to survive and flourish. In order to survive and flourish people must be able to deal with stress effectively. One such mechanism that allows people to manage stress effectively is coping. Coping refers to all thoughts and behaviors that an individual deploys to manage a problem and the negative emotions the problem causes (Folkman and Lazarus, 1980).

Aldwin (2007) suggested that the rationale for studying coping is because coping can reduce and even diminish the effects of stress, and that there will be individual differences in responses to stress. It is therefore unsurprising that coping has received considerable interest among academics over a number of years in the domain of sport, but there is still confusion regarding conceptualizing this construct.

Voluntary versus Involuntary Responses to Stress

A salient issue within the conceptualization of coping relates to the contrast between the responses to stress that involve conscious effort and responses to stress that are automaticized, which are not under conscious control (Compas, Connor-Smith, Saltzman, Harding Thomsen, and Wadsworth, 2001). Some coping scholars from the mainstream literature (e.g., Coyne and Gottlieb, 1996; Skinner, 1995) have argued that coping should involve *all* responses to relieve stress, including both voluntary and involuntary responses. Alternatively, others have suggested that coping is limited to responses to stress that involve conscious effort (e.g., Compas et al., 2001; Lazarus and Folkman, 1984; Rudolph, Dennig, and Weisz, 1995). Connor-Smith, Compas, Wadsworth, Harding Thomsen, and Saltzman (2000) suggested that voluntary responses to stress are directed towards regulating cognitive, behavioral, emotional, or physiological responses stress.

There are some similarities between voluntary and involuntary responses to stress. Both involuntary and voluntary reactions are aroused when there is psychological disequilibrium. Furthermore, both voluntary and involuntary responses to stress serve to decrease negative affect and allow the individual to return to a sense of emotional well-being as soon as possible (Cramer, 1998). Although there are commonalities between voluntary responses to stress, coping scholars have proposed a number of arguments of why both involuntary and voluntary responses to stress should not be conceptualized as coping.

Not including involuntary acts as coping permits a much more concise definition of coping. If involuntary responses are included within this construct, coping would involve everything that an individual does in response to stress, making it very hard to measure (Lazarus, 1999; Lazarus and Folkman, 1984). For example, Aldwin (2007) suggested that involuntary emotional responses (e.g., crying) are not a coping response, but an emotional reaction. Conversely, expressing an emotion such as shouting at a team mate in response to stress has a purpose and could potentially be considered a coping strategy. However, if involuntary responses were conceptualized as coping, emotional reactions such as coping would have to be classified as coping. Secondly, people experience volitional and involuntary responses differently and are able to distinguish between behaviors and thoughts that are under control and those that are beyond their control (Skinner, 1995). It would therefore seem appropriate to distinguish volitional stress responses as coping, but not involitional responses. Involitional responses to stress include defense mechanisms. A defense mechanism refers to cognitions that alter or change the truthful perception and individual has, in order to protect the person from experiencing too much anxiety (Cramer, 1998). However, both Cramer (2000) and Lazarus (2000b) stated that involitional responses to stress should be differentiated between volitional responses to stress. Finally, voluntary and involuntary processes may react differently to interventions that are designed to teach people to manage responses to stress. Such interventions can only indirectly influence involuntary processes (Compas et al., 2001). As such, we believe that only volitional acts that are directed towards managing stress should be considered as coping.

Management Skills

Aldwin (2007) suggested that it is important to differentiate coping with management skills, so that this psychological process is not mistakenly called coping. A management skill is a thought or behavior that has been established out of learning to cope with a problem, but is performed so often to the extent that it becomes a routine. Such behaviors or thoughts are often performed in the in the absence of stress and are therefore no longer coping strategies, but are indeed management skills (Aldwin and Brustrom, 1996). For instance, two athletes called Paul and Michael, who recently participated in a tennis competition, used visualization prior to hitting a serve. However, Paul was not experiencing any stress, but merely used this strategy because it was part of his routine and it was something his coach had encouraged him to do. Conversely, Michael was experiencing stress when he used visualization, just before hitting a serve. In this hypothetical example, visualization could be classified as coping strategy for Michael, but not Paul. Visualization for Paul was not an attempt to cope; rather it was what Aldwin (Aldwin, 2007; Aldwin and Brustrom) termed a management skill. The key differences between these examples relates to stress (stress vs. no stress) and the act of visualizing (non-routine vs. routine). Therefore, to determine whether an athlete was coping or not, researchers should ensure that athletes (a) have or are experiencing stress and (b) the purpose of the strategy was to reduce stress.

Classifying Coping

Although the literature within the coping domain has evolved rapidly in recent years, so has the divergence in terms of how it has been classified. In part, this has stemmed from researchers such as Pearlin and Schooler (1978) who stated that "coping needs more detailed specification…because of the bewildering richness of behaviour relevant to it." With the above in mind, it is imperative for researchers and practitioners to gain a better understanding to how coping is currently classified across varying populations (i.e., childhood, adolescence, adulthood, or old age; see Chapter 6, by Hoar and Evans for more details) and attempt, where appropriate, to move towards a common set of coping classifications. The following will provide an insight to the varying classifications of coping, and where relevant, will include sport specific examples.

Prior to discussing the varying classifications of coping, it is important to consider that researchers have frequently debated whether to consider general coping dimensions (also referred to as macro-level approaches) or specific categories of coping (also referred to as micro-level coping dimensions; Connor-Smith, 2000; Crocker, Kowalski, and Graham, 1998; Hoar, Kowalski, Gaudreau, and Crocker, 2006). This chapter will focus on the macro- level of coping with references to the micro levels being made within each classification. Further to this, Skinner, Edge, Altman, and Sherwood, (2003) reported three distinctions of coping: (1) functions of coping, (2) varying ways of coping, and (3) higher order categories. The following will work through each distinction and detail the coping categories.

FUNCTIONS OF COPING

Problem- and Emotion-Focused Coping

The most commonly reported functions of coping are those that relate to either problem- or emotion-focused coping. Problem-focused coping is reported as that which is "aimed at managing or altering the problem causing the distress" while emotion-focused coping reflects efforts to "regulate emotional responses to the problem" (Lazarus and Folkman, 1984, p.150). Within problem-focused coping, it is likely that individuals will attempt to seek information, plan strategies and set goals. For example, in their work examining coping strategies of golfers, Nicholls and Polman (2008) reported strategies such as shot planning the shot and conducting pre-shot routines as typical problem-focused strategies, whilst Reeves, Nicholls, and McKenna (2009) identified increases in effort and communicating to others as problem-focused approaches within a soccer context. Typical examples of emotion-focused strategies include those such as relaxation, meditation and seeking emotional support. Indeed Nicholls and Polman (2008) reported visualization to enhance relaxation and using positive appraisals as forms of emotion-focused coping. Social support and venting emotions have also been labeled amongst the vast array of emotion-focused approaches (see Reeves et al., 2009).

Appraisal-Focused Coping

Despite the preferences by researchers to refer to problem- and emotion-focused coping with regularity, a further category within the functions of coping has also emerged, namely appraisal coping (Cox and Ferguson, 1991). Here, Moos and Billings (1982) asserted that appraisal-focused coping referred to efforts made towards redefining the meaning of the situation. Consequently, athletes would be advised to reappraise situations from, for example, perceived 'threatening' situations towards more of a 'challenge' situation. A typical scenario could be a performer who has experienced difficulty in certain environmental conditions and rather than appraising the environment as a 'failure-inducing environment' they would be advised to employ a coping strategy that enables them to approach the environment in a challenging manner.

Despite the widespread employment of problem- and emotion-focused coping and to a lesser degree, appraisal coping, Skinner et al. (2003) suggest that such classifications should no longer be employed. The argument here being that researchers have treated the coping types as being mutually exclusive which in turn has lead to an oversimplification of the way in which coping operates. Further to this Lazarus (1996) commented that ways of coping are not to be labeled as functions and instead, problem, emotion, and appraisal approaches should be referred to as action types that have functions, especially given that action types often serve more than one function.

WAYS OF COPING

Approach Verses Avoidance Coping

The most commonly presented ways of coping reflect those of approach and avoidance coping and in short refer to the "cognitive and emotional activity that is oriented either toward or away from threat" (Roth and Cohen, 1986, p.813). More specifically, approach coping involves confronting the stressor and then deliberately attempting to reduce it via strategies that enable the taking of direct action, increased effort and planning. Examples of this have been reported by Holt and Dunn (2004) in their study of female soccer players where responses to performance mistakes (stressor) included making an extra effort and arriving early for practice sessions and to then employ mental preparation strategies to improve focus within the practice session. In contrast, avoidance coping includes both psychological (e.g., cognitive distancing) and behavioral (e.g., removing self from the situation) efforts to disengage from the situation (Krohne, 1993, 1996). Similar to approach-coping, avoidance coping has also been reported in a number of coping studies in sport. For example, Thelwell, Weston, and Greenlees (2007) in their study of stress and coping in professional cricket batters reported batters to either 'ignore the situation,' 'avoid the issue,' and make excuses for the performance' so that they did not have to confront the stressor.

While much of the literature reporting 'ways of coping' refer to the approach and avoidance terminology, other variants of this categorization have used terminology such as monitoring verses blunting (Miller, 1987; Miller, Brody, and Summerton, 1988), sensitization verses repression (Byrne, 1964), and information seeking verses information avoiding (Peterson and Toler, 1986). With regard to monitoring verses blunting, individuals may employ a high level of monitoring where they scan the environment for threat-relevant information. This requires the individual seeking information about a stressful event and could be exemplified in a sporting scenario by an athlete who is warming up for a performance and scanning the environment for a player whom they have struggled against before. As such, they are searching for information that is high in potential threat. Alternatively, the opposite could apply where individuals are classed as being low in monitoring when they ignore and avoid threat-relevant information. A related example of this is when an athlete decides against reading about a performer whom they have struggled against in the past. With regard to blunting, individuals who are high in this approach will make efforts to cognitively distract themselves from threat-relevant cues and as such will engage in distracting activities. A typical example of this would be the use of an iPod (to listen to music or to watch themselves in action on a video) to distract themselves from what is going on around them to enhance focus on themselves. On the contrary, an individual towards the lower end will demonstrate a lack of effort to cognitively distract themselves from threat-relevant situations and will not engage in distracting activities.

A further variation on approach and avoidance coping is that of sensitization verses repression coping. Sensitization refers to individuals approaching threatening stimuli and not repressing the associated affect. Repression coping is symbolized by individuals avoiding threatening stimuli and repressing negative affect. Yet another view to this way of coping is that of the information seeking verses information avoiding distinction. Information seeking refers to efforts made by the individual to acquire information regarding the stressor, such as asking questions and using observation. Contrary to this, information avoiding reflects the efforts made to avoid information relating to the stressor and may be associated with an absence of behaviours relating to information seeking. In sport, such coping approaches are often adopted where information relating to, for example, opponents, conditions, environments, and officials is often sought after. Although the generic terms of approach and avoidance coping are popular with researchers, it is very much the case that the requests for greater specificity from authors such as Pearlin and Schooler (1978) has resulted in widespread variance of the distinction.

Active Verses Passive Coping

Another frequently reported way of coping falls within the active verses passive distinction (Peterson, 1989; Rudolph, Dennig, and Weisz, 1995). In short, active coping is where the individual demonstrates a willingness to encounter information via asking questions and observing preparation. An example of this within sport would be a performer who is prepared to find out information regarding a forthcoming encounter. Such information may relate to the environment that they will compete in, the likely behaviour of the opponents, typical challenges that will face them, or the officials for the competition. Put together, such coping affords the individual the opportunity to prepare for the potential eventualities that they may experience. On the contrary, passive coping is explained by individuals having a tendency to avoid or deny stress where they would ignore information during preparation. Illustrations of this would include situations where performers are happy to turn up and perform, where in essence they are not enabling themselves to become embroiled in behaviors that trigger stress responses. For example, if a performer had experienced performance difficulties against a particular opponent before, it may be that they attempt to ignore all information relating to the performance, and in particular the potential opponent until the very last minute prior to performance. As such, the passive coping enables them to withstand any of the stress responses that may relate to the performance.

Behavioral Verses Cognitive Coping

A further distinction of coping is of behavioral and cognitive coping (Compas, Connor, Saltzman, Harding, Thomson, and Wadsworth, 1999; Rudolph et al. 1995). Behavioral coping refers to the external mode of coping such as seeking support, information seeking, and the employment of direct efforts to maintain control whereas cognitive coping reflects the ability to employ internal modes of coping such as diversionary thinking or attempts to divert thoughts away from the stressor and positive cognitive restructuring (Curry and Russ, 1985; Worchel, Copeland, and Barker, 1987). An example of behavioral and cognitive coping could be encapsulated within a pre-performance routine where athletes engage in appropriate actions and thoughts in an attempt to enable them to focus on relevant stimuli prior to performance rather than inappropriate stimuli such as potential stressors.

Engagement Versus Disengagement Coping

There has also been a vast amount of research that examined the distinction between engagement and disengagement coping (e.g., Ebata and Moos, 1991; Long, 1998; Tobin, Holroyd, Reynolds, and Wigal, 1989). Essentially, engagement coping involves the individual responding in a manner that is oriented toward the stressor or towards emotions and thoughts related to the stressor. On the contrary, disengagement coping relates to situations where the responses are oriented away from the stressor or the related cognitions and emotions. Whilst there is a resemblance to approach and avoidance ways of coping, the engagement-disengagement dimension is broader due to avoidance representing only one way in which the individual can disengage. As such, it was commented that the engagement-disengagement distinction was overly broad and necessitated a focus on more distinct subtypes of coping then that previously presented (e.g., Connor-Smith et al. 2000). As a consequence, Gaudreau, Ali, and Marivain (2005) in their work with marathon runners developed an enhanced approach to the engagement-disengagement distinction, where they proposed three ways of coping that included task-oriented coping (e.g., thought control, seeking support, and logical analysis), distraction-oriented (e.g., distancing and mental distraction) and disengagement-oriented coping (e.g., venting of unpleasant emotions and disengagement/resignation). While the three ways of coping were proposed as being appropriate macro-level dimensions of coping for the population under scrutiny, the authors did air caution to the appropriateness of the dimension across all sporting activities.

Alternative Ways of Coping

In addition to the aforementioned approaches that have received attention within the literature, there are some additional ways of coping that are worthy of mentioning. The first is that of the control verses escape distinction which has been referred to as the 'proactive take-charge approach' verses the 'staying clear of the person or situation' (Latack and Havlovich, 1992). Closely matching this distinction is the proactive way of coping that has been referred to as "efforts undertaken in advance of a potentially stressful event to prevent it or modify its form before it occurs" (Aspinwall and Taylor, 1997). A penultimate way of coping is reflected in the social verses solidarity distinction. Here Latack and Havlovich (1992) refer to coping attempts that include the involvement of others verses those that are conducting alone. Although sparsely reported, this approach may be employed in sporting situations where for example individuals attempt to surround themselves with others to benefit from the potential distractions that they might bring or the support that they provide or prefer to isolate themselves from others because the very reasons mentioned as potential benefits of the social form of coping create further stress responses. A final way of coping is that of alloplastic verses autoplastic coping. Perez and Reicherts (1992) assert that this reflects the coping efforts made by an individual to change the environment compared to those made towards changing the self. In sporting situations, it is likely that the alloplastic form of coping would be inappropriate given that the environments in which athletes perform are either fixed or dynamic in nature, meaning that the individual has a limited ability to influence the environment in which they perform due to its constraints having been previously identified.

HIGHER ORDER CATEGORIES OF COPING

Primary Verses Secondary Coping

The final set of distinctions with regard to coping reflects those that are hierarchical in nature. To this end, the most frequently reported are those that are based on a primary-secondary model of control (Rothbaum Weisz, and Snyder, 1982; Weisz, McCabe, and Dennig, 1994). Previously, researchers employed the phrases assimilation and accommodation coping, instead of primary and secondary control coping (e.g., Brandtstädter and Renner, 1990). Primary control is defined as coping that is "designed to influence objective events or conditions" while secondary control is that which is "aimed at maximizing one's fit to current conditions." Relinquished control reflects "the absence of any coping attempt" (Rudolph et al., 1995, pp. 331). As outlined by Connor-Smith et al. (2000), this approach is most commonly employed by viewing the primary and secondary distinction as a pair of higher order categories that include lower order ways of coping. For example, lower order categories for primary control coping often include instrumental action and problem solving (similar to that reported in problem-focused coping) while lower order categories for secondary control coping include cognitive restructuring or self-talk relating to situation acceptance. As such, this approach is regarded as being the only model that enables the assessment of coping responses and goals as distinct constructs. Although not readily employed within sport, a performer dealing with a performance error may describe a primary coping response ("try not to do what I did last time") and a primary control goal ("so I can do it correctly this time and show what I can do"), a secondary control coping response ("try not to think about what happened last time") and a secondary control goal ("so I can focus on what I need to do this time and keep the worries about the last performance away"), a primary control coping response ("discuss the issue with the coach") and a secondary control goal ("so he /she can reassure me that I am doing the right thing"), or a secondary control coping response ("think about the excitement of doing it well and succeeding") and a primary control goal ("so that I just go and do what I need to without thinking too much," c.f. Rudolph et al., 1995).

ASSESSING COPING STRATEGIES AS DIMENSIONS

A possible limitation of assessing coping at the dimensional level is that a single coping strategy could be classified within more than one dimension (Compas, Worsham, Ey, and Howell, 1996; Lazarus, 1999; Skinner et al., 2003), making it very difficult to accurately classify a coping strategy within a dimension. For example, Phil may plan a supplementary training schedule due to the distress he is experiencing from a lack of fitness. This would appear to be an example of coping that should be classified within the task-orientated or problem-focused dimension of coping. However, Phil may have also been trying to distract himself by devising a plan, so this strategy could have also been classified in the distraction-orientated dimension. Indeed, Lazarus (1999) suggested that even though it may seem straightforward or "seductive" to classify coping strategies within distinct dimensions, they are seldom separated if ever. Researchers should consider this issue when categorizing coping.

CONCLUDING REMARKS

Despite differences among researchers with regards to classifying both voluntary and involuntary or just voluntary responses to stress, we feel that behaviors or thoughts should only be considered coping if they are volitional response to stress. Additionally, there are a number of different ways to classify coping, which have widely been ignored within the sport literature. A recent review by Nicholls and Polman (2007) revealed that over 80% of published studies adhered to the framework of coping proposed by Lazarus and Folkman (1984) and thus adopted the problem- and emotion-focused classification of coping. In order to gain more insight into coping among athletes researchers could consider classifying coping within the different frameworks.

REFERENCES

Aldwin, C. M. (2007). *Stress, coping and development: An integrative perspective* (2nd ed.). New York: Guilford Press.

Aldwin, C. M., and Brustrom, J. (1997). Theories of coping with chronic stress: Illustrations from the health psychology and aging literatures. In B. Gottlieb (Ed.), *Coping with chronic stress* (pp. 75-103). New York: Plenum Press.

Brandtstädter, J., and Renner, G. (1990). Tenacious goal pursuit and flexible goal adjustment: Explication and age-related analysis of assimilative and accommodative strategies of coping. *Psychology and Aging, 5,* 58-67.

Byrne, D. (1964). Repression-sensitization as a dimension of personality. In B.A. Maher (Ed.), *Progress in experimental personality research* (Vol. 1, pp. 169-220). New York: Academic Press.

Compas, B. E., Connor, J. K., Osowiecki, D., and Welch, A. (1997). Effortful and involuntary responses to stress: Implications for coping with chronic stress. In B.J. Gottlieb (Ed.), *Coping with chronic stress* (pp. 105-130). New York: Plenum Press.

Compas, B. E., Connor, J. K., Saltzman, H., Thomson, A. H., and Wadsworth, M. E. (1999). Getting specific about coping: Effortful and involuntary responses to stress in development. In M.Lewis and D. Ramsay (Eds.), *Soothing and stress* (pp. 229-256). New York: Cambridge University Press.

Compas, B. E., Connor-Smith, J. K., Saltzman, H., Harding Thomsen, A., and Wadsworth, M. E. (2001). Coping with stress during childhood and adolescence: Problems, progress, and potential in theory and research. *Psychological Bulletin, 12,* 87-127.

Compas, B. E., Worsham, N., Ey, S., and Howell, D. C. (1996). When mom or dad has cancer: II Coping, cognitive appraisals, and psychological distress in children of cancer patients. *Health Psychology, 15,* 167-175.

Connor-Smith, J. K., Compas, B. E., Wadsworth, M. E., Thomsen, A. H., and Saltzman, H. (2000). Responses to stress in adolescence: Measurement of coping and involuntary stress responses. *Journal of Consulting and Clinical Psychology, 68,* 976–992.

Cox, T., and Ferguson, E. (1991). Individual differences, stress and coping. In C.L. Cooper and R. Payne (Eds.), *Personality and stress: Individual differences in the stress process* (pp. 7-30). Chichester, UK: Wiley.

Coyne, J. C., and Gottlieb, B. J. (1996). The mismeasure of coping by checklist. *Journal of Personality, 64,* 959-991.

Cramer, P. (1998). Coping and defense mechanisms: What's the difference? *Journal of Personality, 66,* 895-918.

Cramer, P. (2000). Defense mechanisms in psychology today: Further processes for adaptation. *American Psychologist, 55,* 637-646.

Crocker, P. R. E., and Graham, T. R. (1995). Coping by competitive athletes with performance stress: Gender differences and relationships with affect. *The Sport Psychologist, 9,* 325-338.

Crocker, P. R. E., Kowalski, K. C., and Graham, T. R. (1998). Measurement of coping strategies in sport. In J.L. Duda (Ed.), *Advances in sport and exercise psychology measurement* (pp. 149-161). Morgantown, WV: Fitness Information Technology.

Curry, S. L., and Russ, S. W. (1985). Identifying coping strategies in children. *Journal of Clinical Child Psychology, 14,* 61-69.

Ebata, A. T., and Moos, R. H. (1991). Coping and adjustment in distressed and healthy adolescents. *Journal of Applied Developmental Psychology, 12,* 33-54.

Eubank, M., and Collins D. (2000). Coping with pre- and in-event fluctuations in competitive state anxiety: A longitudinal approach. *Journal of Sports Sciences, 18*, 121-131.

Folkman, S., and Lazarus, R. S. (1980). An analysis of coping in a middle-aged community sample. *Journal of Health and Social Behavior, 21,* 219-239.

Gaudreau, P., and Blondin, J-P. (2002). Development of a questionnaire for the assessment of coping strategies employed by athletes in competitive sport settings. *Psychology of Sport and Exercise, 3,* 1-34.

Gaudreau, P., Ali, M. E., and Marivain, T. (2005). Factor structure of the coping inventory for competitive sport with a sample of participants at the 2001 New York marathon. *Psychology of Sport and Exercise, 6,* 271-288.

Giacobbi, P. R., Foore, B., and Weinberg, R. S. (2004). Broken clubs and expletives: The sources of stress and coping responses of skilled and moderately skilled golfers. *Journal of Applied Sport Psychology, 16,* 166-182.

Gould, D., Eklund, R. C., and Jackson, S. A. (1993). Coping strategies used by US Olympic wrestlers. *Research Quarterly for Exercise and Sport, 64,* 83-93.

Haney, C. J., and Long, B. C. (1995). Coping effectiveness: A path analysis of self-efficacy, control, coping and performance in sport competitions. *Journal of Applied Social Psychology, 25,* 1726-1746.

Hoar, S. D., Kowalski, K. C., Gaudreau, P., and Crocker, P. R. E. (2006). A review of coping in sport. In S. Hanton and S.D. Mellalieu (Eds.), *Literature reviews in sport psychology.* New York: Nova.

Holt, N. L., and Dunn, J. G. H. (2004). Longitudinal idiographic analyses of appraisal and coping responses in sport. *Psychology of Sport and Exercise, 5,* 213-222.

Krohne, H. W. (1993).Vigilance and cognitive avoidance as concepts in coping research. In H.W. Krohne (Ed.), *Attention and avoidance: Strategies in coping with aversiveness.* (pp. 19-50). Seattle, WA: Hogrefe and Huber.

Krohne, H. W. (1996). Individual differences in coping: In M. Zeidner and N.S. Endler (Eds.), *Handbook of coping: Theory, research, and application* (pp. 381-409). New York: Wiley Lazarus, R. S. (1999). *Stress and emotion: A new synthesis.* New York: Springer.

Latack, J. C., and Havlovich , S. J. (1992). Coping with job stress: A conceptual evaluation framework for coping measures. *Journal of Organizational Behavior, 13,* 479-508.

Lazarus, R. S. (1996). The role of coping in the emotions and how coping changes over the life course. In C. Maletesta-Magni and S.H. McFadden (Eds.), *Handbook of emotion, adult development, and aging* (pp.289-306). New York: Academic Press.

Lazarus, R. S. (2000a). How emotions influence performance in competitive sports. *The Sport Psychologist, 14*, 229-252.

Lazarus, R. S. (2000b). Toward better research on stress and coping. *American Psychologist, 55*, 665-673.

Lazarus, R. S., and Folkman, S. (1984). *Stress, appraisal and coping.* New York: Springer.

Long, B.C. (1998). Coping with workplace stress: A multi-group comparison of female managers and clerical workers. *Journal of Counseling Psychology, 45,* 65-78.

Miller, S. M. (1987). Monitoring and blunting: Validation of a questionnaire to assess the styles of information seeking under threat. *Journal of Personality and Social Psychology, 52,* 345-353.

Miller, S. M., Brody, D. S., and Summerton, J. (1988). Styles of coping with threat: Implications for health. *Journal of Social Psychology, 54,* 142-148.

Moos, R. H., and Billings, A. G. (1982). Conceptualizing and measuring coping resources and coping processes. In L. Goldberger and S. Breznitz (Eds.), *Handbook of stress: Theoretical and clinical aspects* (pp. 212-230). New York: Free Press.

Nicholls, A. R., Backhouse, S. H., Polman R.C. J., and McKenna, J. (2009). Stressors and affective states among professional rugby union players. *Scandinavian Journal of Medicine and Science in Sports, 19,* 121-128.

Nicholls, A. R., Holt, N. L., and Polman, R. C. J. (2005). A phenomenological analysis of coping effectiveness in golf. *The Sport Psychologist, 19,* 111-130.

Nicholls, A.R., and Polman, R.C.J. (2008). Think aloud: Acute stress and coping strategies during golf performances. *Anxiety, Stress, and Coping, 21,* 283-294.

Pearlin, L. I., and Schooler, C. (1978). The structure of coping. *Journal of Health and Social Behavior, 19,* 2-21.

Perrez, M., and Reicherts, M. (1992). *Stress, coping, and health.* Seattle, WA: Hogrefe and Huber.

Peterson, L. (1989). Coping by children undergoing stressful medical procedures: Some conceptual, methodological, and therapeutic issues. *Journal of Consulting and Clinical Psychology, 57,* 380-387.

Peterson, L., and Toler, S. M. (1986). An information seeking disposition in child surgery patients. *Health Psychology, 4,* 343-359.

Reeves, C.W., Nicholls, A. R., and McKenna, J. (2009) Stressors and coping strategies among early and middle adolescent premier league academy soccer players: Differences according to age. *Journal of Applied Sport Psychology, 21,* 31-48.

Roth, S., and Cohen, L. J. (1986). Approach, avoidance, and coping with stress. *American Psychologist, 41,* 813-819.

Rothbaum, F., Weisz, J. R., and Snyder, S. S. (1982). Changing the world and changing the self: A two-process model of perceived control. *Journal of Personality and Social Psychology, 42,* 5-37.

Rudolph, K. D., Dennig, M. D., and Weisz, J. R. (1995). Determinants and consequences of children's coping in the medical setting: Conceptualization, review, and critique. *Psychological Bulletin, 118,* 328-357.

Scanlan, T. K., and Lewthwaite, R. (1984). Social psychological aspects of competition for male youth sport participants: I. Predictors of competitive stress. *Journal of Sport Psychology, 6,* 208-226.

Skinner, E. A. (1995). *Perceived control, motivation, and coping.* Thousand Oaks, CA: Sage.

Skinner, E.A., Edge, K., Altman, J., and Sherwood, H. (2003). Searching for the structure of coping: A review and critique of category systems for classifying ways of coping. *Psychological Bulletin, 129,* 216-269.

Smith, R. E., Ptacek, J. T., and Smoll, F. L. (1992). Sensation seeking, stress, and adolescent injuries: A test of stressbuffering, risk-taking, and coping skills hypotheses. *Journal of Personality and Social Psychology, 62,* 1016_/24.

Thelwell, R. C., Weston, N. J. V., and Greenlees, I.A. (2007). Batting on a sticky wicket: Identifying sources of stress and associated coping strategies for professional cricket batsmen. *Psychology of Sport and Exercise, 8,* 219-232.

Tobin, D. L., Holroyd, K. A., Reynolds, R. V., and Wigal, J. K. (1989). The hierarchical factor structure of the Coping Strategies Inventory. *Cognitive Therapy and Research, 13,* 343-361.

Weisz, J R., McCabe, M. A., and Dennig, M .D. (1994). Primary and secondary control among children undergoing medical procedures: Adjustment as a function of coping style. *Journal of Consulting and Clinical Psychology, 62,* 324-332.

Worchel, F. F., Copeland, D. R., and Barker, D. G. (1987). Control-related coping strategies in pediatric oncology patients. *Journal of Pediatric Psychology, 12,* 25-38.

In: Coping in Sport: Theory, Methods, and Related Constructs   ISBN: 978-1-60876-488-4
Editor: Adam R. Nicholls   © 2010 Nova Science Publishers, Inc.

Chapter 2

COPING ACROSS TIME, SITUATIONS, AND CONTEXTS: A CONCEPTUAL AND METHODOLOGICAL OVERVIEW OF ITS STABILITY, CONSISTENCY, AND CHANGE

Patrick Gaudreau and Dave Miranda
University of Ottawa, Canada

ABSTRACT

Coping has been qualified as "constantly changing" and the process-oriented approach has been the dominant paradigm in the sport-related coping literature. Yet, the constantly changing properties of the coping construct remain under-specified in current definition, theory, and research on coping, both in the sport domain and in general psychology. What does it mean to assume that coping constantly changes? This chapter formulates a useful distinction between stability and consistency in coping utilization. Also, it proposes that coping can be studied across four levels of analysis (i.e., time, situation, context, or life in general) using both a state-like and a trait-like scope of analysis. This chapter delineates some of the many meanings attached to the notion of variability and stability/consistency by drawing on recent advances in personality theory. Empirical evidence from the sport literature are reviewed to demonstrate the normative/absolute, differential/relative, idiographic, idiographic/nomothetic, and structural stability/consistency and variability of the coping construct. It is argued that coping can combine intricate characteristics of stability, consistency, and change. Not all athletes change their coping across time and even the "changers" vary in both the magnitude and direction of their change in coping utilization and psychological adjustment. Such multinomial patterns of change highlights the need of moving beyond the sole reliance on traditional analyses of change and the need to abandon the dogmatic and nomothetic debate about the trait-like versus state-like nature of coping. This chapter concludes by presenting sophisticated quantitative approaches with potential of shedding new lights regarding the antecedents and consequences of individual differences in longitudinal coping utilization.

INTRODUCTION

Coping can combine intricate characteristics of stability, consistency, and change, although the latter became the dominant paradigm. Indeed, in one of its most authoritative definitions, coping is conceptualized as the "constantly changing cognitive and behavioral efforts to manage specific external and/or internal demands that are appraised as taxing or exceeding the resources of the person" (Lazarus and Folkman, 1984, p. 141). Accordingly, a recent systematic review by Nicholls and Polman (2007a) revealed that over 80% of coping studies in the sport domain have been strongly influenced by such process-oriented definition. But first of all, what does it mean to assume that coping *constantly changes*? Does it mean that we expect all individuals to change their coping actions homogeneously or should we expect heterogeneity from individual differences in the magnitude and direction of change over time and situations? What are the different conceptual meanings tied to the seemingly opposite notions of stability/consistency and change in coping utilization across time, situations, and contexts? What does the literature reveal about stability and consistency of coping in the sport domain? Unfortunately, such fundamental questions have received limited attention in the coping literature in sport. Therefore, it is important to revisit some underlying assumptions of the influential *transactional approach*, as they were initially articulated by Lazarus and Folkman (1984).

Distinguishing Stability and Consistency in Coping

The model of Lazarus and Folkman (1984) encourages the examination of state-like coping, which represents the *"actual or momentary utilization of coping strategies in a particular situation at a particular point in time"* (Lazarus and Folkman, 1984, p. 297). On the basis of this paradigm, researchers interested in delineating the changing properties of coping responses are invited to measure the same individuals across multiple times, situations, or contexts. In research settings precluding the use of longitudinal methodologies, researchers are encouraged to ask individuals to report what they did to manage the requirements of a specific situation. For instance, the Coping Function Questionnaire (Kowalski and Crocker, 2001) requires participants to report their coping effort in reference to the most stressful situation experienced in the past 12 months. Similarly, the Coping Inventory for Competitive Sport (Gaudreau and Blondin, 2002) instructs athletes to report how they have been coping during their last sport competition. Even the seminal qualitative research of Gould, Eklund, and Jackson (1993) asked elite athletes to report their coping efforts used to manage the requirements of the Olympic Games. Overall, these measurement strategies, albeit relying on cross-sectional methodologies, can be considered as attempts to capture coping in a particular situation at a particular point in time.

Although research has been skewed in favor of this process orientation, it can be argued that the "constantly changing" properties of coping remain under-specified in the definition of Lazarus and Folkman (1984). After all, what is exactly meant when asserting that coping constantly changes, does it entail that coping should change across time within the unfolding of a given situation or across situations as they are compared within a particular life domain? For such matters, the classic distinction between *stability vs. consistency* holds great promise for clarifying the changing properties of coping (for a review, see Fleeson and Noftle, 2008). This distinction is not novel in the sport-related coping literature (Schutz, 1998). Nonetheless, this distinction necessitates further specifications to account for an array of possible situations of interest for both researchers and practitioners.

Stability or the lack of thereof, refers to the extent to which individuals are coping in a similar manner across time within the same situation or context. For instance, a research program could examine how athletes cope across multiple sport competitions over the course of a season (Louvet, Gaudreau, Menaut, Genty, and Deneuve, 2007, 2009) or how they manage the requirements of training across distinct training sessions (Crocker and Isaak, 1997).

Consistency can take several forms (Fleeson and Noftle, 2008). One form of consistency represents the extent to which individuals cope in a similar manner across distinct situations within a particular life domain (*within-domain cross-situational consistency*). As such, a research program could compare coping across multiple sport-related situations such as competition, training, and conflicting interpersonal relationships. Traditionally, researchers have examined this form of consistency by asking participants to report a series of challenging/stressful situations to compare their coping utilization across these events (e.g., Bouffard and Crocker, 1992; Giacobbi Jr. and Weinberg, 2000). Another instance of consistency would represent the examination of coping across distinct situations across different contexts (*cross-domain cross-situational consistency*). Hence, a researcher might examine how students-athletes cope with the distinct requirements of specific situations in the sport and academic domains (Sellers, 1995; Sellers and Peterson, 1993). More globally, it is also possible to examine consistency across distinct life domains by asking individuals to report how generally cope in sport, school, part-time work, relationships with a romantic partner, and friendships (*cross-domain consistency*).

The process-oriented approach has fruitfully encouraged researchers to embrace a fine-grained outlook to the study of coping (Somerfeld, 1997). For instance, Folkman and Lazarus (1985) proposed that situations can be divided in naturally occurring stages with distinct demands likely to generate changes in coping utilization. For instance, achievement-related stressors such as sport competitions, school exams, and job interviews can be divided in pre-situation, intra-situation, and post-situation phases likely to render changes in coping utilization (*within-situation consistency*). Research in both school and sport has taken advantage of this natural segmentation to examine the within-situation patterning of coping during the unfolding of sport competition (Gaudreau, Blondin, and Lapierre, 2002; Gaudreau, Lapierre, and Blondin, 2001) and academic examination (e.g., Carver and Scheier, 1994; Raffety, Smith, and Ptacek, 1997). Similarly, situations such as surgeries (e.g., Sorlie and Sexton, 2001) and cancer treatments (e.g., Carver, Pozo, Harris, Noriega, and et al., 1993) all subsume distinct phases in which individuals face distinct demands likely to render changes in coping utilization. Research in the sport domain has examined coping across distinct phases of physical rehabilitation following injuries (e.g., Udry, 1997). Another example in the sport domain would be the examination of coping across naturally occurring performance episodes (Beal, Weiss, Barros, and MacDermid, 2005) such as periods in hockey, lanes in bowling, holes in golf, or innings in baseball. Crocker and Isaak (1997) relied on such an episodic approach in which coping of swimmers was examined across three distinct swim meets during a sport competition.

As depicted herein, the study of coping across time, situations, and domains is a multifaceted enterprise propelled by the impetus to examine what people actually do during a given time frame, in a precise situation, or in a specific context. The study of both stability and consistency is useful to understand how coping unfolds across time and how it manifests itself across situations and contexts. The finer-grained approach is also commendable as it provides rich and precise descriptions of coping across subcomponents of a particular stressful situation. It is our contention that all types of stability/consistency are required for a complete understanding of the coping construct. Researchers are invited to choose the approach that is compatible with their research question and amenable to empirical testing, rather than judging a particular approach as inherently and definitively favorable or unfavorable on the basis of some dogmatic thinking.

Trait and State Coping: Distinguishing Level and Scope of Analysis

Despite their strong interest for a situational approach, Lazarus and Folkman (1984) originally conceived coping as a multi-level construct that could be measured both at the trait and state levels. In this context, dispositional/trait coping represents the usual or recurrent utilization of coping strategies across contexts, situations, and time. Rather than providing contradictory information to the situational/state approach, it can be argued that dispositional/trait and situational/state coping are yielding a complementary portrait of the overall "person × situation" transaction residing at the core of the coping construct. However, a critical distinction is needed between *level of analysis* and *scope of analysis*. Coping, like many psychological constructs (e.g., Vallerand, 1997), can be organized by four nested levels of analysis: time, situation, context, and life in general. Time points are nested in situations which, in turn, are nested in contexts or life domains. Also, the sums of all life domains and the overall judgment about one's life in general can be taken to represent general coping.

In contrast, the *scope of analysis* distinguishes between what a person is actually doing (state) versus what he or she usually does (disposition/trait). A researcher might study either the actual or the habitual ways of coping across the four levels of analysis (see Table 1). For example, the study of habitual coping is not limited to the overarching level of general coping. This notion is consistent with the possible integration between the concepts of personality state and personality trait which are complementary rather than opposing constructs (e.g., Funder, 2008; Mischel and Shoda, 2008; Roberts and Pomerantz, 2004). For instance, trait anxiety has been conceived as representing both a generalized disposition to experience anxiety in one's life and a more contextualized tendency to feel anxious in a particular situation (e.g., competition, test, and social interaction). The two concepts can be complementary if one considers that trait anxiety is actually an overarching dimension, which can provide a parsimonious summary for consistent patterns of anxiety across specific situations (Smith, Smoll, and Wiechman, 1998). Similarly, as Table 1 indicates, the study of state coping is not limited to the first levels of analysis (i.e., time or situation) as researchers may examine how someone is currently coping with the demands of a particular situation, a particular context, or one's general life. Similarly, trait coping is applicable across the situational, contextual, and general levels of analysis. At the situational level, a researcher could ask athletes to report their habitual coping during sport competitions (*dispositional coping at the situational level*).

Table 1. Integration of Trait and State Coping Across Levels of Analysis

Levels of analysis	Scopes of analysis Dispositional/trait Situational/state	
Time	Athletes' habitual coping in a specific phase of sport competitions (e.g., before the events)	Athletes' actual coping in a specific phase of a given sport competition
Situation	Athletes' habitual coping with sport competitions	Athletes' actual coping at a given sport competition
Context	Habitual coping of athletes within the sport domain	Actual coping of athletes within the sport domain
Global	Habitual coping of athletes across all spheres of living	Actual coping of athletes across all spheres of living

The level of analysis is situational with a dispositional scope capturing habitual ways of responding across various occurrences of the same situation across time. For instance, Hurst and colleagues (2009) recently adapted the Coping Inventory for Competitive Sport (Gaudreau and Blondin, 2002) to measure how athletes typically cope during sport competitions. Also, questionnaires have been adapted and validated with a focus on how athletes cope when experiencing a performance slump (Eklund, Grove, and Heard, 1998; Grove, Eklund, and Heard, 1997). At the contextual level, one might examine the habitual coping of athletes in the sport domain (*dispositional coping at the contextual level*). The level of analysis is contextual with a dispositional scope that encompasses habitual ways of coping across all situations in the sport domain. The Coping Scale for Korean Athletes (Yoo, 2000) typifies this approach by measuring usual ways of coping when experiencing stressful events in the athletic life. Finally, at the general level, research could examine the habitual coping of an athlete across all spheres of living (*dispositional coping at the general level*).

On a final note, the distinction between dispositional/trait and situational/state coping has theoretical bearings beyond measurement and conceptual issues (e.g., Krohne, 1996). Dispositional coping can be seen as the *structure* (macro-analysis) likely to influence the *process* of how a person actually responds to a specific situation at a particular point in time (micro-analysis). Despite preference for a state approach at the situational levels, Lazarus and Folkman (1984) clearly delineated the need to consider trait and state coping. Accordingly, they noted that "structure and process are both necessary for an understanding of coping" (Lazarus and Folkman, 1984, p. 298) as they might provide complementary information about the complex nature of human adaptation. Dispositional coping has been found to predict coping measured at the situational level (Carver, Scheier, and Weintraub, 1989). In the sport domain, correlations ranging from .52 to .80 have been reported between dispositional and state versions of the MCOPE Inventory using a small sample of college athletes (Giacobbi Jr. and Weinberg, 2000).

In addition, Anshel and Anderson (2002) also found significant correlations between the dispositional coping styles of table tennis players and their situational coping strategies enacted to manage an acute stressful event.

Four Types of Stability/Consistency in Longitudinal Research

The idea that "coping constantly changes" is more complex than it appears. At first glance, change and stability/consistency seem opposite and hardly reconcilable phenomena. This section delineates some of the many meanings attached to the notion of variability and stability/consistency by drawing on recent advances in personality theory (e.g., Caspi, Roberts, and Shiner, 2005; Roberts and Pomerantz, 2004) and quantitative methodology (e.g., Affleck, Zautra, Tennen, and Armeli, 1999; Meredith, 1993; Nagin, 2005) to present four distinct meanings of stability/consistency in coping utilization.

Nomothetic Stability/Consistency: Absolute and Differential Analyses

Differential Stability/Consistency. The nomothetic approach focuses on overall trends in longitudinal coping utilization using two classes of statistical indicators: Correlational and mean-level. Correlations (e.g., test-retest correlations, intra-class correlations) can be used to estimate *differential stability, also labelled rank-order or relative stability*. Differential stability represents the extent to which individual differences are consistent across time. In other words, this form of stability/consistency represents the degree to which the relative positioning of individuals in a group on a particular variable is maintained over time or situations (e.g., Caspi et al., 2005). Research concerning *differential stability* revealed that individual differences in the coping of soccer players (Louvet et al., 2007) and referees (Louvet et al., 2009) are only moderately stable across competitive events over a season. Also, two studies on the *differential within-situation consistency* revealed that individual differences in the coping of competitive golfers are not very stable across stages of a sport competition (Gaudreau et al., 2002; Gaudreau et al., 2001). Likewise, coping changes across situations in different life domains (*cross-domain cross-situational consistency*) with moderate correlations between academic and athletic coping strategies of university student-athletes (Sellers and Peterson, 1993). This particular result indicates that an athlete who is amongst the most frequent user of task-oriented coping during sport might not be amongst the most frequent users of such coping in an academic domain. Overall, it can be argued that individual differences in coping utilization are somewhat varying across time in the same situation, across stages of a situation, and across distinct situations from different life domains.

Absolute Stability/Consistency. Mean-level analyses have been employed to examine *normative stability*, also labelled *absolute or mean-level stability*. Normative stability represents the degree to which a sample, on average, increases, decreases, or remains stable on a particular variable across time (e.g., Caspi et al., 2005). Several studies have relied on MANOVAs and generalizability theory to evaluate the normative stability of coping in sport.

Inconsistent results have been found regarding the *normative stability* of coping across time within the same situation among athletic samples. The average level of coping utilization of soccer players did not significantly change across three competitions during the course of a season (Louvet et al., 2007). Similar results were obtained with swimmers across three training periods (Crocker and Isaak, 1997). In a sample of soccer referees, however, disengagement-oriented coping and seeking social support significantly decreased during the season whereas problem-focused coping remained stable (Louvet et al., 2009). In contrast, a study following athletes across four measurement points revealed that only task-oriented coping was significantly decreasing across competitions (Fletcher, 2008). Diary methodologies have also been used to examine coping of a small group of athletes across using intensive data collection ranging from 28 to 31 days during the competitive season (Nicholls, 2007; Nicholls and Polman, 2007b). Although statistical analyses were not reported, the graphical illustration of the data provided evidence to support the mean-level change of coping across time.

At least two studies have examined whether athletes cope in a similar manner across distinct situations within a particular life domain (*within-domain cross-situational consistency*). Giacobbi Jr. and Weinberg (2000), asked athletes to report two challenging/stressful situations. No inferential statistics were conducted but the means and standard deviations were reported, thus allowing the calculation of standardized effect size (Cohen, 1992). As such, results indicates that coping was mostly consistent across the situations, with Cohen's *d* effect size ranging from -0.17 to 0.07 (absolute average = 0.05). Alternatively, Bouffard and Crocker (1992) reported substantial changes in coping utilization of individuals with physical disabilities across three situations, during a six-month period. In a similar vein, the study of Sellers (1995) examined *cross-domain cross-situational consistency* by comparing the coping of student-athlete across a school and sport stressor. Results indicated that only three out of nine coping strategies were not used consistently across the stressors. Yet, the standardized effect size ranged from 0.03 to 1.03 (absolute average 0.40), thus indicating that small sample size may had contributed to some non-significant results.

A few studies have adopted a finer-grained approach. Two studies that examined the *normative within-situation consistency* of coping revealed that the mean-level utilization of a majority of coping strategies changed across stages of a sport competition (Gaudreau et al., 2002; Gaudreau et al., 2001). Similar results were obtained across stages of physical rehabilitation (Udry, 1997) and across three distinct meets of a swimming competition (Crocker and Isaak, 1997).

Integrating the Differential and Absolute Stability/Consistency. Limited research has simultaneously examined differential and absolute stability in the same sport study. Intriguingly, Louvet et al. (2007) outlined that coping could manifest a moderate level of differential stability (thus leaving room for some level of change) that is coupled with an absolute stability in coping utilization across time. Failure to examine both types of stability in a given data set could result in incomplete and misleading conclusions as normative stability of coping can co-exist in the presence of differential instability, and vice versa (Caspi et al., 2005; Roberts and Pomerantz, 2004). Firstly, in situations where half of a sample respectively increases and the other half decreases their coping effort to the same extent, the two patterns of change cancel each other out, thus yielding absolute stability and rank-order instability. Secondly, in situations where the coping effort of most individuals increases (or decreases) to the same extent, everyone conserve the same positioning in the group whereas the average level of the group significantly increases (or decreases), thus yielding rank-order stability combined with absolute instability. At first glance, these results might seem counterintuitive. In combination, these results suggest that change is characterized by multinomial heterogeneity with both its magnitude and direction substantially varying across individuals (Nagin, 1999), an issue that will be further explained in an upcoming section of this chapter.

Idiosyncratic Stability/Consistency: Individual-Level Analyses

Idiographic Longitudinal Profile. At the opposite end of the nomothetic approach, some researchers have conducted idiographic longitudinal studies. For instance, four athletes recorded their stressful situations, coping, and cognitive appraisals across multiple points over a season (Holt and Dunn, 2004). A chronologically-ordered idiographic profile was created to illustrate the sequential patterning coping for each athlete during the first six weeks of the season. In-depth information can be gained by following a single individual across time and situations (Nesselroade and Molenaar, 1999). Future research could incorporate advanced modeling strategies for dynamic repeated measures single case studies, such as the dynamic P-technique factor analysis (Jones and Nesselroade, 1990).

Relative Change Index. The analysis of idiosyncratic stability/consistency is not limited to case studies or small samples. Analyses, such as the reliable change index, can be used to determine whether each individual in a large-scale longitudinal study has changed over and above what would be attributable to mere measurement error (Christensen and Mendoza, 1986). For instance, a recent study in educational setting revealed that performance-approach goals were normatively stable during a semester (Fryer and Elliot, 2007). Yet, results of analyses using the reliable change index revealed distinct longitudinal patterns of achievement goals with 34% of the students increasing, 46% decreasing, and 20% remaining stable across time. Overall, these three distinct and heterogeneous profiles of change were cancelling each other out in the normative stability analyses. Without considering change at the individual level, these researchers would have erroneously concluded that achievement goals were not changing when, in fact, they did change for a majority of students albeit in a different manner. Coping researchers could easily incorporate relative change index in future longitudinal studies.

Nomothetic-Idiosyncratic Stability/Consistency: Longitudinal Trajectories Analyses

Nomothetic and idiosyncratic approaches provide important and complementary information. Lazarus and Folkman (1984) strongly advocated their integration into nomothetic-idiosyncratic designs. The goal of the nomothetic-idiosyncratic approach is "to observe individuals repeatedly intra-individually and do inter-individual comparisons" (Lazarus and Folkman, 1984, p. 301-302). In other words, this approach combines "how the person varies from its own mean" (intra-individual variability) and "how each person's pattern of variability differs from the group mean" (inter-individual differences in variability). During the last decade, the growing dissemination of longitudinal quantitative methodologies has facilitated the modeling of individual differences in intra-individual change in applied research. Several modeling approaches, such as linear growth modeling (Duncan, Duncan, and Strycker, 2006), multilevel modeling (e.g., Affleck et al., 1999), growth mixture modeling (Jung and Wickrama, 2007), and latent class growth modeling (e.g., Nagin, 2005) are now available to examine the individual differences in the rate and/or direction of change across time and situation. Growth mixture modeling and latent class growth modeling are particularly useful when individuals are expected to vary on both the magnitude and direction of their change across time and situation (Raudenbush, 2001), such as in the example of performance-approach achievement goals (Fryer and Elliot, 1999). Andruff, Carraro, Thompson, Gaudreau, and Louvet (2008) have recently published a tutorial to delineate the conceptual underpinnings and practical applications of latent class growth modeling. Louvet et al. (2009, p. 126) have summarized the impetus of latent class growth modeling by saying that:

> "LCGM offers a systematic framework to discover the number and the shape of the developmental trajectories of coping utilization or any other psychological variables by creating latent classes that are unobservable subgroups of people with different patterns of change and stability (Nagin,1999, 2005). People within the same latent trajectory are homogeneous in their longitudinal pattern of change or stability on a certain variable (e.g., problem-focused coping). In contrast, individuals in different subgroups possess different developmental courses on a specific variable. These trajectories represent prototypical profiles of development on a given criteria over time, thus summarizing inter-individual differences in change into a limited number of meaningful subgroups of people (Nagin, 2005)"

Two recent studies relied on latent class growth modeling to examine multinomial heterogeneity in longitudinal coping utilization (Louvet et al., 2007, 2009). The findings revealed that not all soccer players or soccer referees changed the coping strategies they deployed across time and not all "changers" were changing in the same direction. For instance, it was found that 55% of the soccer players maintained a moderate level of task-oriented coping whereas 5% and 40%, respectively, increased and decreased their use of task-oriented coping. Similar results were reported for other coping dimensions for both soccer players and soccer referees. Another study with young hockey players revealed the existence of distinct longitudinal trajectories of positive and negative affective states during a period surrounding team selection, an important turning point event in the seasonal course of a hockey season (Gaudreau, Amiot, and Vallerand, 2009).

Latent class growth modeling is a promising approach for the study of coping and emotions. Clearly, not all athletes change how they cope across time and even the "changers" vary in both the magnitude and direction of their change in coping utilization and psychological adjustment. Traditional analyses may fail to uncover the complex multinomial heterogeneity in change. Such pattern of change highlights the need of moving beyond the sole reliance on traditional analyses of change and the need to abandon the dogmatic and nomothetic debate about the trait-like versus state-like nature of coping. The idiographic-nomothetic approach offers a useful platform to start examining why some people are changing their coping utilization more than others (antecedents of individual differences in change) and what are the consequences associated with distinct longitudinal trajectories of coping utilization.

Construct Stability/Consistency: Longitudinal Confirmatory Factor Analyses

Longitudinal studies, including those using the idiographic-nomothetic approach, revolve around the implicit assumption that coping remains *qualitatively invariant* or *structurally stable* across measurement points. This fundamental assumption has rarely been addressed in sport-related research (Conroy, Metzler, and Hofer, 2003). However, longitudinal methodologists consider the demonstration of longitudinal factorial invariance as a prerequisite to unbiased estimation of differential, normative, and idiosyncratic stability/consistency (Schutz, 1998; Vandenberg and Lance, 2000). The patterns of change observed in a sample could reflect mere measurement error or the instability of the construct itself rather than true "behavioral changes," thus outlining the importance of ensuring that the overall structure of the construct remains relatively stable/consistent across time and situations.

Structural stability or consistency is inferred through a close examination of the similarity or statistical invariance of the correlations among the set of variables (Caspi et al., 2005). Longitudinal confirmatory factor analysis is a premium platform to evaluate structural invariance of latent constructs (e.g., Conroy et al., 2003; Schutz, 1998). At least three conditions must be attained to ensure unbiased estimation of rank-order, normative, and idiographic-nomothetic stability/consistency. Firstly, *configural invariance* is attained when coping can be measured with the same number of items that are all loading on the same factor across measurement points. In other words, configural invariance is achieved whenever the pattern of fixed and freed loadings is invariant across measurement time. The lack of configural invariance would indicate that the conceptual core of the coping construct qualitatively differs across measurement points, thus biasing all other potential examination of stability. Secondly, *metric invariance* is reached when the strength of the relation between the items and the latent factor (i.e., factor loading) is not significantly different across the different measurement points. Metrical invariance is important to ensure that the conceptual meaning of a coping dimension remains stable/consistent across measurement points. Thirdly, *scalar invariance* consists of testing the invariance of the score of a manifest variable (e.g., item) when the latent factor equals zero (i.e., intercept) to ensure that measurement biases are longitudinally consistent. Therefore, scalar invariance provides additional guarantee that mean-level differences represent true change rather than systematic measurement bias occurring at a particular measurement point.

Little empirical attention has been allocated to the longitudinal factorial invariance of sport-related coping questionnaires. A study by Louvet et al. (2009) examined the factorial invariance of the Ways of Coping Questionnaire with a sample of soccer referees across three competitions in a season. Results supported the configural invariance of the three coping dimensions (i.e., problem-focused, avoidance, seeking support). The metric invariance was supported for 23 of 25 items whereas scalar invariance was corroborated for 22 of 25 items across three measurement points. Another study by Fletcher (2008) obtained comparable results with a sample of female athletes completing the Coping Inventory for Competitive Sport after four sport competitions, over a 10-week period.

Overall, these results provide some evidence for the longitudinal stability of the factorial structure of coping, thus implying that coping in the sport domain can be measured reliably across measurement points. Early research on coping have prematurely celebrated the changing nature of coping with flamboyant titles such as "If it changes, it must be a process" (Folkman and Lazarus, 1985). Parker, Endler, and Bagby (1993) have summarized several limitations about coping measures under the title: "If it changes it might be unstable". The satirical title was meant to convey the message that observed variations in coping might be the mere reflection of measurement error. Hence, it is encouraging to observe that two sport-related coping instruments have succeeded the stringent empirical test of longitudinal factorial invariance.

Advances in the Modeling of Change: Opportunities for Coping Researchers

As noted earlier, individual differences exist regarding the magnitude and direction of change in longitudinal coping utilization. Not all athletes change nor do all athletes who change how they cope change in the same direction. Future research could start examining the antecedents and consequences associated with distinct longitudinal patterns of coping utilization. This section presents quantitative approaches with potential of shedding new lights in the sport-related coping literature. Other approaches are available and could also be explored. As noted by Nagin and Tremblay (2005, p. 150), "the complexity of studying developmental trajectories is too great to be left to any one statistical method."

Advances in Latent Class Growth Modeling (LCGM)

Predictors. LCGM can be used to examine the predictors of distinct longitudinal trajectories of coping. In LCGM, a predictor is a variable that is likely to influence the likelihood of belonging to a specific longitudinal trajectory compared to other trajectories. A recent study examined the longitudinal trajectories of positive and negative affective states over a six-month period (Gaudreau et al., 2009). Three trajectories of negative affect were observed in this study with one adaptive-healthy trajectory representing hockey players with lowest levels of negative affect throughout the measurement points. Results indicated that high academic identity and need satisfaction in addition to low athletic identity substantially increased the likelihood of membership in the more healthy-adaptive trajectory, compared to the other two less adaptive trajectories of negative affective states. Similar studies could be performed on longitudinal trajectories of coping to determine if theoretically-driven antecedents (e.g., personality, motivation, self-concept, cognitive appraisals, or the social environment) could influence the likelihood of belonging to a trajectory of high and stable utilization of task-oriented coping, for instance, compared to low and unstable usage of such coping.

Dual-trajectories. Another application of LCGM (Jones and Nagin, 2007) considers the joint probabilities of membership on the longitudinal trajectories of distinct "behaviors." For instance, a researcher could measure coping, state cognitive anxiety, self-determined motivation, and perceived parental pressure across multiple points during a season. LCGM would allow the identification of distinct longitudinal trajectories for each of the four psychological constructs. In turn, a dual-trajectory model could be implemented to examine whether the likelihood of belonging to a particular trajectory of coping (compared to other coping trajectories) is significantly influenced by membership into a specific longitudinal trajectory of self-determined motivation, for instance. Each of the following research questions could be examined using a dual-trajectory LCGM: What are the odds of belonging to a trajectory of decreased task-oriented coping if an athlete belongs to a trajectory of decreased self-determined motivation? What are the odds of belonging to a trajectory of increased disengagement-oriented coping if an athlete belongs to a trajectory of increased cognitive state anxiety? What are the odds of membership into a trajectory of decreased disengagement-oriented coping if an athlete belongs to a trajectory of decreased perceived parental pressure?

Outcomes. LCGM also offers a useful platform to examine the potential outcomes of longitudinal coping trajectories. The approach is highly similar to the approach described for the inclusion of predictors. In LCGM, an outcome is a variable measured at the end of a study which is influenced by the likelihood of belonging to a specific longitudinal trajectory compared to other trajectories. Jones and Nagin (2007) offered a nice illustration of this modeling technique.

Multilevel Analyses of Intensive Longitudinal Data

Multilevel modeling is another useful quantitative method for the examination of coping across multiple times, particularly in intensive longitudinal data collected in daily-diary or experience-sampling studies (e.g., Affleck et al., 1999; Tennen, Affleck, Armeli, and Carney, 2000). Up to now, most research on the antecedents and consequences of sport-related coping has focused on between-person associations. For instance, the extant literature indicates that athletes using high levels of task-oriented coping are more likely to attain their goals, to experience positive affective states, and to feel more satisfied than their counterparts using low levels of such coping (Hoar, Kowalski, Gaudreau, and Crocker, 2006). Albeit important, these results provide little information about the within-person associations between coping and outcomes such as a performance, affective states, or symptoms of burnout. Future research is needed to determine whether individual athletes' are performing better than their own personal average on days or events during which they are using task-oriented coping to a greater extent than their own average utilization of such strategy (e.g., Beal et al., 2005; Daniels and Harris, 2005)

Density Distribution

The focus on within-person variability does not have to be made at the expense of individual differences. As depicted earlier in this chapter, research on both state-like and trait-like coping are needed to provide complementary understanding on momentary and habitual ways of coping, respectively. The field of personality seems to have nearly ended the "person versus situation" debate insofar as they are able to integrate traits (structure) and states (process) to explain how personality displays both within-person stability and change (e.g., Fleeson, 2001, 2004; Funder, 2008).

Short term longitudinal experience-sampling studies have shed light on related "person × situation" synthesis as they indicated that personality traits can actually represent the central tendency from the density of everyday life distributions of corresponding personality-related states (Fleeson, 2001). As such, the within-person results of Fleeson (2001) have indicated that an individual usually experiences all levels of each personality variables (low to high ends on the Big Five traits) as to form a within-person normally-shaped distribution of related states. On the one hand, these results brought support to the notion of trait consistency, given that the mean of the distributions were reliable indicators of individual differences in terms of how much people behaved similarly across situations. On the other hand, these same results provided simultaneous support to the notion of change, because the variability (standard deviations) was also a reliable indicator of the extent to which people behaved differently across situations.

As the classic position of many personality researchers has often strived to explain (e.g., Epstein, 1979; Fleeson and Noftle, 2008) not only do traits represent meaningful aggregates of states, they can be reliably predicted (Fleeson, 2001) and be potent predictors of health, psychological, and social outcomes (Ozer and Benet-Martinez, 2006). In terms of sport research, this implies that although a single coping state might be weakly related to personality (Connor-Smith and Flachsbart, 2007), finding consistent patterns of coping states might be useful in order to create empirical scores of trait coping that become significant predictors of global life outcomes (Lazarus, 1999). For instance, basketball coaches tend to promote a pattern of coping behaviours that increases the likelihood of making a maximum of free throws (average performance), not necessarily of making the last free throw that could tie the final game in double overtime while visiting the current champion team (situational performance). In sum, the level of analysis of coping needs to be reasonably adjusted to the types of outcomes that could inform coaches and practitioners about the possible roles of both state and trait coping.

In the short term, it might be difficult to intervene on changing trait coping, as it is more stable and develops more slowly. Hence, most practitioners would argue in favour of focusing interventions on the management of everyday coping states as they might be more amenable to immediate change. In turn, a coping trait can develop from an aggregate of coping states that itself becomes stable as a result of repeated learning/training. The point here is that it would not be psychologically economical for both athletes and their training staff to perpetually learn and readjust their coping behaviors in every single sport situation. As recurrent patterns of coping states occur, it is plausible that a coping trait also develops – for the better or worse. In the long term, promoting the development of certain coping traits can also contribute to global well-being, a multifaceted outcome which effect may ripple across life domains.

CONCLUSION

As reviewed in this chapter, evidence suggests that coping responses changes across times, situations, and contexts. Recent developments and applications of multivariate modeling strategies have lead researchers to acknowledge the substantial amount of inter-individual differences in both the magnitude and direction of change in coping utilization. In other words, not all athletes change the coping strategies they use. Furthermore, the changes in coping utilization may take many distinct forms for different subgroups of individuals. Despite these advances, research has yet to fully examine the antecedents and the consequences of individual differences in longitudinal coping utilization. Moving from a focus on between-person associations to a paradigm that examines individual differences in within-person associations might be informed by recent development in the study of episodic self-regulation, emotion, and achievement (Beal et al., 2005).

From an applied standpoint, the changeability of coping utilization is certainly encouraging. Some individuals might be more prone than others to adapt or adjust their use of coping according to the evolving nature of their environment. Yet, interventions could be devised to teach athletes how to cope with the requirements of a specific stressful situation or to adapt their coping efforts according to the changing demands of their multiple life strivings. Interventions might provide valuable information about the role of social agents in the process leading to coping modifications as well as about the affective, motivational, and performance outcomes resulting from modifications in coping utilization. Research and intervention need to be regularly integrated. Theories and the extent literature on sport-related coping can be used to develop and evaluate interventions. In turn, empirically-driven interventions can be used to evaluate and refine theories.

Finally, applied sport psychology could move towards evidenced-based practices which will require coping researchers to examine the causal effect of coping in experimental studies. It is important to bear in mind that even the most sophisticated statistical methods for longitudinal studies remain correlational, as causality is usually dependent on experimental or quasi-experimental research designs. Demonstrating the causal role of coping within a natural context will be needed to eventually contribute to the well-being of athletes and society in general. The innovative area of developmental psychopathology is informative as how to device studies that can test the causality of correlational results from longitudinal studies in natural settings. As such, evaluations of prevention programs with experimental, quasi-experimental, and randomized control trial nested within a longitudinal follow-up, can demonstrate causality of etiological theories by manipulating the presence, frequency, or intensity of protective factors across groups of participants with equivalent risk factors (e.g., Howe, Reiss, and Yuh, 2002). Overall, research on coping has tremendous potential to inform coaches and applied sport psychologists to facilitate the development of evidence-based practices insofar as sport researchers are willing to explore and implement a mixture of sophisticated research designs. Again, as noted by Nagin and Tremblay (2005, p. 150), "the complexity of studying developmental trajectories is too great to be left to any one statistical method."

AUTHOR NOTE

This chapter was supported by a grant from the Social Sciences and Humanities Research Council of Canada awarded to the first author and by a scholarship for postdoctoral research from the *Fonds Québécois de la Recherche sur la Société et la Culture* awarded to the second author.

REFERENCES

Affleck, G., Zautra, A., Tennen, H., and Armeli, S. (1999). Multilevel daily process designs for consulting and clinical psychology: A preface for the perplexed. *Journal of Consulting and Clinical Psychology, 67*, 746-754.

Andruff, H., Carraro, N., Thompson, A., Gaudreau, P., and Louvet, B. (2008). Latent class growth modelling: A tutorial. *Tutorials in Quantitative Methods for Psychology, 5*, 11-24.

Anshel, M. H., and Anderson, D. I. (2002). Coping with acute stress in sport: Linking athletes' coping style, coping strategies, affect, and motor performance. *Anxiety, Stress and Coping, 15*, 193-209.

Beal, D. J., Weiss, H. M., Barros, E., and MacDermid, S. M. (2005). An episodic process model of affective influences on performance. *Journal of Applied Psychology, 90*, 1054-1068.

Bouffard, M., and Crocker, P. R. (1992). Coping by individuals with physical disabilities with perceived challenge in physical activity: Are people consistent? *Research Quarterly for Exercise and Sport, 63*, 410-417.

Carver, C. S., Pozo, C., Harris, S. D., Noriega, V., and et al. (1993). How coping mediates the effect of optimism on distress: A study of women with early stage breast cancer. *Journal of Personality and Social Psychology, 65*, 375-390.

Carver, C. S., and Scheier, M. F. (1994). Situational coping and coping dispositions in a stressful transaction. *Journal of Personality and Social Psychology, 66*, 184-195.

Carver, C. S., Scheier, M. F., and Weintraub, J. K. (1989). Assessing coping strategies: A theoretically based approach. *Journal of Personality and Social Psychology, 56*, 267-283.

Caspi, A., Roberts, B. W., and Shiner, R. L. (2005). Personality development: Stability and change. *Annual Review of Psychology, 56*, 453-484.

Christensen, L., and Mendoza, J. L. (1986). A method of assessing change in single subject : An alternative of the RC index. *Behavior Therapy, 17*, 305-398.

Cohen, J. (1992). A power primer. *Psychological Bulletin, 112*, 155-159.

Connor-Smith, J. K., and Flachsbart, C. (2007). Relations between personality and coping: A meta-analysis. *Journal of Personality and Social Psychology, 93*, 1080-1107.

Conroy, D. E., Metzler, J. N., and Hofer, S. M. (2003). Factorial invariance and latent mean stability of performance failure appraisals. *Structural Equation Modeling, 10*, 401-422.

Crocker, P. R., and Isaak, K. (1997). Coping during competitions and training sessions: Are youth swimmers consistent? *International Journal of Sport Psychology, 28*, 355-369.

Daniels, K., and Harris, C. (2005). A daily diary study of coping in the context of the job demands-control-support model. *Journal of Vocational Behavior, 66*, 219-237.

Duncan, T. E., Duncan, S. C., and Strycker, L. A. (2006). *An introduction to latent variable growth curve modeling (2nd edition)*. Mahwah, NJ: Lawrence Erlbaum.

Eklund, R. C., Grove, J. R., and Heard, N. P. (1998). The measurement of slump-related coping: Factorial validity of the COPE and modified-COPE inventories. *Journal of Sport and Exercise Psychology, 20*, 157-175.

Epstein, L. H. (1979). The stability of behavior. I: On predicting most of the people much of the time. *Journal of Personality and Social Psychology, 37*, 1097-1126.

Fleeson, W. (2001). Toward a structure- and process-integrated view of personality: Traits as density distribution of states. *Journal of Personality and Social Psychology, 80*, 1011-1027.

Fleeson, W. (2004). Moving personality beyond the person-situation debate: The challenge and the opportunity of within-person variability. *Current Directions in Psychological Science, 13*, 83-87.

Fleeson, W., and Noftle, E. E. (2008). Where does personality have its influence? A supermatrix of consistency concepts. *Journal of Personality, 76*, 1355-1385.

Fletcher, R. (2008). Longitudinal factorial invariance, differential, and latent mean stability of the Coping Inventory for Competitive Sports. In M. P. Simmons and L. A. Foster (Eds.),

Sport and Exercise Psychology Research Advances (pp. 293-306). New York: Nova Publisher.

Folkman, S., and Lazarus, R. S. (1985). If it changes it must be a process: A study of emotion and coping across three stages of a college examination. *Journal of Personality and Social Psychology, 48*, 150-170.

Fryer, J. W., and Elliot, A. J. (2007). Stability and change in achievement goals. *Journal of Educational Psychology, 99*, 700-714.

Funder, D. C. (2008). Persons, situations, and person-situation interactions. In O. P. John, R. W. Robins and L. A. Pervin (Eds.), *Handbook of Personality, Theory and Research* (Third ed., pp. 568-580). New York: Guilford.

Gaudreau, P., Amiot, C. E., and Vallerand, R. J. (2009). Trajectories of affective states in adolescent hockey players: Turning point and motivational antecedents. *Developmental Psychology 45*, 307-319.

Gaudreau, P., and Blondin, J.-P. (2002). Development of a questionnaire for the assessment of coping strategies employed by athletes in competitive sport settings. *Psychology of Sport and Exercise, 3*, 1-34.

Gaudreau, P., Blondin, J.-P., and Lapierre, A.-M. (2002). Athletes' coping during a competition: Relationship of coping strategies with positive affect, negative affect, and performance-goal discrepancy. *Psychology of Sport and Exercise, 3*, 125-150.

Gaudreau, P., Lapierre, A.-M., and Blondin, J.-P. (2001). Coping at three phases of a competition: Comparison between pre-competitive, competitive, and post-competitive utilization of the same strategy. *International Journal of Sport Psychology, 32*, 369-385.

Giacobbi Jr., P. R., and Weinberg, R. S. (2000). An examination of coping in sports: Individual trait anxiety differences and situational consistency. *The Sport Psychologist, 14*, 42-62.

Gould, D., Eklund, R. C., and Jackson, S. A. (1993). Coping strategies used by U.S. Olympic wrestlers. *Research Quarterly for Exercise and Sport, 64*, 83-93.

Grove, J., Eklund, R. C., and Heard, N. (1997). Coping with performance slumps : Factor analysis of the Ways of Coping in Sport Scale. *Australian Journal of Science and Medicine in Sport, 29*, 99-105.

Hoar, S. D., Kowalski, K. C., Gaudreau, P., and Crocker, P. R. E. (2006). A review of coping in sport. In S. Hanton and S. D. Mellalieu (Eds.), *Literature reviews in sport psychology* (pp. 47-90). New York: Nova Science Publishers.

Holt, N. L., and Dunn, J. G. H. (2004). Longitudinal idiographic analysis of appraisal and coping responses in sport. *Psychology of Sport and Exercise, 5*, 213-222.

Howe, G. W., Reiss, D., and Yuh, J. (2002). Can prevention trials test theories of etiology? *Development and Psychopathology, 14*, 673-694.

Hurst, J., R., Thompson, A., Visek, A. J., Fisher, B., and Gaudreau, P. (2009). Towards a dispositional version of the Coping Inventory for Competitive Sport. *Manuscript submitted for publication*.

Jones, B. L., and Nagin, D. S. (2007). Advances in group-based trajectory modeling and an SAS procedure for estimating them. *Sociological Methods and Research, 35*, 542-571.

Jones, J. C., and Nesselroade, J. R. (1990). Multivariate, replicated, single-subject, repeated measures designs and P-technique factor analysis: A review of intraindividual change studies. *Experimental Aging Research, 16*, 171-183.

Jung, T., and Wickrama, K. A. S. (2007). An introduction to latent class growth analysis and growth mixture modeling. *Social and Personality Psychology Compass*, 302-317.

Kowalski, K. C., and Crocker, P. R. (2001). Development and validation of the Coping Function Questionnaire for adolescents in sport. *Journal of Sport and Exercise Psychology, 23*, 136-155.

Krohne, H. W. (1996). Individual differences in coping. In M. Zeidner and N. S. Endler (Eds.), *Handbook of coping : Theory, research, and applications* (pp. 381-409). New York: Wiley.

Lazarus, R. S. (1999). *Stress and emotion: A new synthesis*. New York: Springer.

Lazarus, R. S., and Folkman, S. (1984). *Stress, appraisal, and coping*. New York: Springer.

Louvet, B., Gaudreau, P., Menaut, A., Genty, J., and Deneuve, P. (2007). Longitudinal patterns of stability and change in coping across three competitions: A latent class growth analysis. *Journal of Sport and Exercise Psychology, 29*, 100-117.

Louvet, B., Gaudreau, P., Menaut, A., Genty, J., and Deneuve, P. (2009). Revisiting the changing and stable properties of coping utilization using latent class growth analysis: A longitudinal investigation with soccer referees. *Psychology of Sport and Exercise, 10*, 124-135.

Meredith, W. (1993). Measurement invariance, factor analysis and factorial invariance. *Psychometrika, 58*, 525-543.

Mischel, W., and Shoda, Y. (2008). Toward a unified theory of personality: Integrating dispositions and processing dynamics within the cognitive-affective processing system. In O. P. John, R. W. Robins and L. A. Pervin (Eds.), *Handbook of personality, theory and research* (Third ed., pp. 208-241). New York: Guilford.

Nagin, D. S. (1999). Analyzing developmental trajectories: A semiparametric, group-based approach. *Psychological Methods, 4*, 139-157.

Nagin, D. S. (2005). *Group-based modeling of development*. Cambridge, MA: Harvard University Press.

Nagin, D. S., and Tremblay, R. E. (2005). Further reflections on modeling and analyzing developmental trajectories: A Response to Maughan and Raudenbush. *Annals of the American Academy of Political and Social Science, 602*, 145-154.

Nesselroade, J. R., and Molenaar, P. C. M. (1999). Pooling lagged covariance structures based on short, multivariate time series for dynamic factor analysis. In R. H. Hoyle (Ed.), *Statistical strategies for small sample research* (pp. 224-251). Thousand Oaks: Sage.

Nicholls, A. R. (2007). A longitudinal phenomenological analysis of coping effectiveness among Scottish international adolescent golfers. *European Journal of Sport Science, 7*, 169-178.

Nicholls, A. R., and Polman, R. C. J. (2007a). Coping in sport: A systematic review. *Journal of Sports Sciences, 25*, 11-31.

Nicholls, A. R., and Polman, R. C. J. (2007b). Stressors, coping, and coping effectiveness among players from the England under-18 rugby union team. *Journal of Sport Behavior, 30*, 199-218.

Ozer, D. J., and Benet-Martinez, V. (2006). Personality and the prediction of consequential life outcomes. *Annual review of Psychology, 57*, 401-421.

Parker, J. D., Endler, N. S., and Bagby, M. R. (1993). If it changes, it might be unstable: Examining the factor structure of the Ways of Coping Questionnaire. *Psychological Assessment, 5*, 361-368.

Raffety, B. D., Smith, R. E., and Ptacek, J. (1997). Facilitating and debilitating trait anxiety, situational anxiety, and coping with an anticipated stressor: A process analysis. *Journal of Personality and Social Psychology, 72*, 892-906.

Raudenbush, S. W. (2001). Comparing personal trajectories and drawing causal inferences from longitudinal data. *Annual Review of Psychology, 52*, 501-525.

Roberts, B. W., and Pomerantz, E. M. (2004). On traits, situations, and their integration: A developmental perspective. *Personality and Social Psychology Review, 8*, 402-416.

Schutz, R. W. (1998). Assessing the stability of psychological traits and measures. In J. L. Duda (Ed.), *Advances in sport and exercise psychology measurement* (pp. 393-408). Morgantown, WV: Fitness Information Technology.

Sellers, R. M. (1995). Situational differences in the coping processes of student-athletes. *Anxiety, Stress, and Coping, 8*, 325-336.

Sellers, R. M., and Peterson, C. (1993). Explanatory style and coping with controllable events by student-athletes. *Cognition and Emotion, 7*, 431-441.

Smith, R. E., Smoll, F. L., and Wiechman, S. A. (1998). Measurement of trait anxiety in sport. In J. L. Duda (Ed.), *Advances in sport and exercise psychology measurement* (pp. 105-127). Morgantown, WV: Fitness Information Technology.

Somerfeld, M. R. (1997). The utility of systems models of stress and coping for applied research: The case of cancer adaptation. *Journal of Health Psychology, 2*, 133-151.

Sorlie, T., and Sexton, H. C. (2001). The factor structure of the "Ways of Coping Questionnaire" and the process of coping in surgical patients. *Personality and Individual Differences, 30*, 961-975.

Tennen, H., Affleck, G., Armeli, S., and Carney, M. A. (2000). A daily process approach to coping: Linking theory, research, and practice. *American Psychologist, 55*, 626-636.

Udry, E. (1997). Coping and social support among injured athletes following surgery. *Journal of Sport and Exercise Psychology, 19*, 71-90.

Vallerand, R. J. (1997). Toward a hierarchical model of intrinsic and extrinsic motivation. In M. Zana (Ed.), *Advances in experimental social psychology* (Vol. 29, pp. 271-360). New York: Academic Press.

Vandenberg, R. J., and Lance, C. E. (2000). Review and synthesis of the measurement invariance literature: Suggestions, practices, and recommendations for organizational research. *Organizational Research Methods, 3*, 4-69.

Yoo, J. (2000). Factorial validity of the coping scale for Korean athletes. *International Journal of Sport Psychology, 31*, 391-404.

PART II. METHODOLOGICAL ISSUES IN COPING: COLLECTING COPING DATA AND IMPLICATIONS

In: Coping in Sport: Theory, Methods, and Related Constructs   ISBN: 978-1-60876-488-4
Editor: Adam R. Nicholls   © 2010 Nova Science Publishers, Inc.

Chapter 3

TRADITIONAL AND NEW METHODS OF ASSESSING COPING IN SPORT

Adam R. Nicholls[1] and Nikos Ntoumanis[2]
[1]University of Hull, UK
[2]University of Birmingham, UK

ABSTRACT

Over recent years, a variety of different methods have been employed in sport to measure coping among athletes. A large volume of research has used traditional methods such as questionnaires and interviews. However, more recently researchers have adapted different techniques from the mainstream psychology literature such as concept maps, diaries, think aloud protocols. One method that has not been used in sport, but has potential is Ecological Momentary Assessment. The purpose of this chapter is to describe the various methods used to assess coping, illustrate how each method can be used, and discuss its strengths and limitations.

INTRODUCTION

Researchers within the sport psychology literature have adopted a variety of methods, both qualitative and quantitative, to explore how athletes cope with stress in relation to athletic competition. Different methods allow researchers to address different research questions. It is therefore imperative that the correct methods of measuring coping are selected in relation to the question that coping scholars wish to address. Early studies on coping within the sport domain were quantitative in methodology and relied on questionnaires, followed by an emergence of interview studies. More recently different techniques, such as diaries, concept maps, and think aloud protocols, have been developed and/or adapted from other contexts to assess coping in sport. Another method, ecological momentary assessment, which has not been used within the sport literature to assess coping, will be reviewed in this chapter due to its potential relevance for sport research.

Questionnaires

The most frequently used questionnaires to assess coping in sport are the Inventaire des Stratégies de Coping en Compétition Sportive (ISCCS; Coping Strategies in Sport Competition Inventory), the Modified COPE inventory (MCOPE), and the Coping Function Questionnaire (CFQ). All three questionnaires were developed using a theoretically-based approach and rely, to a different extent, on Lazarus and Folkman's (1984) conceptual framework and Carver and Scheier (1989) COPE measure. Some initial evidence for the psychometric properties of the three instruments has been provided in the literature, however, all three could benefit from further psychometric testing and improvements.

Coping Strategies in Sport Competition Inventory (ISCCS)

The ISCCS was developed by Gaudreau and Blondin (2002) and has been primarily tested with French-speaking athletes. Gaudreau and Blondin quite rightly argued for the need of sport-specific measures of coping, as measures developed in other contexts might have low relevance or predictive validity in sport settings. The development of the ISCCS item pool was very extensive, involving a review of relevant literatures from sport and other areas of psychology, and pilot testing of item content with athletes, coaches, and sport psychology researchers. In contrast to the other two questionnaires reviewed here, the ISCCS includes a number of basic psychological skills (e.g., imagery and self-talk) which Gaudreau and Blondin argued are relevant in terms of understanding how athletes cope with stress. Using a sample of 306 Canadian athletes (M age = 17.4; SD= 2.15) from a variety of sports and competitive levels, Gaudreau and Blondin used a sequential confirmatory factor analysis (CFA) approach to reduce an initial pool of 95 items to 39 items measured on a 5-point scale (1= *not used at all*; 5= *used very much*). Ten factors were hypothesized: thought control, mental imagery, relaxation, effort expenditure, logical analysis, seeking support, venting of unpleasant emotions, mental distraction, disengagement/resignation, and social withdrawal. Gaudreau and Blondin showed that the 10 first-order factor model had better fit indices than those of alternative models (i.e., two- and three-factor ones describing more general dimensions of coping). Although the incremental fit indices (i.e., CFI and TLI) were slightly below recommended cut-off levels (Hu and Bentler, 1999), given the complexity of the factor model and the number of items analysed, these fit indices should be considered as satisfactory. Gaudreau and Blondin suggested that the first six factors are aspects of task-oriented coping and the latter six factors are indicators of emotion-oriented coping, however, they did not test such a hierarchical factor model.

Gaudreau and Blondin (2002) also reported satisfactory internal reliability coefficients for most ISCCS subscales. Further, the authors provided some evidence of concurrent validity by correlating the ICSS subscales with subscales from the MCOPE and the Ways of Coping Questionnaire (Folkman and Lazarus, 1985), although some of the correlations were not in the expected direction. Evidence of predictive validity was also offered by correlating the ISCCS subscales with cognitive appraisal and affective variables. Further evidence for the predictive validity of the ISCCS has been provided by Gaudreau and Blondin (2004), and Nicholls, Polman, Levy and Backhouse (2008), showing associations between coping strategies and measures of optimism, pessimism, goal attainment and affect.

As with all instrument development efforts, sample-specific modifications to obtain a good model fit need to be cross-validated with independent samples. Unfortunately, there has been only one other study that has examined the factorial structure of the ISCCS with an independent sample. Gaudreau, Ali and Marivain (2005) used 366 French marathon runners, from a very diverse age and competitive level background, to cross-validate the ISCCS. Preliminary data screening and reliability analysis resulted in the removal of 10 items and one factor (imagery), thus the cross-validation of the ISCCS version reported by Gaudreau and Blondin (2002) was not possible. Employing again a sequence of CFA's, Gaudreau et al. provided support for a 28-item nine-factor model. However, acceptable model fit was obtained only when 4 pairs of residuals were allowed to correlate. Although the authors defended these post-hoc correlations, correlated errors are problematic as they indicate high item overlap and possible item redundancy (as also acknowledged by Gaudreau and Blondin, 2002). Furthermore, Gaudreau et al. examined the hierarchical structure of the ISCCS and advocated support for a three second-order factor model (i.e., task-, distraction- and disengagement-oriented coping). However, the hierarchical model was problematic as it included a first-order factor (i.e., mental distraction) which cross-loaded on two second-order factors (i.e., distraction and task coping), and also had correlated error terms. Further, the fit of the hierarchical model was marginal and very similar to the fit of alternative first-order factor models.

Very little additional evidence has been reported in the literature regarding the psychometric properties of the ISCCS. Amiot, Gaudreau, and Blanchard (2004) presented the results of an exploratory factor analysis of the original 10-factor model with a predominantly French-speaking sample. Their analysis was carried out on the 10 subscale scores and not on the individual items. In contrast to the three higher-order factor model proposed by Gaudreau et al. (2005), Amiot et al. reported a two-factor model solution with task-and disengagement-oriented coping factors. In conclusion, there is no consensus in the literature as to the optimal number of items, first-order and second-order factors of the ISCCS.

Modified COPE Inventory

Unlike the ISCSS, the MCOPE has been predominantly used with English-speaking samples. The scale was first presented by Crocker and Graham (1995) and relies heavily on Carver and Scheier's (1989) COPE inventory. In fact, 9 of the 12 subscales of the MCOPE are taken from the COPE with modifications in the wording of some items to make them more applicable to sport: active coping, seeking social support for instrumental reasons, planning, seeking social support for emotional reasons, denial, humour, behavioural disengagement, venting of emotions and suppression of competing activities. Some of these strategies are also assessed by the ISCSS. The three other subscales of the MCOPE are based on previous sport-specific coping research and are self-blame, wishful thinking and increasing effort. Each item is scored on a 5-point scale (1= *used not at all/very little*, 5= *used very much*). Crocker and Graham tested the MCOPE with a sample of 377 athletes from a diverse background in terms of age, sport, and competitive experience. The athletes were asked to recall a recent situation in which they experienced performance difficulties or felt under pressure to perform. Cronbach internal reliability coefficients were satisfactory for all subscales except the one tapping denial (alpha =.42). The authors reported conceptually meaningful relationships between some of the coping strategies and positive and negative affect. Rather surprisingly, Crocker and Graham did not examine the factorial structure of the MCOPE.

This limitation was subsequently addressed by Eklund, Grove, and Heard (1998) who examined the factorial structure of both the COPE and MCOPE with a large diverse sample of 621 Australian athletes. A strength of this study was the employment of a cross-validation procedure which involved randomly splitting the large sample into two equal sub-samples and cross-validating the findings from the first sub-sample with the second sub-sample. The stressor under examination was performance slumps (i.e., unexplained significant reductions in performance levels). Eklund et al. utilised CFA procedures to compare the fit of a 12-factor MCOPE model against alternative models which had 11 and 10 factors respectively, derived by combining some of the subscales of the MCOPE. The model fit of all examined models was very similar but the authors argued for the 10-factor model which was more parsimonious and did not have very high factor correlations. In this 10-factor model the strategies of planning and active coping were combined, as well as the two social support subscales. However, an inspection of the incremental fit indices (unfortunately, other important fit indices such as the RMSEA and the SRMR were not reported) suggests that the 10-factor model fits very modestly and has considerable room for improvement. This was also noted by Eklund et al. Surprisingly, the fit indices of the COPE which was not modified for sport settings and which included more factors (14) were better than those of the MCOPE. Unfortunately, the hierarchical structure of the MCOPE was not tested by Eklund et al. The Cronbach alpha coefficients for all subscales were acceptable.

Although the MCOPE has room for improvement, there have been no other studies testing and improving its psychometric properties. Such studies are clearly needed. However, various other studies in the literature have offered support for the predictive validity of the MCOPE by showing conceptually meaningful relationships between coping and achievement motivation indices (Ntoumanis, Biddle and Haddock, 1999), competitive trait anxiety (Giacobbi and Weinberg, 2000), performance goal discrepancy and positive/negative affect (Gaudreau, Blondin, and Lapierre, 2002).

Coping Function Questionnaire (CFQ)

Unlike the ISCCS and the MCOPE, the CFQ taps general coping functions as opposed to specific coping strategies. The questionnaire was first presented by Kowalski and Crocker (2001) who tested its validity and reliability in two samples of adolescent athletes. The CFQ assesses three coping functions: problem-focused, emotion-focused and avoidance. Kowalski and Crocker argued that assessing general coping functions can aid researchers to examine how coping changes over time and across situations. In contrast, coping behaviours, as for example those targeted by the ISCCS and the MCOPE, can be too specific to the sample or situation under examination and this can hinder any efforts for generalising findings. However, an inspection of the CFQ items indicates that they actually tap specific coping behaviours (e.g., increasing effort, planning, behavioural disengagement) which might be more relevant to some sport situations than others.

Crocker and Graham initially developed a pool of 30 items based on the coping literature in sport and other life domains. The number of items was reduced to 19 via pilot testing involving athletes and researchers in sport psychology. The first sample used by Crocker and Graham consisted of 126 high school students of seemingly low competitive level. The students were asked to rate the coping items by referring to the most stressful situation they experienced in the previous year in their sport or in another physical activity setting. Interestingly, for each coping item there were separate measures of frequency, duration and effort, however, the scores from these scales were highly correlated. Further, all ratings related to avoidance coping exhibited poor internal reliability. The scale was subsequently modified by Crocker and Graham by rewording, adding and deleting items, and by keeping ratings related to frequency of coping only. It is unfortunate that the ratings for duration and effort were dropped based on the results obtained from a small sample of a seemingly low competitive standard, but one can appreciate that short scales are likely to have higher participant completion rates and perhaps more accurate responses.

The modified CFQ was tested by Kowalski and Crocker (2001) with an independent sample of 835 students of non-specified competitive status. The questionnaire contained 18 items scored on a 5-point scale (1= *not at all*; 5= *very much*). CFA of a three-factor model, performed first separately and then simultaneously across gender, provided very modest fit indices, indicating considerable room for improvement. The authors identified an item that could improve model fit but they were reluctant to delete it. It is surprising that no subsequent studies have further tested the factorial structure of the CFQ. The internal reliability coefficients for all three coping functions were above .80. Lastly, Kowalski and Crocker (2001) offered evidence of the concurrent validity of the CFQ by correlating its subscales with scales from the COPE, the MCOPE and the Life Situations Inventory (Feifel and Strack, 1989). Evidence for the predictive validity of the CFQ in adolescent samples has been provided by Kowalski, Crocker, Hoard and Niefer (2005), and Bolgar, Janelle, and Giacobbi (2008), by relating its subscales with measures of control beliefs, perceived stress and trait anger. Lastly, Hanton, Neil, Mellalieu and Fletcher (2008) used the CFQ with adult athletes (18-36 years) and found that current-elite athletes used more problem-focused and emotion-focused coping, and perceived such coping responses as more effective, than past-elite athletes.

Interviews

There are three types of interviews: structured, semi-structured, and unstructured. Within structured interviews all participants are asked the same questions in exactly the same order. When a semi-structured interview is used participants are asked the same questions, but the order can fluctuate depending on the interviewer who also may wish to explore different avenues that may arise during the interview (Patton, 2002). If the aim of a piece of research is to compare the findings of participants, either a structured or unstructured interview is preferable as the participants will be asked the same questions Finally, interviews that adopt an unstructured approach are guided by the participant and his/her responses (Patton, 2002). Unstructured interviews are more suitable to research questions in which the researcher places less emphasis on comparing the responses of participants. This is because the interviews are participant-driven. In theory, 10 interviews could be conducted that could have completely different content. Virtually all interview studies that have assessed coping in sport utilized a semi-structured interview.

In order to illustrate the processes of conducting an interview study in coping, a recent example from the sport psychology literature will be described in detail. Holt and Hogg (2002) explored stressors and coping strategies among a sample of 10 female soccer players who were about to participate in the 1999 World Cup. Before the interviews were conducted, two pilot interviews were carried out to ensure that the interview guide was suitable. Semi-structured interviews, which lasted between 45 and 60 minutes, were conducted by the lead author during a residential training camp. Participants were initially asked some general background questions relating to their career and the training camp. Questions were centered on a performance framework, which was used to determine the stressors the players had experienced. When the players had described the stressors they had experienced they were asked "How did you/are you dealing with that" (p. 257) to explore the coping strategies used.

Holt and Hogg (2002) analyzed their data in accordance with the framework provided by Maykut and Morehouse (1994). All interviews were transcribed verbatim and individual meaning units relating to stressors and coping strategies were identified. Similar meaning units (e.g., stressors and coping strategies) were grouped and given a phrase that summarized the essence of each meaning unit within that category. To ensure the accuracy of these groupings, each meaning unit was scrutinized using the constant comparative method (Glaser and Strauss, 1967). Following this procedure, the authors discussed the themes that had been derived from analyzing the data. An external auditor with previous experience in sport psychology and qualitative research examined categories and early versions of the manuscript. In order to ensure the goodness of the data triangulation (Patton, 2002) was conducted where: (a) interview data was corroborated via observations from the lead author who was a sport psychologist in the camp, (b) member-checks to ensure what happened had been accurately reported in the research (Lincoln and Guba, 1985), and (c) checking whether information was factually correct with the governing body for soccer.

Four main stressor categories were reported, which included coaches, demands of international soccer, competitive stressors, and distractions. To manage these stressors, the players reported using a variety of different coping strategies that were categorized as reappraising (e.g., positive self-talk), use of social resources (e.g., family support), performance behaviors (e.g., on field task communication), and blocking (e.g., blocking irrelevant stimuli).

A potential issue with interviews (and questionnaires for that matter) is whether athletes are able to accurately remember how they coped when recalling coping strategies. For instance, Gould, Eklund, and Jackson (1993) interviewed wrestlers about how they coped during an Olympic Games six months after the competition had finished. Many interview studies in the sport psychology literature do not report the period between the stressful event and the recall of the coping strategies. Stone et al. (1999) compared momentary assessments coping reports over 48 hours with retrospective reports of coping that took place immediately after the momentary assessments had finished, among a non-athletic sample. Participants retrospectively underreported cognitive coping, whereas they over reported behavioral strategies. Around 30% of participants failed to retrospectively report items they had reported on the momentary assessments. Furthermore, 30% of participants reported items that were not reported on the momentary assessments, despite the same questionnaires being used. It appears that participants may forget, underreport, or over-report when retrospectively recalling coping strategies (Folkman and Moskowitz, 2004). This finding is supported by other researchers from the mainstream psychology literature (e.g., Ptacek, Smith, Espe, and

Raffety, 1994; Smith, Leffingwell, and Ptacek, 1999), who found that with passage of time people provide less accurate coping accounts. Indeed, Ptacek et al. (1994) found evidence to suggest the validity of coping strategies recalled over a recall period between 5-day to 12-day period is questionable. Therefore, interviews to assess coping should be conducted as close to the stressful event as possible and within a 5-day period to ensure that the data is valid.

Concept Maps

Concept maps proposed by Novak and Gowin (1984) are node-link diagrams that represent concepts or relationships between different variables. In a sporting context, concept maps have been used to explore stressors and coping among athletes (e.g., Holt and Mandigo, 2004; Nicholls, Polman, Levy, Taylor, and Cobley, 2007). In these two studies each concept map consisted of six numbered blank boxes in which participants were able to report their data. Participants were asked to recall stressors (see Figure 1) and the corresponding coping strategies they used to manage each stressor, by reporting the coping strategy used in the corresponding numbered box (see Figure 2).

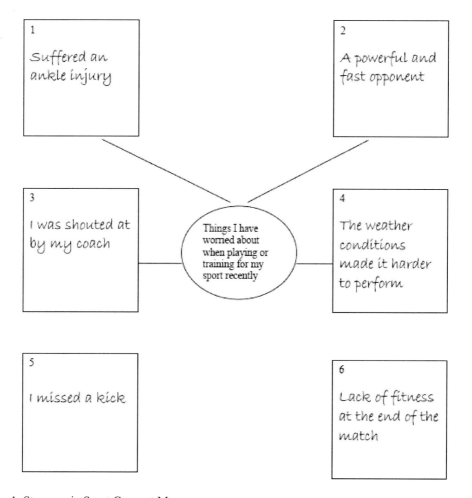

Figure 1. Stressors in Sport Concept Map.

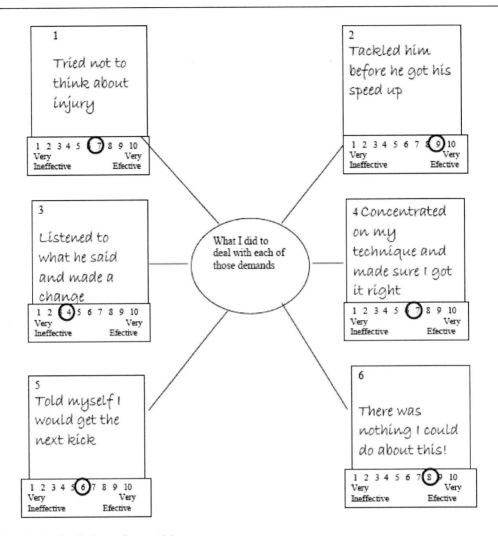

Figure 2. Coping in Sport Concept Map.

For instance, in the example provided the athlete reported injury as a stressor in Box 1 of the stressor concept map (see Figure 1) and coped with this stressor by blocking out thoughts of the injury (see Box 1, Figure 2).

Similar to questionnaires, concept maps are relatively quick to complete. Athletes should be able to complete a pair of stressor and coping concept maps within 15 to 20 minutes, which means it is possible to generate large amounts of data. Unlike questionnaires, the responses of participants are not pre-determined, so athletes' responses are not constrained.

With regard to analyzing data generated from concept maps, a variety of qualitative and quantitative procedures can be carried out. The initial phase is to transcribe the data from the concept maps. Nicholls et al. (2007) identified individual meaning units from the stressor and coping concept maps and grouped similar meaning units together. A descriptive label that reflected the meaning of each theme was given to each unit, in accordance with Maykut and Morehouse (1994). Following this procedure, a range of statistical tests can be used.

Although the studies by Holt and Mandigo (2004) and Nicholls et al. (2007) have only explored the relationship between stressors and coping, other variables could be introduced.

Other components of stressors and coping could also be explored, such as stressor intensity, stressor controllability, coping effectiveness, and coping automaticity. For instance, other concept maps could include constructs appraisals and emotions. A potential limitation of using concept maps relates to the open-ended format of the questions. Unlike interviews, participants do not have somebody to provide them with prompts, which may limit the responses provided. Furthermore, this type of data will be vulnerable to memory decay associated with the retrospective recall of coping (e.g., Stone et al., 1999). It is therefore essential that researchers minimize the delay between the stressful event and the recall of the stressors and the coping strategies in the concept maps to within 5-day period.

Diaries

A recent systematic review revealed that over 80% of sport psychology coping studies adopted the transactional approach (Nicholls and Polman, 2007a). In an attempt to reduce the recall period and to tap into the dynamic nature of coping, scholars have utilized diaries to assess coping on a daily basis (Porter and Stone, 1996). This allows coping to be compared over various time periods in relation to different events that may be occurring. A variety of different diaries have been developed and modified in the research by Nicholls and colleagues. Some of these diaries have used an open-ended question format (e.g., Nicholls 2007; see Figure 3) or a mixture of open-ended questions, checklists (e.g., Nicholls, Holt, Polman, and James, 2005) and Likert-type scales (e.g., Nicholls, Holt, Polman, and Bloomfield, 2006; Nicholls, Jones, Polman, and Borkoles, 2009; Nicholls and Polman, 2007b; see Figure 4).

The different components of the diaries are analyzed differently. The stressor checklist, based upon Anshel (1996), was tallied to provide a frequency for each stressor. As stress and coping are measured over repeated time points in diary designs, stressor frequencies can be measured within different periods of the study (Nicholls, Holt, Polman, and James, 2005; Udry, 1997). For example, in the 31-day study by Nicholls et al. (2005), there were five periods of five days (e.g., days 1–5, 6–10, 11–15, 16–20, and 21–25) and one period of six days (e.g., days 26-31). The open-ended coping responses and open-ended stress responses have been analyzed inductively in accordance with guidelines suggested by Maykut and Morehouse (1994). With regards to analyzing the Likert-type scales used for measures such as coping effectiveness, means can be calculated by adding the coping effectiveness score for each time a coping strategy was employed and then dividing the total score by the frequency of times a strategy was deployed to provide an overall coping effectiveness score. Furthermore, the mean coping effectiveness of different strategies can be calculated in response to different stressors, by adding up the coping effectiveness Likert-type scale scores for each coping strategy in response to a specific stressor and dividing the total by the frequency of times the coping strategy was deployed.

A concern of using diaries over a prolonged period of time relates to a high drop-out rate, which was up to 60% among participants, observed in the studies by Nicholls and colleagues (e.g., Nicholls et al., 2006; Nicholls, Holt, Polman, and James, 2005; Nicholls and Polman, 2007b). It is inevitable that athletes will get injured, especially those from physically demanding sports, but researchers must try hard to enhance adherence to diary studies.

Saturday, 10th APRIL

PRACTICE/ COMPETITION [please circle].

Type of competition CLUB/ COUNTY/ NATIONAL/ INTERNATIONAL [Please circle if appropriate]

1.What stressors have you faced today during golf (please list and describe)?

Missing putts- I missed some really short putts today. There was one where I had chance for birdie and I missed it.

Opponents- Today my playing partners were playing really well and that worried me a bit

Mistakes- I made a few mistakes today which cost me a top 10 finish. I found it hard to get my club selection right because of the strong wind conditions

2.What did you do to manage these stressors?

I went through my putting routine, and tried to hit positive putts.
I focused on my own game and tried to ignore what my opponent was doing
I tried to block out each mistake that I had made and tried to be positive for my next shot

3. Which of the coping strategies you used today were the most effective/helped you the most?

When I focused on my own game it really helped as I could concentrate more

4.Why do you think these strategies were particularly effective/helpful?

Just because you can think more clearly about what you are going to do yourself and it takes the pressure off not thinking about how they are doing

5.Were there any things that you did or attempted to manage stress which was not very effective/helpful?

Trying to block out my mistakes was not very helpful at all.

6. Why did these strategies not help?

They did not really work as all I could think about was the wrong club selection to the 5th green which cost me the chance of a birdie and was the reason why I made a double bogey. I was thinking about this shot for the rest of my round

Figure 3. Open-ended Stressor and Coping Sheet.

Techniques to reduce drop could involve only giving participants diaries for seven days at a time (e.g., Polman, Nicholls, Cohen, and Borkoles, 2007), meeting participants on a regular basis, or if this is not possible sending SMS messages (e.g., Nicholls, Levy, Grice, and Polman, in press). Although diary methods reduce the period of recall which increases the validity of the data (e.g., Stone et al., 1999), Folkman and Moskowitz (2004) suggested that daily measures of coping do not allow people time for reflection, with regard to their coping.

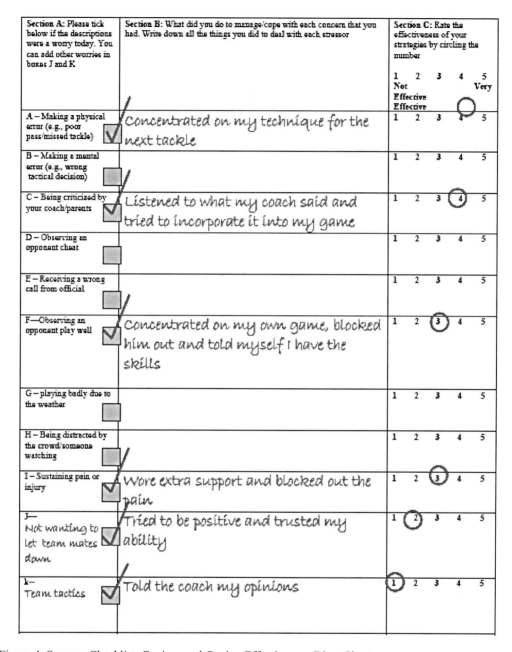

Section A: Please tick below if the descriptions were a worry today. You can add other worries in boxes J and K	Section B: What did you do to manage/cope with each concern that you had. Write down all the things you did to deal with each stressor	Section C: Rate the effectiveness of your strategies by circling the number 1 2 3 4 5 Not Very Effective Effective
A – Making a physical error (e.g., poor pass/missed tackle) ✓	*Concentrated on my technique for the next tackle*	1 2 3 ④ 5
B – Making a mental error (e.g., wrong tactical decision)		1 2 3 4 5
C – Being criticized by your coach/parents ✓	*Listened to what my coach said and tried to incorporate it into my game*	1 2 3 ④ 5
D – Observing an opponent cheat		1 2 3 4 5
E – Receiving a wrong call from official		1 2 3 4 5
F—Observing an opponent play well ✓	*Concentrated on my own game, blocked him out and told myself I have the skills*	1 2 ③ 4 5
G – playing badly due to the weather		1 2 3 4 5
H – Being distracted by the crowd/someone watching		1 2 3 4 5
I – Sustaining pain or injury ✓	*Wore extra support and blocked out the pain*	1 2 ③ 4 5
J— Not wanting to let team mates down ✓	*Tried to be positive and trusted my ability*	1 ② 3 4 5
k— Team tactics ✓	*Told the coach my opinions*	① 2 3 4 5

Figure 4. Stressor Checklist, Coping, and Coping Effectiveness Diary Sheet.

Think Aloud Protocols

An alternative method to diaries that enables coping to be measured longitudinally and to reduce the period of recall even further is a think aloud protocol (Ericsson and Simon, 1980). In order to assess such fluctuations, repeated measurements on the same person are taken. According to Ericsson and Simon (1993) there has been an increase in the use of verbal data to assess cognitive processes in many areas of psychology. Given that coping is a cognitive process (e.g., Lazarus, 1999), think aloud would appear to be a suitable method of assessing coping. Ericsson and Simon proposed three different levels of verbalizations, which: (a) determine the type of data collected, and (b) influence the effect that verbalizing may have on athletic performance.

Verbalizations of thoughts are classified as Level 1 and Level 2 verbalizations, whereas verbalizations of specific information, such as reasons or explanations, are known as Level 3 verbalizations (Ericsson and Simon, 1993). The difference between Level 1 and Level 2 lies in the cognitive processes involved in verbalization. Verbalizations of thoughts that are already verbal and do not need transforming, but simply to be vocalized (e.g., a thought that relates to the performance of an opponent, such as "Christopher is playing well today") is a case of Level 1 verbalizations. Conversely, thoughts that require transformation so it can verbalized are referred to as Level 2 verbalizations. This would include, for example, verbalizing images (e.g., "the coach looks annoyed today").

Ericsson and Simon (1993) reviewed the effects of verbalizations on performance. Although none of the reviewed studies were sport-based, their findings revealed that Level 1 and Level 2 verbalizations had no undermining effect on performance. In contrast, Level 3 verbalizations had a negative impact on performance. Caution is therefore warranted before asking athletes to provide Level 3 verbalizations, until research has examined the impact these verbalizations in non-competitive environments. If a study wants to explore either Level 1 or Level 2 verbalizations, participants should be instructed to say what they are thinking during a specific task or event and not to explain their thoughts.

A recent study by Nicholls and Polman (2008) used a think aloud protocol to explore stress and coping during six holes of golf, via Level 2 Verbalizations. Before the data collection commenced, the participants received instructions and took part in some think aloud exercises. To ensure that Level 2 verbalizations were obtained, the participants were instructed not explain their thoughts, but say what they were thinking. Participants were asked to talk continuously throughout the six holes of golf other than when they were just about to draw their club back for a shot, and resume talking straight after the shot completion. The participants were told that if they were quiet for more than 20 seconds, they would be asked to continue thinking aloud by the researcher who walked behind the golfers. As such, with the exception of the researcher, each participant performed alone.

Following the completion of the warm up exercise the participant was wired up to a digital voice recorder, with a microphone attached to their collar. All digital files were transcribed verbatim and then subjected to protocol analysis (Ericsson and Simon, 1993). Transcripts were checked for relevance and consistence. Verbalizations are considered relevant if they relate to the task and consistent if they flow with previous verbal data. Verbal data that is not deemed relevant to the task or inconsistent with previous verbalizations is removed. Ericsson and Simon's protocol analysis was then adapted to specifically assess stress and coping using an inductive analysis procedure (e.g., see Maykut and Morehouse, 1994). Similar meaning units (e.g., coping strategies) were grouped together and a rule of inclusion, that summarized the essence of each meaning unit, was written for each coping strategy. This was then discussed with other members of the research team. Once this was carried out stressors and coping strategies were tallied. The final procedure was member-checking (Lincoln and Guba, 1985), in which participants received a chronologically ordered profile of coping strategies and are asked to comment upon the accuracy of their report. Overall, the results of Nicholls and Polman (2008) revealed that stressors and coping strategies varied across the six holes of golf. Additionally, golfers reported up to five stressors before deploying a coping strategy.

Think aloud protocols are useful if a researcher intends to explore coping over time. Data can be tallied across different time periods (e.g., holes within golf or laps within motor racing), so that frequencies can be established over time. Although think aloud protocols reduce the time between the stressful event and the recall of the corresponding coping strategies to a few seconds, a potential issue relates to whether the verbalizations reported as stressors actually caused the participants stress, which then has implications with regards to whether the subsequent strategies can be classified as coping. (see Krathwohl, 1993, for an explanation of credibility). Construct validity could be assessed by comparing the verbal reports with other measurements, such physiological measurements of stress (e.g., heart rate or blood pressure). Further, data from think aloud protocols could be compared with those obtained from sport-specific stress and coping inventories administered after the event. Finally, think aloud will only be suitable for a limited number of sports, due to the requirements of the protocol. In sports such as soccer or basketball it would be virtually impossible for athletes to verbalize their thoughts whilst sprinting.

Ecological Momentary Assessment

Another method that has been used to assess coping, although not among athletic populations, is ecological momentary assessment (EMA; Larson, Csikszentmihalyi, and Graef, 1980). With this method participants are given electronic "bleepers" that go off at either random or predetermined times and the participants have to answer a series of questions (Aldwin, 2007). A potential limitation of this method within a sporting context relates to the timing of the beeps. If the bleeper goes off at inconvenient times during competition it may be impossible for the athlete to complete the questions they are supposed to answer. This method may therefore be more suitable to explore organizational stressors, whereby athletes could complete EMA assessments outside of competition. Furthermore, the questions have to be very brief, which may limit the usefulness of findings generated. Similar to diaries and think aloud protocols, a potential strength of this approach is the reduced period between the stressful event and the recall of the coping strategies used to manage such stressors. However, participants have less time for reflection, with regards to how they coped (Folkman and Moskowitz, 2004).

CONCLUSION

A variety of diverse techniques have been used to assess coping among athletes. Before deciding which method to use, it is essential that one considers the research question that needs to be addressed. If the research question is directed towards examining individual experiences of coping, then interviews or open-ended diaries and think aloud protocols will be more suitable. In contrast, questionnaires or concept maps might be more suitable if the aim of the research is to make generalisations among large groups of athletes. All of the methods have strengths and limitations, as mentioned in this chapter.

A common observation for all three scales reviewed in this chapter is that there have been a surprisingly very small number of studies testing their psychometric properties. Many coping researchers have utilised these scales without examining how valid the scales are with their own data. This is rather worrying as the coping responses included in these questionnaires might vary in relevance as a function of factors such as the timing of the assessment (e.g., before or after a competition), the type of sport, the nature of the stressor or individual differences. For example, coping responses such as analysing past performances or using relaxation techniques might not be possible in fast-paced sports or during competition. The low or no-usage of certain strategies might result in very low mean scores and potentially floor effects when associating the scores from these scales with various antecedents and outcome variables. It seems that it might be counter-productive to attempt to identify for each scale a definite number of items and factors that would generalise across moderators such as type of sport, culture, stressors, or timing of assessments. Thus, it is strongly suggested that future studies on coping should subject to CFA the coping instruments they use so that researchers can develop a better understanding of which coping strategies or functions are more relevant to different stressors or samples.

REFERENCES

Aldwin, C.M. (2007). *Stress, coping and development: An integrative perspective* (2nd ed.). New York: Guilford Press.

Amiot, C.E., Gaudreau, P., and Blanchard, C.M. (2004). Self-determination, coping, and goal attainment in sport. *Journal of Sport and Exercise Psychology, 26*, 386-411.

Anshel, M. H. (1996). Coping styles among adolescent competitive athletes. *Journal of Social Psychology, 136,* 311-324.

Bolgar, M. R., Janelle, C., and Giacobbi, P. R. (2008). Trait anger, differences among adolescent tennis players. *Journal of Applied Sport Psychology, 20,* 73-87.

Crocker, P. R. E., and Graham, T. R. (1995). Coping by competitive athletes with performance stress: Gender differences and relationships with affect. *The Sport Psychologist, 9,* 325-338.

Crocker, P. R. E., Kowalski, K. C., and Graham, T. R. (1998). Measurement of coping strategies in sport. In J. L. Duda (Ed.), *Advances in sport and exercise psychology measurement* (pp. 149-161). Morgantown, WV: Fitness Information Technology.

Eklund, R. C., Grove, R. J., and Heard, P. N. (1998). The measurement of slump-related coping: factorial validity of the COPE and the Modified-COPE inventories. *Journal of Sport and Exercise Psychology, 20,* 157–175.

Ericsson, K. A., and Simon, H. A. (1980). Verbal reports as data. *Psychological Review, 3,* 215-251.

Ericsson, K. A., and Simon, H. A. (1993). *Verbal reports as data.* Cambridge, MA: MIT Press.

Feifel, H., and Strack, S. (1989). Coping with conflict situations: Middle-aged and elderly men. *Psychology and Aging, 4,* 26-33.

Folkman, S., and Lazarus, R. S. (1985). If it changes it must be a process: Study of emotion and coping during three stages of a college examination. *Journal of Personality and Social Psychology, 48,* 150-170.

Folkman, S., and Moskowitz, J. T. (2004). Coping: Pitfalls and promise. *Annual Review of Psychology, 55,* 745-774.

Gaudreau, P., and Blondin, J. P. (2002). Development of a questionnaire for the assessment of coping strategies employed by athletes in competitive sport settings. *Psychology of Sport and Exercise 3,* 1-34.

Gaudreau P, Blondin J. P. (2004). Different athletes coping differently during sport competition: A cluster analysis of coping. *Personality and Individual Differences 36,* 1865-77.

Gaudreau, P., El Ali, M., and Marivain, T. (2005). Factor structure of the coping inventory for competitive sport with a sample of participants at the 2001 New York marathon. *Psychology of Sport and Exercise, 6,* 271-288.

Glaser, B.G., and Strauss, A. (1967). *The discovery of grounded theory.* Chicago, IL: Aldine.

Gould, D., Eklund, R. C., and Jackson, S. A. (1993). Coping strategies used by US Olympic wrestlers. *Research Quarterly for Exercise and Sport, 64,* 83-93.

Hanton, S., Neil, R., Mellalieu, S. D., and Fletcher, D. (2008). Competitive experience and performance status: An investigation into multidimensional anxiety and coping. *European Journal of Sport Science, 8,* 143-152.

Holt, N. L., and Hogg, J. M. (2002). Perceptions of stress and coping during preparations for the 1999 women's soccer world cup finals. The Sport Psychologist, 16, 251 – 271.

Holt, N. L., and Mandigo, J. L. (2004). Coping with performance worries among male youth cricket players. *Journal of Sport Behavior, 27,* 39-57.

Holt, N. L., and Sparkes, A. C. (2001). An ethnographic study of cohesiveness in a college soccer team over a season. *The Sport Psychologist, 15,* 157-172.

Hu, L., and Bentler, P. M. (1995). Evaluating model fit. In R. H. Hoyle, *Structural equation modeling: Concepts, issues, and applications* (pp. 76–99). Thousand Oaks, CA: Sage.

Kowalski, K. C., and Crocker, P. R. (2001). Development and validation of the Coping Function Questionnaire for adolescents in sport. *Journal of Sport and Exercise Psychology, 23,* 136-155.

Kowalski, K. C., Crocker, P. R., Hoar, S. D., and Niefer, C. B. (2005). Adolescents' control beliefs and coping with stress in sport. *International Journal of Sport Psychology, 36,* 257-272.

Krathwohl, D.R., (1993). *Methods of educational and social science research: An integrated approach.* White Plains, NY: Longman.

Larson, R., Csikszentmihalyi, M., and Graef, R. (1980). Mood variability and the psychosocial adjustment of adolescents. *Journal of Youth and Adolescence, 9,* 469-490.

Lazarus, R. S. (1999). *Stress and emotion: A new synthesis.* New York: Springer.

Lazarus, R. S. (2000). Toward better research on stress and coping. *American Psychologist, 55,* 665-673.

Lazarus, R. S., and Folkman, S. (1984). *Stress, appraisal and coping.* New York: Springer.

Lincoln, Y. S., and Guba, E. G. (1985). *Naturalistic Inquiry.* Newbury Park, CA: Sage.

Maykut, P., and Morehouse, R. (1994). *Beginning qualitative research: A philosophic and practical guide.* Philadelphia: Falmer Press.

Nicholls, A. R. (2007). A longitudinal phenomenological analysis of coping effectiveness among Scottish international adolescent golfers. *European Journal of Sport Science, 7,* 169-178.

Nicholls, A. R., Hemmings, B., and Clough, P. J. (in press). Stressors, coping, and emotion among international adolescent golfers. *Scandinavian Journal of Medicine and Science in Sports.*

Nicholls, A. R., Jones, C. R., Polman, R. C. J., and Borkoles, E. (in press). Stressors, coping, and emotion among professional rugby union players during training and matches. *Scandinavian Journal of Medicine and Science in Sports.*

Nicholls, A. R., Holt, N. L., and Polman, R. C. J. (2005). A phenomenological analysis of coping effectiveness in golf. *The Sport Psychologist, 19,* 111-130.

Nicholls, A. R., Holt, N. L., Polman, R. C. J., and Bloomfield, J. (2006). Stressors, coping, and coping effectiveness among professional rugby union players. *The Sport Psychologist, 20,* 314-329.

Nicholls, A. R., Holt, N. L., Polman, R. C. J., and James, D. W. G. (2005) Stress, coping, and coping effectiveness among international adolescent golfers. *Journal of Applied Sport Psychology, 17,* 333-340.

Nicholls, A. R., Levy, A. R., Grice, A., and Polman, R. C. J. (in press). Stress appraisals, coping, and coping effectiveness among international cross country runners during training and competition. *European Journal of Sport Science.*

Nicholls, A. R., and Polman, R.C.J. (2007a). Coping in sport: A systematic review. *Journal of Sports Sciences, 25,* 11-31.

Nicholls, A. R. and Polman, R. C. J. (2007b). Stressors, coping and coping effectiveness among players from the England under-18 rugby union team. *Journal of Sport Behavior, 30,* 199-218.

Nicholls, A. R., and Polman, R. C. J. (2008). Think aloud: Acute Stress and coping during golf performances. *Anxiety, Stress, and Coping, 21,* 283-294.

Nicholls, A. R., Polman, R. C. J., Levy, A. R., and Backhouse, S. H. (2008). Mental toughness, optimism, pessimism, and coping among athletes. *Personality and Individual Differences, 44,* 1182-1192.

Nicholls, A. R., Polman, R.C. J., Levy, A. R., Taylor, J. A., and Cobley, S. P. (2007). Stressors, coping, and coping effectiveness: Gender, sport type, and skill differences. *Journal of Sports Sciences, 25,* 1521-1530.

Novak, J. D., and Gowin, D. B. (1984). *Learning how to learn.* Cambridge: Cambridge University Press.

Patton, M. Q. (2002). *Qualitative research and evaluation methods.* Thousand Oaks, CA: Sage.

Polman, R. C. J., Nicholls, A. R., Cohen, J. and Borkoles, E. (2007). The influence of game location and outcome on behaviour and mood states among professional rugby league players. *Journal of Sports Sciences, 25,* 1491-1500.

Porter, L. S., and Stone, A. A. (1996). An approach to assessing daily coping. In M. Zeidner and N. S. Endler (Eds.), *Handbook of coping: Theory, research, and applications* (pp. 133-150). New York: Wiley.

Ptacek, J. T., Smith, R. E., Espe, K., and Raffety, B. (1994). Limited correspondence between daily coping reports and retrospective coping recall. *Psychological Assessment, 6,* 41-48.

Smith, R. E., Leffingwell, T. R., and Ptacek, J. T. (1999). Can people remember how they coped? Factors associated with discordance between same-day and retrospective reports. *Journal of Personality and Social Psychology, 76,* 1050-1061.

Smith, R. E., Smoll, F. L., and Wiechman, S. A. (1998). Measurement of trait anxiety in sport. In J. L. Duda (Ed.), *Advances in sport and exercise psychology measurement* (pp. 105-127). Morgantown, WV: Fitness Information Technology.

Stone, A. A., Schwartz, J. E., Neale, J. M., Shiffman, S., Marco, C., Hickcox, M., Paty, J., Porter, L. S., and Cruise, L. J. (1999). A comparison of coping assessed by ecological momentary analysis and retrospective recall. *Journal of Personality and Social Psychology, 74,* 1670-1680.

Udry, E. (1997). Coping and social support among injured athletes following surgery. *Journal of Sport and Exercise Psychology, 19,* 71-90.

In: Coping in Sport: Theory, Methods, and Related Constructs   ISBN: 978-1-60876-488-4
Editor: Adam R. Nicholls   © 2010 Nova Science Publishers, Inc.

Chapter 4

COPING: RESEARCH DESIGN AND ANALYSIS ISSUES

Peter R.E. Crocker[1], Amber D. Mosewich[1], Kent C. Kowalski[2] and Leah J. Besenski[2]

[1]University of British Columbia, Canada
[2]University of Saskatchewan, Canada

ABSTRACT

This chapter reviews the various quantitative and qualitative research questions and methods that have been asked and used within coping in sport literature to date. We also discuss quantitative and qualitative research methods that could be used, but are generally not used or underrepresented, to better understand coping in sport. To this end, we discuss quantitative research designs predominantly focusing on mediation, moderator models, and multilevel and multilevel longitudinal modeling of coping. We also discuss various issues relevant to qualitative research including the need for prolonged time in the field, consideration of the number of participants, bracketing, and methods of data collection, analysis, and representation.

INTRODUCTION

How can we advance our understanding of the coping process in sport? The previous three chapters addressed some fundamental conceptual and measurement issues about coping in sport. Subsequent chapters will tackle a host of specific areas such as development, gender, ethnicity, personality, motivation, emotions, and performance related topics. Clearly this indicates that coping is a complex issue. All of the chapters reveal that our present understanding of coping in sport is primarily informed by two inter-connected areas – theory and research. Sport researchers have conducted numerous studies, using both quantitative and qualitative methods. The complexity of factors that impact coping, as well as the outcomes of coping, makes designing and analyzing a strong coping study very challenging. Nevertheless, such challenges are necessary to triumph over if we are to comprehend the coping process.

The purpose of this chapter is to identify key research issues about design and analysis in sport coping studies. Research design often presupposes a thorough understanding of theoretical, conceptual, or empirical knowledge about coping. As highlighted in the previous chapters, however, this knowledge is still developing. Research methods themselves are often rooted in assumptions that are laden with limitations (Denzin and Lincoln, 2003; Okasha, 2000). To even address these assumptions would require an additional chapter. Thus, any particular research method cannot provide absolute clarity about any question concerning coping. However, if approached with scientific caution and humility, solid research designs and the ensuing analysis of data can facilitate our appreciation of coping in sport. In this chapter we will highlight (a) the importance of developing a sound research question, (b) how particular research questions may require specific designs and analyses, and (c) the use of both quantitative and qualitative methods in coping research. Through the chapter we will provide examples of research design and analyses in coping from the literature, identifying both strong and questionable methods and analyses, and underscoring specific strengths and limitations.

Developing Strong Research Questions

Strong research and knowledge development in coping in sport requires the formulation of strong research questions. A fundamental question is what is coping and how does it fit into a larger picture of self-regulation and adaptation in sport? This issue has been discussed in Chapter 1 by Nicholls and Thelwell and other recent reviews (Hoar Kowalski, Gaudreau, and Crocker, 2006; Nicholls and Polman, 2007), so we will not belabour it in any detail. Coping is typically defined in most sport studies using Lazarus and Folkman's (1984) characterization that coping consists of responses (behavioral, cognitive, and emotional) to manage internal or external demands that are evaluated as taxing or exceeding the resources of the athlete. There are other definitions (see Compas, Conner, Osowiecki, and Welch, 1997; Skinner, 1999), but there is an emerging opinion that coping involves regulating stress and emotion by mobilizing and coordinating many self-regulation systems involving motor behaviour, cognitions, attention, emotion, and physiological processes (see Skinner and Zimmer-Gembeck, 2007). Thus, to make significant increases in our understanding coping in sport will require a determination of how all these systems work together to allow the athlete to adapt, or even fail to adapt, to the demands of sport. This is no small challenge. Therefore a first step in developing strong research questions would be to become familiar with the key conceptual questions covered in many of the excellent chapters in this book as well as the emerging coping and general self-regulation literature (e.g., Aldwin, 2007; Baumeister and Vohs, 2004; Skinner and Zimmer-Gembeck, 2007).

When we examine coping in sport, we need to determine what the athlete is coping with, what factors determine the selection of specific coping actions, and what constitutes the outcomes of coping. Some of these topics have been covered in previous chapters, but we believe these three aspects need to be considered when developing research studies. First, athletes will use coping responses to manage the various demands (stressors) of sport that threaten or challenge athletes' goals, values, and beliefs. These stressors can have different temporal qualities such as being acute, intermittent, or chronic. The stressors can be categorized at macro-levels such as social, interpersonal, emotional, physical, psychological, and organizational (Gould, Finch, and Jackson, 1993; Hanton and Fletcher, 2005; Kowalski and Crocker, 2001) or operationalized at more micro-levels such as a specific injury, performance goals, coach, referee or teammate conflict, media or significant other expectations, specific technical demands, performance mistakes, and emotional states related to competition (Anshel, Williams, and Williams, 2000; Holt and Hogg, 2002; Nicholls and Polman, 2008). The particular stressor is also embedded in a stressor context (sport type and sport situation) that will demand and constrain the specific types of coping responses. For example, some sports like ice hockey tolerate players verbally venting at referees whereas other sports like volleyball have very low tolerance levels for such behaviour. Thus, the same type of stressor (perceived bad call by the referee) is moderated by context (sport) to restrict the range of possible coping responses. These relationships are further moderated by cultural standards. For example, baseball managers in North America often engage in a somewhat ritualized verbal and expressive venting display when confronting umpires over disputed calls. Such behaviour is rarely displayed in Japan. We believe that coping research that does not specify the characteristics of the stressor are unlikely to provide significant contributions to the sport coping literature in the 21st century.

What other factors, besides the type and context of the stressor, are likely to impact coping in sport? As captured by the various chapters in this book, there are numerous antecedents including personality, knowledge, coping skills repertoire, skill level, global and sport specific culture (values and beliefs), motivation, gender, social support, sport experience, and other environmental demands, to name a few. These personal and situational factors create personal meaning and subsequent appraisals (threat, harm/loss, challenge, perceived control, future expectancies, and coping options) to influence coping (Lazarus, 1991a, 1991b, 1991c, 1999; Aldwin, 2007). Coping can produce varied adaptive and maladaptive outcomes related to emotional experience and expression, performance, social functioning, burn-out, injury, career transitions, and lifestyle management. Thus, it appears that researchers should develop coping studies that consider not only stressor factors but also some key antecedents and/or outcomes.

With so many factors to consider, it would be impossible for any particular study to provide a definitive understanding of coping in sport. Thus, what type of study design and analysis will make a significant contribution to the field? Are quantitative or qualitative methods, or even mixed methods, appropriate? Unfortunately there are no easy answers! We believe research design and analysis should be driven by a strong research question that is guided by empirical, theoretical, or rationale driven formulations. In the following sections, we will discuss various research designs and analyses that could have or actually have been used to examine specific research questions related to coping in sport. Obviously we cannot cover all the coping research in the field but we have selected specific examples of designs and analyses that seek to answer questions including simple descriptive studies, group differences (such as gender, sport type, and level of competition), direct prediction models, and mediation and moderator modeling examining the effects of particular variables on coping and coping outcomes. We will also briefly describe the use of different types of designs including experimental, quasi-experimental, and passive observation (correlation), as well as discuss the merits and limitations of cross-sectional and prospective designs. For the ease of organization, we will start with descriptive studies that will include both quantitative and qualitative examples. This will be followed by two separate major sections section on quantitative and qualitative designs and analyses.

Descriptive Research Designs

There are a number of sport coping studies that are primarily descriptive or exploratory in nature. While this type of research cannot yield causal or predictive claims, it can play an important foundational role in understanding coping. Because coping is such a complex process influenced by multiple person and societal variables, it is important to acknowledge that there are likely to be unique aspects of coping that need to be described for particular sport populations and contexts. Increased comprehension about the coping process in a particular circumstance, such as athletes in a certain sport facing a particular stressor, may provide preliminary information about coping and help provide direction for future research.

Descriptive or exploratory studies can take the form of qualitative or quantitative design, or a combination of the two (known as mixed methods research), depending on the goal of the research and the research question. Data collected can be longitudinal or cross-sectional and participants can provide information either prospectively or retrospectively. Surveys, interviews, and observations are common methods of descriptive research. For example, Gould et al. (1993) employed qualitative methodologies to identify and describe the coping strategies used by national champion figure skaters and to explore the relationship between coping strategies and sources of stress. Former Senior U. S. National figure skaters were interviewed using a series of open-ended and guided questions about stressors and coping with the demands of being a national champion level figure skater. Content analysis procedures revealed a number of coping dimensions including rational thinking and self-talk, positive focus and orientation, social support, time management and prioritization, precompetitive mental preparation and anxiety management, training hard and smart, isolation and deflection, and ignoring the stressor(s).

Quantitative methods can also yield specific information about a particular group or setting, but accomplishes the task using a different approach. For example, Yoo (2000) examined coping in a group of Korean athletes using a culturally-specific coping measure. Exploratory and confirmatory factor analyses were conducted to test the fit of a coping model specifically for Korean athletes. While providing validation for the measure, this study also provides a description of the coping processes employed by Korean athletes. In addition to the commonly cited components of coping in work with North American athletes (problem-focused, emotion-focused, and avoidance coping), Yoo also identified that transcendental coping (a culturally-specific psychological control strategy employed by Koreans in times of adversity) is an important component to assess if one is to adequately measure and understand coping in Korean athletes.

As with any research approach, descriptive research has both advantages and limitations. Descriptive research can yield specific information about the group or situation being studied. However, this also means that the results may not be generalizable across different samples and contexts. Additionally, causal claims cannot be generated from descriptive research. Descriptive studies can provide other useful information, just from a different perspective. Descriptive studies typically address questions such as who, what, where, when, and why. These questions are often valuable when looking at variables that cannot be controlled, or when looking at variables that have not been previously considered in research. Nevertheless, it is critical that coping researchers justify the use of descriptive studies and how such studies will further our understanding of coping in sport.

QUANTITATIVE RESEARCH DESIGNS

There are several different types of research designs used in quantitative studies of coping.[1] These designs have varying strengths in determining the causal relationship among variables in the coping process. A causal relationship essentially reflects a condition that is necessary to produce an effect on a given outcome (Thomas, Nelson, and Silverman, 2005). Three conditions are necessary to establish causality. First, there must be a temporal relationship between variables such that the causal agent occurs before the effected variables. Second, there must be systematic covariation between the variables such that changing one variable is associated with a systematic change in the other variable. Third, it is important to rule out alternative plausible hypotheses. Keeping these three conditions in mind, we can evaluate the strengths of particular research designs.

At a general level there are three primary designs used in quantitative studies of coping: experimental, quasi-experimental, and passive observation (correlational) designs. In both experimental and quasi-experimental studies, key "causal" variables are manipulated to effect change in dependent variables. In experimental studies, all three conditions of causality can be satisfied, whereas quasi-experimental studies can often only satisfy the first two conditions. The lack of random assignment of participants to experimental conditions in quasi-experimental studies creates many threats to internal validity. In observational studies, there is no systematic variable manipulation but simply the passive observation and measurement of key variables. Thus, only the condition of systematic covariation can be satisfied. Despite this weakness, the great majority of coping studies in sport are observational. What this type of approach does often offer, however, is an important first step in identifying whether or not the data is consistent with plausible causal models and the identification of potentially key variables that could be playing a role in a causal chain.

Coping research studies can also be categorized as being cross-sectional and prospective longitudinal. Cross-sectional designs involve measuring variables from a number of athletes at one particular time. These designs provide a "snap-shot" of the relationships among variables that are thought to remain consistent over time and among all members of the target population. Researchers can use data from such studies to establish correlations and predictive relationships among variables in the coping process (e.g., Crocker and Graham, 1995), as well as examine differences among groups based on categories such as level of experience, gender, cultural group, and sport type. Advantages of this method include decreased data collection time and typically larger sample sizes (because sample attrition over time is not an issue). They also often provide critical first steps in exploring the plausibility of causal models, which is important because of the time and resources necessary to conduct strong experimental studies. However, these advantages come at a cost because cross-sectional designs do not allow for a direct test of causal models due to the loss of temporal ordering of variables. Also, cross-sectional designs make looking developmental issues associated with the coping process particularly difficult. While different age or maturity groups might differ on a number of developmental markers, it is difficult to rule out

---

[1] There are several types of designs that will not be covered because of space restrictions. These include cohort designs (both longitudinal and cross-sectional), cross-over designs, longitudinal case studies, and retrospective longitudinal designs. We will also not consider coping instrument development and assessment.

alternative hypotheses that propose any group differences found simply reflect differences on variables other than development.

In contrast, prospective longitudinal designs involve repeated measurement of the same variables over periods of time. Some prospective studies might only measure different variables at specific time periods (see Gaudreau and Antl, 2008). The time period can range from being relatively short (e.g., over the phases of a competition), to intermediate (e.g., over the course of several competitions or a season), to very long (e.g., several years or decades). Using a longitudinal design allows the researcher to look at various features of the data including: (a) changes in the distribution of individual differences over time (covariance stability), (b) the consistency of relationships among variables at specific time intervals, (c) whether changes in specific variables covary over time, (d) whether stable variables (like personality) influence dynamic variables (like coping) at different time periods, and (e) differences in the prediction of cross-sectional and longitudinal data (Crocker, Kowalski, Hoar, and McDonough, 2003; Gaudreau and Antl, 2008; Gollob and Reichardt, 1987). There are a few longitudinal studies examining such issues as determining distinct trajectories for coping, examining how personality and motivation influence goal attainment and coping, and differences in the stability of coping in training and competition (Gaudreau, and Antl, 2008; Crocker and Isaak, 1997; Louvet, Gaudreau, Menaut, Genty, and Deneuve, 2007). Although prospective longitudinal designs are more powerful than cross-sectional studies, they still cannot establish causal relationships. The main difference between prospective longitudinal designs and true and quasi experimental designs is the absence of manipulation of the independent variable. Without manipulation of the independent variable, all a researcher knows is *how* variables covary over time; not specifically *why* those variables covary. Similar to cross-sectional designs, this makes it difficult to rule out an alternative hypothesis proposing that any change in outcome is a result of a third variable. Also, the directionality in the relationship can be difficult to ascertain. For example, if it was found that stress and avoidance coping are positively related over time, it is difficult to know whether it was the stress or the avoidance coping that came first. And in many cases these types of relationships are bidirectional, such that avoidance coping might be a way for an athlete to cope with increased stress, but at the same time that same avoidance strategy could be a catalyst for more stress.

Research Questions

Comparing coping by different groups. A basic research question is determining whether differences in coping can be partially explained by group differences. Numerous studies have examined categories such as gender, ethnicity or nationality, chronological or maturational age, sport type, sport experience, skill or playing level, and even playing position within a particular sport (e.g., Anshel, Williams, and Hodge, 1997; Crocker and Graham, 1995; Kristiansen, Roberts, and Abrahamsen, 2008; Meyers, Stewart, Laurent, LeUnes, and Bourgeious, 2008; Nicholls, Polman, Levy, Taylor, and Cobley, 2007; Philippe, Seiler, and Mengisen, 2004; Yoo, 2001). Since most quantitative studies use instruments that produce interval or quasi-interval score scores, the statistical analysis is usually fairly straightforward using *t*-test, one-way ANOVA, or factorial ANOVA, and possibly discriminant analysis. In some cases, researchers have examined group differences in the frequency of a selected coping strategy for a particular type of stressor (see Goyen and Anshel, 1998; Hoar, Crocker, Holt, and Tamminen, 2009). Chi-square analysis is the appropriate test for such nonparametric data. Overall, these studies allow researchers to determine if coping differs across levels of a particular group or groups, or whether there are more complex interactions such as gender by skill level.

Group differences provide a glimpse about coping in sport. Remember, one goal of design and analysis is to explain individual differences in coping. There are, however, limitations to studies that simply report group differences in coping. First, although a group effect may explain some of this individual variability in coping, most group effect sizes are small. This leaves much of the variability in coping unexplained. Second, simple group effects (e.g., gender or age) often provide no insight into the underlying mechanisms governing coping in sport. It is uncertain whether group effects are due to differences across the groups in other key variables that are theoretically linked to coping. These variables could include the type of stressor, the importance of the stress transaction, the sporting and social culture values pertaining to appropriate and inappropriate responses, the athlete's cognitive maturity and knowledge structures, as well as the perceived intensity, threat, or challenge of the stressor. Thus, researchers need to measure or control many of these features. In fairness to some authors, they have attempted to measure and analyze the effects of some of these factors. Third, the great majority of studies use cross-sectional, passive observation designs with all the limitations associated with such designs. Therefore, to a large extent, comparing coping in different groups has provided little insight, and often conflicting findings about coping in sport (see the chapters on gender and development).

Examining Coping in Predictive Models

Most quantitative coping research reported in this book use predictive models to examine theoretical relationships. These predictive models could include simple direct effects, simple mediation or moderator effects, multiple mediator or moderator effects, and mediated moderator or moderated mediator effects, as well as more complicated multilevel models (see Aguinis, 2004; Baron and Kenny, 1986; MacKinnon, Fairchild, and Fritz, 2007 for discussion of these various types of models in psychological research). Coping studies using some of these predictive model designs have included both cross-sectional and longitudinal designs, with constructs represented as either manifest or latent variables. Specific statistical tests can include multiple regression, path analysis, structural equation modeling (SEM), and latent growth analysis. The research design and analysis strategy should be primarily driven by the particular research question; however, all designs and analysis strategies have inherent limitations. We will review some particular designs using examples from sport coping research and coping theory.

Simple direct effects models. Simple predictive models typically either examine the direct effects of key antecedents (e.g., stressors, appraisals, experience, skill level, social support) on the prediction of coping or how coping predicts particular outcomes like emotions, burnout, and performance (e.g., Crocker and Graham, 1995; Grove, and Heard, 1997). They do not examine the impact of potential mediators or moderators. For example, Crocker and Graham (1995) investigated how coping predicted positive and negative affect in 235 female and male athletes who experience performance goal frustration. Coping was assessed by a modification of Carver, Scheier, and Weintraub's (1989) COPE instrument. A multiple regression analysis found five unique coping variable solutions for both positive and negative affect.

Simple predictive models are limited in many ways. First, they are often cross-sectional passive observation designs; thus, causality cannot be inferred. In the Crocker and Graham study is not possible to determine if coping is caused by the specific affective states, if affective states are caused by coping, or if scores for both constructs are caused by another variable(s). Further, direct effects models are not able to determine if theoretically meaningful variables (e.g., stressor types, gender, or personality) moderate the relationships in the simple model or if other variables are mediating effects. These limitations hold for all studies investigating simple direct effect models. Since most stress and coping models propose complex relationships (mediation and moderation) among key variables such as gender, personality, external resources, stressors, appraisal, coping, and outcomes (see the other chapters in this book), simple predictive studies are unlikely to provide meaningful information about the coping process.

Mediator and Moderator Models in Sport Coping

This book highlights that there are many potential mediator and moderator models that will impact the relationship between stressors and sporting outcomes. For example, coping is posited to mediate the relationship between threatening stressors and outcomes (Lazarus, 1991). Further, the strength of the relationship between key variables like stressors and coping may vary across levels of other another variable like gender (Hoar et al., 2006; Tamres, Janicki, and Helgeson, 2002). Thus, gender may moderate the relationship between stressors and coping. Since mediation and moderation effects are inherent in stress and coping models, it is critical that researchers understand some key aspects and differences between these designs and associated analysis strategies. We do not intend, nor would it be possible, to cover all the potential relationships and possible ways to assess these relationships. First, we will address mediation followed by moderation models.

Mediation. Mediation models are causal models that propose the effects of an independent variable or variables on a dependent variable or variables are caused by one or more mediator variables (Baron and Kenny, 1986; Hoyle and Kenny, 1999). Mediation models can become very complicated, involving multiple levels as well as moderator variables (see Edwards and Lambert [2007] and MacKinnon et al. [2007] for a more complete discussion of these models). We will focus on more simple models involving (a) one mediator with one independent and one dependent variable and (b) two mediators between multiple independent and dependent variables.

A simple mediation model involving an opponent, task-oriented coping, and an athlete's performance is shown in Figure 1. In Figure 1(a), the stressor of the opponent (X) has a direct or total effect (c) on an athlete's performance (Y). This is the direct effect model. In Figure 1(b), the model considers the mediating effect of task-oriented coping (M). Researchers could use hierarchical multiple regression, path analysis, or SEM to analyze the model. Baron and Kenny (1986) have described the steps involved in examining mediation (an excellent website on this matter is: http://davidkenny.net/cm/mediate.htm).

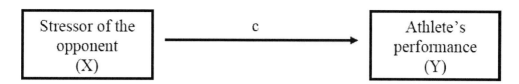

Figure 1a. Direct effect model.

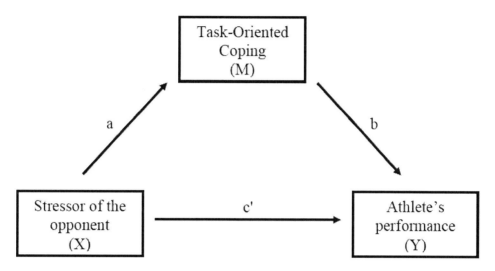

Figure 1b. Simple mediation model.

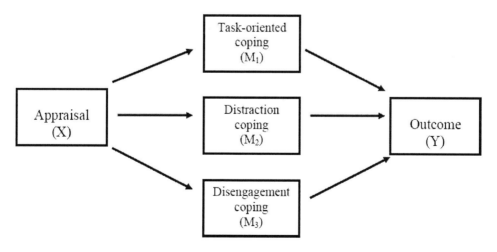

Figure 1c. Multiple mediators model.

Essentially, there should be significant relationships between the opponent and coping ('a' coefficient) and coping and performance ('b' coefficient). When you statistically control for coping, the total effect (c') between the opponent (X) and performance (Y) should be reduced (partial mediation) or extinguished (total mediation). The amount of mediation can be measured through the use of the Sobel Test or through bootstrapping procedures available on many statistical programs (see Preacher and Hayes, 2008).

An example of simple mediation is the cross-sectional study by Puente-Diaz and Anshel (2005) examining the mediating effects of perceived controllability on the relationship between culture and coping in American and Mexican high-school tennis players. They assessed coping to the most stressful situation in tennis using a modification of Carver et al.'s (1989) COPE and examined mediation separately for each coping scale. Following Baron and Kenny's (1986) guidelines and using the Sobel Test to measure mediation, Puente-Diaz and Anshel found evidence that perceived controllability mediated the relationship between culture (nationality was used as a proxy measure of culture) and active coping. There was no evidence that appraisal mediated culture and coping relationships involving the strategies of planning, denial, or positive reinterpretation.

Some researchers have proposed a simple mediation model (and even complex models), but have used incorrect analytic procedures. For example, a well cited study by Hammermeister and Burton (2001) proposed to examine how coping mediated the relationship between threat appraisal and state anxiety in endurance athletes (runners and cyclists). Unfortunately, they used stepwise regression to predict anxiety. Such an analysis produces an equation that shows how a linear combination of variables (appraisal and coping) predicts coping. Their findings provide no insight on how coping mediates the appraisal-anxiety relationship.

Most coping models indicate that there could be multiple mediators between stressors, appraisals, and outcomes. As covered in Chapter 1, coping can be categorized in multiple categories. Since athletes can use multiple coping strategies or coping functions to manage stressful sport transactions, it might be useful to model these coping effects in a multiple mediator model (see Figure 1c). This allows the researcher to determine the mediating effects of multiple types of coping on outcomes.

An interesting example of such multiple mediators is the Gaudreau and Antl (2008) study that investigated how coping mediated the effects of self-determined and non-self-determined motivation on goal attainment and life satisfaction in 186 French Canadian athletes from multiple sports. Their prospective study was even more complex in that they considered how the two types of motivation mediated the effects of dispositional perfectionism and life satisfaction (see Figure 2). Such a design allowed Gaudreau and Antl to look at a number of mediated relationships and examine both direct and indirect effects. We will highlight just a few finding here. Using structural equation modeling, they found evidence that the two types of motivation partially mediated the relationship between perfectionism and coping. They also found evidence that goal attainment mediated the relationship between both task and disengagement coping-oriented coping with change in life satisfaction. An important point is that the causal model tested was based on research questions that arose from considering the motivational and perfectionism literatures.

Mediation models have great potential to provide insight into the coping process in sport. However, there are a number of limitations that need to be considered. The use of passive observation designs, whether cross-sectional or prospective, is problematic in determining causal relationships. If the mediator is not manipulated then it is not possible to discount reverse causal effects (i.e., outcome causes the supposed mediator). Prospective studies have some advantage over cross-sectional studies in that mediators can be measured before outcomes. For example, Gaudreau and Antl (2008) measured perfectionism and motivation before coping and goal attainment. However, goal attainment, life satisfaction, and coping were measured at the same time.

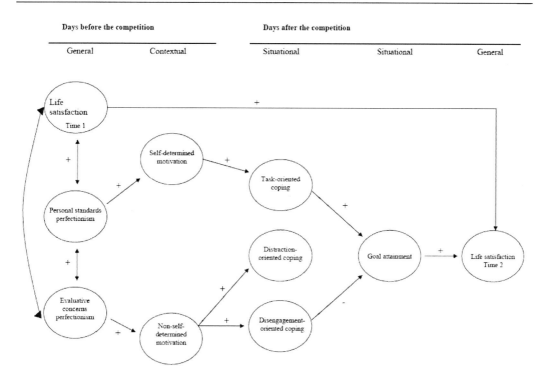

Figure 2. Hypothesized model of the relationships between dispositional perfectionism, contextual motivation, situational coping, goal attainment, and life satisfaction (from Gaudreau and Antl, 2008). (+ indicates a positive relationship, - indicates a negative relationship).

Thus, it becomes difficult to rule out reverse causal effects between goal attainment and life satisfaction. In many stress and coping studies, it might be difficult to measure variables at different time points given that they occur in such a dynamic fashion. In many cases, researchers can only determine if results are consistent with theoretical models.

Moderator models. The coping literature identifies several potential moderators that could influence coping-outcome relationships including personality, gender, ethnicity or cultural values, and social support (see Aldwin, 2007; Lazarus, 1999). Moderator models determine if the relationship between an independent variable and a dependent variable varies across levels of a second or moderator variable. For example, gender may moderate the relationship between confrontational coping and emotion when managing a poor decision by a referee. That is, the relationship between confrontational coping and emotion is significantly different between males and female athletes. If this is a plausible hypothesis, one would test it by considering the interaction effects between coping and gender in explaining differences in emotion scores in addition to these effects produced by the main effects of gender and coping.

When examining moderator effects, it is assumed that the independent variable and the moderator are unrelated or independent. That is, changing confrontation should not have any effect on gender. This seems self-evident with these particular variables but it may create some challenges when considering other moderator variables like social support and coping effectiveness. Depending on the nature of the independent and moderator variables (categorical or continuous), moderators can be analyzed by a number of different statistical techniques including factorial ANOVA, moderated hierarchical regression, or multi-group SEM. The necessary steps to perform and interpret moderation models using various statistical techniques are described in several excellent publications (Aguinis, 2004; Aiken and West, 1991; Baron and Kenny, 1986; Hopwood, 2007).

An example of a moderator model in the coping literature is the work by Ntoumanis and Biddle (1998) who investigated whether coping effectiveness moderated the effects of coping strategies on affect (emotional experience) in 356 British athletes. Because they measured several coping strategies (using a modification of the COPE instrument) and the effectiveness of each strategy, they used a series of separate moderated hierarchical regression analyses. Both the independent variable (coping) and the moderator (effectiveness of the specific strategy) were entered first in the regression analysis, followed by the interaction term (effectiveness X coping). Moderator effects were inferred if the interaction term made a significant increase in the prediction of affect. Ntoumanis and Biddle reported moderator effects for several relationships including the coping strategies of seeking social support, venting of emotions, and behavioural disengagement.

Moderator models also have the potential to forward our understanding of coping in sport. These models can be combined with mediators to look at even more complex relationships proposed in the coping literature (mediated moderation or moderated mediation models). There are limitations and key assumptions in using moderator models, many of which are stated in the section on mediation models. These include the need to manipulate causal variables, the limitation of cross-sectional designs, and the role of other causal variables. The assumption of independence between the independent and moderator variable is critical. For example, one can question whether coping and coping effectiveness (Ntoumanis and Biddle, 1998) are unrelated. Again, it is important to make sure the model is consistent with the research question.

Multilevel and multilevel longitudinal modeling of coping. Most quantitative sport coping research is cross-sectional and focuses on the individual level of analysis. Sport coping data, however, is primarily multi-level in nature. Athletes are typically embedded in teams, training groups, and sporting organizations. Even these latter variables occur in larger groupings such as geopolitical regions. Thus, coping and other individual level variables in the coping process are nested in contexts or groups. For example, individual coping responses to a common stressor (e.g., perceived cheating by an opponent) might be influenced by group coping norms (within a team) or sporting coping norms (within a specific sport). Therefore, although a person's coping might be impacted by their gender, values, and goals, it is informative to know the gender composition, values, and goals of the team.

In essence, multilevel analysis seems to determine if contextual factors can tell us more about the coping process compared to individual level analyses. Multilevel analysis has increased over the last decade in sport and exercise psychology (see Cresswell and Eklund, 2006; Duncan, Duncan, Strycker, and Chaumeton, 2004). There has been little research, however, that has investigated multilevel effects in sport coping. There are several excellent publications that outline multilevel technique (see Bickel, 2007; Heck and Thomas, 2008).

There are few quantitative longitudinal analyses of the sport coping process (e.g., Louvet et al., 2007). This is surprising since such designs have several advantages over cross-sectional designs. Longitudinal designs allow the analysis of inter-individual change (latent or manifest group mean analysis) and intra-individual change. Intra-individual change is critical since researchers can study not only how single variables change within a person but more importantly how theoretically related variables change systematically. Multilevel longitudinal models can be utilized since variable scores are nested within individuals over time (Heck and Thomas, 2008).

Multilevel longitudinal designs are optimal for examining dynamic stress and coping processes, especially if key variables can be manipulated. Even using passive observation techniques, researchers can vary the time period between assessments (Amiot, Blanchard, and Gaudreau, 2008), with recent studies examining daily processes. For example, Holtzman and Delongis (2007) studied how a spouse's response influenced the relationship between pain, negative affect, and catastrophizing coping in rheumatoid arthritis patients. Participants were interviewed twice daily by telephone. The analysis looked at several potential models of how morning scores on the variables could predict evening scores after accounting for two levels of personal factors. The details of such analyses are far too detailed for this chapter, but the design and analysis features associated with multilevel longitudinal designs should be strongly considered by sport coping researchers (see Heck and Thomas, 2008; Singer and Willett, 2003 for details of longitudinal analyses). Such designs and analyses will be challenging in sport settings; however, these approaches offer many potential benefits for improving our understanding of coping in sport.

QUALITATIVE RESEARCH DESIGNS

There is a growing recognition and use of qualitative research methods in coping in sport research over recent years. So much so, that approximately half of the studies published on coping in sport since 2006 can be categorized under the broad rubric of "qualitative research." The emergence of qualitative methods as a better way understand the coping process in sport might be a natural progression of the field, as coping is dynamic, complex, multifaceted, and contextual; and hence, particularly well-suited to qualitative methodologies. Making coping even more difficult to understand is that it is embedded within an emotion process, a process for which a consensus definition also seems to elude us despite over a century of debate.

In many ways the trajectory of research on coping in sport might reflect Richard Lazarus' own journey towards an understanding of the emotion process. Lazarus (1999) stated, "I have developed a new viewpoint about the best research strategy for the emotions" (p. 193). His critique was aimed largely at his own previous thinking that a systems approach was a practical and effective strategy that added to the knowledge and understanding of a complex system like emotion. A systems approach proposes causal antecedents, such as person and environment variables, which are mediated by processes like appraisal and coping and lead to intermediate and long-term effects. Most telling of his change in thinking he boldly wrote:

> There are also too many antecedent, mediating, and outcome variables to deal with for an adequate test of this strategy. I believe the good idea of doing research within a systems theory framework is likely to fail. And restricting one's research to a modest number of variables to make it more practical reduces the value of systems thinking and research (p. 195).

The alternative he proposed was to take a narrative approach to the emotions, whereby a dramatic plot or story of an emotion is constructed in relation to a provoking action and followed through the continuing transaction. He proposed that from the telling of life stories of individuals, prototypes for each emotion could be constructed that "portrays how the emotion is typically aroused in most or all persons who experience the emotion as well as how it is coped with and expressed" (p. 207); and he emphasized that narratives across people need to focus both on what is common as well as divergent in the narrative for each emotion. Most relevant to the current chapter, he concluded that such an approach could be directed specifically to any aspect of the emotion process, including coping.

Narrative inquiry, while acknowledged recently as having particularly promising application to sport and exercise psychology (e.g., Smith and Sparkes, 2009), represents one qualitative approach to research. In an attempt to bring together the vast diversity in qualitative methods, Creswell (2007) organized the different ways of conducting qualitative research into five approaches--narrative, phenomenological, grounded theory, ethnographic, and case study. While describing the defining characteristics of each approach is beyond the scope of the present chapter, qualitative research on coping in sport is generally dominated by the use of case study and phenomenological approaches focused on better understanding coping with various stressors and emotions in sport. Recent studies predominantly focus on coping with performance-related competition stressors (e.g., Buman, Omli, Giacobbi, and Brewer, 2008; Kristiansen, Roberts, and Abrahamsen, 2008; Nicholls, 2007a; Nicholls and Polman, 2008; Nieuwenhuys, Hanin, and Bakker, 2008; Thelwell, Weston, and Greenlees, 2007); but range broadly from coping with athletic injury (e.g., Thing, 2006), to coaching (e.g., Thelwell, Weston, Greenlees, and Hutchings, 2008), to general sport participation (e.g., Uphill and Jones, 2007), to retirement from sport (e.g., Lally, 2007). Rather than adhering to a single tradition of inquiry many authors cite the use of research methods that borrow upon multiple qualitative approaches as part of their research strategy. Such combinations include phenomology-grounded theory (e.g., Buman et al., 2008), case study-phenomenology (e.g., Holt, 2003; Nicholls, 2007b), ethnography-narrative (Thing, 2006), and case study-phenomenology-narrative (Nieuwenhuys et al., 2008); whereas others do not explicitly state a specific tradition of inquiry used within in their qualitative approach (e.g., Nicholls and Polman, 2008; Thatcher and Day, 2008; Thelwell et al., 2007).

Research Issues

Prolonged time in the field. Collectively, qualitative research on coping in sport raises a number of important methodological issues. One issue is how long the researcher should spend in the research environment. A number of studies rely on a single time-point of data collection in which participants recall past stressors and reflect on coping strategies used. For example, Thatcher and Day (2008) used single time-point interviews to better understand 16 national level trampolinists' most stressful competitive experience over the past two years. Thing (2006) coupled single time-point interviews with prolonged participant observation over a 1.5-year period in a private physiotherapy clinic in her study on female athletes' experiences after anterior cruciate ligament injury. By the time of the interviews, she had spent at least six months observing each participant in the field and took field notes on over 200 consultations. In contrast, a number of researchers have used multiple time-point interviews. Lally (2007) interviewed six university student athletes about their sport experiences one month into their last season of competition followed by interviews on identity and retirement one month and one year following the season. Similarly, in Holt, Berg, and Tamminen's (2007) study on female volleyball player's patterns of appraisal, coping, and coping effectiveness, athletes were interviewed before and after a final playoff tournament.

Spending prolonged time in the field is often one of the criteria used to evaluate the merits of a qualitative research study (e.g., Creswell, 2009). Furthermore, Janesick (2000) suggested that "qualitative design demands that the researcher stay in the setting over time" (p. 386). Despite this, qualitative research on coping in sport tends toward briefer engagements with participants and typically employs only formal interviews. This is particularly problematic for understanding a dynamic construct like coping, which in essence reflects an individual's adaptational struggle over time. Towards this end, it is hard to envision more time in the field not being beneficial in the understanding of participants' experience. The challenge, however, is that spending prolonged time in the field can clearly be a difficult task and can require substantial personal and monetary resources.

Number of participants. When considering the challenges associated with collecting data over time, a second issue to consider is the number of participants that should be included in the study. Just as the amount of time spent with participants in qualitative research depends on available time and resources, sample size is also contingent upon these same practical issues as well as the research question being asked. For example, Nicholls (2007b) used a single-participant case study design to explore the longitudinal stress and coping experiences of an international golfer during a training program for coping. The single-participant design allowed for a rich understanding of the golfer's coping experiences because information was collected over an extended period of time using interviews, audio-diary, and a coping training program. While single-participant designs are the exception, qualitative studies on coping in sport predominantly range between three and 20 participants. A noteworthy exception is Buman et al.'s (2008) examination of 57 elite marathon runners' experiences of coping with periods of extreme stress. While Buman et al.'s design provided for a breadth for understanding collective coping, a cost was to understanding the adaptational struggle of any specific individual. This becomes even more evident in Park's (2000) study on coping strategies used by 180 Korean athletes, because while they used quotes from individual athletes to highlight coping themes, the results of the research are (necessarily) focused predominantly on the numbers and percentages of particular coping strategies rather than the coping of individuals. In sum, there is a delicate balance that must be struck between attempts to understand the breadth of coping across individuals and the depth of meaning in individual coping attempts. As a result, thoughtful consideration needs to be given to the number of participants in qualitative studies on coping in sport. If the number of participants entirely obscures individual meaning, a significant advantage of using qualitative approaches will likely be lost. At times knowing the number or percentage of participants (as often reported in coping research) is important, while at other times this might be quite secondary to knowing how and/or why a strategy or set of strategies were used. Hence, qualitative research should not be judged exclusively on the number of participants in the study; instead, the number of participants needs to appropriate to the goals and research questions of a given study.

Data collection methods. The most prominent data collection method in qualitative research on coping in sport is the one-on-one interview. However, some have included multiple one-on-one interviews (e.g., Holt, 2003; Holt et al., 2007; Lally, 2007; Niewenhuys et al., 2008), or combined one-on-one interviews with focus groups (e.g., Giacobbi et al., 2004) and observation (e.g., Thing, 2006). Alternative approaches include the use of audio-diaries and think aloud procedures. For example, Nicholls (2007b) had an international-level adolescent golfer maintain an audio-diary over 21 days and reflect on the stressors experienced and coping strategies used during seven competitive rounds of golf. Similarly, Holt and Dunn (2004) had four female soccer players maintain audio-diaries over a 6-week period in which they provided detailed descriptions of the stressors they experienced and the coping strategies utilized. Similar to audio-diaries but occurring in real-time, Nicholls and Polman (2008) had five adolescent golfers engage in think aloud techniques to record participants' verbalizations of thoughts over six holes of golf.

Other methods used in qualitative research are noticeably absent in the coping in sport literature, such as photovoice and videotaping. Photovoice, a technique in which participants take photographs as representations of their experiences, allows the researcher to perceive the world from the viewpoint of the participants through the use of visual images (Wang and Burris, 1997). Photovoice turns the focus of the research process towards the eyes and experiences of the participants through their photography and provides them the opportunity to reflect upon and critique their experiences. A method like photovoice seems particularly promising for a dynamic and complex construct like coping because the visual image could act as a metaphor and entry point into their experiences. Maybe even more surprising is that video has not been used in studies as a way to assist in understanding the coping process. Lazarus (1999) suggested that videotaping episodes and having participants reflect upon those experiences could benefit understanding of emotion narratives. This could be beneficial in the coping in sport research because many studies rely on retrospective recalls of events gone by. For example, Holt et al. (2007) had volleyball players recall their anticipated and actual appraisals and coping before and after a final playoff tournament. As part of the participants' reflections on the tournament events, what if they had had video of themselves to watch as they reconstructed their experiences in the tournament? However, this type of approach is likely more appropriate and practical for understanding coping in more acute events rather than long-term chronic stressors.

Bracketing. Due to the relational nature of qualitative research and inevitable "hands-on" approaches to data collection, researchers using qualitative methods are typically encouraged to engage in critical self-reflection, or bracketing, in order to identify how their own personal experiences and values impact the research process (Creswell, 2009). In accordance, many researchers using qualitative methods to study coping in sport bracket their experiences and biases in an attempt to maintain a level of objectivity in their research (e.g., Lally, 2007; Thatcher and Day, 2008; Uphill and Jones, 2007). In Nicholls, Holt, and Polman's (2005) study on international golfers' coping, a reflexive journal was kept by the first author "...to help 'bracket' his personal experiences and consider the influence of his personal values and golfing experiences on the research" (p. 120). Another example is Dale (2000) who engaged in multiple reflexive activities before and during his exploration into the experiences of seven elite decathletes' most memorable performances. Prior to interviewing participants, Dale engaged in a bracketing interview with a skilled qualitative researcher not involved in the study and shared personally memorable performances in sport and personal notions of elite decathletes' experiences. He suggested this process of bracketing process "...minimizes researcher bias by creating more awareness of preconceived notions regarding the topic" (p. 21). Dale also maintained a daily log in which he reflected on personal experiences of the study in order to separate his own experiences from those of the participants.

Angen (2000) suggested that attempting to separate one's experiences from the research study by being self-reflexive might actually be a misguided attempt to obtain objective distance between the researcher and the study. Rather, she said that reflexivity is a way to acknowledge the role of the researcher in qualitative research studies and as a way to value the researcher's own contribution to understanding. The existing knowledge, history, and experience that qualitative researchers bring to their studies should be viewed as thoughtful elaboration on interpretations of meaning that may vary from one researcher's perspective to another (Haverkamp, 2005). Rather than creating biased subjectivity, incorporating the researcher's previous experiences into the research process may provide additional and/or unique perspectives that might otherwise be neglected if the researcher attempts to remain distant from the study. There are opportunities in coping in sport literature to embrace researcher experience as a way to enrich the written text. Although Holt and Dunn (2004) acknowledged the first author's former role as a sport psychology consultant for the soccer team prior to individual interviews as beneficial to gaining entry, building rapport, and contextualize data, it is not clear how that previous experience shaped the subsequent themes and written results. On the other hand, although they did not use the term bracketing, Holt and Dunn's research is one of the few studies that seems to really accept the philosophical stance that research on lived experience is inherently an interpretative process and that the context of the research cannot fully be bracketed out (see Gearing, 2004 for a further discussion of this issue). The challenges associated with bracketing and the ways researchers make themselves known in written texts, especially in phenomenology, has been acknowledged for many years (see LaVasseur, 2003, for a review of bracketing in phenomenology). What remains is the need for authors to provide a more clear picture of how the researcher and participant(s) come together to co-create meaning and understanding of coping in sport, rather than using the term bracketing as something that comes across as "methodologically superficial or vague" (Gearing, 2004, p. 1429).

Methods of data analysis and representation. Most qualitative studies on coping in sport use a fairly consistent form of data analysis and data representation whereby interviews are transcribed verbatim, coded for content, themes are developed, and presented in a way that generally describes the theme supported by participant quotations. The specific form of this theme development and representation can differ, however. While the themes developed are often done by a single researcher, in their study on sources of stress and associated coping strategies for professional cricket batsmen, Thelwell et al. (2007) had two of the authors read, code, and develop themes independently and then meet to develop higher-order meaning dimensions. A third researcher, not involved in earlier phases of data collection and analysis, subsequently examined the steps taken by the previous two researchers to help develop the final themes. A similar process was used by Buman et al. (2008) in their study of recreational marathon runners; however, they added an additional step by having a separate sample of four experienced marathon runners conduct a focus group interview to review the themes that were developed.

A strength of qualitative research on coping in sport is the adherence to systematic, thorough, and well-supported analysis strategies. However, a weakness seems to be the absence of an acknowledgement and embracing of human imagination and creativity as a potentially valuable way to construct meaning. The range of analysis strategies is surprisingly small and there is a general absence of arts-based analysis strategies in the coping in sport literature. Strategies like poetic transcription, for example, which "…involves word reduction while illuminating the wholeness and interconnections of thoughts" (Glesne, 1997), are noticeably absent but could potentially add a great deal to the ways researchers try to make meaning out of interview transcripts. Sullivan (2005) argued that the visual arts in particular can be described as a form of research and that "...for understanding requires knowledge to be created from which explanations can be extracted: To create, the researcher has to enter the realm of imagination, to take on the possible, as well as the plausible, and probable" (p. 115). He suggested the real benefit of visual knowing specifically is that it can allow us to come to new understandings, especially in the context of what is already known. As far as we could discern in our review of the literature, none of the studies on coping in sport used visual art forms as a way to create meaning from the experiences of others. While visual representations are often a part of the presentation of the results, such as Holt et al. (2007) who presented a visual matrix of individual volleyball players' appraisal patterns, artistic mediums are seldom used (or at least explicitly acknowledged) in the actual data analysis process, even though creative synthesis has been acknowledged as an important part of qualitative inquiry (Patton, 2002).

Similarly, there is also surprisingly little variety in the way qualitative research results on coping in sport are presented in the literature. We say surprisingly because coping seems particularly well-suited for alternative ways of representation as a result of its critical role in human emotional experience. One of the biggest decisions in the presentation of qualitative results is whether to organize results around composite themes, with quotes of individuals to highlight the themes, or organize the data around each individual in the study. While the presentation of themes is the standard choice, Holt and Dunn (2004) presented "chronologically-ordered idiographic profiles" in their study on four high performance female soccer players. The narrative of each woman was organized around the athlete's goals followed by her main "stressor theme" (e.g., leadership abilities, team performance, injury, and fitness). Across the various qualitative studies, as the number of participants increases the representation of specific individuals within the study is less common and more challenging to present. Holt et al. (2007) addressed this challenge by showing coping responses of all 10 women volleyball players in a matrix briefly summarizing each participant's age, goals, pre-tournament anticipated appraisals and coping, and post-tournament appraisals and coping. Within the text they then presented more detailed individual profiles for three athletes to demonstrate effective, partially effective, and ineffective coping. Taking a slightly different approach in their study with 16 trampolinists, Thatcher and Day (2008) presented a presence/absence matrix of incidence of stress properties for each athlete, but then presented an integrated narrative of each stress property (highlighted by quotations from individuals). Clearly, the choice of representation of data within themes or across individuals is a balance between the desire to present commonalities across individuals and each individual's unique coping efforts.

Another writing choice that must be made is how best to present the overall narrative of the research itself. A review of the qualitative research on coping in sport reveals the dominance of a format that is very akin to the writing-up of traditional quantitative research studies. The typical format is one in which the literature review is presented; the participants are introduced; the method is overviewed; the results are presented (typically theme-by-theme with quotations of individuals to highlight exemplars of those themes); and then the results, implications, limitations, and future directions are discussed. While this type of approach can be effective in presenting evidence to allow the reader to evaluate criteria often used to judge the effectiveness of qualitative research (e.g., peer review processes, member-checking, time in the field, data analysis approach, etc.), a weakness is that it might not be the most effective way to present an in-depth, engaging, rich narrative of coping in sport. Richardson (2000) discussed her use of "aesthetic merit" as one criteria she considers when reviewing papers, and asks herself questions such as whether the piece succeeds aesthetically and whether the text is artistically shaped, satisfying, complex, and not boring. Although she discussed it specifically in the context of creative analytic practice, the criteria of aesthetic merit might be considered more earnestly within the coping and sport literature. Thing (2006) provided an excellent example of an engaging text that not only presents female athletes' injury experiences, but also the research process and her role as co-creator of meaning making within her study. She breaks from a traditional presentation of coping in sport by intricately weaving the grand narrative of her research throughout, often moving in and out among conclusions, methods, participant experiences, and the extant literature. As a result, she forms a narrative of the women's injury experience that is neither shallow nor lifeless, and very much seems to embrace the goal of providing a potential prototype narrative of the injury experience – which Lazarus (1999) envisioned as a potentiality of research on emotion.

CONCLUSION

Coping is certainly a complex process. This point is illustrated by the multitude of design and analysis options to explore coping in sport that were presented in this chapter. There are many other studies in the literature that were not mentioned in this chapter that further support this point. The direction one takes in the choice of research design and analysis depends largely on the research question. Researchers are encouraged to follow a path that best suits their question, but at the same time recognize the various strengths and limitations of their approach. They should also not be afraid to approach the task with creativity, ingenuity, and logic aimed at better understanding coping in sport. We encourage a greater focus on well-designed experimental studies that allow for stronger tests of causal relationships among variables in the coping process, as well as studies that embrace the potential of qualitative methods to provide a richer understanding of the complexity of coping in sporting lives.

REFERENCES

Aguinis, H. (2004). Regression analysis for categorical moderators. New York: Guilford.

Amiot, C. E., Blanchard, C. M., and Gaudreau, P. (2008). The self in change: A longitudinal investigation of coping and self-determination process. *Self and Identity*, 7, 204-224.

Aiken, L. S., and West, S. G. (1991). Multiple regression: Testing and interpreting interactions. Newberg Park, CA: Sage.

Aldwin, C. M. (2007). Stress, coping, and development: An integrative approach (2nd ed.). New York: Guilford.

Angen, M. J. (2000) Pearls, pith, and provocation. Evaluating interpretive inquiry: Reviewing the validity debate and opening the dialogue. *Qualitative Health Research*, 10, 378-395.

Anshel, M. H., Williams, L. R. T., and Hodge, K. (1997). Cross-cultural and gender differences on coping style in sport. *International Journal of Sport Psychology*, 28, 141-156.

Anshel, M. H., Williams, L. R., and Williams, S. M. (2000). Coping style following acute stress in competitive sport. *Journal of Social Psychology*, 140, 751-73.

Baron, R. M., and Kenny, D. A. (1986). The moderator-mediator variable distinction in social psychological research: Conceptual, strategic, and statistical considerations. *Journal of Personality and Social Psychology*, 51, 1173-1182.

Baumeister, R. F., and Vohs, K. D. (2007). Encyclopedia of social psychology. *Thousand Oaks*, CA: Sage Publications.

Bickel, R. (2007). Multilevel analysis for applied research: It's just regression! New York: Guilford Press.

Buman, M. P., Omli, J. W., Giacobbi Jr., P. R., and Brewer, B. W. (2008). Experiences and coping responses of "hitting the wall" for recreational marathon runners. *Journal of Applied Sport Psychology*, 20, 282-300.

Carver, C. S., Scheier, M. F., and Weintraub, J. K. (1989). Assessing coping strategies: A theoretically based approach, *Journal of Personality and Social Psychology*, 56, 267–283.

Compas, B. E., Conner, J., Osowiecki, D., and Welch, A. (1997). Effortful and involuntary responses to stress: Implications for coping with chronic stress. In B.H. Gottlieb (Ed.), Coping with chronic stress. New York: Plenum.

Creswell, J. W. (2007). Qualitative inquiry and research design: Choosing among five approaches (2nd ed.). *Thousand Oaks*, CA: Sage.

Creswell, J. W. (2009). Research design: Qualitative, quantitative, and mixed methods approaches (3rd Ed.). *Thousand Oaks*, CA: Sage.

Cresswell, S. L., and Eklund, R. C. (2006). Changes in athlete burnout over a thirty-week "rugby year". *Journal of Science and Medicine in Sport*, 9, 125-134.

Crocker, P. R. E. and Graham, T. R. (1995). Coping by competitive athletes with performance stress: Gender differences and relationships with affect. The Sport Psychologist, 9, 325-338.

Crocker, P. R. E. and Isaak, K. (1997). Coping during competitions and training sessions: Are youth swimmers consistent? *International Journal of Sport Psychology, 228,* 355-369.

Crocker, P.R.E., Hoar, S.D., McDonough, M., Kowalski, K.C., Niefer, C. (2003). Emotional experiences in youth sport. In M.R. Weiss (Ed.), Developmental sport and exercise psychology: A lifespan perspective. Morgantown, WV: Fitness Information Technology Inc.

Crocker, P. R. E., Kowalski, K. C., Hoar, S. D., and McDonough, M. H. (2003). Emotion in sport across adulthood. In M.R. Weiss (Ed.), Developmental sport and exercise psychology: A lifespan perspective. Morgantown, WV: Fitness Information Technology Inc.

Dale, G. A. (2000). Distractions and coping strategies of elite decathletes during their most memorable performances. *The Sport Psychologist*, 14, 17-41.

Denzin, N. K., and Lincoln, Y. S. (2003). Strategies of qualitative inquiry. *Thousand Oaks*, CA: Sage.

Duncan, S. C., Duncan, T. E., Strycker, L. A., and Chaumeton, N. R. (2004). A multilevel approach to youth physical activity research. *Exercise and Sport Sciences Reviews*, 32, 95-99.

Edwards, J. R., and Lambert, L. S. (2007). Methods for integrating moderation and mediation: A general analytical framework using moderated path analysis. *Psychological Methods*, 12, 1-22.

Gaudreau, P., and Antl, S. (2008). Broad dimensions of perfectionism: Examining change in life-satisfaction and the mediating role of motivation and coping. *Journal of Sport and Exercise Psychology*, 30, 356-382.

Gearing, R. E. (2004). Bracketing in research: A typology. *Qualitative Health Research*, 14, 1429-1452.

Giacobbi, P. R., Jr., Lynn, T. K., Wetherington, J. M., Jenkins, J., Bodendorf, M., and Langley, B. (2004). Stress and coping during the transition to university for first-year female athletes. *The Sport Psychologist*, 18, 1-20.

Glesne, C. (1997). That rare feeling: Re-presenting research through poetic transcription. *Qualitative Inquiry*, 3, 202-221.

Gollob, H. F., and Reichardt, C. S. (1987). Taking account of time lags in causal models. *Child Development*, 58, 80–92.

Gould, D., Finch, L. M., and Jackson, S. A. (1993). Coping strategies used by national champion figure skaters. *Research Quarterly for Exercise and Sport*, 64, 453-468.

Goyen, M. J., and Anshel, M. H. (1998). Sources of acute competitive stress and the use of coping strategies as a function of age and gender. *Journal of Applied Developmental Psychology,* 19, 469-486.

Grove, J. R., and Heard, N. P. (1997). Optimism and sport confidence as correlates of slump-related coping among athletes. *The Sport Psychologist*, 11, 400-410.

Hammermeister, J. J., and Burton, D. (2001). Stress, appraisal, and coping revisited: Examining the antecedents of competitive state anxiety with endurance athletes. *The Sport Psychologist*, 15, 66-90.

Hanton, S. and Fletcher, D. (2005). Organizational stress in competitive sport: More than we bargained for? *International Journal of Sport Psychology*, 36, 273-283.

Haverkamp, B. E. (2005). Ethical perspectives on qualitative research in applied psychology. *Journal of Counseling Psychology*, 52, 146-155.

Heck, R. H., and Thomas, S. L. (2008). An introduction to multilevel modeling technique (2nd ed.). New York: Routledge. Holt, N. L. (2003). Coping in professional sport: A case study of an experienced cricket player. *Athletic Insight*, 5, 1-11.

Hoar, S. D., Crocker, P. R. E., Holt, N. L., and Tamminen, K. A. (2009). Gender differences in adolescent athletes. Coping differences with interpersonal stressors in sport: More similarities than differences? Manuscript submitted for publication.

Hoar, S. D., Kowalski, K. C., Gaudreau, P., and Crocker, P. R. E. (2006). A review of coping in sport. In S. Hanton and S. Mellalieu (Eds.), Literature reviews in sport psychology (pp. 47-90). Hauppauge, NY: Nova Science Publishers.

Holt, N. L. (2003). Coping in professional sport: A case study of an experienced cricket player. *Athletic Insight*, 5, 1-11.

Holt, N. L., Berg, K.-J., and Tamminen, K. A. (2007). Tales of the unexpected: Coping among female collegiate volleyball players. *Research Quarterly for Exercise and Sport*, 78, 117-132.

Holt, N. L., and Dunn, J. G. H. (2004). Longitudinal idiographic analyses of appraisal and coping responses in sport. *Psychology of Sport and Exercise*, 5, 213-222.

Holt, N. L., and Hogg, J. M. (2002). Perceptions of stress and coping during preparations for the 1999 women's soccer world cup finals. *The Sport Psychologist*, 16, 251-271.

Holtzman, S., and DeLongis, A. (2007). One day at a time: The impact of daily satisfaction with spouse responses on pain, negative affect and catastrophizing among individuals with rheumatoid arthritis. *Pain*, 131, 202-213.

Hopwood, C. J. (2007). Moderation and mediation in structural equation modelling: Applications for early intervention research. *Journal of Early Intervention*, 29, 262-272.

Hoyle, R. H., and Kenny, D. A. (1999). Statistical power and tests of mediation. In R. H. Hoyle (Ed.), Statistical strategies for small sample research. Newbury Park: Sage.

Janesick, V. J. (2000). The choreography of qualitative research design: Minuets, improvisations, and crystallization. In N. K. Denzin and Y. S. Lincoln (Eds.), Handbook of qualitative research (2nd ed.) (pp. 379-399). *Thousand Oaks*, CA: Sage.

Kowalski, K. C., and Crocker, P. R. E. (2001). The development and validation of the Coping Function Questionnaire for adolescents in sport. Journal *of Sport and Exercise Psychology*, 23, 136-155.

Kristiansen, E., Roberts, G. C., and Abrahamsen, F. E. (2008). Achievement involvement and stress coping in elite wrestling. *Scandinavian Journal of Medicine and Science in Sports*, 18, 526-538.

Lally, P. (2007). Identity and athletic retirement: A prospective study. *Psychology of Sport and Exercise,* 8, 85-99.

Lazarus, R. S. (1991a). Cognition and motivation in emotion. *American Psychologist*, 46, 352-367.

Lazarus, R. S. (1991b). Emotion and adaptation. New York: Oxford University Press.

Lazarus, R. S. (1991c). Progress on a Cognitive-Motivational-Relational Theory of Emotion. *American Psychologist*, 46, 819-834.

Lazarus, R. S. (1999). Stress and emotion: A new synthesis. New York: Springer.

Lazarus, R. S., and Folkman, S. (1984). Stress, appraisal, and coping. New York: Springer.

LeVasseur, J. J. (2003). The problem of bracketing in phenomenology. *Qualitative Heath Research,* 13, 408-420.

Louvet, B., Gaudreau, P., Menaut, A., Genty, J., and Deneuve, P. (2007). Longitudinal patterns of stability and change in coping across three competitions: A latent class growth analysis. *Journal of Sport and Exercise Psychology*, 29, 100-117.

MacKinnon, D. P., Fairchild, A. J., and Fritz, M. S. (2007). Mediation analysis. *Annual Review of Psychology,* 7, 83-104.

Meyers, M. C., Stewart, C. C., Laurent, C. M., LeUnes, A. D., and Bourgeois, A. E. (2008). Coping skills of Olympic developmental soccer athletes. *International Journal of Sports Medicine*, 29, 987-993.

Nicholls, A. R. (2007a). A longitudinal phenomenological analysis of coping effectiveness among Scottish international adolescent golfers. *European Journal of Sport Science*, 7, 169-178.

Nicholls, A. R. (2007b). Can an athlete be taught to cope more effectively? The experiences of an international-level adolescent golfer during a training program for coping. *Perceptual and Motor Skills*, 104, 494-500.

Nicholls, A. R., Holt, N. L., and Polman, R. C. J. (2005). A phenomenological analysis of coping effectiveness in golf. *The Sport Psychologist*, 19, 111-130.

Nicholls, A. R., and Polman, R. C. J. (2007). Stressors, coping and coping effectiveness among players from the England under-18 rugby union team. *Journal of Sport Behavior, 30,* 119-218.

Nicholls, A. R., and Polman, R. C. J. (2008). Think aloud: Acute stress and coping strategies during golf performances. *Anxiety, Stress, and Coping*, 21, 283-294.

Nicholls, A. R., Polman, R. C. J., Levy, A., Taylor, J. A., and Cobley, S. P. (2007). Stressors, coping, and coping effectiveness: Gender, sport type, and ability differences. *Journal of Sports Sciences, 25,* 1521-1530.

Nieuwenhuys, A., Hanin, Y. L., and Bakker, F. C. (2008). Performance-related experiences and coping during races: A case of an elite sailor. *Psychology of Sport and Exercise, 9,* 61-76.

Ntoumanis, N., and. Biddle, S. J. H. (1998). The relationship of coping and its perceived effectiveness to positive and negative affect in sport. P*ersonality and Individual Differences*, 24, 773-788.

Okasha, S. (2002). Philosophy of science: A very short introduction. Oxford: Oxford University Press.

Park, J.-K. (2000). Coping strategies used by Korean national athletes. *The Sport Psychologist,* 14, 63-80.

Patton, M. Q. (2002). Qualitative research and evaluation methods (3rd ed.). *Thousand Oaks*, CA: Sage.

Philippe, R. A., Seiler, R., and Mengisen, W. (2004). Relationships of coping style to sport. *Perceptual and Motor Skills*, 98, 479-486.

Preacher, K. J., and Hayes, A. F. (2008). Asymptotic and resampling strategies for assessing and comparing indirect effects in multiple mediator models. *Behavior Research Methods*, 40, 879-891.

Puente-Diaz, R., and Anshel, M.H. (2005). Sources of acute stress, cognitive appraisal, and coping strategies among highly skilled Mexican and U.S. competitive tennis players. *Journal of Social Psychology*, 145, 429-446.

Richardson, L. (2000). Writing: A method of inquiry. In N. K. Denzin and Y. S. Lincoln (Eds.), Handbook of qualitative research (2nd ed.) (pp. 923-948). *Thousand Oaks*, CA: Sage.

Singer, J.D., and Willett, J. B. (2003). Applied longitudinal data analysis: Modeling change and event occurrence. New York: Oxford University Press.

Skinner, E. A. (1999). Action regulation, coping, and development. In J. B. Brandtstadter and R. M. Lerner (Eds.), Action and self-development (pp. 465-503). *Thousand Oaks*, CA: Sage.

Skinner, E. A., and Zimmer-Gembeck, M. J. (2007). The development of coping. *Annual Review of Psychology*, 58, 119-144.

Smith, B., and Sparkes, A. C. (2009). Narrative inquiry in sport and exercise psychology: What can it mean, and why might we do it? Psychology of Sport and Exercise, 10, 1-11.

Sullivan, G. (2005). Art practice as research: Inquiry in the visual arts. *Thousand Oaks*, CA: Sage.

Tamres, L., Janicki, D., and Helgeson, V. S. (2002). Sex differences in coping behavior: A meta-analytic review. *Personality and Social Psychology Review*, 6, 2-30.

Thatcher, J., and Day, M. C. (2008). Re-appraising stress appraisals: The underlying properties of stress in sport. *Psychology of Sport and Exercise*, 9, 318-335.

Thelwell, R. C., Weston, N. J. V., and Greenlees, I. A. (2007). Batting on a sticky wicket: Identifying sources of stress and associated coping strategies for professional cricket batsmen. *Psychology of Sport and Exercise*, 8, 219-232.

Thelwell, R. C., Weston, N. J. V., Greenlees, I. A., and Hutchings, N. V. (2008). Stressors in elite sport: A coach perspective. *Journal of Sport Sciences*, 26, 905-918.

Thing, L. F. (2006). "Voices of the broken body." The resumption of non-professional female players' sports careers after anterior cruciate ligament injury. The female player's dilemma: Is she willing to run the risk? *Scandinavian Journal of Medicine and Science in Sports,* 16, 364-375.

Thomas, J. R., Nelson, J. K., and Silverman, S. J. (2005). Research methods in physical activity (5th ed.). Champaign, IL: Human Kinetics.

Uphill, M. A., and Jones, M. V. (2007). Antecedents of emotions in elite athletes: A cognitive motivational relational theory perspective. *Research Quarterly for Exercise and Sport*, 78, 79-89.

Wang, C. C., and Burris, M. (1997). Photovoice: Concept, methodology, and use for participatory needs assessment. Health Education and Behavior, 24, 369-387.

Yoo, J. (2001). Coping profile of Korean competitive athletes. *International Journal of Sport Psychology, 32*, 290-303.

Yoo, J. (2000). Factorial validity of the Coping Scale for Korean Athletes. *International Journal of Sport Psychology*, 31, 391-404.

PART III: COPING AND MODERATING VARIABLES

In: Coping in Sport: Theory, Methods, and Related Constructs   ISBN: 978-1-60876-488-4
Editor: Adam R. Nicholls   © 2010 Nova Science Publishers, Inc.

Chapter 5

GENDER AND COPING IN SPORT: DO MALE AND FEMALE ATHLETES COPE DIFFERENTLY?

Mariana H. Kaiseler[1] and Remco C.J. Polman[2]
[1]University of Derby, UK
[2]University of Central Lancashire., UK

ABSTRACT

The aim of this chapter was to systematically review the recent literature (1990 to February 2009) on gender and coping in sport. In particular we examined gender differences in coping, whether males and females differed in the appraisal of stressors (e.g., stress intensity and perceived control of stress), and examined evidence for the situational and dispositional hypothesis among athletes. A detailed literature search of SPORTdiscus, Medline, PSYCHinfo, PSYCHarticles, yielded 16 studies spanning 19 years. Thirteen of these studies found gender differences in coping among athletes. However, the findings of these studies are equivocal and questionable, because important constructs such as type of the stressors and stressor appraisals were not controlled for in these studies. It is suggested that poor methodologies are preventing researchers from addressing the issue of whether male and female athletes cope differently and the underlying reasons for any such differences.

INTRODUCTION

In a recent review on coping in sport, Nicholls and Polman (2007) discussed the importance of gender as a possible variable that may influence coping among athletic populations. In support of this idea, a meta-analysis by Tamres, Janicki and Helgeson (2002) found evidence for the commonly held belief that males and females differ in the coping strategies they use. Nevertheless, little is known about the influence of gender in the sport context and findings appear to be equivocal. In this chapter we will review the recent literature on the influence of gender on coping and highlight some of the limitations of the previous research which might explain the ambiguous results in the sport domain. Finally, we will provide some implication for future research in this area.

Social stereotypes exist, which suggest that females are nicer and more nurturing than males (Eagly, Mladinic, and Otto, 1991). A meta-analysis by Dindia and Allen (1992) showed that females share more personal information about their lives, thoughts, and feelings than males. Females also express negative feelings, such as sadness and depression, more than males (Zeman and Garber, 1996), whereas males express anger more than females (Clark and Reis, 1988). Furthermore, as suggested by Lippa (2005), males and females may express and experience emotions differently as males are more sensitive to internal cues and females are more sensitive to external cues. Generally, females express their emotions through many different modalities: facial expression, verbal expression, and physiology. This line of research suggests that females are more likely to cope with stress using emotion-focused coping strategies.

It is unclear whether gender differences in emotional expression are learned or innate. Some evidence has emerged (Grossman and Wood, 1993) suggesting that the expression of emotions is larger in males and females, who have stronger stereotypes about gender and emotions. This suggests that gender differences in emotional expression may be explained by the social role theory rather than innate differences (Eagly, Wood, and Johannesen-Schmidt, 2004).

Tamres et al. (2002) attributed gender differences in coping to biological reasons rather than the social category of gender. In particular, the pituitary hormone oxytocin could be a potential explanation for biological differences. The release of oxytocin during times of stress is associated with down regulation of the sympathetic nervous system and facilitation of the parasympathetic nervous system (Tamres et al.). As suggested by Taylor et al. (2000), this neuroendocrine activity is associated by a pattern of tend-and-befriend rather than fight-or-flight. Since females have a larger oxytocin activity this could explain why they are more likely to use social support as a coping strategy. It is not clear from the previous research whether observed gender differences in coping are innate or learned, however, it is evident that there are characteristic differences among males and females that affect the coping strategies males and females use.

DISPOSITIONAL HYPOTHESIS VS. THE SITUATIONAL HYPOTHESIS

The *dispositional hypothesis* suggests that males and females have different underlying characteristics that cause men and women to cope differently (Tamres et al., 2002). These underlying differences can be biological or social in nature and include variations in emotional expression, social support seeking, responses to stress, and socialization. The situational hypothesis (Tamres et al.), also referred to as role constraint theory (Rosario, Schinn, Morch, and Huckabee, 1988), suggests that situations influence coping behaviours. Differences in coping behavior in this view are the result of the dissimilar roles males and females occupy in society and the different stressors they encounter. According to this theory, if males and females were treated the same and gender stereotypes were abolished; many behavioral gender differences would disappear. Advocates of the situational hypothesis theory view gender as not being something a person is born with; rather it is something a person learns during life (West and Zimmerman, 1991).

It is well accepted that males and females occupy different roles in society, with females being more responsible for childcare and domestic duties, whereas males for income-producing work (Eagly et al., 2004). In sport settings relatively little is known about how social roles influence males and females. Previous research in American society has suggested that participation in sport is primarily a masculine activity (Czisma, Wittig, and Schurr, 1988). Additionally, sport participation appears to intensify masculine characteristics such as competitiveness and achievement (Birrel, 1983) and is a way for American males to pursue and achieve a masculine gender role identity (Anthrop and Allison, 1983). American society perceives that being female and an athlete as incompatible (Desertrain and Weiss, 1988). As suggested by Czisma et al. (1988), these phenomena may result in female athletes experiencing a conflict between personal gender values and societal expectations of femininity. No support for the gender role conflict has been found in the literature in sport settings (Miller and Levy, 1996). Nevertheless, Hoar, Kowalski, Gaudreau, and Crocker (2006) suggested that future research analyzing gender and coping in sport should be aware of how social roles may interact and affect coping.

Previous research has often not defined a common stressor among male and female athletes, nor has it assessed the appraisal process in terms of stress intensity and perceptions of control. Gender differences found could be due to the fact that males and females face different stressors in sport or appraise the same stressors differentially (Tamres et al., 2002). In this way, the dispositional hypothesis would predict that gender differences in coping will be found across situations and social roles whereas the situational hypothesis/role constraint theory predicts that gender differences will disappear when males and females would face the same stressor and take on similar social roles (Sigmon, Stanton, and Snyder, 1995).

To get a better insight on the role of gender on coping in sport, we decided conduct a systematic review of the recent literature, that included research from January 1990 to February, 2009. The inability to cope with stress in sport is a significant factor in the failure of athletes to function fully in many types of athletic performance (Lazarus, 2000). As suggested by previous research (Hammermeister and Burton, 2004; McLeod, Kirkby, and Madden, 1994; Yoo, 2001), gender appears to be a moderator variable influencing the stress and coping process. It is therefore essential that researchers, coaches, and sport psychology practitioners have a greater understanding of gender as a moderator variable influencing the stress and coping process in sport in order to develop successful psychological interventions. Our review examined gender differences in coping, whether males and females differed in the appraisal of stressors (e.g., stress intensity and perceived control of stress), and examined evidence for the situational and dispositional hypothesis among athletes.

The methodology used for the systematic review was based on the guidelines described by Chalmers and Haynes (1995), Lloyd Jones (2004), and Mulrow (1995). Guidelines for taxonomy and reporting were also provided by an editorial on literature reviews published in the Psychological Bulletin (Cooper, 2003). Studies were considered for inclusion if they provided quantitative or qualitative data on gender differences in coping in sport and had been published as full papers. As recommended by Knipschild (1995), studies were been excluded if they were published as abstracts or conference proceedings. Studies were excluded if the mean age of participants was less than 18 years old. All studies were obtained through electronic searches on SPORTdiscus, Medline, PSYCHinfo, PSYCHarticles (1990 to February 2009).

As recommended by Lloyd Jones (2004) and Meade and Richardson (1997), sifting was carried out in three stages. Papers were first reviewed by title, then by abstract, and finally, by full text, apart from those at each step that did not satisfy the inclusion criteria (Lloyd Jones, 2004). We used the key word *coping* in combination with *gender* and *sex* and with *sport* and *exercise*. From the initial search, 7451 papers were removed after reading their title during the first stage of sifting. Following this stage, 104 articles were scanned by abstract and 88 were excluded from the study at this stage of sifting. A total of 36 papers were screened, of which 23 were excluded. Additionally, the reference lists of all papers read were checked for relevant studies. Based on this another nine studies were screened, six of which were excluded. In total 16 papers were included in the systematic review (see Table 1).

Of the 16 papers in this systematic review, 15 (95%) were quantitative and one (5%) was qualitative, using concept maps (see Table 1). The number of males in the quantitative studies ranged from 31 to 332 (mean = 181.5, *SD* = 212.8). The number of females in the quantitative studies ranged from 20 to 332 (mean = 176, *SD* = 220.6). The mean age of males participants in the quantitative studies ranged from 18.1 to 33.8 (weighted means = 23.1, Pooled *SD* = 6.4). The mean age of females participants in the quantitative studies ranged from 18.1 to 36.9 (Weighted means = 22.7, Pooled *SD* = 6.4). The number of participants in the qualitative study was 749. The mean age of participants in the qualitative studies was 19.8 years for both males and females.

Of the 16 papers in this systematic review, nine used the transactional perspective to analyze coping whereas four studies used the trait perspectives. Surprisingly, in three studies it was unclear what perspective was adopted by the researchers. It is believed that this limitation can result in poor research designs to investigate the coping process. In agreement with this, Aldwin (2007) suggested that the theoretical orientation adopted by researchers investigating coping directs the type of factors considered influencing the coping process.

The methodology used to define the nature of the stressor differed across the studies reviewed, some adopted an experimenter defined approach (*n* = 7), whereas others adopted a self-selected approach (*n* = 8), and in one cases the nature of the stressor was not reported (e.g., Bebetsos and Antoniou, 2003). In the experimenter defined studies, athletes reported what they usually did to cope with commonly experienced stressors in their respective sport (i.e. making an error, pain, or an opponent cheating). One study used classifications such as such as performance-related and coach-related stressors (Anshel and Sutarso, 2007). These criteria were suggested to result in a meaningful generalization of the athletes coping strategies (McCrae, 1992).

Two studies defined the event or the time that athletes should refer to (Campen and Roberts, 2001; Hammermeister and Burton, 2004). Five studies (Crocker and Graham, 1995; McLeod et al., 1994; Pensgard and Roberts, 2003; Philipe et al., 2004; Yoo, 2001) asked participants to 'refer to a situation where they experienced problems in performance.' A study by Nicholls et al. (2007) used concept maps and asked participants to describe a maximum of six worries that they have experienced over the past two weeks.

Table 1. Gender and coping in sport: A summary

Study	Participant Information	Method and Framework	Instrumentation	Type of Stressors	Stress Intensity Appraisal	Control Appraisal	Gender Differences
Anshel and Sutarso, 2007	N = 331 (176M; 156F) Age: 21.6 years Former and current sport competitors from various high school sports	Quantitative Trait	SAS Study specific coping inventory 3 dimensions *AppBeh, AppCog, AvCog*	Experimenter defined: Performance and coach related-	Yes	No	When facing a performance related stressors females used more AppBeh, whereas males were more likely to use AppBeh, followed by AppCogn but not AvCog. Study did not control for stress intensity appraisal when comparing gender differences in coping.
Anshel and Kassidis, 1997	N = 190 (93M; 97F) Age: 18-44 years Basketball players from various levels	Quantitative Transactional	Miller BSC CSIA	Experimenter defined	Yes	Yes	For the stressor missing a 'lay up' males used more approach coping than the females. Stress intensity and control appraisal were not used as control variables when comparing gender differences in coping.
Anshel et al., 1998	N = 477 (288M; 189F) Age: 15.8- 20.3 years National + club athletes from variety of sports	Quantitative Not specified	Study specific coping Survey	Experimenter defined	No	No	Gender differences existed for each source of stress. Males used more approach coping after each acute stressor. Overall, males and females were more similar, than different in coping patterns.
Anshel et al., 1997	N = 633 (290M; 359F) Club to international athletes from USA (n = 296), Age: 20.7 years; Australia (n=337) Age: 20.6 years	Quantitative Trait	Study specific Coping inventory (134 items)	Experimenter defined	No	No	Female athletes employed more approach-emotion coping strategies than males.
Anshel et al., 2001a	N = 251 (174M; 77F) Age: 23.7 years Athletes from a variety of sports. Level not reported.	Quantitative Transactional	CSIA	Experimenter defined	No	No	Females used more avoidance coping than males for the crowd stressor. Coping with acute stress was more similar than different between genders.

Table 1. (Continued)

Study	Participant Information	Method and Framework	Instrumentation	Type of Stressors	Stress Intensity Appraisal	Control Appraisal	Gender Differences
Anshel et al., 2001b	N = 251 (174M; 77F) Age: 23.7 years Athletes from a variety of sports. Level not reported.	Quantitative Transactional	CSIA	Experimenter defined	No	No	No coping differences reported.
Bebetsos and Antoniou, 2003	N = 85 (44M; 41F) Age: 22.3 years National badminton players	Quantitative Not specified	GVAC-28	Not relevant	No	No	No gender differences in psychological skills.
Campen and Roberts, 2001	N = 51 (31M; 20 F) Age: 37 years Recreational runners	Quantitative Transactional	Study specific coping Inventory CSAI-2 STAI	Self selected but related to upcoming competition	Yes (state Anxiety)	No	No gender differences on anxiety measure. Females were more likely to use social supportive strategies than males. Did not control for appraisal in coping analysis.
Crocker and Graham, 1995	N = 377 (208M; 169F) Age: 20.5 years Regional to national athletes from variety of sports	Quantitative Transactional	COPE PANAS PGI	Self selected	Yes (goal incongruence)	No	Females used higher levels of SESS and increasing effort to manage goal frustration. Did not control for stress appraisal in coping analysis.
Goyen and Anshel, 1998	N = 65 (37M; 28F) Age: 26.6 years Club athletes	Quantitative Transactional	Study specific Coping Survey	Experimenter defined	Yes	No	Gender differences in stressor type and stress intensity. Males reported more problem-focussed coping than females, whereas females reported more emotion-focused coping. Did not control for appraisal in coping analysis.
Hammermeister and Burton, 2004	N = 315 (209M; 106F) Club to professional tri-athletes, age: 35 years: Distance runners, age: 38 years; Cyclists, Age: 28 years	Quantitative Transactional	EADBQ CESQ PTCEGI PCCEGTI CSAI-2	Self selected but related to upcoming event	Yes	Yes	Males and females do not differ on types and degree of threat. Howevef females perceived less control over environmental threats than did males. Females used more emotion-focussed and males more problem-focused coping. Did not control for appraisal in coping analysis.
McLeod et al., 1994	N = 73 (43M; 30F) Age: 22.9 years Elite basketball players N = 133 (84M; 49F) Age: 23.8 years Non-elite basketball players	Quantitative Not specified	WOCS	Self selected	No	No	Females reported greater use of seeking social support.

Study	Participant Information	Method and Framework	Instrumentation	Type of Stressors	Stress Intensity Appraisal	Control Appraisal	Gender Differences
Nicholls et al., 2007	N = 749 (455M; 294F) Age: 19.8 years Athletes from different sports and skill levels	Qualitative Transactional	Concept maps	Self selected	No	No	Females used problem-focused coping more frequently than males.
Pensgard and Roberts, 2003	N = 69 (50M; 20F) Age: 25.2 years Elite athletes from Winter Olympic sports	Quantitative Transactional	POSQ COPE	Self selected	No	No	High ego orientation was associated with less use of active coping and planning strategies among females and more use of denial, but not male athletes.
Philippe et al., 2004	N = 80 (44M; 36F) Age: 23.1 years Athletes from different sports and skill levels	Quantitative Trait	CISS	Self selected	No	No	Males showed higher task focused coping than females.
Yoo, 2001	N = 532 (332M; 200F) Age: 21.2 years Elite and non elite athletes from various sports	Quantitative Trait	CSKA	Self selected	No	No	Males were more likely to use problem-focused coping than females, whereas females reported higher transcendent and EFC.

Note: SAS = Sources of Acute stress (Fisher and Zwart, 1982); Miller BSC = Behavioural style scale (Miller, 1987); CSIA = Coping Style Inventory for Athletes (Roth and Cohen framework); GVAC-28 = Greek Version of Athletic Coping-28 (Goudas et al., 1998); AARS = Adolescent Anger Rating Scale (Burney, 2001); EFC-= Emotion Focused Coping; PFC = Problem Focused Coping; CDS II = Causal Dimensions Scale II; COPE= Coping Inventory (Carver et al., 1989); PA = Positive Affect; NA = Negative Affect; SESS = Seeking social support for emotional reasons; PANAS = Positive and Negative Affect Schedule (Watson, Clark, and Tellegen., 1988); PGI = Performance goal incongruence (Crocker and Graham, 1995); CICS- Coping Inventory for Competitive Sport (Gaudreau and Blondin, 2002); EADBQ = Endurance Athlete Demographic and Background Questionnaire (Hammermeister and Burton, 2001); CESQ = Coping with Endurance Sports Questionnaire (Hammermeister and Burton, 2001); PTCEG1 = Perceived Threat to Competitive Endurance Goals (Hammermeister and Burton, 2001); PCCEGTI = Perceived Controllability of Competitive Endurance Goals Inventory (Hammermeister and Burton, 2001) ; CSAI-2 = Competitive State Anxiety Inventory- 2 (Martens, Burton, Vealey, Bump, and Smith, 1990); STAI = State Trait Anxiety Inventory (Spielberg et al., 1983); Self Esteem - Rosenbergs' Self Esteem Scale (Rosenberg, 1965); MCOPE = Modified Version of the COPE (Crocker and Graham, 1995); Self efficacy – Bandura (1997); WOCS = Ways of Coping with Sport; CISS= Coping Inventory for stressful situations (Endler and Parker, 1990); POSQ- Perception of Success Questionnaire (Roberts, Treasure, and Balague, 1998); SARRS = Social and Athletic Readjustment Rating Scale; ALES= Athletic Life Experiences Survey; ACSI= Athletic Coping Skills Inventory (Smith, Schutz, Smoth, and Ptaceck, 1995); CSKA = Coping Scale for Korean Athletes (Yoo, 2000).

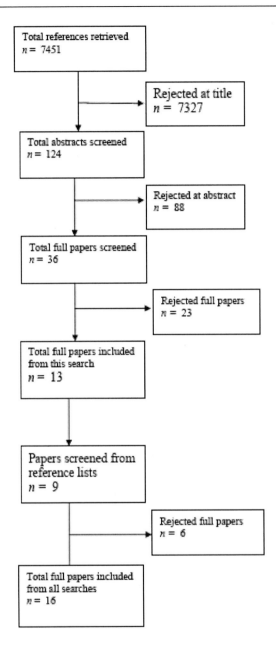

Figure 1. Summary of study selection and exclusion – all electronic literature searched.

It is believed that differences in coping strategies found in these studies may be the result of different performance stressors experienced by the male and female athletes (Ptaceck, Smith, and Zanas, 1992). In order to advance the research concerning gender differences in coping, it is essential that the nature of the stressor remain constant for male and female athletes in order to reduce possible gender differences in stressor type influencing the selection of coping strategies.

As suggested by Tamres et al., (2002) when comparing male and female coping behavior, it is crucial to determine how severity of the stressor among males and females. Surprisingly, from the 16 studies reviewed only six assessed stress intensity and only two of these studies measured perceptions of control over the stressful encounter. However, none of these studies controlled for stress intensity or perceived control appraisal when comparing the use of coping strategies reported by the male and female athletes.

Research from personality literature has provided insight into gender differences in relation to stress. Previous research has shown that females tend to have higher levels of neuroticism (Costa, Terraciano, and McCrae, 2001; Feingold, 1994) and high levels of neuroticism have been associated with higher levels of stress (Gunthert, Cohen, and Armelli, 1999). This suggests that females may be more likely to experience a stressful situation with higher levels of stress intensity than males. If this is the case, than this would be a possible explanation for differences in coping behaviour rather than gender per se. For example, the higher use of emotion-focused coping strategies reported by female athletes might be due to the fact that they first regulate their emotional arousal before adopting problem-focused coping strategies to deal with the stressor. Hence, it is difficult for individuals to make rational and logical decisions when they are in heightened emotional state. In such situations it would be advantageous to first lower emotions before invoking problem-focused coping strategies. Similarly, control perceptions have also been associated with the use of different coping strategies. For example, it has been found in situations in which the individuals perceive control it is more advantageous to use problem-focused coping strategies whereas emotion-focused coping strategies are better used in situations which are perceived as uncontrollable (Zakowski, Hall, Klein, and Baum, 2001).

We found that 12 studies explicitly analyzed gender differences in coping, whereas the remaining four studies examined gender differences in coping on a *post-hoc* basis. That is, gender differences were not part of the initial aim of these investigations. Partial support was found for the common belief that males and females differ in coping preferences in sport settings. However, conclusions towards gender coping preferences seem to be equivocal. From the 13 studies finding gender differences in coping, only three (e.g., Goyen and Anshel, 1998; Hammermeister and Burton, 2004; Yoo, 2001) supported the widely held belief that males use more problem-focused coping than females, who use more emotion-focused coping strategies than males in sport. In some studies males were found to use more problem-focused coping, but no differences in emotion-focused coping were observed (Anshel and Kassidis, 1997; Anshel et al., 1998; Anshel and Sutarso, 2007; Philippe et al., 2004). Other studies found gender differences in relation to emotion-focused coping, but not problem-focused coping (Anshel et al., 1997; Campen and Roberts, 2001; Crocker and Graham, 1995; McLeod et al., 1994). Conversely, the study (Nicholls et al., 2007) found that females used more problem-focused coping and no gender differences regarding the use of emotion-focused coping were reported.

From the seven studies that found males use more problem-focused coping, three assessed coping at the dimensional level. In these studies it was reported that males used more approach-cognitive coping (Anshel and Sutarso, 2007), task-orientated coping (Philippe et al., 2004), and problem-focused coping than females (Yoo, 2001). Four studies assessed coping at both the dimensional and strategy level. These studies found that males used more approach-coping (Anshel and Kassidis, 1997; Anshel et al., 1998) and problem-focused coping (Hammermeister and Burton, 2004; Goyen and Anshel, 1998) than the females.

Seven studies reported that females used more emotion-focussed coping strategies than the male athletes. One of these studies measured coping only at the dimensional level and found females scoring higher on emotion-focussed coping than the males (Yoo, 2001). Two studies measured coping only at the strategy level and found that females were more likely to use 'social supportive strategies' (Campen and Roberts, 2001; McLeod et al., 1994). The other four studies which assessed coping both at the dimensional and strategy level found that females used more approach-emotion coping strategies such as 'I felt anger toward the stressor' (Anshel et al., 1997), and emotion-focused coping strategies such as 'seeking emotional social support' (Crocker and Graham, 1995), 'positive reinterpretation, emotional social support, and dissociation' (Hammermeister and Burton, 2004) than the males. One study by Pensgard and Roberts (2003) analyzed coping only at the strategy level and as a function of ego-orientation. They found that females high in ego orientation reported more use of denial as a coping strategy in comparison to the males. Finally, a study by Yoo (2001) reported an additional, culturally specific, higher order coping category, 'transcendental coping,' which according to Yoo is similar to avoidance coping. However, it does not involve denial or attempts to avoid stress. In this study females used more transcendental coping than males.

The grouping of distinct coping categories under broad dimensions such as problem- or emotion-focused coping may be the reason for the equivocal findings regarding gender and coping among athletes. Additionally, as suggested by Tamres et al. (2002), gender differences may be limited to one or two strategies of these broad dimensions. Also, the studies included in the present systematic review adopted different higher-order dimensions to categorize the coping strategies used by athletes, making coping making comparisons difficult if not impossible. Finally, the studies used different questionnaires to assess coping, some of which were developed for the particular study (e.g., Anshel et al., 1998; Anshel et al., 1997; Anshel and Sutarso, 2007), which is another reason why meaningful comparisons difficult.

We also examined the evidence for both the situational and dispositional hypothesis in sport. Only four studies of those included in this systematic review (e.g., Crocker and Graham, 1995; Hammermeister and Burton, 2004; Philippe et al., 2004; Yoo, 2001), related their findings to gender theory. All four of these studies found gender differences in coping among athletes, and three of them in sport and three of them (Hammermeister and Burton, 2004; Philippe et al., 2004; Yoo, 2001) claimed that their findings supported the socialization model, and thus the dispositional hypothesis. The other study by Crocker and Graham (1995) suggested that the design of their study did not allow them to adequately test the dispositional hypothesis or the situational hypothesis as this research did not examine whether males and females experienced a common stressors.

The studies by Yoo (2001) and Philippe et al. (2004) reported gender differences in coping without males and females experiencing a common stressor, it is believed that their interpretation are therefore spurious. In the Hammermeister and Burton (2004) study, males and females appeared to be threatened to the same degree and experienced similar levels of cognitive and somatic anxiety in response to those threats. However, this study found that males and females differed in perceptions of control. Although females perceived less control over environmental threats than males, stress appraisal was not considered when analysing coping. This is an important issue because there has been consistent evidence that the perceived control an individual has over a stressful event influences coping. For example, problem-focused coping strategies are more widely used in situations appraised as being controllable. On the other hand, emotion-focused coping is more widely reported when the individual has low controllability of stressful situation (Zakowski et al., 2001). This is because low controllability increases emotional distress and emotion-focused coping strategies mange such distress (Aldwin, 1991). Therefore, it could be suggested that, the authors conclusion that females use more emotion-focused coping whereas males use more problem-focused coping strategies was a consequence of stress appraisal rather than coping. Sport stressors could be perceived different by males and females because of socialization processes. Some authors have suggested that attitudes and values involved in the 'sport' role (i.e., competitiveness, autonomy, and achievement) may interact with gender roles and maximize traditional masculine gender-roles and minimize traditional feminine roles (Gill, 2003; Miller and Levy, 1996). In this way males could be encouraged to intensify their attitudes and behaviors in sport, whereas female athletes may experience conflict between the values and proscribed behaviours associated with sport and the societal expectations of femininity (Czisma et al., 1988; Hoar et al., 2006; Miller and Levy, 1996). Hammermeister and Burton (2004) suggested that females may perceive less control over sport stressors than males, because sport is likely to be more amenable to personal control for males than females. If this is the case, gender differences in coping observed in this study should be explained by the role constraint theory or situational hypothesis (Tamres et al. 2002) rather than dispositional reasons as suggested by the authors. Although previous research (Anthrop and Allison, 1983; Archer and McDonald, 1990; Miller and Levy, 1996) failed to support the gender role conflict in female athletes, future studies in this area could explore whether social roles in sport influence gender differences in coping. In addition, nature of the stressor and stress appraisal should also be contemplated when investigating gender differences in coping with stress in sport.

CONCLUSION

In order to reach conclusions of whether males and females differ in coping in sport, future studies need to use a stronger theoretical framework to investigate gender and address methodological issues which may have affected previous findings. Although we found that most of the studies reviewed found gender differences in coping with stress, the findings of these studies are equivocal and questionably. Important aspects such as nature of the stressor, and stressor appraisal, were not controlled for in any of the studies reviewed, limiting the answer to the question whether gender differences in sport are actually due to dispositional reasons or to situational aspects.

Understanding more about male and female coping preferences in sport is important and can assist both researchers and applied practitioners with developing strategies to teach males and females to cope more effectively with stress in sport and as such improve performance or increase satisfaction. The past literature has a number of methodological and theoretical limitations, which makes it difficult to draw any firm conclusions regarding any possible gender differences in relation to coping. Male and female athletes appear to use different coping strategies; however, it is unclear whether such differences are the consequence of underlying biological/social differences or situational aspects.

It is important that future studies make use of a common stressors experienced by male and female athletes (Nicholls and Polman, 2007). Sport, in this respect, is unique in that males and females tend to experience similar stressor (Nicholls et al., 2007). However, experiencing a similar stressor is not sufficient, the way, male and female athletes appraise this stressor is also of crucial importance. Primary appraisal can be assessed by how much stress the event causes (stress thermometer). As suggested previously, this is an important issue. Tamres et al. (2002), in their meta-analysis, found that females appraise stressors as more severe than males. In terms of secondary appraisal, perceptions of control over the stressful event as well as control over one's internal state (emotions) would be important. As suggested by Tamres et al. (2002), the best way to determine whether stressor appraisal accounts for gender differences is to analyze if gender differences disappear when stress appraisal is controlled for in a statistical analysis.

REFERENCES

Aldwin, C. M. (1991). Does age affect the stress and coping process? Implications of age differences in perceived control. *Journal of Gerontology, 46,* 174-180.

Aldwin, C.M. (2007). *Stress, coping and development: An integrative perspective* (2nd Ed.). London: Guilford Press.

Anshel, M. H., Jamieson, J., and Raviv, S. (2001a). Cognitive appraisals and coping strategies following acute stress among skilled competitive male and female athletes. *Journal of Sport Behavior, 24,* 75-94.

Anshel, M. H., Jamieson, J., and Raviv, S. (2001b). Coping with acute stress among male and female Israeli athletes. *International Journal of Sport Psychology, 32,* 271-289.

Anshel, M. H., and Kassidis, S. N. (1997). Coping style and situational appraisals, as predictors of coping strategies following stressful events in sport as a function of gender and skill level. *British Journal of Psychology, 88,* 263-276.

Anshel, M. H., Porter, A., and Quek, J. (1998). Coping with acute stress in sport as a function of gender: An exploratory study. *Journal of Sport Behavior, 21,* 363-376.

Anshel, M. H., and Sutarso, T. (2007). Relationships between sources of acute stress and athletes' coping style in competitive sport as a function of gender. *Psychology of Sport and Exercise, 8,* 1-24.

Anshel, M.H., Williams, L.R.T., Hodge, K. (1997). Cross-cultural and gender differences on coping style in sport. *International Journal of Sport Psychology, 28,* 141-156.

Anthrop, J., and Allison, M. T. (1983). Role conflict and the high school female athlete. *Research Quarterly for Exercise and Sport, 54.* 104-111.

Archer, J., and McDonald, M. (1990). Gender roles and sports in adolescent girls. *Leisure Studies, 9,* 225-240.

Bandura, A. (1997). *Self-efficacy: The exercise of control.* New York: Freeman.

Bebetsos, E., and Antoniou, P. (2003). Psychological skills of Greek badminton athletes. *Perceptual and Motor Skills, 97,* 1289-1296.

Birrel, S. (1983). The psychological dimensions of female athletic participation. In M. Boutilier and L. San Giovanni (Eds.), *The sporting woman,* (pp.49-91) Champaign, IL: Human Kinetics.

Burney, D.A. (2001). *Adolescent Anger Rating Scale: Professional Manual* Psychological Assessment Resources , Lutz, FL.

Campen, C., and Roberts, D.C. (2001). Coping strategies of runners: Perceived effectiveness and match to precompetitive anxiety. *Journal of Sport Behaviour, 24,* 141-161

Carver, S., Scheier, M.F., and Weintraub, J.K. (1989). Assessing coping strategies: A theoretically based approach, *Journal of Personality and Social Psychology, 56,* 267–283.

Chalmers, I., and Haynes, B. (1995). Reporting, updating, and correcting systematic reviews of the effects of health care. In I. Chalmers and D. G. Altman (Eds.), *Systematic reviews* (pp. 86 – 95). London: BMJ Publishing Group.

Clark, M. S., and Reis, H. T. (1988). Interpersonal processes in close relationships. *Annual Review of Psychology, 39,* 604-672.

Cooper, H. (2003). *Editorial. Psychological Bulletin, 129,* 3–9.

Costa, P.T., Jr., Terraciano, A., and McCrae, R.R. (2001). Gender differences in personality across cultures: Robust and surprising results. *Journal of Personality and Social Psychology, 81,* 322-331.

Crocker, P. R. E., and Graham, T. R. (1995). Coping with competitive athletes with performance stress: Gender differences and relationships with affect. *The Sport Psychologist, 9,* 325-338.

Czisma, K., Wittig, A., and Schurr, K. (1988). Sport stereotypes and gender. *Journal of Sport and Exercise Psychology, 10,* 62-74.

Desertrain, G.S., and Weiss, M.R. (1988). Being female and athletic: A cause for conflict? *Sex Roles, 18,* 567-582.

Dindia, K., Allen, M. (1992). Sex differences in self disclosure: A meta-analysis. *Psychological Bulletin, 112,* 106-124.

Eagly, A. H., Mladinic, A., and Otto, S. (1991). Are women evaluated more favorably than men? An analysis of attitudes, beliefs, and emotions. *Psychology of Women Quarterly, 15,* 203-216.

Eagly, A.E., Wood, W., and Johannesen-Schmidt, M.C. (2004). Social theory of sex differences and similarities. In A.H. Eagly, A. E. Beall, and R.J. Stenberg (Eds), *The psychology of gender* (2nd ed. pp. 269-295). New York: The Guilford Press.

Endler, N.S. and Parker, J.D.A., (1990). Multidimensional assessment of coping: A critical evaluation. *Journal of Personality and Social Psychology, 58,* 844–854.

Feingold, A. (1994). Gender differences in personality: A meta-analysis. *Psychological Bulletin, 116,* 429-456.

Gaudreau, P., and Blondin, J.P. (2002). Development of a questionnaire for the assessment of coping strategies employed by athletes in competitive sport settings. *Psychology of Sport and Exercise, 3,* 1-34.

Goudas, M., Theodorakis, Y., and Karamousalidis, G. (1998). Psychological skills in basketball: Preliminary study for development of a Greek form of the Athletic Coping Skills Inventory-28. *Perceptual and Motor Skills, 86,* 59–65.

Goyen, M.J., and Anshel, M.H. (1998). Sources of acute competitive stress and use of coping strategies as a function of age and gender. *Journal of Applied Developmental Psychology, 19,* 469-86.

Gill, D.L. (2003). Gender and cultural diversity across the lifespan. In M. R. (Weiss (Ed.), *Developmental sport and exercise psychology: A lifespan perspective* (pp. 475-501) Morgantown, WV: Fitness Information Technology.

Grossman, M., and Wood, W. (1993). Sex differences in intensity of emotional experience: A social role interpretation. *Journal of Personality and Social Psychology, 65,* 1010-1022.

Gunthert, K.C., Cohen, L.H., and Armeli,S. (1999). The role of neuroticism in daily stress and coping. *Journal of Personality and Social Psychology, 77*, 1087-1100.

Hammermeister, J., and Burton, D. (2004). Gender differences in coping with endurance sports: Are men from Mars and women from Venus? *Journal of Sport Behavior, 27*, 148-164.

Hoar, S.D., Kowalski, K.C., Gaudreau, P., and Crocker, P.R.E. (2006). A review of coping in sport. In S. Hanton and S. D. Mellalieu (Ed.), *Literature Reviews in Sport Psychology* (pp. 47-90). New York: Hauppauge.

Knipschild, P. (1995). Some examples of systematic reviews. In. I Chalmers and D. G. Altman (Eds.), *Systematic reviews* (pp. 9 – 16). London: BMJ Publishing Group.

Lazarus, R.S. (2000). How emotions influence performance in competitive sports. *The Sport Psychologist, 14*, 229 – 252.

Lippa, R.A. (2005). *Gender, nature, and nurture.* New Jersey: Lawrence Erblaum Associates, Inc.

Lloyd Jones, M. (2004). Application of systematic review methods to qualitative research: Practical issues. *Journal of Advanced Nursing, 48,* 271 – 278.

Martens, R., Burton, D., Vealey, R.S., Bump, L.A., and Smith D. (1990). Development and validation of the Competitive State Anxiety Inventory-2. In R. Martens, R. S. Vealey, and D. Burton (Eds.), *Competitive anxiety in sport* (pp. 117-190). Champaign, IL: Human Kinetics.

McLeod, S.L., Kirkby, R.J., and Madden, C.C. (1994). Coping in basketball: Differences according to ability and gender. *European Journal for High Ability, 5*, 191-198.

McCrae, R.R. (1992). Situational determinants of coping. In B.N. Carpenter (Ed.), *Personal coping: Theory research, and application.* Westport, CT: Praeger.

Meade, M.O., and Richardson, W.S. (1997). Selecting and appraising studies for a systematic review. *Annals of Internal Medicine, 127*, 531 – 537.

Miller, J.L., and Levy, G.D. (1996). Gender role conflict, gender typed characteristics, self-concepts, and sport socialization in female athletes and nonathletes. *Sex Roles, 35,* 111-122.

Mulrow, C.D. (1994). Rationale for systematic reviews. In I. Chalmers and D. G. Altman (Eds.), *Systematic reviews* (pp. 1 – 8). London: BMJ Publishing Group.

Murlow, C.C. (1994). Systematic reviews: Rationale for systematic reviews. British Medical Journal, 309, 597 – 599.

Nicholls, A.R., and Polman, R.C.J. (2007). Coping in sport: A systematic review. *Journal of Sport Sciences, 25,* (1) 11-31.

Nicholls, A.R., Polman, R.C.J., Levy, A., Taylor, J.A., and Cobley, S.P. (2007). Stressors, coping, and coping effectiveness: Gender, sport type, and ability differences. *Journal of Sports Sciences*, 25, 1521-1530.

Pensgard, A.M., and Roberts, G.C. (2003). Achievement goal orientations and the use of coping strategies among winter Olympics. *Psychology of Sport and Exercise, 4*, 2 101-116.

Philippe, R.A., Seiler, R., and Mengisen, W. (2004). Relationship of coping styles with type of sport. *Perceptual and Motor Skills, 98*, 479-486.

Ptacek, J.T., Smith, R.E., and Zanas, J. (1992). Gender, appraisal, and coping: A longitudinal analysis. *Journal of Personality, 60*, 747-770.

Roberts, G.C., Treasure, D.C. and Balagué, G. (1998). Achievement goals in sport: the development and validation of the Perception of Success Questionnaire. *Journal of Sport Sciences*, *16*, 337-347.

Rosario, M., Shin, M., Morch, H., and Carol, B.H. (1988).Gender differences in coping and social supports: Testing socialization and role constraint theories. *Journal of Community Psychology 16,* 55-69.

Rosenberg, M. (1965). *Society and the Adolescent Self-Image.* Princeton, New Jersey: Princeton University Press.

Sigmon, S.T., Stanton, A.L., and Snyder, C.R. (1995). Gender differences in coping: a further test of socialization and role constraint theories. *Sex Roles, 33,* 565-587.

Smith, R.E., Schutz, R.W., Smoll, F.L., and Ptacek, J.T. (1995). Development and validation of a multidimensional measure of sport-specific psychological skills: The Athletic Coping Skills Inventory-28. *Journal of Sport and Exercise Psychology*, *17*, 379.

Spielberg, C.D. (1983). *Manual for the State-Trait Anxiety Inventory. Revised Edition..* Consulting Psychologists Press: Palo Alto, CA.

Tamres, L.K., Janicki, D., and Helgeson, V.S. (2002). Sex differences in coping behavior: A meta-analytic review and an examination of relative coping. *Personality and Social Psychology Review 6,* 2-30.

Taylor, S.E., Klein, L.C., Lewis, B.P., Gruenewald, T.L., Gurung, R.A.R. and Updegraff, J. A. (2000). Biobehavioral responses to stress in females: Tend-and-befriend, not fight-or-flight. *Psychological Review, 107*, 411-429.

Watson, D., Clark, L.A. and Tellegen, A. (1988). Development and validation of brief measures of positive and negative affect: the PANAS scales. *Journal of Personality and Social Psychology, 54*, 1063-1070.

West, C., and Zimmerman, D.H. (1991). Doing gender. In. J. Lorber and S. A. Fareel (Eds). *The social construction of gender* (pp.13-37). Thousand Oaks, CA: Sage.

Yoo, J. (2001). Coping profile of Korean competitive athletes. *International Journal of Sport Psychology, 32,* 290-303.

Zakowski, S.G., Hall, M.H., Klein, L.C., and Baum, A. (2001). Appraisal control, coping, and stress in a community sample: A test of the Goodness-of-Fit hypothesis. *Annals of Behavioral Medicine, 23*, 158-165.

Zeman, J., and Garber, J. (1996). Display rules for anger, sadness, and pain: It depends on who is watching. *Child development, 67*, 957-973.

In: Coping in Sport: Theory, Methods, and Related Constructs   ISBN: 978-1-60876-488-4
Editor: Adam R. Nicholls   © 2010 Nova Science Publishers, Inc.

Chapter 6

ATHLETES' COPING ACROSS THE LIFESPAN

Sharleen D. Hoar and M. Blair Evans
University of Lethbridge, Alberta, Canada

ABSTRACT

The past twenty-five years of sport psychology research has witnessed a burgeoning amount of attention to the study of coping. However, there have been few attempts to understand how athletes' coping changes across the lifespan. This chapter provides knowledge about the development of coping as it is studied in sport psychology. Specifically, three lines of research are reviewed: (a) the direct study of age-related differences in athletes' coping, (b) the indirect study of age-related differences in athletes' coping, and (c) maturation differences in athletes' coping. A developmental agenda for the study of coping in sport is offered. We conclude the chapter by addressing future directions for sport research.

INTRODUCTION

Coping and development seem inherently inter-connected. No account of coping is complete without acknowledging the central role that age-graded factors play in shaping an individual's adaptation to stress....Likewise, no account of development is complete without consideration of how individuals respond to stress (Skinner and Edge, 2002, p. 77).

During the 2008 Summer Olympic games in Beijing, China the age of four female gymnasts came into question. As of 1997, the Federation Internationale de Gymnastique (FIQ) has ruled that athletes who were at least 16 years of age within the calendar year are eligible to compete at the most elite-level competition. After being subjected to multiple age-inquires, the FIQ and the International Olympic Committee found that the four gymnasts had met the age requirements and were eligible to compete at the 2008 summer Olympic games (Clarke, 2008). Like that of gymnastics there are other sports that impose age restrictions on athletes' eligibility to participate at the most elite levels of competition. For example, the International Skating Union (ISU) imposes age restrictions on figure skaters and speed skaters. Additionally, the National Hockey League mandates that professional players be 18 years of age by September 15th of the year in which the athlete wishes to compete. The age restrictions imposed by these sport organizations (and others) are not designed to level the playing field in terms of skill or physical advantages. Rather, these age restrictions are imposed to protect child athletes from physical and psychological injury and exploitation associated with the most elite levels of sport (Van Anderson, 1997).

It is well established among the developmental research that children and adolescents do not think like, nor do they behave like miniature adults (Newman Kingery, Roblick, Suveg, Grover, Sherrill et al., 2006). Gould (1982) observed that sport scholars "Too often [we] erroneously assume that psychological processes and theories that have been based on research with adults automatically transfer to younger age groups" (p. 12). Moreover, old and very old adults also do not think like, nor act like their younger counterparts (Aldwin, Sutton, Chiara, and Spiro, 1996). Accordingly, sport researchers such as Gould (1982) and Weiss and Bredemeier (1983) have long advocated for a developmental perspective for studying socio-psychological processes associated with sport participation in general, and with children and youth in particular. Sport scholars have not heeded this call for a developmental perspective to the study of coping and positive adaptive processes. Developmental studies in the literature are scant (Hoar, Kowalski, Crocker, and Gaudreau, 2006). In their extensive review of the coping literature, sport scholars Nicholls and Polman (2007) concluded that "Research concerning child and adolescent coping in sport appears to be relatively underdeveloped" (p. 18). Additionally, we could not locate one published study examining the coping process of older-aged adult sport participants. Without developmental data, sport researchers' efforts to improve adaptive coping with individuals in these groups is likely to miss the mark. It has also been suggested that developmental study, particularly with youth sport participants, is important for talent identification and the development of expertise (Holt and Dunn, 2004; Nicholls and Polman, 2007).

In this chapter we present a developmental agenda for studying sport participants' coping processes and review the field's current state of knowledge about coping processes achieved during various stages of lifespan. The chapter is organized into several sections. First, we present several images of athletes' coping across the lifespan. These cases serve the purpose of illustrating key quantitative and qualitative shifts in coping that are observed with age. We will use these images to illustrate key concepts discussed in the chapter. Next we present a research agenda for studying developmental changes in coping across an athletes' lifespan through a discussion of key changes in coping found within the general developmental literature. In the third section we engage in a discussion of the changes that occur in athletes' coping process across the lifespan. Finally, we provide conclusions and directions for future research.

IMAGES OF ATHLETE'S COPING ACROSS THE LIFESPAN

Daniel – 13-Year-Old Male Track and Field Competitor

This was basically the first year that I have done competitive track and I knew that there was really fast kids that were in this competition. I was pretty nervous before the race. My only strategy for the race was to try to get the inside lane before the start. When the gun went off there were some people that went off sprinting and I knew that they would probably run out of energy. So I was in the bottom couple of runners and then after about 50 or 60 metres I decided that it was a really slow pace and I knew that I could run faster so I jumped into one of the outside lanes and passed a ton of people. At 200 metres left in the race there were two leaders and one kid that was slowing down. I could tell that he was out of energy so I passed him. I remember thinking about how well I was doing and that I had sold myself short. I then I wondered what all my friends and family who are watching thought about how well I am doing. Then as we went around the corner and there were about 60 metres left in the race, I guess the guy had a lot of energy because he started sprinting. I did not want to let him get a head of me so I started to sprint too. I just barely got ahead of him and beat him by just, like, half a second. I ended up coming in third. I was pretty happy about that. After the race I waited around and talked to my friends and my mom. I was just kind of amazed at how well I did, because I ended up with a time that was way faster than personal best.

Emilia – 20-Year-Old Female Rugby Player

This game was about defending our championship. It's hard playing at home. I find that I have so many distractions with family and friends present and I am just so comfortable that I'm not as focused on the tasks as I should be. I was really thinking to focus on what I had to do myself and to just pay attention to the little things, like getting a good warm-up. For me I find that music is really big in helping me focus. I have different lists on my IPOD. There are songs that get me pumped up. There are certain songs that I play – one song in particular that makes me think of how to tackle, other songs make me really think of being a team player. Another thing that I do is talk to the girl on my team who plays the same position as me. We talk about our strengths and the things that we can do on the field during the game. It is really important for me to have a good warm-up too. Rather than scanning who was in the crowd, I tried to pretend that I was somewhere else where I didn't know anyone and to be in the moment.

Ruby – 43-Year-Old Female Triathlete

I remember that I was *really* nervous and full of adrenalin when I got into the pool for the warm-up. I think I swam 100 metres faster than I had ever swam 100 metres before; I needed to try to settle down and just focus and try to not be distracted by what was going on. During the swim I tried to stay present in my head for every lap of the swim portion. It is really difficult for me to not let my head get away from me and come up with self-defeating thoughts, like oh you still have 1100 metres to go and you feel [like] this [bad]. Towards the end of the swim, about 400 or 500 metres, I put out a little more effort and tried to go faster. When I finished the swim, I came out of the pool and I remember they called my swim time. I was shattered because I felt like I had swam faster than I had before and I had convinced myself that I was swimming an exceptionally fast pace. I was actually quite slow. As I ran to the transition are for the bike portion I was already planning how I was going to make up the time. Once out on the [bike] course I tried to keep an even pace. Self-defeating thoughts entered my mind when people passed me and I rationalized that I didn't need to feel bad because that person was a 20 year-old male or a 40 year-old male who I wasn't competing against. But if it was a 40 year-old female than I would be really bummed at myself and try to push harder.

Thomas – 72 Years-Old Golfer

Since I retired six years ago I have been participating in a golf tournament to raise money for my hospital. The morning of the tournament, there wasn't any real anxiety. I was interested to get to the golf course early enough to get in some putting. You can usually tell how well your game is going to go by how well you can putt. My putting that morning was good. I also decided before the tournament that I was going to use a cart. The course is quite hilly and I didn't want to walk. I was feeling confident about my golf and that I would be able to contribute to the team score…. I remember that there was some anxiety at the first hole. There is always anxiety with the first hole. There are people around you and things like that. I usually foul up the first hole and in my mind I tell myself that my tournament starts at the second hole. That is how I rationalize that failure…. I shot 119, I was hoping for 113. I had a few holes with snowmans [8 shots] on them. I think that the bad shots happened because I am just not a good golfer. I go into these tournaments to help raise money not to play par golf. I did have several holes that I was either under-par or under-par with my handicap. I don't remember why those holes went well and the others didn't. In the end I wasn't pleased with my score, but I remembered why I was playing. It was competitive, yes, and I wasn't pleased with my result; but I got to get up, enjoy breathing in the good fresh air, get some exercise with some guys I like to golf with, and raise money for my hospital.

A DEVELOPMENTAL AGENDA FOR STUDY OF COPING IN SPORT

A lifespan perspective defines development as all the physical, cognitive, emotional, and psychological *changes* that humans undergo over a lifetime (Horn, 2004; Weiss and Raedeke, 2004). Thus, *change-over-time* is central to a developmental examination of coping. Lerner (2002) warns scholars not to equate development with change. Developmental change must meet at least two criteria. First, developmental change must be systematic and organized in character. Second, the nature of change must be successive in character. That is, changes that are seen at a later point in time are at least in part, influenced by the changes that occurred at an earlier time. A lifespan perspective considers continuity and change from infancy through to older adulthood (see Baltes, Lindenberger, and Staudinger, 1998).

Developmental researchers use the terms flexible, differentiated, appropriate, selective, reflective, considered, organized, constructive, measured, modulated, sturdy, and autonomous to describe the quantitative (i.e., amount) and qualitative (i.e., structural) changes observed in coping across the lifespan (Skinner and Zimmer-Gembeck, 2007; Weiss and Raedeke, 2004). For example, the term 'differentiated' most commonly describes quantitative change. That is, athletes' coping is more or less differentiated. Going back to the coping images, it is recognized that all four athletes used self-talk as a coping strategy in the management of competitive stress. Relative to Daniel and Thomas, Emilia's (athlete with the most athletic experience) and Ruby's (middle-aged adult) self-talk was more differentiated in the sense that both women used a larger variety of self-talk coping effort instances. Qualitative change describes structural changes that occur in coping over time. As coping develops across the lifespan, coping undergoes reorganization that gives rise to unique constellations of coping actions that serve a specific coping function (Skinner and Zimmer-Gembeck, 2007). School-aged children are likely to use behavioral coping strategies to distract themselves from a stressful event (Seiffge-Krenke, 1995). Older children and young adolescents who have more mature cognitive abilities will distract him/herself using both behavioral and cognitive based coping strategies (Fields and Prinz, 1997). Sport researchers adopting a developmental approach to studying coping seek to describe, explain, predict, and control for the systematic quantitative and qualitative changes in athletes' coping.

To study developmental change, most developmental scholars specialize in smaller segments of the lifespan such as children, adolescents, young adulthood, middle-age, and older-age. These smaller segments are referred to as *developmental stages* and each stage is understood to be a period of life that is characterized by a specific underlying maturational organization (i.e., biological, cognitive, social, and affective factors) that differentiates it from the preceding and succeeding stages (Newman and Newman, 1999). The development of coping is affected by maturational changes in physiology, perception, memory, cognition, language, emotion, self-perceptions, motivation, social comparison, and social relationships (see Fields and Prinz, 1997; Newman Kingery et al., 2006; Skinner and Zimmer-Gembeck, 2007). Furthermore, a lifespan development orientation recognizes that humans develop within social contexts that have distinct norms and agendas (Skinner and Edge, 1998). Children's coping environments are different than that of adults (Fields and Prinz, 1997). In sport, children have limited amounts of control over their circumstances and must depend on adult (i.e., parent and coach) support. Understanding the differences in development of coping across the lifespan requires considering the *interaction* between an individuals' state of maturational organization and their social context.

ATHLETE'S COPING ACROSS THE LIFESPAN

Information about the development of coping across the lifespan is emerging (Nicholls and Polman, 2007; Skinner and Zimmer-Gembeck, 2007). Three main lines of research can be observed. First, developmental researchers have examined *age-related* changes in coping. To delineate the developmental stages most relevant to understanding the development of coping across the lifespan 'age' is a proxy variable for maturation, as the maturational mechanisms (i.e., changes in physiology, socio-cognition, and emotion) underlying the key developmental stages in the development of coping are not fully understood (Fields and Prinz, 1997; Weiss and Raedeke, 2004). Thus, the following age-periods are used to describe developmental stages in coping across the lifespan: (a) school-age childhood, ages 6 to 11 years; (b) early adolescence, 12 to 14 years; (c) middle adolescence, 15 to 17 years; (d) late adolescence and college-age, 18 to 22 years; (e) early adulthood, 23 to 35 years, (f) middle-aged adulthood, 36 to 59 years; and (g) older adulthood, 60 to 75 years (Holt, Hoar, and Fraser, 2005; Skinner and Zimmer-Gembeck, 2007; Weiss and Bredemeier, 1983). Included in this first line of research are studies that *directly* compare the coping processes of individuals at different developmental stages in the lifespan. Examining the past twenty years of coping sport research, five studies could be located (i.e., Bebestos and Antoniou, 2003; Gëczi, Bognar, Toth, Sipos, and Fudedi, 2008; Goyen and Anshel, 1998; Nicholls, Polman, Morely, and Taylor, 2009; Reeves, Nicholls, and McKenna, 2009) whose primary purpose was to examine age-related differences in coping.

Table 1. Listing of Sport Coping Research Reviewed for Different Developmental Stages over the Lifespan

Developmental Stage	Age Range (years)	No. of Studies	Study Reference
School-age children	6 – 11	2	Anshel and Delany (2001); Holt and Mandigo (2004).
Early adolescent	12 – 14	4	Crocker and Isaak (1997); Eubank and Collins (2000), Gould, Wilson, Tuffey, and Lochbaum, (1993); Hoar, Crocker, Holt, and Tamminen (2009)
Middle adolescent	15 – 17	10	Crocker, Alderman, and Smith (1988); Gal-or, Tenenbaum, Furst, and Shrtzer (1986); Gaudreau, Lapierre, and Blondin (2001); Gould, Udry, Tuffey, and Loehr, (1996); Kowalski and Crocker (2001); Manuel, Shilt, Curl, Smith, DuRant, Lester et al. (2002); Nicholls (2007); Nicholls, Holt, Polman, and James (2005); Rider and Hicks (1995); Smith, Smoll, and Ptacek (1990)
Older adolescent	18 – 22	19	Anshel, Porter, and Quek (1998); Anshel, Williams, and Hodge (1997); Giacobbi, Foore, and Weinberg (2004); Giacobbi, Lynn, Wetherington, Jenkins, Bodenforf, and Langley (2004); Giacobbi and Weinberg (2000); Haney and Long (1995); Hatzigeorgiadis (2006); Holt (2003); Holt, Berg, and Tamminen (2007); Kim and Duda (2003); Krohne and Hindel (1988); Lally (2007); Ntoumanis and Biddle (1998); Ntoumanis and Biddle (2000); Ntoumanis, Biddle, and Haddock (1999); Ridnour and Hammermeister (2008); Stanley, Pargman, and Tenenbaum (2007); Wang, Marchant, and Morris (2004); Williams and Krane (1992)
Early adult	23 – 34	13	Arathoon and Malouff (2004); Cresswell and Hodge (2004); Dale (2000); Dugdale, Eklund, and Gordon (2002); Gaudreau and Blondin (2004); Hoar and Flint (2008); Holt and Dunn (2004); Kadlcik and Flemr (2008); Madden, Jeffrey, and Brown (1990); Pensgaard and Duda (2003); Pensgaard and Roberts (2003); Pensgaard and Ursin (1998); Thelwell, Weston, and Greenlees (2007)
Middle-aged adult	35 – 59	3	Burman, Omli, Giacobbi, and Brewer (2008); Frey (2007); Wolfson and Neave (2007)
Older-aged adult	60 - 75	1	Evans, Link, and Hoar (2009)

A second line of research in the developmental study of coping across the lifespan is to systematically review and compare across bodies of coping literature whose samples have been constrained to a specific developmental stages (Aldwin, 2007; Compas, Connor-Smith,

Saltzman, Thomsen, and Wadsworth, 2001; Fields and Prinz, 1997; Holt et al., 2005). Though this line of research *indirectly* studies age-related change, it has received the most attention in the developmental literature.

Table 1 lists the sport studies whose samples can inform about coping at developmental stages across the lifespan. We remind readers that these studies were not designed to explicitly capture development. Additionally, embedded within the age-categories are different mechanisms of physical, cognitive, and social development affecting the stress and coping process. Nevertheless, considering these studies together can be informative in capturing age-related differences in coping (Skinner and Zimmer-Gembeck, 2007).

Finally, the third line of research within the developmental coping literature is to study *maturation-related* difference in coping. In sport, one study was recently published comparing coping across individuals of different biological maturational status (Nicholls et al., 2009).

Direct Study of Age-Related Differences in Athletes' Coping

Reeves et al. (2009) compared the types of competitive stressors and coping strategies reported by early adolescent male academy soccer players to their middle adolescent counterparts. Data was collected using interview procedures. Results revealed that middle adolescent soccer players' stress is more complex than younger players in two important ways. First, the older soccer players reported more stressful events than the younger players. Second, older players had qualitatively different competitive stressors than the younger players. For example, early adolescents reported making errors, the opposition, team performances, and family as prominent stressors. Middle adolescents reported making errors, team performance, coaches, selection, contractual stressors, social evaluation, and playing at a higher level as important sources of stress. Coping also changed with age. Specifically, coping shifted in function and became more diversified with age. Problem-focused coping, the most frequently applied functional category of coping for both groups, consisted of different types of coping efforts. Early adolescent problem-focused coping efforts primarily consisted of behavioral performance and increased concentration. While middle adolescents reported problem-focused coping instances of behavioral performance and increased concentration, problem-focused coping also consisted of increased effort, learning/reflection, and positive thinking/self-talk. Instances of emotion-focused coping emerged during middle adolescence. Early adolescents used more avoidance coping instances than did middle adolescents. Nicholls et al. (2009) also examined adolescent age-related changes in coping. The 527 adolescents sampled ranged in age from 11 to 19 years. Significant correlation results between chronological age and coping strategy use implied that younger athletes use more mental imagery, effort expenditure, and resignation than older athletes, and that older athletes use more venting of emotions compared to younger athletes. No significant relations emerged between chronological age and perceived coping effectiveness of a specific coping strategy.

Goyen and Anshel (1998) compared the coping responses from 74 middle adolescent athletes (M_{age} = 15.4 years) to the coping responses of 65 young adult athletes (M_{age} = 26.6 years). In comparison to young adults, middle adolescents reported higher levels of stress associated with competitive interactions with others. Middle adolescents primarily relied on three types of coping efforts ("I concentrated on what to do next", "I put my anger into my game," and "I thought about how I would change the situation"), whereas adults were more diversified in the selection of coping responses. More recently, age-related differences in coping between players of a U-18 Hungarian national team hockey team and a young adult national team were examined (Gëczi et al. 2007). The young adult hockey players reported higher usage of peaking under pressure and freedom from worry compared to the younger counterparts. It was also reported that the older players had lower state anxiety scores in response to competing in a world tournament than the middle adolescent players.

In summary, the direct study of age-related differences has informed about quantitative and qualitative shifts in the development of athletes' coping across the developmental stages of early adolescence to young adulthood. Early adolescent athletes' organize coping efforts differently than older athletes. In particular, early adolescent athletes' smaller and less developed coping repertoires primarily consist of behavioral types of coping actions. With age (and presumably maturation) older adolescents have access to and increasingly use cognitive forms of coping efforts in the application of coping strategies. This pattern is strengthened in early adulthood. Athletes' young and old perceive coping efforts to be appropriate (i.e., effective) to manage the types of competitive stress faced at specific developmental stages.

Indirect Study of Age-Related Differences in Athletes' Coping

School-age children's coping. Two studies examine the coping of children under the age of twelve years. Holt and Mandigo (2004) studied 33 male cricket participants ($M_{age} = 11.9$ years). The athletes' coping responses to competitive stress were primarily behavioral in nature, such as focusing on the technical points of their sport skill. 43% of coping responses were found to serve an emotion-focused purpose, while 41% of the coping responses served a problem-focused purpose, and 16% of coping responses were designated as 'no-coping'. Anshel and Delany (2001) interviewed 52 youth sport participants between the ages of 10 and 12 years regarding stressful situations in competition and the associated coping strategies applied in the management of stress. Results of the study revealed that children's positive (i.e., challenge) appraisal was associated with increased approach coping while a negative (i.e., threatening) appraisal was associated with increased avoidance coping. The results of this research imply that older children's coping may be related more to the type of appraisals made about the stressful context rather than the actual or perceived demands of the stressful event.

Early adolescent athletes' coping. Sport studies considered in this developmental stage include participants between the ages of ten to sixteen years of age. No published studies exclusively focus on the early adolescent age period of twelve to fourteen years. Each of the four studies are reviewed consist of a sample mean ranging between twelve to fourteen years.

Early adolescent athletes rely on behavioral coping strategies to manage stressful competitive events. In addition, early adolescents who view their pre-competitive anxiety as facilitative for performance (i.e., positive appraisal) report higher coping levels (problem-focused and emotion-focused coping) compared to those early adolescents who view anxiety to be debilitative (i.e., negative appraisal, Eubank and Collins, 2000). This is a pattern that is similar to that seen at the younger school-age developmental stage.

Hoar et al. (2009) surveyed 575 early adolescent sport participants (aged 11 to 15 years) management of a self-selected interpersonal stressful event in sport. The most frequently cited coping strategies included seeking social support (relative frequency of 19.0% of coping instances), active coping (relative frequency of 21.7% of coping instances), and mental disengagement (relative frequency of 18.7% of coping instances). The least frequently cited coping strategies were isolating activities, and the cognitive strategies of seeking spiritual support, planning, and cognitive reappraisal. This result suggests the emergence of cognitive-based coping (i.e., mental disengagement, cognitive reappraisal, and planning) and some reorganization of the coping repertoire (i.e., use of mental disengagement) during this stage of development.

Early adolescent athletes may have difficulties discussing coping responses on open-ended surveys and during interviews. A number of studies reveal that athletes at this developmental stage consistently cite a limited number of coping strategies (Eubank and Collins, 2000; Gould et al., 1993; Hoar et al., 2009). For example, Hoar et al. reported that athletes cited an average of two to three coping strategies on an open-ended questionnaire. Young adolescent athletes acknowledge an insufficient coping repertoire for managing the types of sport stress that is encountered (Gould et al.). While the types of coping strategies (i.e., cognitive-based coping strategies) are more available to an early adolescent (due to increased abstract cognitive thinking, Compas et al., 2001), athletes at this stage of development have not fully integrated these strategies and do not understand how to effectively apply such coping strategies. For example, Gould et al. reported that while parents and teachers made the youth sampled more aware of certain types of coping strategies that could be used to manage their sport stress, such as relaxation, the athletes felt that the adults didn't inform how to effectively execute the strategies.

Early adolescents apply multiple coping functions to a single coping strategy (Hoar et al., 2009). Lazarus (1991) theorized that coping strategies are capable of serving more than one function. For example, Daniel's isolation from others before his race served both a problem-focused function (e.g., to focus on his strategy of where to stand at the start) and emotion-focused function (e.g., to calm his nervous feelings). Though Daniel did not explicitly state that his isolation served an avoidance function, one may speculate that his isolation also helped him to physically avoid interacting with his competitors and potentially increasing his nervousness. Taken further, it is plausible that Daniel did not choose to execute other coping strategies at that precompetitive stage because the coping effort (i.e., isolation) efficiently served his coping function needs. Thus, no other strategies were required.

Crocker and Isaak (1997) found mixed evidence that early adolescents' coping is situational-based. Results revealed that though competitive swimmers (aged 10 to 16 years) primarily relied on active coping efforts to manage competitive stress, coping efforts changed across the three different races. In contrast, early adolescents exhibited stable coping patterns across time in the training environment.

In sum, sport research reveals that athletes at this development stage approach stressful sport situations with a limited coping repertoire. That is, most athletes rely on a few behavioral coping strategies to manage stressful sport events, such as active coping. Further, coping efforts appear to serve multiple coping functions. Not all early adolescent athletes, however, fit this profile. The empirical literature shows that some early adolescent athletes use a wider array of both behavioral and cognitive-based strategies according perceived effectiveness of strategy and the situational context (Crocker and Isaak, 2997; Hoar et al., 2009).

Middle adolescence athletes' coping. Ten studies are reviewed that examined the coping efforts of athletes between the ages of fourteen and eighteen years of age. It has been suggested that middle adolescence is a critical stage of development for the acquisition of a mature coping repertoire (e.g., Aldwin, 2007; Nicholls and Polman, 2007; Seiffge-Krenke, 1995):

> At about age 15 in Seiffge-Krenke's data, adolescence seems to be marked by the development of cognitive processes from simple, concrete, and more self-centered thinking to complex, abstract, and relational thinking. Early adolescents who operate at earlier level of social cognitive maturity are, for example, unlikely to differentiate between sources of support. They are less able to recognize the links between current behavior and long-range outcomes and they are possibly more motivated by self-centered needs. In contrast, late adolescents, having already reached more mature social cognitive level, select social support strictly in accordance to the problem at hand, consider current options more often, think about the future consequences of their actions, and reflect about their position with respect to the perspectives of others (Lazarus, 1999, pp. 181-182).

In a series of studies with middle adolescent male golfers, Nicholls and his colleagues assessed athletes stress and coping experiences in competitive golf using daily diary procedures. Results of these studies revealed that the athletes used a wide array of coping efforts that were primarily cognitive in nature. As expected, individual differences in athletes coping was evident, although some commonalities could be identified. Among a sample of eleven international male golfers (M_{age} = 16.4 years) common coping strategies cited included blocking (a form of cognitive avoidance), increased concentration, and technical adjustments (Nicholls, Holt, Polman, and James, 2005). Taken together, the results from these studies imply that middle adolescent athletes have an expanded coping repertoire in comparison to younger athletes and display individual differences in the types of coping strategies employed.

Middle adolescent sport participants are capable of distinguishing between at least three different coping functions (i.e., problem-focused coping, emotion-focused coping, and avoidance coping) that their coping efforts serve (Kowalski and Crocker, 2001). Male middle adolescent golfers are reported to use more problem-focused coping efforts than emotion-focused or avoidance coping to manage stress associated with competitive golf (Nicholls et al., 2005). It is cautioned that this latter finding may be specific to the male gender and should not be generalized to all middle adolescent athletes. Commencing in early adolescence, males show an increased tendency for problem-focused and avoidance coping efforts compared to females (Aldwin, 2007; Hoar et al., 2009; Nicholls and Polman, 2007).

Middle adolescent athletes vary the types of coping strategies applied during different phases of a competitive event. Gaudreau et al. (2001) found that 33 male middle adolescent athletes' coping (age range from 15 to 19 years) changed across the phases of competition (i.e., 2 hours prior to event, immediately following the event, and 24 hours following the event). Specifically, changes were observed in the utilization of increased effort, wishful thinking, active coping/planning, suppression of competing activities, seeking social support, and behavioral disengagement.

There is some evidence that middle adolescent athletes are able to discern between the instances when a specific coping strategy is more or less effective. Nicholls (2007) also observed important differences in perceived effectiveness. Middle adolescent golfers judged the effectiveness of a coping effort differently in accordance to different appraised demands of the situation. Thus, despite the objective similarity between two coping situations, golfers stated different levels of effectiveness for the coping effort as used in each situation.

Some research suggests that links middle adolescent athletes' coping with functional (i.e., sport performance), emotional (i.e., affective states), and psychosomatic (i.e., athletic injury and burnout) outcomes. An early study revealed that middle adolescent military students with superior parachute jumps utilized more cognitive coping efforts prior to making the jump compared to that of the students with less skilled jumps (Gal-or et al., 1986).

Gould et al. (1996) found important coping differences were associated with burnout. These researchers compared young tennis players (M_{age} = 16.4 years) who burned out of elite tennis (n = 30) compared to those who were still actively participating (n = 32). Specifically, athletes' responses on the COPE inventory (Carver, Scheier, and Weintraub, 1989) revealed that burned out tennis players were less likely to use planning and positive reinterpretation and growth compared to active tennis players. Evidence also exists that middle adolescent athletes with low coping skill are at increased risk for the occurrence of athletic injury, particularly if social support resources are also evaluated to be low (Rider and Hicks, 1995; Smith et al., 1990). While poor coping skills is demonstrated to be an important contributor of athletic injury among middle adolescent athletes, poor coping skill does not appear to influence affective experience of being injured. Manuel et al. (2002) did not find a relationship between an injured middle adolescent athletes coping skill and the severity of depression incurred from the injury.

Compared to earlier developmental stages, middle adolescent athletes show a marked increase in the number and types of coping actions available within the individual's coping repertoire. Social-cognitive maturation that occurs during this developmental stage enables the adolescent increased access to more cognitive forms of coping. Proficiency with cognitive coping efforts facilitates a reorganization of the coping repertoire so that cognitive forms of coping are used in conjunction with the behavioral forms of coping efforts developed at earlier developmental stages. There is also an increase in the number of coping strategies cited to manage a stressful situation. Also, there is an increase in both intra-individual and inter-individual differences in coping used across different phases of competitive events and different types of competitive events. This finding implies that coping at this developmental stage is situational in nature, and is determined by the demands of the context. There is some evidence for types of coping that have an enhancing effect for middle adolescents' sport experiences.

Older adolescent athletes' coping. The nineteen studies reviewed included those which sample is limited to older adolescent athletes between the ages of 18 and 22 and/or post-secondary student-athlete sample. Though this latter category of studies often included individuals who could be classified in both the middle adolescent and early adult phase of development, the mean age fell within the older adolescent phase of development and thus, was deemed appropriate for this review.

Comparatively more coping research has occurred at this stage of development than the other stages. Athletes at this developmental stage are considered to possess (or are in the process of developing) highly adaptive coping skills that render achievement at the most elite levels of sport. Developmental coping literature advances that biological and psychosocial maturation combined with relevant sport experiences give rise to mature forms of coping (Aldwin, 2007; Skinner and Zimmer-Gembeck, 2007). The intense study of athletes' coping at this stage of development is important for informing sport professionals and practitioners about aspects of coping that can and should be emphasized and shaped in aspects of athletic training of younger athletes.

In general, older adolescent athletes use a wide array of coping strategies to manage stressful events in sport (Giacobbi, Foore, et al., 2004; Holt et al., 2007). Athletes use behavioural- and cognitive-based strategies that are directed towards traditional coping functions; including problem-focused, emotion-focused, approach, and avoidance. Qualitative case studies demonstrate individual differences in the breadth of athletes' coping. One study examining collegiate female volleyball players' coping with tournament play revealed that the oldest and/or most experienced players used the largest array of coping strategies in their stress management and rated their coping effective in comparison to the younger and least experienced players (Holt et al., 2007). This result infers that athletes' coping continues to develop during the older adolescent stage, particularly in regards to the diversity and breadth of coping efforts, which then can be used to effectively manage the demands of the stressful situation.

Older adolescent athletes' coping is flexible and is linked to person variables, personal resources, types of environmental stressors, and the temporal phase of the stressful event. Older adolescent athletes' coping is influenced by gender (e.g., Anshel et al., 1998; Wang et al., 2004), trait anxiety (Giacobbi and Weinberg, 2000), state anxiety and confidence (Ntoumanis and Biddle, 2000; Williams and Krane, 1992), perceived control (e.g., Haney and Lane, 1995; Kim and Duda, 2003), and motivational goal orientation (e.g., Ntoumanis et al., 1999).

Personal resources, such as competent social support providers, are also important for older adolescent athletes' coping (Giacobbi, Lynn, et al., 2004; Hoar and Flint, 2008). Hoar and Flint surveyed University athletes' intentions to seek social support from various support providers when faced with a hypothetical loss-time injury. Athletes' intentions differed according to the type of social support provider (and the perceived resources available from that type of social agent) and the stage of injury recovery. Giacobbi et al. reported a similar finding from data collected with interviews from female University student-swimmers transitioning to post-secondary level competition. Early in the academic year, the swimmers responded to stress with social forms of emotion-focused coping (i.e., social support, venting to others, humor/fun). As the school year progressed the participants increased trust in their coaches' support and sought the coaches' support as a primary coping strategy.

Older adolescent athletes' coping is specific to the social context (Anshel et al., 1998; Ntoumanis et al., 1999). Ntoumanis and his colleagues surveyed 356 British University athletes (M_{age} = 20.8 years) from a variety of different sports. Results of the study revealed a relationship between avoidance and emotion-focused coping and high ego and high performance oriented training climates.

The research examining the perceived effectiveness of late adolescent athletes' coping has been insightful. Interviews with 10 female collegiate volleyball players revealed that when coping efforts did not include behavioral-avoidance strategies, coping was viewed to be effective for managing tournament competition (Holt et al., 2007). The use of behavioral-avoidance strategies rendered perceptions of less effective or ineffective coping by the sample. Kim and Duda (2003) surveyed 722 Division I student-athletes from the US (M_{age} = 20.0 years) and Korea (M_{age} = 19.7 years). It was found that both active/problem-focused coping and avoidance/withdrawal coping were perceived to be effective for managing sport competition; but had different effects on long-term outcomes. Specifically, active/problem-focused coping was shown to have a positive relation with sport satisfaction, enjoyment, and desire to continue (sport participation). Opposite relations were found between the long-term outcomes and avoidance/ withdrawal coping. Similar findings have been reported from other collegiate samples (Haney and Long, 1995; Ntoumanis and Biddle, 1998). Collectively, these results suggest that older adolescents athletes *evaluate* the effectiveness of avoidance and cognitive distraction coping efforts in relation to temporal proximity of desired outcomes. When immediate performance is of interest for the athlete, avoidance may be viewed to be effective. However, if performance satisfaction and enjoyment, distal outcomes, is of interest, avoidance coping is likely to be viewed to be ineffective. Objectively, older adolescent athletes' perceptions about avoidance coping efforts on performance may be accurate. Two experimental studies have demonstrated that an avoidance coping style is associated improved performance (Stanely et al., 2007; Wang et al., 2004). In summary, athletes' coping at this stage of development is more differentiated, more organized, more flexible, and more selective than at earlier developmental stages. All earlier changes in coping are strengthened enabling athletes to effectively cope with stressful competitive demands associated with elite levels of sport.

Young adult athletes' coping. Thirteen studies examined the coping efforts of athletes between the ages of 23 and 32 years of age. Studies are differentiated between two groups of athletes. The first group has received the most attention and includes the athletes who are active in or have just retired from international (e.g., Commonwealth and Olympic games) and professional level competition. The second group consists of 'club' level athletes.

In general, there is considerable diversity in early adult athletes' coping. The diversity in coping is associated with person factors such as motivation orientation, anxiety, and self-confidence; as well as contextual factors such as the types of stressors encountered (Cresswell and Hodge, 2004; Dale, 2000; Dugdale et al., 2002; Holt and Dunn, 2004; Kadlcki and Flemr, 2008; Pensgaard and Roberts, 2003). As a consequence, athletes at this stage in the lifespan appear to use a wide array of coping strategies. Further, there is a marked increase in the types of coping effort instances identified. For example, Thelwell et al. (2007) interviewed nine male professional cricket batsmen who reported 228 distinct types of coping effort instances that could be categorized into 10 higher-order coping strategies for managing eight different stress events faced as a result of their sport participation. This finding is in line with developmental coping researchers' observations that hundreds of distinct coping effort instances can be identified among adult samples (Skinner and Zimmer-Gembeck, 2007).

Thelwell et al. (2007) noted that of the 10 coping strategies, four coping strategies were primarily used, giving the appearance of coping stability (i.e., using similar strategies across different types of stressors). Upon deeper examination, it was revealed that the types of coping effort instances that represented a high-order coping strategy differed qualitatively in accordance with the type of stressor. A batsman who was managing the stress associated with being in the crease reported using the coping strategy 'self-talk' in the sense that his coping effort instance was *to tell myself to focus* [on his form]. The same athlete, also reported using 'self-talk' to manage the stress of poor past batting performances leading to a negative scout report through the coping effort instance of *telling myself what it is that I can do* (Thelwell et al.). This study provides evidence that at this stage of the lifespan there is both a quantitative and qualitative shift in the types of coping instances used to manage a stressful competitive situation.

The extensive research of early adult athletes' coping provides challenges to finding commonalities. Group-level analyses has revealed that the types of coping efforts most often used in the management of international level competition includes problem-focused and emotion-focused coping strategies of acceptance, increasing effort, planning, imagery/visualization, confidence in self, being aware of and focusing on the 'keys,' and consistency in executing performance plans (Dale, 2000; Dugdale et al., 2002; Thelwell et al., 2007). When athletes retire from international level competition keeping in touch with sport (as an institution), stress and energy management efforts, seeking social contacts, and other life activities are seen as important coping strategies (Kadlcki and Flemr, 2008). Madden et al. (1990) reported that highly stressed club basketball athletes used increased effort and resolve, problem-focused coping, social support seeking, and wishful thinking to manage competitive stress to a greater extent than less stressed players. It is concluded that early adult athletes' coping includes a multitude of cognitive efforts and, to a lesser extent, behavioral efforts that are directed towards problem-focused and emotion-focused coping functions.

Coping efforts that focus early adult athletes' attention and efforts towards mastering international-level competitive demands is facilitative for performance (Gaudreau and Blondin, 2002; Pensgaard and Duda, 2003). Further, when athletes view coping efforts to be effective in the context of a specific stressful event, athletes are more likely to report positive affect (Arathoon and Malouff, 2004; Pensgaard and Duda, 2003). In summary, athletes' coping at this stage of development does not appear much different from that during late adolescence. The coping described in this body of studies is differentiated, organized, flexible, and selective.

Middle-aged adult sport participants' coping. Three studies are reviewed that examined the coping processes of athletes' and sport participants' between the ages of 35 to 59 years of age. Each study in this review has focused attention on identifying the stressors and the type of coping efforts utilized for a specific type (or role) of sport participant including: male English soccer referees (Wolfson and Neave, 2007), male and female head coaches of U.S. Division I sport teams (Frey, 2007), and male and female recreational marathon runners (Buman et al., 2008).

Similar to the younger adult cohort, middle-aged adults apply a diversity of coping effort instances for managing stressful events in sport. Across the studies, there was an emphasis on the use of cognitive based strategies directed towards an emotion-focused coping function. This result, however, is likely due to the role of the sport participant studied and the types of stressors managed. For example, male English soccer players reported using confidence-building cognitions, and self-reflective cognitions to cope with the negative comments made by players, coaches and the spectators (Wolfson and Neave, 2007). The recreational marathon runners reported utilizing a constellation of coping strategies that were both behavioral (e.g., taking sustenance and seeking social support) and cognitive (e.g., mental reframing) in nature to manage 'hitting the wall'.

Older-aged adult athletes' coping. No published studies could be located in the sport literature examining the coping processes of adults aged sixty years or older. There is increasing popularity among adults and older adults to participate in organized sport at the master-level of competition. At the sixth World Masters Games held in Edmonton, Canada, more than 20, 000 adults participated in over 27 different sports (Baker, 2007). Thus, given the perceived importance of sport among individuals within this developmental cohort and the impact of coping on the psycho-social experience of sport, this is an evident gap in the literature where future study is needed.

In an unpublished study, Evans et al. (2009) recently explored the coping strategies used by 262 older-aged athletes (M_{age}=68.1 years) managing a self-selected stressor associated with a provincial senior winter games. Participants completed open-ended assessments inquiring about a self-selected stressor and the ways that the athlete coped with the event. Inductive analysis revealed that the most prevalent stressors were: meetinging performance standards-task, meeting performance expectations of others, winning/socially comparing well, and novelty concerns. Active coping, seeking social support, planning, and general health enhancing behaviours were the most common coping strategies. Athletes primarily directed coping efforts towards an emotion-focused coping function. Age comparisons within the sample were also conducted. Older athletes (70+ years) reported lower feelings of stress and used fewer coping strategies compared to the late middle-age athletes (55 to 65 years). Older and late middle age athletes could be distinguished by the stressors experienced (meeting performance standards, and logistical and novelty concerns) as well as the coping strategies used (planning and health enhancing behaviours).

Physical Maturation Changes in Athletes' Coping

Developmental researchers warn that although developmental processes are age related, development is not age-dependent. It is, therefore, important to identify, describe, and explain how other maturational indices affect changes in athletes' coping over time.

Nicholls et al., (2009) examined the influence of pubertal hormonal changes on 527 adolescents athletes' coping efforts and the perceived effectiveness of coping to manage competition. Based on their scores on the Physical Development Scale (Petersen, Crockett, Richards, and Boxer, 1988), male and female athletes were classified into one of four pubertal states: beginning-pubertal, mid-pubertal, advanced-pubertal, and post-pubertal. It was hypothesized that athletes with advanced development would perceive their coping as more effective than do less mature athletes. Results revealed few differences in adolescents' coping. Less mature athletes' (i.e., pre-pubertal and mid-pubertal) reported increased use of mental imagery, distancing, and mental distraction coping strategies in comparison to the more mature athletes (i.e., advanced-pubertal and post-pubertal). Mid-pubertal athletes reported using resignation more than athletes classified in the other pubertal status groups. More mature athletes reported greater perceived effectiveness of mental distraction than the less mature athletes. Gender did not moderate the relationship between pubertal status and coping strategy use or perceived coping effectiveness.

DIRECTIONS FOR FUTURE RESEARCH

There are several gaps in the research that limit our knowledge of the developmental process of athletes' (and, more in general, sport participants') coping. As outlined in our review, very few sport coping studies exist that select participants based on specific developmental criteria (e.g., age, sport experience, and maturational characteristics), compare age groups at key stages of coping development, and follow individuals longitudinally (Holt et al., 2005; Weiss and Bredemeier, 1983). Accordingly, fundamental questions about the development of coping remain unanswered (Holt et al., 2005; Nicholls and Polman, 2007; Skinner and Zimmer-Gembeck, 2007).

Developmental coping researchers have long understood that the nature of coping is 'developmental' (Aldwin, 2007; Compas, 1998; Lazarus, 1999; Skinner and Edge, 1998). A developmental structure implies that coping is a system that potentially progresses from diffuse to differentiated, from uncoordinated to integrated, from reactive to proactive autonomic regulation (Skinner and Zimmer-Gembeck, 2007). Yet, as Skinner and Zimmer-Gembeck observe, "it has proven surprisingly difficult to realize a developmental agenda for the study of coping" (p. 121). A developmental perspective requires coping researchers to study (a) how the fundamental dimensions or coping change, and/or remain stable with development, (b) the aspects of maturation and social context that influence the acquisition and use of coping responses, (c) what constitutes effective coping and how is coping effectiveness related to the social context and individual coping differences, and (d) the aspects of coping that are changeable through intervention as well as the aspects of coping that are less amendable to change (Compas, 1998). Further, it is recognized that the lack of a developmentally based definition of coping, and a theoretical framework to guide research efforts will continue to impede advancing knowledge of the developmental nature of coping (Compas, 1998; Horn, 2004; Skinner and Edge, 1998).

Traditionally, developmental (and sport) coping research is grounded in the transactional perspective of stress and coping (Lazarus and Folkman, 1984) with developmental understandings evolving from studies of age-related differences (Compas, 1998; Skinner and Zimmer-Gembeck, 2007). Age is operationalized to represent particular states of physiological, cognitive, and social maturation. It is argued that age-related research provides important descriptive evidence of the changing nature of coping across the lifespan but does not advance understanding about the underlying mechanisms that are important for positive adaptation and effective coping during the various developmental stages of the lifespan (Aldwin, 2007; Holt et al., 2005). Thus, developmental coping researchers argue that a transactional perspective is inadequate for advancing *developmental* coping research (Aldwin, Sutton, and Lachman, 1996; Holt et al., 2005; Skinner and Edge, 1998). A central concern is that the standard conceptualization of coping is not "developmentally friendly." Skinner and Zimmer-Gembeck (2007) state that developmentally friendly definitions provide a conceptualization of coping that provide theoretical links to other developing systems, and guide the investigation of how developmental components underlying coping combine to shape the emergence of new coping abilities at successive ages. To meet this need, Compas et al., (2001) offered a more developmentally friendly conceptualization of coping, whereby coping is considered to be "conscious volitional efforts to regulate emotion, cognition, behavior, physiology, and the environment in response to stressful events or circumstances" (p. 89). Other developmental definitions have also advanced in the literature (see Eisenberg, Fabes, and Guthrie, 1997; Skinner, 1999). This advancement has prompted increased calls for the developmental study of coping both within the general coping and the sport coping fields. Echoing the recommendation of Holt et al. (2005), future study of developmental coping within the sport context should be guided by a conceptualization of coping that is developmentally friendly.

What theoretical framework may be appropriate for the developmental study of coping in sport? Based on advancements in the developmental coping literature, sport researchers may benefit from applying theoretical frameworks that examine emotion regulation constructs (e.g., Compas et al., 2001; Eisenberg et al., 1997; Skinner and Zimmer-Gembeck, 2007). In particular, dual-model process models are advanced. Dual-process models of coping posit that the major components of coping (e.g., stress reactions and action regulation) have different underlying temperamental bases and developmental timetables (see Skinner and Zimmer-Gembeck, 2007).

In addition to adopting a developmentally friendly conceptualization of coping, sport coping scholars should strive to plan developmentally appropriate research studies where sample participants are selected according to developmental criteria (e.g., sport experience, maturation characteristics, and age), and utilize a longitudinal research design. Schutz and Park (2004) emphasize that to understand human development, one must repeatedly observe individuals over a period of time. Within the body of sport coping research reviewed in this chapter, approximately 10% of the studies utilized a longitudinal design. Though this statistic is common to developmental study of other psychological constructs within the field of sport and exercise psychology, it is inadequate for advancing knowledge about developmental processes in sport (Weiss and Raedeke, 2004). Descriptive and experimental cross-sectional studies permit conclusions about *differences* (Schutz and Park). Undoubtedly a number of psychological and social context factors exist that are not developmental which result in individual differences in athletes' coping. Only through longitudinal studies can valid inferences be made about *change* and *patterns of change* (Schutz and Park).

CONCLUSION

When examining developmental shifts or change in athletes' coping, researchers are advised to explore patterns of change at the level of the individual rather than establishing normative patterns of change in athletes' coping in sport environments. At the normative group-level of analysis, simple descriptive studies reporting changes in coping provide only a superficial glimpse into the complex coping process. Future research needs to incorporate important advancements in data analysis techniques, such as multi-level modeling and latent growth modeling. These statistical techniques can account for change at both the individual and group levels and will provide for a more informative account of developmental features of athletes' coping. Additionally, case study and other types of qualitative research designs are important for providing deep and rich descriptive evidence of athletes' coping in sport at an idiographical level. Recall that the coping images of the four athletes (Daniel, Emilia, Ruby, Thomas) were each imbedded in a complex socio-personal context. These images, combined with an appropriate theoretical framework, will provide important information about the organization, differentiation, selection, and flexibility of athletes' coping across the lifespan.

REFERENCES

Aldwin, C. M. (2007). *Stress, coping, and development (2ⁿᵈ ed.)*. New York: Guildford Press.

Aldwin, C. M. , Sutton, K. J., Chiara, G., and Spiro, A. (1996). Age differences in stress, coping, and appraisal: Findings from the Normative Aging Study. *Journals of Gerontology: Psychological Sciences and Social Sciences, 51B*, 179 -188.

Aldwin, C. M., Sutton, K. J., and Lachman, M. (1996). The development of coping resources in adulthood. *Journal of Personality, 64*, 837 – 871.

*Anshel, M. H., and Delany, J. (2001). Sources of acute stress, cognitive appraisals, and coping strategies of male and female child athletes. *Journal of Sport Behavior, 24*, 329 - 353.

*Anshel, M. H., Porter, A., and Quek, J. J. (1998). Coping with acute stress in sport as a function of gender: An exploratory study. *Journal of Sport Behavior, 21*, 363 - 377.

*Anshel, M. H., Williams, L. R. T., and Hodge, K. (1997). Cross-cultural and gender differences on coping style in sport. *International Journal of Sport Psychology, 28*, 128 – 143.

*Arathoon, S. M., and Malouff, J. M. (2004). The effectiveness of a brief cognitive intervention to help athletes cope with competition loss. *Journal of Sport Behavior, 27*, 213 - 229.

Baker, J. (2007). Sport and physical activity in the older athlete. In P. R. E. Crocker (ed.) *Sport Psychology: A Canadian perspective* (pp. 295 - 314). Toronto, Canada: Pearson.

Baltes, P. B., Lindenberger, U., and Staudinger, U. M. (1998). Life-span theory in developmental psychology. In W. Damon (Series Ed.) and R. M. Lerner (Volume Ed.), *Handbook of child psychology: Vol. 1. Theoretical models in human development* (5ᵗʰ ed., pp. 1029 – 1143). New York: Wiley.

Bebetsos, E., and Antoniou, P. (2003). Psychological skills of Greek badminton athletes. *Perceptual and Motor Skills, 97*, 1289 – 1296.

*Buman, M. P., Omli, J. W., Giacobbi, P. R., and Brewer, B. W. (2008). Experiences and coping responses of "Hitting the Wall" for recreational marathon runners. *Journal of Applied Sport Psychology, 20*, 282 - 300.

Carver, C. S., Scheier, M. F., and Weintraub, J. K. (1989). Assessing coping strategies: A theoretically based approach. *Journal of Personality and Social Psychology, 56*, 267 – 283.

Clarke, L. (2008, October 1). FIG: 2008 Gymnasts were of age. Washington Post. http://voices.washingtonpost.com/olympics/2008/10/fig_2008_gymnasts_were_of_age_2.html. Retrieved July 4, 2009.

Compas, B. E., (1998). An agenda for coping research and theory: Basic and applied development issues. *International Journal of Behavioral Development, 22*, 231-237.

Compas, B. E., Connor-Smith, J. K., Saltzman, H., Thomsen, A. H., and Wadsworth, M. E. (2001). Coping with stress during childhood and adolescence: Problems, progress, and potential in theory and research. *Psychological Bulletin, 127*, 82-127.

*Cresswell, S., and Hodge, K. (2004). Coping skills: role of trait sport confidence and trait anxiety. *Perceptual and Motor Skills, 98*, 433 - 438.

*Crocker, P. R. E., Alderman, R. B., and Smith, F. M. (1988). Cognitive-Affective Stress Management Training with high performance youth volleyball players: Effects on affect, cognition, and performance. *Journal of Sport and Exercise Psychology, 10*, 448 - 460.

*Crocker, P. R. E., and Isaak, K. (1997). Coping during competitions and training sessions: Are youth swimmers consistent? *International Journal of Sport Psychology, 28*, 355 - 369.

*Dale, G. A. (2000). Distractions and coping strategies of elite decathletes during their most memorable performances. *The Sport Psychologist, 14*, 17 – 41.

*Dugdale, J. R., Eklund, R. C., and Gordon, S. (2002). Expected and unexpected stressors in major international competition: Appraisal, coping, and performance. *The Sport Psychologist, 16*, 20 - 33.

Eisenberg, N., Fabes, R. A., and Guthrie, I. K., (1997). Coping with stress: The roles of regulation and development. In S. A. Wolchik and I. N. Sandler (Eds.) *Handbook of children's coping: Linking theory and intervention* (pp. 41 -70). New York: Plenum.

*Eubank, M., and Collins, D. (2000). Coping with pre- and in-event fluctuations in competitive state anxiety: A longitudinal approach. *Journal of Sports Sciences, 18*, 121 - 131.

*Evans, M. B., Link, C., and Hoar, S. D. (2009). *The stressors and coping efforts associated with master-level competition: A developmental population overlooked?* Unpublished manuscript.

Fields, L, and Prinz, R. J. (1997). Coping and adjustment during childhood and adolescence. *Clinical Psychological Review, 17*, 937 – 976.

*Frey, M. (2007). College coaches' experiences with stress--"Problem Solvers" have problems, too. *The Sport Psychologist, 21*, 38 - 57.

*Gal-or, Y., Tenenbaum, G., Furst, D., and Shrtzer, M. (1986). Effects of self-control and anxiety on training performance in young and novice parachuters. *Perceptual and Motor Skills, 60*, 743 - 746.

*Gaudreau, P., and Blondin, J. P. (2004). Differential associations of dispositional optimism and pessimism with coping, goal attainment, and emotional adjustment during sport competition. *International Journal of Stress Management, 11*, 245 – 269.

*Gaudreau, P., Lapierre, A. M., and Blondin, J. P. (2001). Coping at three phases of a competition: Comparison between pre-competitive, competitive, and post-competitive utilization of the same strategy. *International Journal of Sport Psychology, 32*, 369-385.

Gëczi, G. B., Bognar, J. Z, Toth, L.S., Sipos, K. I. and Fugedi, F. G. (2008). Anxiety and coping of Hungarian national ice hockey players. *International Journal of Sports Science and Coaching, 3*, 277-285.

*Giacobbi Jr., P., Foore, B., and Weinberg, R. S. (2004). Broken clubs and expletives: the sources of stress and coping responses of skilled and moderately skilled golfers. *Journal of Applied Sport Psychology, 16*, 166 -182.

*Giacobbi Jr., P. R., Lynn, T. K., Wetherington, J. M., Jenkins, J., Bodenforf, M., and Langley, B. (2004). Stress and coping during the transition to university for first-year female athletes. *The Sport Psychologist, 18*, 1 - 20.

*Giacobbi, Jr., P. R., and Weinberg, R. S. (2000). An examination of coping in sport: Individual trait anxiety differences and situational consistency. *The Sport Psychologist, 14*, 42 – 62.

*Gould, D. (1982). Sport psychology in the 1980s: Status, direction, and challenge in youth sports research. *Journal of Sport Psychology, 4,* 203-218.

*Gould, D., Udry, E., Tuffey, S., and Loehr, J. (1996). Burnout in competitive junior tennis players: I. A quantitative psychological assessment. *The Sport Psychologist, 10,* 322 - 340.

*Gould, D., Wilson, C. H., Tuffey, S., and Lochbaum, M. (1993). Stress and the young athlete. *Pediatric Exercise Science, 5,* 286 - 297.

Goyen, M. J., and Anshel, M. H. (1998). Sources of acute competitive stress and use of coping strategies as a function of age and gender. *Journal of Applied Developmental Psychology, 19,* 469 – 486.

*Haney, C. J., and Long, B. C. (1995). Coping effectiveness: A path analysis of self-efficacy, control, coping and performance in sport competitions. *Journal of Applied Social Psychology, 25,* 1726 – 1746.

*Hatzigeorgiadis, A. (2006). Approach and avoidance coping during task performance in young men: The role of goal attainment expectancies. *Journal of Sports Sciences, 24,* 299 - 307.

*Hoar, S. D., Crocker, P. R. E., Holt, N. L., and Tamminen, K. A. (2009). *Gender differences in adolescent athletes' coping with interpersonal stressors in sport: More similarities than differences?* Manuscript submitted for publication.

*Hoar, S. D., and Flint, F. (2008). Determinants of help-seeking intentions in the context of athletic injury recovery. *International Journal of Sport and Exercise Psychology, 6,* 157 - 175.

Hoar, S. D., Kowalski, K. C., Gaudreau, P., and Crocker, P. R. E. (2006). A review of coping in sport. In S. Hanton and S. Mallalieu (Eds.), Literature reviews in sport psychology (pp. 53 – 103). Hauppauge, NY: Nova Science Publishers.

*Holt, N. L. (2003). Coping in professional sport: A case study of an experienced cricket player. *Athletic Insight, 5.* Article 1 (available at http://www.athleticinsight.com/ Vol5Iss1/CricketPlayerCoping.htm; accessed June 16, 2009)

*Holt, N. L., Berg, K. J., and Tamminen, K. A. (2007). Tales of the unexpected: coping among Female collegiate volleyball players. *Research Quarterly for Exercise and Sport, 78,* 117 - 132.

*Holt, N. L., and Dunn, J. G. H. (2004). Longitudinal idiographic analyses of appraisal and coping responses in sport. *Psychology of Sport and Exercise, 5,* 213 – 222.

Holt, N. L., Hoar, S., and Fraser, S. N. (2005). How does coping change with development? A review of childhood and adolescence sport coping research. *European Journal of Sport Sciences, 5,* 25 – 39.

*Holt, N. L., and Mandigo, J. L. (2004). Coping with performance worries among male youth cricket players. *Journal of Sport Behavior, 27,* 39 - 57.

Horn, T. S. (2004). Lifespan development in sport and exercise psychology: Theoretical perspectives. In M. R. Weiss (Ed.), *Developmental sport and exercise psychology: A lifespan perspective* (pp. 27 -71). Morgantown, WV: Fitness Information Technology.

*Kadlcik, J., and Flemr, L. (2008). Athletic career termination model in the Czech. *International Review for the Sociology of Sport, 43,* 251 - 269.

*Kim, M. S., and Duda, J. L. (2003). The coping process: Cognitive appraisals of stress, coping strategies, and coping effectiveness. *The Sport Psychologist, 17,* 406 – 425.

*Kowalski, K. C., and Crocker, P. R. E. (2001). Development and validation of the Coping Function Questionnaire for adolescents in sport. *Journal of Sport and Exercise Psychology, 23,* 136 - 155.

*Krohne, H. W., and Hindel, C. (1988). Trait anxiety, state anxiety, and coping behavior as predictors of athletic performance. *Anxiety Researcher, 1,* 225 – 234.

*Lally, P. (2007). Identity and athletic retirement: A prospective study. *Psychology of Sport and Exercise, 8,* 85 - 99.

Lazarus, R. S. (1991). *Emotion and adaptation.* New York: Oxford University Press.

Lazarus, R. S. (1999). *Stress and emotion: A new synthesis.* New York: Springer.

Lazarus, R. S., and Folkman, S. (1984). *Stress, appraisal, and coping.* New York: Springer Publishing.

Lerner, R. M. (2002). *Concepts and theories of human development* (3rd ed.). Mahwah, NJ: Lawrence Erlbaum.

*Madden, C. C., Jeffery, J., and Brown, D. F. (1990). The influence of perceived stress on coping with competitive basketball. *International Journal of Sport Psychology, 21,* 21 – 35.

*Manuel, J. C., Shilt, J. S., Curl, W. W., Smith, J. A., DuRant, R. H., Lester, L., et al. (2002). Coping with sports injuries: An examination of the adolescent athlete. *Journal of Adolescent Health, 31,* 391 - 393.

Newman, B. M., and Newman, P. R. (1999). *Development through life. A psychosocial approach* (7th ed.). Belmont, CA: Wadsworth Publishing Company.

Newman Kingery, J., Roblek, T. L., Suveg, C., Grover, R. L., Sherrill, J. T., and Bergman, R. L. (2006). They're not just "little adults": Developmental considerations for implementing cognitive-behavioral therapy with anxious youth. *Journal of Cognitive Psychotherapy: An International Quarterly, 20,* 263 - 273.

*Nicholls, A. R. (2007). A longitudinal phenomenological analysis of coping effectiveness among Scottish international adolescent golfers. *European Journal of Sport Science, 7,* 169 - 178.

*Nicholls, A. R., Holt, N. L., Polman, R. C. J., and James, D. W. G. (2005). Stress, coping among international adolescent golfers. *Journal of Applied Sport Psychology, 17,* 333 - 340.

Nicholls, A. R., and Polman, R. C. J. (2007). Coping in sport: A systematic review. *Journal of Sports Sciences, 25,* 11 – 31.

Nicholls, A. R., Polman, R., Morley, D., and Taylor, N. J. (2009). Coping and coping effectiveness in relation to a competitive sport event: Pubertal status, chronological age, and gender among adolescent athletes. *Journal of Sport and Exercise Psychology, 31,* 299 – 317.

*Ntoumanis, N., and Biddle, S. J. H. (1998). The relationship of coping and its perceived effectiveness to positive and negative affect in sport. *Personality and Individual Differences, 24,* 773 – 778.

*Ntoumanis, N., and Biddle, S. J. H. (2000). Relationship of intensity and direction of competitive anxiety with coping strategies. *The Sport Psychologist, 14,* 360 - 371.

*Ntoumanis, N., and Biddle, S. J. H., and Haddock, G. (1999). The mediating role of coping strategies on the relationship between achievement motivation and affect in sport. *Anxiety, Stress, and Coping, 12,* 299 – 327.

*Pensgaard, A. M., and Duda, J. L. (2003). Sydney 2000: The interplay between emotions, coping, and the performance of Olympic-level athletes. *The Sport Psychologist, 17,* 253 – 267.

*Pensgaard, A. M., and Roberts, G. C. (2003). Achievement goal orientations and the use of coping strategies among winter Olympians. *Psychology of Sport and Exercise, 4,* 101 – 116.

*Pensgaard, A. M., and Ursin, H. (1998). Stress, control, and coping in elite athletes. *Scandinavian Journal of Medicine and Science in Sports, 8,* 183 - 189.

Petersen, A. C., Crockett, L., Richards, M., and Boxer, A. (1988). A self-report measure of pubertal status: Reliability, validity, and initial norms. *Journal of Youth and Adolescence, 17,* 117 – 133.

Reeves, C. W., Nicholls, A. R., and McKenna, J. (2009). Stressors and coping strategies among early and middle adolescent premier league academy soccer players: Differences according to age. *Journal of Applied Sport Psychology, 21,* 31 – 48.

*Rider, S. P., and Hicks, R. A. (1995). Stress, coping, and injuries in high school male and female athletes. *Perceptual and Motor Skills, 81,* 499 – 503.

*Ridnour, H., and Hammermeister, J. (2008). Spiritual well-being and its influence on athletic coping profiles. *Journal of Sport Behavior, 31,* 81 - 92.

Schutz, R. W., and Park, I. (2004). Some methodological considerations in developmental sport and exercise psychology. In M. R. Weiss (Ed.) *Developmental sport and exercise psychology: A lifespan perspective* (pp. 73 – 99). Morgantown, WV: Fitness Information Technology.

Seiffge-Krenke, I. (1995). *Stress, coping, and relationships in adolescence.* Mahwah, NJ: Lawrence Erlbaum.

Skinner, E. A. (1999). Action regulation, coping, and development. In J. B. Brandtstädter, and R. M. Lerner (Eds.), *Action and self-development* (pp. 465 – 503). Thousand Oaks, CA: Sage.

Skinner, E. A., and Edge, K. (1998). Reflections on coping and development across the lifespan. *International Journal of Behavioral Development, 22,* 357-366.

Skinner, E. A., and Zimmer-Gembeck, M. J. (2007). The development of coping. *Annual Review of Psychology, 58,* 119 – 144.

*Smith, R. E., Smoll, F. L., and Ptacek, J. T. (1990). Conjunctive moderator variables in vulnerability and resiliency research: Life stress, social support and coping skills, and adolescent sport injuries. *Journal of Personality and Social Psychology, 58,* 360 - 370.

*Stanley, C. T., Pargman, D., and Tenenbaum, G. (2007). The effect of attentional coping strategies on perceived exertion in a cycling task. *Journal of Applied Sport Psychology, 19,* 352 - 363.

*Thelwell, R. C., Weston, N. J. V., and Greenlees, I. A. (2007). Batting on a sticky wicket: Identifying sources of stress and associated coping strategies for professional cricket batsmen. *Psychology of Sport and Exercise, 8,* 219 - 232.

Van Anderson. (1997). Female gymnasts: Older – and healthier? *The Physician and Sportsmedicine, 25,* 25 - 26.

*Wang, J., Marchant, D., and Morris, T. (2004). Coping style and susceptibility to choking. *Journal of Sport Behavior, 27,* 75 - 92.

Weiss, M. R., and Bredemeier, B. J. (1983). Developmental sport psychology: A theoretical perspective for studying children in sport. *Journal of Sport Psychology, 5,* 216 - 230.

Weiss, M. R., and Raedeke, T. D. (2004). Developmental sport and exercise psychology: Research status on youth and directions toward a lifespan perspective. In M. R. Weiss (Ed.) *Developmental sport and exercise psychology: A lifespan perspective* (pp. 1 – 26). Morgantown, WV: Fitness Information Technology.

*Williams, J. M., and Krane, V. (1992). Coping styles and self-reported measures of state anxiety and self-confidence. *Journal of Applied Sport Psychology, 4*, 134 – 143.

*Wolfson, S., and Neave, N. (2007). Coping under pressure: Cognitive strategies for maintaining confidence among soccer referees. *Journal of Sport Behavior, 30*, 232 - 247.

* = reference used in review of literature

In: Coping in Sport: Theory, Methods, and Related Constructs   ISBN: 978-1-60876-488-4
Editor: Adam R. Nicholls   © 2010 Nova Science Publishers, Inc.

Chapter 7

CULTURAL DIFFERENCES IN COPING WITH STRESS IN SPORT: THEORY AND PRACTICE

Mark H. Anshel

Middle Tennessee State University, TN, U.S.

ABSTRACT

This chapter addresses an area of coping with sport stress that has been relatively neglected; the influence of culture in the coping process. Culture reflects the customary practices and language associated with a particular racial or ethnic group, and influences a person's view of the world based on shared social beliefs and values. In competitive sport, culture reflects the athlete's values, psychological needs, expectations, habits, thought patterns, behavioral tendencies, and identity of a group that promote certain goal-directed actions that are accepted as "right" (i.e., appropriate) or "wrong" (i.e., inappropriate). Why should we be surprised when athletes from different cultures differ in their respective ways of coping with stress? Why, also, should be expect athletes of all cultures to experience and respond to stressful events in a similar manner? This chapter reviews selected studies on coping with sport stress. Far more studies have examined athletes from various countries, but relatively few studies in the sport coping literature have examined differences between cultures. It is concluded that culture serves as both a moderator and a mediator variable in various studies in attempting to improve our understanding of the factors that affect the coping process in sport.

INTRODUCTION

The process of coping with stress in sport is complex and multidimensional. The coping process begins with an experience, event, or detection of a stimulus that the athlete interprets as stressful. If the athlete does not interpret an experience as stressful, therefore, coping becomes unnecessary; there is no perceived stress. Numerous authors have contended that half of the stress we experience in life would not exist if we "simply" failed to interpret so many situations, events, and experiences as stressful (Schafer, 1996).

Experiencing stress, in both acute (i.e., short-term) and chronic (i.e., long-term) forms, is inherent – and even necessary - in competitive sport. Examples of acute stress, discussed at length later, include making a physical or mental error, receiving a penalty (or "bad" call) from the referee/umpire, performance the athlete judges as "poor," experiencing pain or an injury, vocal disapproval from spectators, and a reprimand from one's coach. Chronic stress examples include mental or physical fatigue (perhaps due to poor sleep), a poor relationship with a coach or teammate, physical discomfort or pain, and ongoing poor performance (e.g., slumping, failure to meet performance goals). The objective of athletes and coaches is not to eradicate stress from the sport environment, but to improve our ability to manage it. Managing stress is accomplished by reflected by effective coping. One factor, referred to in the research literature as a "moderating variable," that strongly influences the coping process in sport is the athlete's culture.

Each of us is unique. We bring an array of personal characteristics, thoughts, emotions, and behavioral patterns to any given situation, including the sport environment. While the area of coping in sport has received increased attention by researchers and practitioners in recent years, there has been relatively little examination of the moderating and mediating variables that influence the coping process. As discussed later, culture can be either a mediating or moderating variable, and therefore, is particularly important because of the wide variability with which individuals respond to stress. While the primary aim of researchers is to generalize findings to the general population, the focus of sports participants and the practitioners with whom they consult is to identify and be sensitive to individual differences and the unique characteristics (e.g., skill level, sport type, gender, or culture) that each athlete brings to the sport contest.

The primary purpose of this chapter, therefore, is to examine the role of one unique attribute – culture - in the process of coping with sport stress, and the implications for the effective use of coping skills in managing stressful events. In particular, this chapter will consist of four sections: (a) defining the concepts of psychosocial stress (as opposed to biological or somatic stress), appraisal, and coping, (b) an overview of the coping process in sport using the approach-avoidance coping framework, (c) the influence of cultural differences as a moderator variable in the coping process, and (d) implications for cultural differences in the use of effective cognitive and behavioral coping strategies and interventions in sport for coaches and athletes.

DEFINING RELEVANT CONCEPTS

What Is Culture?

Wong, Wong, and Scott (2006) define culture as "the customary practices and language associated with a particular racial or ethnic group" (p. 1). To Brislin (1990), "culture refers to widely shared ideals, values, formation, and uses of categories, assumptions, about life, and goal-directed activities that become unconsciously or sub-consciously accepted as right and correct by people who identify themselves as members of a society" (p. 11). It would appear obvious, therefore, that the sport environment creates an array of events and situations perceived differently by athletes from different cultures, and that their reactions to these events and situations would also differ, perhaps significantly.

Perhaps one reason for virtually ignoring the role of culture in examining the sport coping process is that sport psychology researchers have tended to follow the paths previously taken in general psychology in depicting the coping process as a function of personal (i.e., traits, orientations or behavioral tendencies) and situational factors (i.e., sources of stress, cognitive appraisals, or sport type), while anthropologists consider the cultural context in which stress is experienced and appraised as highly relevant, even predictive, of a person's coping responses. As Aldwin (2007) contends, culture is entrenched within an individual's emotional system to make certain coping styles, and the use of certain coping strategies, comfortable and culturally sanctioned.

Aldwin (2007) states, compellingly, that "the influence of culture on the stress and coping process is so pervasive that it is little noticed" (p. 245). Her claim that researchers and practitioners have failed to recognize the striking difference between how one expects others to react and how they actually behave resonates in the sport psychology literature. Examining cultural differences in the coping in sport literature has been surprisingly rare. Therefore, attempts to understand the coping process in the existing sport psychology research literature have failed to consider culture as a moderating variable, thereby limiting subsequent recommendations for effective coping in sport. As indicated earlier, the primary focus of this chapter, therefore, is to examine the evidence that indicates the extent to which culture influences the coping process in competitive sport.

Psychosocial Stress

It is important to differentiate the components and properties of stress in order to determine the role of culture in the coping process. Stress has both physical and psychosocial forms. Schafer (1996), reflecting the traditional stress literature, defines stress as "arousal of mind and body in response to demands made on them" (p. 6). Psychosocial stress, on the other hand, is derived from a person's thoughts, that is, an individual's interpretation of a situation as unpleasant. The source of this interpretation could be due to the lack of personal resources (e.g., confidence, self-control, self-esteem, or mental toughness) or due to an imposing, difficult environment (Lazarus, 1999). The importance of acknowledging differences between physical (somatic) and psychosocial forms of acute stress in sport is that: (a) they warrant different types of coping strategies, (b) they influence the coping process in different ways, and (c) culture influences psychosocial stress far more than physical/somatic stress. Another unique quality of psychosocial stress is that it can be categorized into positive and negative forms.

Psychosocial stress has both positive and negative properties. While some individuals consider the words, "positive stress" an oxymoron, that is, a contradiction in terms, others (e.g., Lazarus, 1999; Loehr and Schwartz, 2003; Selye, 1974; Shafer, 1996) contend that stress can be positive because it has performance-enhancing properties. Selye pioneered the concept of "eustress" as a "positive form of stress. While "distress" infers a negative or unpleasant experience, perhaps as a function of "too much" or "too little" stress, eustress is beneficial to the individual by elevating arousal level and other desirable and constructive cognitions to the "optimal" level.

Along these lines and more recently, Shafer, for instance, contends "stress can be helpful as well as harmful. Positive stress can provide zest and enjoyment, as well as attentiveness and energy for meeting deadlines, entering new situations, coping with emergencies, achieving maximum performance, and meeting new challenges" (p. 16). Loehr (1990) contends that positive stress has energy-producing properties, in which energy is expended and results in expanding one's physical, mental, and emotional capacity. To these authors, then, the positive component of stress is to produce growth and enhance achievement and performance excellence.

Inherent in understanding the role of positive stress in sport is the concept of *voluntary recovery*. As Selye (1974), a pioneer in stress research, has noted, and supported more recently by Loehr and Schwartz (2003), all forms of stress are alleviated when the individual voluntarily takes planned intermittent brakes. Recovery, according to Loehr and Schwartz, is anything that causes energy to be renewed or recaptured. Because recovery has the effect of re-energizing the organism, the person feels more invigorated to maintain optimal energy and performance for a longer period of time. To use a cliché, less is more. Stress has its positive qualities if we balance physical exertion with recovery breaks. The inter-exchange between effort (i.e., stressful physical exertion) interpolated with periods of voluntary recovery is called *oscillation* (Loehr and Schwartz, 2003). According to these authors, failure to engage in voluntary recovery, even of a few minutes, may result in *involuntary recovery*, in which cognitive, motoric, or physiological processes of the human organism deteriorate as a function of overuse. This breakdown manifests as sickness, disease, and extreme physical or mental fatigue.

Acute and Chronic Stress

Understanding the coping process, particularly with respect to cultural differences, is partially dependent on the type of stress with which the athlete is exposed. Stress has been typically categorized as either acute (short-term) and chronic (long-term). Acute stress is defined as an incident, event, experience, or stimulus that an individual appraises as unpleasant or challenging. Chronic stress, on the other hand, reflects persistent experiences, events, or situations that the person considers challenging or unpleasant (Richards, 2004). Traditionally, coping in sport has been studied with respect to chronic stress. In more recent years, however, researchers have attempted to understand the coping process with respect to acute stress (see Hoar, Kowalski, Gaudreau, and Crocker, 2006; Nicholls and Polman, 2007; Richards, 2004, for recent reviews). The differentiation between acute and chronic stress is important, because they require different types of coping strategies for optimal effectiveness in reducing stress intensity and enhancing sport performance (Gottlieb, 1997). One area of uncertainty and inconsistency in the extant coping in sport literature is the study of coping styles, as opposed to coping strategies.

Coping Styles and Strategies

While the concepts of coping *styles* and coping *strategies* have been discussed in other chapters of this book, it is important to acknowledge these concepts, which have been wrongly used interchangeably at time in the previous literature, with respect to cultural differences. Coping style, a disposition that reflects behavior over time, is learned, and reflects a person's pattern, or consistency, of thoughts, emotions, or behaviors in responding to stress. In the context of competitive sport, coping style refers to the athlete's preference, or tendency, to use certain types of coping strategies across time, in response to the same type of stressor, or following different types of stressful events (Krohne, 1993). Examples of coping styles, including the strategies that represent them, are problem-focused and emotion-focused coping (Lazarus and Folkman, 1984), approach and avoidance coping (Anshel, 1996; Suls and Fletcher, 1985), monitoring and blunting (Miller, 1989), attention and distraction coping (McCrae, 1992), sensitization and desensitization, and engagement and disengagement coping (Carver, Scheier, and Weintraub, 1989).

Coping strategies, on the other hand, is a state or situational measure. It consists of the athlete's use of one or more cognitive or behavioral attempts at reducing perceived stress intensity. An athlete's coping *style* consists of several coping *strategies* that can be categorized according to similar characteristics. Sample coping strategies are "planning the next response or strategy," "distracted myself from the situation," and "asked the referee/coach for clarification or more information."

Of particular importance in this chapter is that coping styles are highly related to the athlete's cultural norms, expectations, and common practices, whereas the use of coping strategies are more situationally-defined (Anshel et al., 2001; Chun, Moos, and Cronkite, 2006). To understand how culture is a mediating factor in strongly influencing the athlete's coping style, it is important to acknowledge that coping with stress is an emotional process. Emotions are unique to certain cultures (Mauro, Sato, and Tucker, 1992). The authors contend that "emotions cannot be defined without reference to a social context" (p. 301), in other words, the influence of culture.

As Anshel et al. (2001) concluded from their review of the coping literature, "surprisingly, the area of cultural influences on the coping process has been virtually ignored in sport psychology" (p. 67). In one rare study in this area, discussed in greater detail later, Anshel, Williams, and Hodge (1997) found significant cultural differences in coping *style* between U.S. and Australian athletes using the approach-avoidance coping style framework as a function of the type of stressful event. Australians were more prone to avoidance coping then their U.S. counterparts. While far more cross-cultural coping in sport research is needed to examine consistent differences in the athletes' coping style (rather then the use of coping strategies), the results of limited studies (see Anshel et al., 2001, for a brief review) suggest that some cultures emphasize avoidance coping styles, while other cultures are more approach oriented. Also see reviews by Nicholls and Polman (2007), and Skinner, Edge, Altman, and Sherwood (2003) for clarification of these concepts and recognition of the need for further study in this area.

Culture as a Mediating and Moderating Variable

It is important to know the ways in which culture influences cognitive, emotional, and behavioral outcomes by examining the inclusion of mediating and moderating variables in the research process (Pederson, 2006). Cultural factors, in particular, often ignored by researchers, may help improve our understanding of the coping process in sport, including the use or non-use, or effectiveness or ineffectiveness of using certain coping strategies in response to particular types of stressful events (Nicholls and Polman 2007).

Mediating variables, also referred to as intervening variables, address the issue that sometimes psychological factors (e.g., motivation, skill level, past experience, learning, culture) influence research outcomes. If a researcher, for instance, wants to examine the effect of mental imagery on some aspect of sports performance, the participant's past experience in using mental imagery will influence its effectiveness. In the area of coping with sport stress, culture may be a mediating variable if it influences the frequency or intensive of experiencing a particular stressor.

Moderating variables, also called categorical variable, are a form of independent variable that cannot be manipulated (e.g., age, race, sex, or culture), but that reflects to determine evidence of a cause-and-effect relationship of the independent and dependent variables is different in the presence of the category (Baron and Kenny, 1986). Culture is a moderating variable when researchers ask if there are group differences between cultures, for instance, comparing Caucasian and Hispanic athletes, or athletes who have been born, reared, and compete in the U.S. versus the UK (Ness Evans, and Rooney, 2008). Culture, then, can serve either as a mediating variable – if, for instance, the researcher addresses cultural differences as one factor that helps explain research outcomes – or a moderator variable if the researcher plans to examine cultural differences on a particular dependent (outcome) variable. The general neglect of culture in the extant coping in sport research is an area of much-needed future research. Mediating and moderating variables are discussed in more detail in Chapter 4, by Crocker, Mosewich, Kowalski, and Besenski.

OVERVIEW OF THE COPING PROCESS IN SPORT USING THE APPROACH-AVOIDANCE FRAMEWORK

Stress Postulates

The coping process begins with the athlete's perceptions of stress in chronic (long-term) or acute (short-term) form. Theorists (e.g., Anshel, 2003; Lazarus and Folkman, 1984; Wheaton, 1997) have generated two postulates, also called assumptions or predictions, about experiencing stress, with direct implications for coping with sport-related stress. The first postulate is that an extreme or unusual external stimulus perceived by the athlete as threatening or harmful will be stressful and cause significant changes in psychological, physiological, and behavioral responses. In sport, this means that the quality of sport performance will be a function of the athlete's coping skills in regulating stress intensity. Coping involves building the athlete's resourcefulness (e.g., confidence, self-control, optimism, or mental toughness) in dealing with the stressor or reduces environmental demands (e.g., removing oneself from the stressful situation, reducing the stressor's importance, use of social support from others; Lazarus, 1990; Wheaton, 1997).

The second postulate is that the failure to cope effectively with short-term, sudden stress leads to long-term, chronic stress and burnout. Examples include ongoing harassment, poor communication, unpleasant relationships, and chronic physical discomfort or pain. Chronic stress reduces efficient information processing, leading to slower, less accurate decision-making. It also contributes to poorer emotional control, which heightens unpleasant emotions such as anxiety and depression, and anger. Long-term effects include reductions in self-esteem, confidence, and perceived self-control (Gottlieb, 1997; Smith, 1986). Unless athletes deploy coping strategies, reduced participation satisfaction, performance, mental withdrawal, and even cessation from further engagement from sport could occur. Thus, athletes who use maladaptive coping skills (e.g., excessive anger or aggression, drug use, smoking, or overeating) or fail to interpret sport-related events accurately and react in a rational manner will likely experience chronic stress and, eventually, may dropout of further sport participation (Smith, 1986). Taken together, these stress postulates provide a foundation on which to understand the meaning of stress in sport, and how to cope with sport-related stress through effective stress and anxiety management.

Another important issue in defining stress concerns it's short-term (acute) versus long-term nature (chronic). An event interpreted by the athlete as stressful is called acute (sudden) stress (Anshel, 1996). Examples of sources of acute stress include a coach reprimand, comments from others, experiencing pain or injury, or making an error. In contrast, a situation interpreted as stressful experienced over a prolonged period of time is called chronic stress (e.g., a poor relationship with a coach, daily pressure to succeed, or unpleasant personal interactions).

Stages of Coping in Sport

While the coping process has been reviewed previously, cultural differences for each stage of coping, particularly in the context of competitive sport, has remained elusive. There is a general consensus in the sport psychology literature, however, about the coping process in sport (e.g., Anshel et al., 2001; Hoar et al., 2006; Nicholls and Polman, 2007; Richards, 2004). A brief overview of these coping "stages," followed by implications for cultural differences at each stage of coping, is warranted. While the coping process begins with detecting a stimulus or experiencing an event, the literature on cultural differences begins with the cognitive appraisal of that stimulus or event.

Cognitive Appraisal

Given the importance of appraisal in determining one's selection and application of coping strategies, cross-cultural research on the appraisal process is surprisingly rare. Nevertheless, the appraisal process is significantly influenced by cultural factors, at least in the non-sport literature. Typically, cognitive appraisal is defined as an individual's subjective assessment of whether or not a particular experience is perceived as stressful, to then to determine one's coping response based on that assessment (Gignac and Gottlieb, 1997). Appraisals, therefore, can be non-stressful (e.g., positive or benign) or stressful. Stress appraisals are usually sub-categorized as positive (e.g., challenging or beneficial) or negative (e.g., harmful or threatening). Only a stressful appraisal requires use of a coping strategy. It is unknown whether athletes possess an *appraisal style*, that is, the tendency of making certain types of appraisals following a stressful encounter.

Harm/loss appraisals, which may be preferred under conditions of low controllability (Dewe, 1992), reflect perceived stress or damage that has already occurred. Sport examples include making a physical or mental error, exposure to unpleasant input from others, being injured or receiving pain.

A *threat* appraisal is a function of the athlete's state anxiety about how the situation might turn out (McCrae, 1992). It consists of expectations of possible future harm or danger often accompanied by unpleasant self-statements such as "What if..." or "I hope...." Examples include uncertainty about the potentially harmful effect of experiencing an injury or an opponent's superior performance, which increases the chances of losing the contest. Sometimes threat appraisals are irrational, based on the athlete's thoughts about worse case scenarios (e.g., "What if my opponent scores" or "What if I get injured?"), or could reflect low confidence (e.g., "I hope my opponent does not play well."). Threat is probably the most common stress appraisal in sport. Sport examples include competing against a superior opponent, performing after experiencing an injury, or returning to competition after rehabilitation. While threat appraisals, per se, are not deleterious to performance success failure to use positive personal resources to meet and overcome threatening stressful events, such as confidence, arousal, positive expectancies, high self-esteem, optimism, and improving self-control, may exacerbate the stressor's effect on the individual's emotional state, perhaps creating additional anxiety (Gottleib, 1997).

A *challenge* appraisal reflects the athlete's determination to confront and overcome the stressful situation. In perceiving a stressful event as challenging, the athlete understands that sport success is contingent on the ability to overcome any obstacle in order to achieve a desirable outcome (Peacock and Wong, 1990). Challenge appraisals often increase the person's perceived control of the stressful event.

A *benefit* appraisal occurs when an athletes appraises that they have gained from a stressful encounter (Lazarus, 1999). Benefit appraisals could include an athlete scoring a goal in soccer, making an important tackle, or being selected for a team. The crucial element of this appraisal is the athlete perceives a gain has occurred.

Controllability is another form of appraisal used by numerous researchers. According to Dewe (1992) and Terry (1991), for example, stressful events appraised as highly controllable will produce different types of coping strategies than low control stressful events. As reviewed later, cognitive appraisals are especially important when examining cultural differences. Each type of appraisal warrants a different type of coping strategy, which is the next step in the coping process.

Use of Coping Strategies

At the heart of the coping process, following cognitive appraisal, is the athlete's conscious use of strategies that should result in reducing or managing the frequency and/or intensive of the stressful event. One framework that accurately reflects coping in the context of competitive sport, and has implications for effective versus ineffective coping responses is approach and avoidance (Krohne, 1993, 1996; Roth and Cohen, 1986). The approach and avoidance coping framework has been studied extensively in general psychology (e.g., Krohne, 1993, 1996; Roth and Cohen, 1986) and sport psychology (e.g., Anshel, 1996; Anshel and Kaissidis, 1997; Anshel and Sutarso, 2007; Anshel and Wells, 2000; Krohne and

Hindel, 1988). Conceptually, approach and avoidance coping has also been studied in sport contexts with respect to cognitive and behavioral sub-dimensions.

Approach coping strategies reflect the intensified intake and processing of unpleasant or threatening information. The selective use of approach coping strategies is aimed to foster perceived control of the situation the athlete perceives as stressful, or may improve one's personal resourcefulness (e.g., confidence, optimism, arousal, or assertiveness) in dealing with stress. This can occur through thoughts (approach-cognitive coping) such as planning or analyzing, or by actions (approach-behavioral coping) such as asking for information or confrontation.

Avoidance coping strategies, on the other hand, reflect a conscious attempt at physically or mentally turning away from the stressful source (Krohne, 1993; Krohne and Hindel, 1988). One objective for using an avoidance coping strategy is to distract the athlete from a particular source of stress. Coping with some stressors consume enormous amounts of attention and energy. The problem is that some stressful events occur at a time when the athlete must attend to the task at hand, and not be distracted by the stressor. Performing in an environment that is "unstable," for instance, European football (U.S. soccer), rugby, and basketball, and in which the performer must respond to uncertain demands, require the athlete to stay focused.

THE ROLE OF CULTURE IN THE SPORT COPING PROCESS

Cultural Influences in the Coping Process

Examining the influence of culture on coping with sport stress is highly relevant to understanding individual differences in the coping process, and acknowledging the role of culture when providing effective stress management programs. It is well-known, for example, that words and non-verbal cues differ between cultures (Brislin, 1990; Hoedaya and Anshel, 2003). In addition, numerous studies have shown that culture is a strong mediator and moderator variable in predicting or explaining sources of stress, identifying coping styles, and the preferred and effective use of coping strategies in response to stressful events, at least in the non-sport literature (see Wong and Wong, 2006). One size does not fit all, to use a cliché; individual differences have to be addressed by researchers and practitioners to determine optimally effective coping skills in sport.

Cultural Differences in Cognitive Appraisals

The role of culture in cognitive appraisals can be seen in a common example in which a person from a one country reacts very differently than their overseas counterpart when eating food that is unfamiliar to them. I had the honor to visit a foreign country in which the seafood on the plate was still moving; the seafood was supposed to be eaten while alive, I was informed [Personal note: The words "fresh seafood" will never mean the same again]. This particular dish was considered a delicacy and part of my host's food culture. I appraised the situation as stressful due, in no small part, to not wanting to insult my hosts. I decided not to indulge in the dish, which was happily devoured by my hosts. Sport competition offers other examples in which the same situation experienced by athletes from different countries will be perceived quite differently.

Mauro et al. (1992) suggest there are three ways culture influences appraisal: (1) differences on how the event is evaluated; (2) the link between the person's evaluation and the emotional response that it creates; and (3) the nature of the person's response(s) associated with an emotional state. In a rare sport stress study in this area, Hoedaya and Anshel (2003) found significant cultural differences between highly skilled, male and female Australian and Indonesian athletes on the intensity of various stressors. Specifically, Indonesians found spectator booing and being ignored by teammates to be significantly more stressful (i.e., higher stress intensity) then their Australian counterparts. Conversely, Australians found "receiving a bad call" to be markedly more stressful then Indonesian athletes. This latter finding supports the heightened respect for game officials often shown by Asian athletes as compared to Western countries. Of course, the athletes' appraisal of stressful events will likely predict the athletes' use of coping strategies. This makes coping also subject to cultural differences.

Cultural Difference in Sport Coping

To examine the role of culture in the coping process in competitive sport, particularly in response to acute stress, we need to examine both coping styles and coping strategies. While there is an apparent dearth of research in this area, there is an existing body of knowledge that supports the contention that culture is a moderator variable of coping styles and strategies.

In one study, for example, Puente-Diaz and Anshel (2005) compared U.S. and Mexican highly skilled male and female tennis players on their respective sources of acute stress, cognitive appraisal, and use of coping strategies. They found that culture significantly predicted the appraisal of perceived controllability and the athletes' subsequent selection of coping strategies for all athletes. In addition, cultural differences were found on these measures, as well as on sources of stress. Specifically, Mexican athletes cited "receiving negative comments," and "injuring myself during the match" as the two most stressful sources. U.S. players, on the other hand, cited "opponent cheating on me" as the most stressful event. Cultural differences in coping were also found, but that appraisal (i.e., perceived controllability) mediated this finding; that is, culture influenced perceived controllability and the use of coping strategies. Higher perceived control was related to greater use of active (i.e., approach) coping. Culture, therefore, indirectly influenced the use of coping strategies as a function of the athletes' appraisal.

In another study, Hoedaya and Anshel (2003) compared Indonesian and Australian athletes on pre-game and game-related sources of acute stress. In response to pregame stress, Indonesians differed markedly from Australians in using "emotional social support" and "denial" following the stressors "seeing significant others," "being ignored by a teammate," "opponent's quality of play," "importance of a particular game," "doubting own performance," and "thinking about family problems." Cultural differences were also found for stress experienced during the game. Indonesians used "denial," "restraint," and "active" coping more so than their Australian counterparts.

The results in the Hoedaya and Anshel study are particularly insightful into why it is important to study cultural differences in sport. Apparently, culture markedly influences an athlete's perception of the sport environment, frequency and intensity of stress appraisals, and evidence of using coping strategies as a function of culture. Understanding the unique characteristics of a culture, in this case Indonesians, might explain research results and the antecedents of cultural differences in coping.

Passchier, Raksadjaya, Sijmons, Goudswaard, Dekker, deVries, and Orlebeke (1991) found that Indonesian culture, more then Western culture, is more likely to value cooperation and consensus than the independence to obtain individual goals, the latter of which is more common in Western culture. More recently, Triandis (1994) found in his review of related literature on cultural influences on social behavior, that Indonesians are more likely to express courtesy and are more "subtle" in expressing disagreement or objection, respectively, than other cultures. There is reason to surmise that the Asian community, in general, share these characteristics, particularly based on the results of studies in Korea (see Anshel et al., 2001, for a review) and China (Anshel and Si, 2008; Gan et al., 2008). Each of these personal characteristics has important implications for understanding individual differences in the coping process in sport.

In another cross-cultural study between U.S. (n = 318) and Asian, specifically Korean, athletes (n = 404), Kim and Duda examined the effectiveness of reported coping responses as a function of the athletes' cognitive appraisals and coping effectiveness. Athletes from both cultures similarly used active (e.g., cognitive restructuring) and avoidance (e.g., emotional calming) coping strategies. Cultural differences also emerged, however. For example, in response to heightened perceived control following stressful experiences, Koreans more often used "behavioral risk coping" and "turning to religion" than their U.S. counterparts. Similar to most cross-cultural studies, however, there were far more similarities then differences between athletes from the different cultures.

Anshel, Williams, and Hodge (1997) compared U.S. and Australian athletes on their use of coping strategies following different sources of stress. They found that U.S. athletes, as compared to their Australian counterparts, tended to use significantly more approach coping strategies (e.g., planning, reflecting on the stressor, obtaining information) then avoidance coping (e.g., discounting the stressor's importance, forgetting).

Researchers (e.g., Anshel and Weinberg, 1996; Kaissidas, Anshel, and Sideridis, 1998) have also examined cultural differences in coping with stress among sports officials. In a qualitative study, for example, Anshel and Weinberg (1996) examined the coping styles of highly skilled Australian and U.S. basketball referees using the approach and avoidance framework. Cultural differences were found in response to an abusive coach or player; U.S. referees were more likely to use an approach coping style (e.g., giving a technical foul), showing relatively little tolerance for coach and player misconduct then their Australian referee counterparts, who considered negative comments as part of the game. Cultural differences were also found in a study comparing Australian and Greek referees. Kaissidas et al. (1998) found cultural differences for stress intensity among different stress sources and for coping responses as a function of the stressor. The authors concluded that Greek officials more often used approach then avoidance coping strategies, as compared to their Australian counterparts. One can speculate, therefore, that higher perceived controllability is related to approach coping, which in turn, effectively lowers the stressor's intensity – "taking control of the game," to use common parlance of the sports officiating literature (Weinberg and Richardson, 1990).

Most coping studies in sport psychology concerned with cultural issues have not involved direct cultural comparisons. Instead, the researchers have examined some aspect of the coping process in sport describing the coping habits of athletes in various countries. For example, two sport coping studies of athletes from the People's Republic of China (Anshel and Si, 2008; Gan, Anshel, and Kim, 2009) identified personal characteristics that provide support for acknowledging cultural differences in the sport coping process. Gan et al., for instance, found that athletes' coping style is a function of the type of stressor and cognitive appraisal, using the perceived controllability framework. Athletes with an approach coping style tended to appraise stressful events as highly controllable, as opposed to competitors with an avoidance coping style. In another study of Chinese male and female athletes, Anshel and Si ascertained coping strategies, using the approach and avoidance coping framework, in response to each of eight different sources of acute stress. Their results supported the transactional coping theory in that athletes' use of coping strategies was a function of the type of stressor.

With respect the cultural characteristics, results of the Anshel and Si (2008) study indicated that elite Asian athletes are more likely to adopt an avoidance, rather then an approach, coping style. Turning one's attention to the next task at hand, learning from the experience, and perceiving the stressor as a normal part of the contest are examples of an avoidance coping style for most stressors. Avoidance coping was especially prevalent in situations of low perceived control (e.g., coach reprimand). The researchers point out that the coach is highly respected in the People's Republic of China, perhaps more so then in Western countries. The following quotation reveals a very clear distinction between Asian and Western coaching behavior, "it is not unusual for sports coaches to use corporal punishment as a means of athlete discipline" (p. 15). The athletes expect, understand, and even appreciate coach criticism as a reflection of the coach's desire to improve their athlete's performance and success. It is reasonable to surmise that Chinese athletes manifest coping patterns of resiliency, hardiness, and resourcesfulness, what Rosenbaum (1990) calls a positive adaptation to stressful events. While there are many examples of coping in sport studies on athletes representing various countries, but do not include cross-cultural comparisons (see Hoar et al., 2006; Nicholls and Polman, 2007; Richards, 2004, for reviews).

Culture is a clear moderator variable that needs to be taken into account in the study and application of coping skills. Cultures do influence cognition, perceptual processes, emotion, and behavior, as indicated in numerous reviews of this literature (see Wong and Wong, 2006). The coach is viewed very differently between the Asian and Western culture. As Anshel and Si (2008) noted, implications of their results strongly indicate that Chinese athletes use an avoidance coping style in response to stressors, especially when the stressful situation is perceived as low control. Park's (2000) study of elite Korean athletes indicated greater use of avoidance coping. Examples included prayer, relaxation, and social support as a form of distraction. Yoo (2000) acknowledges the importance of the unique characteristics of each culture when he developed a 32-item coping scale, called the "Coping Scale for Korean Athletes" (CSKA) that was validated for Korean athletes. Although this scale was validated for Korean athletes, additional research is needed on cross-cultural comparisons using this instrument.

While an athletes' responses to receiving from the coach is unique to each culture, relatively harsh coach behavior, such as a reprimand or any other form of critical feedback, is more often expected and even appreciated by the Asian athlete, as compared to his or her counterparts from Western countries. Use of corporal punishment (i.e., physical abuse, in the parlance of Western observers) would not be tolerated in most countries, but this is the norm in Asian sport, especially at advanced levels (Si, 1995, *Personal communication*). Coach behavior forms another area that requires additional cross-cultural research.

IMPLICATIONS OF CULTURAL DIFFERENCES FOR MANAGING STRESS

What do the existing research findings of cultural comparisons in the sport coping literature tell us about improving athletes' coping skills and managing stress? First, it is important to acknowledge that coping skills and stress management, although often used interchangeably, are not the same concepts. Coping is, by definition, a person's *conscious* attempt to reduce or manage stressful feelings after an event or stimulus has been interpreted as unpleasant. Coping, therefore, follows an experience that has already occurred. Stress management, however, also addresses ways to *prevent* experiencing unpleasant events *before* they occur. As we will see shortly, this is important in controlling the unpleasant outcomes that are inherent in sport settings. If we can help athletes prevent stressful appraisals in response to a stimulus or event in the first place, there will less stress and little need to cope. This will have an enormous positive influence on the athlete's level of energy, satisfaction, and other positive thoughts and emotions. Meichenbaum (1985) refers to this process as *stress inoculation*.

Because stress is inherent in sport, the athlete should anticipate it and practice ways to react accordingly so that there are minimal consequences to stressful experiences. It is also to remember that "some" stress is good, even necessary, for optimal performance. The concept of "positive stress" represents situations that often result in growth, development, and maturation. Therefore, the athlete's goal is to manage, not eliminate, negative forms of stress in sport. As Gignac and Gottlieb contend, "people subjectively assess whether their endeavors help them achieve some degree of success in meeting their coping goals within a specific stressful context" (p. 246). Here are some suggested strategies that take into account cultural differences.

STRESS PREVENTION STRATEGIES

A strategy advanced by Hepburn, Loughlin, and Barling (1997) in the job stress literature is stress prevention – the conscious attempt to avoid experiencing stress before it is perceived. This may seem like common sense, yet, stress prevention is often ignored in sport because athletes – and their coaches – wrongly assume that most stressful events during the contest are common and unalterable. In fact, some stressors are more controllable than others. Making a physical error may be human, but how the athlete perceives negative input from spectators or reacts to receiving a penalty from the referee is firmly under the performer's control. Highly skilled athletes should enter the contest viewing the opponent as a challenge, an opportunity and obligation to demonstrate their own competence, not as a threat. However, as Lehrer and Woolfolk (1993) and Mace (1990) suggestion, characteristics of the athlete's personality, previous experiences, and situational factors should be taken into account when teaching stress prevention strategies (Lehrer and Woolfolk, 1993; Mace, 1990).

ACKNOWLEDGING APPRAISAL STYLE: PREDISPOSITIONAL DIFFERENCES

It is in the athletes' interest to know if they are susceptible to experiencing stress and making stress appraisals. Although evidence of appraisal style has not been studied in sport psychology, if is plausible to surmise that athletes from some cultures would differ from athletes from other cultures in their stress appraisals. Coping style is another factor that may predispose that athlete toward stressful feelings. For example, "approachers" are more susceptible to thinking about stimuli or information that is labeled stressful as opposed to "avoiders," who are more likely to discount or not be as sensitive to such input (Krohne, 1993).

Other orientations such as learned resourcefulness, optimism, self-esteem, perfectionism, self-control, and confidence each influence the athlete's sensitivity and responses to stress. Athletes who acknowledge their typical reactions to situational factors of the competitive event can take precautions toward planning for and learning proper stress management skills.

CONTROLLING ENVIRONMENTAL FACTORS

Coping researchers acknowledge the array of situational and environmental factors strongly influence the coping process. One example of an environmental factor is called *social engineering* (Greenberg, 2004). This coping strategy, located in the stress management literature, consists of the individual taking the initiative to avoid a situation or location that is previously known to alter perceived stress. For instance, an athlete who knows that being in the presence of his or her coach or a teammate will increase the athlete's negative emotion, than one social engineering technique is to avoid close proximity with the coach or teammate. We use social engineering every day when we try to avoid driving in rush hour or in certain high-traffic locations.

Another strategy that serves the similar function of distracting a person from the "storms" of stress and building personal resources in dealing with stress – both chronic and acute - is called *social support*.

Social support consists of interacting with one or more persons who lend emotional (i.e., expressive) or task-related (instrumental) support (Greenberg, 2004). An athlete's teammate, coach, parents, marital or social partner, and even spectators can create an environment that builds a person's resources in dealing with stress.

Effective Coping

One outcome of this chapter is that coping "effectiveness" is partly a function of the expectations, norms, and situations of the athlete's culture. It is generally acknowledged that coping is both purposeful and conscious, therefore, improving one's resourcefulness or reducing external demands in dealing with stressful events are intrinsic to competitive sport. However, some cultures are more "approach oriented," in which strategies such as confrontation, seeking information, and trying to understand the stressor's source(s), are common. Building personal resources, is represented by desirable predispositions such as hardiness, self-control, learned resourcefulness, self-esteem, optimism, and competitiveness (Maddi and Harvey, 2006). Reducing external demands consists of managing the environment so that stressful events are either avoided or confronted, when appropriate (Roth and Cohen, 1986).

Avoidance coping is often more appropriate when there is not sufficient time to address the stressor (e.g., while the ball is in play), when it is early in the contest and the stressor is not perceived as important, when the situation is perceived as uncontrollable (e.g., bad luck, an opponent's superior performance, a coach's reprimand), when the athlete does not have an expressive personality, when the athlete's confidence is low, not does possess an expressive personality, or has an avoidance coping style (Krohne, 1993; Roth and Cohen, 1986).

Some cultures more than others prefer avoidance-type coping styles (Anshel et al., 2001). The Asian community, for example, is more likely to use avoidance coping then their Caucasian counterparts, especially in the U.S. (Chang, Tugade, and Asakawa, 2006). The authors reviewed several studies that "found compelling evidence for greater emotional moderation among members of Asian cultures compared to Caucasian cultures" (p. 447). Examples of *effective* (adaptive) avoidance coping strategies following acute stress in sport include engaging in physical exercise, using various relaxation techniques, using positive self-talk, altering thoughts from irrational to rational beliefs, remembering your skills and other positive qualities, taking a time break, mental distraction, seeing an unpleasant event at temporary, prayer, and psychological distancing, which involves not taking the source of stress seriously or being able to rationalize it (e.g., "that's part of the game," "my opponent is just doing their job," I can't take them seriously; it's just trash talk"). Examples of *ineffective* (maladaptive) avoidance coping, not necessarily conducted during the contest, include excessive use of alcohol or drugs, use of tobacco products, over-consumption of food, displaced aggression (i.e., becoming upset with another person who is not responsible for the problem), and unnecessary risk-taking. For optimal coping effectiveness, athletes may want to balance approach and avoidance coping (Anshel and Sutarso, 2007; Hoar et al., 2006).

CONCLUSION

In conclusion, it is apparent that culture is a factor that strongly influences all components of the coping process. This include athletes' appraisals of sports events and experiences, their coping style, the use of specific coping strategies, and the effectiveness of those strategies. Lonner and Malpas (1994) contend that the main problem in ignoring cultural differences in coping is that researchers and practitioners are subjected to a strongly biased and restricted data base from which they draw conclusions about the coping process. Researchers are beginning to recognize the importance of examining the factors, such as culture, that mediate and moderate coping effectiveness (Nicholls and Polman, 2007). This will allow practitioners to consider cultural differences in prescribing more effective stress management and coping programs.

REFERENCES

Aldwin, C. M. (2007). Stress, coping, and development: An integrative perspective (2nd ed.). New York: Gifford.

Aldwin, C. M., and Revenson, T. A. (1987). Does coping help? A reexamination of the relation between coping and mental health. *Journal of Personality and Social Psychology, 53*, 337-348.

Anshel, M.H. (1996). Examining coping style in sport. *Journal of Social Psychology, 136*, 311-323.

Anshel, M. H. (2003). *Sport psychology:From theory to practice* (4th ed). San Francisco, CA: Benjamin Cummings.

Anshel, M. H. (2005). Strategies for preventing and managing stress and anxiety in sport. In D. Hackfort, J. L. Duda, and R. Lidor (Eds.), *Handbook of research in applied sport and exercise psychology: International perspectives* (pp. 199-215). Morgantown, WV: Fitness Information Technology.

Anshel, M. H., Brown, M., and Brown, D. (1993). Effectiveness of an acute stress coping program on motor performance, muscular tension, and affect. *Australian Journal of Science and Medicine in Sport, 25*, 7-16.

Anshel, M. H., Jamieson, J., and Raviv, S. (2001). Coping with acute stress among male and female Israeli athletes. *International Journal of Sport Psychology, 32*, 271-289.

Anshel, M. H., and Kaissidis, A. N. (1997). Coping style and situational appraisals as predictors of coping strategies following stressful events in sport as a function of gender and skill level. *British Journal of Psychology, 88*, 263-276.

Anshel, M.H., Kim, K.W., Kim, B.H., Chang, K.J., and Eom, H.J. (2001). A model for coping with stressful events in sport: Theory, application, and future directions. *International Journal of Sport Psychology, 32*, 43-75.

Anshel, M. H., and Si, G. (2008). Coping styles following acute stress in sport among elite Chinese athletes : A test of trait and transactional coping theories. *Journal of Sport Behavior, 31*, 3-21.

Anshel, M.H., and Sutarso, T. (2007). Relationships between sources of acute stress and athletes' coping style in competitive sport as a function of gender. *Psychology of Sport and Exercise, 8*, 1-24.

Anshel, M. H., and Weinberg, R. S. (1996). Coping with acute stress among American and Australian basketball referees. *Journal of Sport Behavior, 19*, 180-203.

Anshel, M.H., and Wells, B. (2000). Sources of acute stress and coping styles in competitive sport. *Anxiety, Stress, and Coping: In International Journal, 13*, 1-26.

Anshel, M. H., Williams, L. R. T., and Hodge, K. (1997). Cross-cultural and gender differences on coping style in sport. *International Journal of Sport Psychology, 28*, 141-156.

Baron, R. M., and Kenny, D. A. (1986). The moderator-mediator variable distinction in social psychological research: Conceptual, strategic, and statistical consideration. *Journal of Personality and Social Psychology, 51*, 1173-1182.

Brislin, R. W. (1990). *Applied cross-cultural psychology*. Newbury Park, CA: Sage.

Carver, C. S., Scheier, M. F., and Weintraub, J. K. (1989). Assessing coping strategies: A theoretically-based approach. *Journal of Personality and Social Psychology, 56*, 267-283.

Chang, E. C., Tugade, M. M., and Asakawa, K. (2006). Stress and coping among Asian Americans: Lazarus and Folkman's model and beyond. In P. T. P. Wong and L. C. J. Wong (Eds.), *Handbook of multicultural perspectives on stress and coping* (pp. 1-26). New York: Springer.

Chun, C. A., Moos, R. H., and Cronkite, R. C. (2006). Culture: A fundamental context for the stress and coping paradigm. P. T. P. Wong and L. C. J. Wong (Eds.), *Handbook of multicultural perspectives on stress and coping* (pp. 29-54). New York: Springer.

Compas, B. E., Connor, J., Osowiecki, D., and Welch, A. (1997). Effortful and involuntary responses to stress. In B. H. Gottlieb (Ed.), *Coping with chronic stress* (pp. 105-130). New York: Plenum.

Dewe, P. (1992). The appraisal process: Exploring the role of meaning, importance, control and coping in work stress. *Anxiety, Stress, and Coping, 5*, 95-109.

Eysenck, M. W. (1992). *Anxiety: The cognitive perspective*. Hove, England: Erlbaum.

Gan, Q., Anshel, M. H., and Kim, J. K. (2009). Sources and cognitive appraisals of acute stress as predictors of coping style among male and female Chinese athletes. *International Journal of Sport and Exercise Psychology, 7*, 68-88.

Gignac, M. A. M., and Gottlieb, B. H. (1997). Changes in coping with chronic stress: The role of caregivers' appraisals of coping efficacy. In B. H. Gottlieb (Ed.), *Coping with chronic stress* (pp. 245-268). New York: Plenum.

Gottlieb, B. H. (1997). Conceptual and measurement issues in the study of coping with chronic stress. In B. H. Gottlieb (Ed.), *Coping with chronic stress* (pp. 3-42). New York: Plenum.

Greenberg, J.S. (2004). *Comprehensive stress management* (8th ed.). New York: McGraw-Hill.

Hackfort, D., and Schwenkmezger, P. (1993). Anxiety. In R.N. Singer, M. Murphey, and L.K. Tennant (Eds.), *Handbook of research on sport psychology* (pp. 328-364). New York: Macmillan

Hepburn, C. G., Loughlin, C. A., and Barling, J. (1997). Coping with chronic work stress. In B.H. Gottlieb (Ed.), *Coping with chronic stress* (pp. 343-366). New York: Plenum.

Hoar, S. D., Kowalski, K. C., Gaudreau, P., and Crocker, P. R. E. (2006). A review of coping in sport. In S. Hanton and S. D. Mellalieu (Eds.), *Literature reviews in sport psychology* (pp. 47-90). New York: Nova Science Publishers.

Hoedaya, D., and Anshel, M. H. (2003). Sources of stress and coping strategies among Australian and Indonesian athletes. *Australian Journal of Psychology, 55*, 159-165.

Kaissidas-Rodafinos, Anshel, M. H., and Sideridis, G. (1998). Sources, intensity, and responses to stress in Greek and Australian basketball referees. *International Journal of Sport Psychology, 29*, 303-323.

Kim, M. S., Duda, J. L. (2003). The coping process: Cognitive appaisals of stress, coping, strategies, and coping effectiveness. *The Sport Psychologist, 17, 406-425.*

Krohne, H.W. (1993). Attention and avoidance: Two central strategies for coping with aversiveness. In H.W. Krohne (Ed.), *Attention and avoidance* (pp. 3-18). Seattle, WA: Hogrefe and Huber.

Krohne, H.W. (1996). Individual differences in coping. In M. Zeidner and N.S. Endler (Eds.), *Handbook of coping* (pp. 381-409). New York: John Wiley and Sons.

Krohne, H.W., and Hindel, C. (1988). Trait anxiety, state anxiety, and coping behavior as predictors of athletic performance. *Anxiety Research, 1*, 225-234.

Landers, D. M., and Arent, S. M. (2001). Arousal-performance relationships. In J. M. Williams (Ed.), *Applied sport psychology: Personal growth to peak performance* (pp. 206-228). Mountain View: Mayfield.

Lazarus, R. S. (1990). Theory-based stress measurement. *Psychological Inquiry, 1*, 3-13.

Lazarus, R. S. (1999). *Stress and emotion: A new synthesis.* New York: Springer.

Lazarus, R. S., and Folkman, S. (1984). *Stress, appraisal, and coping.* New York: Springer.

Lehrer, P. M., and Woolfolk, R. L. (1993). Research on clinical issues in stress management. In P.M. Lehrer and R.L. Woolfolk (Eds.), *Principles and practice of stress management* (2nd ed.; pp. 521-538). New York: Guilford.

Loehr, J. E. (1990). The mental game: Winning at pressure tennis. New York: Penguin.

Loehr, J., and Schwartz, T. (2003). *The power of full engagement: Managing energy, not time, is the key to high performance and personal renewal.* New York: Free Press.

Lonner, W. J., and Malpas, R. S. Eds. (1994). *Psychology and culture.* Boston : Allyn and Bacon.

Maddi, S. R., and Harvey, R. H. (2006). Hardiness considered across cultures. In P. T. P. Wong and L. C. J. Wong (Eds.), *Handbook of multicultural perspectives on stress and coping* (pp. 409-426). New York: Springer.

Mauro, R., Sato, K., and Tucker, J. (1992). The role of appraisal in human emotions: A cross-cultural study. *Journal of Personality and Social Psychology, 62*, 301-317.

McCrae, R. R. (1992). Situational determinants of coping. In B.N. Carpenter (Ed.), *Personal coping: Theory, research, and application* (pp. 65-76). Westport, CT: Praeger.

Meichenbaum, D. (1985). *Stress inoculation training.* Elmford, NY: Pergamon Press.

Miller, S. M. (1989). Cognitive informational styles in the process of coping with threat and frustration. *Advances in Behavior Research and Therapy, 11*, 223-234.

Ness Evans, A., and Rooney, B. F. (2008). *Methods in psychological research.* Thousand Oaks, CA: Sage.

Nicholls, A. R., and Polman, R. C. J. (2007). Coping in sport: A systematic review. *Journal of Sports Sciences, 25*, 11-31.

Peacock, E. J., and Wong, P. T. P. (1990). The stress appraisal measure (SAM): A multidimensional approach to cognitive appraisal. *Stress Medicine, 6*, 227-236.

Park, J. K. (2000). Coping strategies used by Korean national athletes. *The Sport Psychologist, 14*, 63-80.

Passchier, J., Raksadjaya, B., Sijmons, R., Goudswaard, P., Dekker, deVries, P. H., and Orlebeke,J. F. (1991). Physiological response to achievement stress in students with high achievement motivation and fear of failure: Are the reactions similar in Amsterdam and Bandung? In N. Bleichrodt and P. J., D. Drenth (Eds.), *Contemporary issues in cross-cultural psychology: Selected papers from a regional conference of the International*

Association for cross-cultural psychology (pp. 297-306). Amsterdam: Swets and Zeitlinger.

Pederson, P. B. (2006). Knowledge gaps about stress and coping in a multicultural context. In P. T. P. Wong and L. C. J. Wong (Eds.), *Handbook of multicultural perspectives on stress and coping* (pp. 579-595). New York: Springer.

Puente-Diaz, R., and Anshel, M. H. (2005). Sources of acute stress, cognitive appraisal, and coping strategies among highly skilled Mexican and U.S. competitive tennis players. *Journal of Social Psychology, 145*, 429-446.

Richards, H. (2004). Coping in sport. In D. Lavallee, J. Thatcher, and M. V. Jones (Eds.), *Coping and emotion in sport* (pp. 29-51). Hauppauge, NY: Nova.

Rosenbaum, M. (1990). *Learned resourcefulness on coping skills, self-control, and adaptive behavior*. New York: Springer.

Roth, S., and Cohen, L. J. (1986). Approach, avoidance, and coping with stress. *American Psychologist, 41*, 813-819.

Schafer, W. (1996). *Stress management for wellness* (3rd. ed). New York: Harcourt Brace.

Selye, H. (1974). *Stress without distress*. Philadelphia: Lippincott.

Smith, R. E. (1986). Towards a cognitive-affective model of athletic burnout. *Journal of Sport Psychology, 8*, 36-50.

Skinner, E. A., Edge, K., Altman, J., and Sherwood, H. (2003). Searching for the structure of coping: A review and critique of category systems for classifying ways of coping. *Psychological Bulletin, 129*, 216-269.

Spielberger, C.D. (1989). *Stress and anxiety in sports*. In D. Hackfort and C.D. Spielberger (Eds.), Anxiety in sports: An international perspective (pp. 3-17). New York: Hemisphere.

Suls, J., and Fletcher, B. (1985). The relative efficacy of avoidant and nonavoidant coping strategies: A meta-analysis. *Health Psychology, 4*, 249-288.

Terry, D. J. (1991). Coping resources and situational appraisals as predictors of coping behavior. *Personality and Individual Differences, 12*, 1031-1047.

Triandis, H. C. (1994). Culture and social behavior. In W. J. Looner and R. S. Malpass (Eds.), *Psychology and culture* (pp. 169-173). Boston: Allyn and Bacon.

Weinberg, R. S., and Richardson, P. A. (1990). *Psychology of officiating*. Champaign, IL: Leisure Press.

Wheaton, B. (1997). The nature of chronic stress. In B.H. Gottlieb (Ed.), *Coping with chronic stress* (pp.43-73). New York: Plenum.

Wong, P. T. P., and Wong, L., C., J. (Eds., 2006). *Handbook of multicultural perspectives on stress and coping* (pp. 1-26). New York: Springer.

Wong, P. T. P., Wong, L. C. J., and Scott, C. (2006). Beyond stress and coping: The positive psychology of transformation. In P. T. P. Wong and L. C. J. Wong (Eds.), *Handbook of multicultural perspectives on stress and coping* (pp. 1-26). New York: Springer.

Woodman, T., and Hardy, L. (2001). Stress and anxiety. In R.N. Singer, H.A. Hausenblas, and C.M. Janelle (Eds.), *Handbook of sport psychology* (2nd ed.; pp. 290-318). New York: John Wiley and Sons.

Yoo, J. (2000). Factorial validity of the coping scale for Korean athletes. *International Journal of Sport Psychology, 31*, 391-404.

Zeidner, M. and Saklofske, D. (1996). Adaptive and maladaptive coping. In M. Zeidner and N. S. Endler (Eds.), *Handbook of coping: Theory, research, applications* (pp. 505-531). New York: John Wiley and Sons.

PART IV: COPING AND RELATED CONSTRUCTS

In: Coping in Sport: Theory, Methods, and Related Constructs   ISBN: 978-1-60876-488-4
Editor: Adam R. Nicholls   © 2010 Nova Science Publishers, Inc.

Chapter 8

PERSONALITY AND COPING IN SPORT: THE BIG FIVE AND MENTAL TOUGHNESS

Remco C. J. Polman[1], Peter J. Clough[2] and Andrew R. Levy[3]
[1]University of Central Lancashire, UK
[2]University of Hull, UK
[3]University of Leeds, UK

ABSTRACT

The role of personality on coping has received scant attention in the domain of sport. However, there are a number of ways how personality might influence coping either directly or indirectly among athletes. Evidence from other life domains is provided suggesting that personality can affect the type and frequency of stressors encountered, the appraisal of the stressor (including stress reactivity), coping, and coping effectiveness. These mechanisms are not independent from each other and suggest that certain personalities are more vulnerable or resistant to stress. In particular, individuals high in neuroticism might experience mood spill-overs and the so called neurotic cascade. Based on the general psychological literature, specific evidence is provided regarding how The Big Five personality dimensions extraversion, neuroticism, agreeableness, conscientiousness, and openness to experiences are related to stressor exposure, appraisal, and coping. We also discuss the role of the sport specific personality construct mental toughness in the stress-coping process. In particular, the different approaches to mental toughness are briefly discussed. A number of studies are discussed that support the notion that more mentally tough athletes are more like to appraise stressful situations as less severe and more under control. Also, mentally tough athletes are more likely to use problem-focused coping strategies to tackle the problem at hand rather than emotion-focused or avoidance coping strategies.

INTRODUCTION

Surprisingly, the role of personality on coping behavior has had little attention in the domain of sport and exercise. Indeed, a recent meta-analysis on this topic by Connor-Smith and Flachsbart (2007) did not contain any sport related studies. However, the large inter-individual differences observed in how athletes cope with stress point towards its importance (e.g., Nicholls, Polman, Levy, Taylor, and Cobley, 2007). In this chapter we will adopt a narrow view of personality and will only examine the role of the Big Five and the sport specific personality trait of mental toughness in relation to coping.

The Lazarus and Folkman (1984) model of stress and coping suggested that coping with stress is a dynamic and recursive process that involves a transaction between a person's internal (e.g., goals and values) and external (e.g., situational) environments. Coping outcomes in turn influence subsequent appraisal as well as the person and environment. Coping and personality in this respect should be viewed as being related to coping, but not identical. That is, there is overlap between coping and personality when a behavioral pattern is trying to manage a particular problem. Hence, personality "creates a person's characteristic patterns of behavior, thoughts, and feelings" (Carver and Scheier, 2008; p. 5), whereas coping can be described as intentional behaviors that are adopted to manage a problem (Leventhal, Suls, and Leventhal, 1993). However, there are differences because patterns of behavior do not just solve problems (Suls and David, 1996). Personality therefore is likely to play a complementary (rather than competing role) in situational coping (Carver, Scheier, and Weintraub, 1989). To this end, DeLongis and Holtzman (2005) have provided a useful conceptual framework in which situational aspects and personality as well as their interaction can be used to guide research in this area (see Figure 1).

From viewing Figure 1 it is clear that there are a number of ways that personality might influence directly or indirectly coping behavior among athletes. There is evidence that personality, through active choice or more involuntary inducement, can influence the probability of people experiencing certain encounters (i.e., the differential exposure hypothesis) and the type of situations that are perceived as being stressful. There is also evidence to suggest that personality can influence the way the stressful encounter is appraised by the individual.

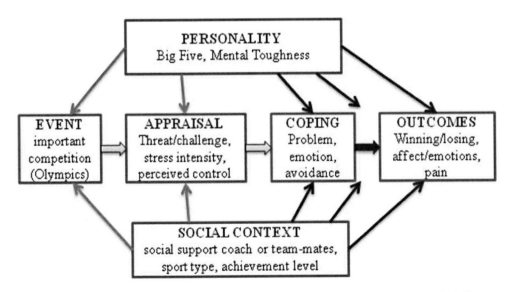

Figure 1. Diagram and conceptual framework how situational aspects and personality could influence coping behavior (adopted from: DeLongis and Holtzman, 2005; p. 3).

Personality also appears to directly influence the selection of coping strategies athletes use, in addition to outcome or the effectiveness of the selected coping strategy or strategies (Semmer, 2006; Suls and Martin, 2005).

Differential Exposure Hypothesis

Depending on their dispositions, athletes may have different probabilities of encountering certain stressors. This might result in athletes encountering the same stressor more often as well as encountering different type of stressors, which Suls and Martin (2005) called the differential exposure hypothesis. There is some indirect evidence and theoretical support from the sport psychology literature that athletes might avoid or approach stressful situations. For example, athletes high in achievement motivation are more likely to engage in achievement situations, whereas athletes low in achievement motivation are more likely to avoid such situations (Atkinson, 1974), which would result in different exposure to stressors. In addition, when an athlete is low in self-confidence (trait or state) or high in state anxiety he or she would be more likely to encounter stressors. In such a situation an athlete is not only more likely to make errors which can cause stress but in turn this might result in more criticism from team-mates or coaches increasing the probability of encountering more stressful events. The mainstream psychology literature focuses on the personality trait neuroticism or negative affectivity when investigating differences in exposure to stressful events. Neuroticism or negative affectivity is associated across time and situations with experiencing negative emotions, distress, anxiety, irritability, pessimism, worry, hostility, and a negative view of oneself, the world, the future, others and an attentional bias towards adverse stimuli. Not surprisingly, individuals high on this trait have been found to experience more negative events more frequently and are more likely to experience interpersonal conflicts (e.g., Bolger and Zuckerman, 1995; Gunthert, Cohen, and Armelli, 1999). Extraverts (or positive affectivity) on the other hand have been found to report more positive events (Zautra, Affleck, Tennen, Reich, and Davis, 2005) and high levels of agreeableness have been associated with fewer social conflicts (Asendorph and Wilpers, 1998).

Personality and Appraisal

Personality may also influence coping behavior indirectly through appraisal of events. As suggested by Semmer (2006), many personality variables are to some extent assessed in terms of their propensity to appraise situations in a given way. For example, from a theoretical perspective it would be predicted that athletes who are more mentally tough or are more optimistic would appraise situations as a challenge whereas athletes who are less mentally tough or who are more pessimistic would appraise situations as a threat. Of course, this will have significant consequences for the subsequent selection of adaptive coping strategies. Hence, when perceiving an event as a threat it is more likely to trigger a stronger emotional response. In such a situation, it might be that the athlete would first have to use an emotion-focused coping strategy to lower emotions before employing an active attempt to solve the problem in a more functional manner (Semmer, 2006). Again, research has mainly focused on individuals high in neuroticism or negative affectivity. As predicted, individuals high on neuroticism, and in particular trait anxiety, appraise events as more harmful or threatening (Eysenck, 1988). As proposed by Guntert et al. (1999), people high in neuroticism would intensify the degree of threat perceived by undesirable events (i.e. primary appraisal), and underestimate their personal resources (secondary appraisal) to cope with the event. Conversely, individuals high on extraversion are associated with positive appraisal of coping resources.

The differential sensitivity hypothesis (Suls and Martin, 2005) suggested that personality variables may influence the stress and coping process by reacting more or less strongly to negative events that are appraised in similar ways. Reactivity is the extent to which a person is likely to show emotional or physical reactions to a stressful event (Bolger and Zuckerman, 1995). The neuroticism/extraversion or negative/positive affectivity distinction is based on the assumption that there are underlying physiological mechanisms that make individuals high on these traits react dissimilar to negative or positive events (Eysenck, 1988; Larsen and Ketelaar, 1991). Individuals with high levels of neuroticism, in this respect, have been shown to "magnify" the impact of negative events (Zautra et al., 2005) and show strong emotional and physiological reactivity to stress (Connor-Smith and Flachsbart, 2007). Conversely, extraverts have been characterized by increased responses to positive events and low stress reactivity (Connor-Smith and Flachsbart, 2007). Of course, in the athletic context it will be difficult to examine stress reactivity. First, in more ecologically valid situations differences in reactivity might be the result of differences in appraisal (Semmer, 2006). Secondly, it will be difficult to establish whether increased physiological arousal is the consequence of stress reactivity or the physical demands of the sport.

Personality and Coping Selection

Research has shown that personality influences coping directly. That is, individuals with certain personality traits tend to use certain coping strategies more often than other people (Carver, Scheier, and Weintraub, 1989). This does not suggest that a particular athlete will always use a particular coping strategy to deal with stress or that situational factors do not play a role. In addition, such findings are not incompatible with Lazarus and Folkman's (1984) model of stress and coping. Individuals will still take into account situational factors to modify their coping and will only show a tendency to use certain coping strategies more often in certain situations. Derryberry, Reed, and Pilkenton-Taylor (2003) have suggested that these direct effects of personality on coping may begin in early childhood, with biologically based appetitive, defensive, and attentional systems providing a framework for coping development. In other words, as suggested by Connor-Smith and Flachsbart (2007), personality may directly influence coping by withdrawal from threats, facilitating approach to rewards, and engagement or disengagement of attention. For example, the high energy and social ability of extraverts may promote the seeking of social support. Neurotics, on the other hand, might use more disengagement coping because of their sensitivity to threats (Conner-Smith and Flachbart, 2007). An important implication for this line of research would be that certain personality traits would not be optimal to perform in competitive sport because of the failure to employ coping strategies which are best suited to deal with stressful situations.

Coping Effectiveness and Outcomes

Personality traits may indirectly influence the effectiveness of coping strategies. In Chapter 14 of this book, Nicholls suggested that coping effectiveness refers to 'degree in which a coping strategy or combination of strategies is or are successful in alleviating stress.' When analyzing the effectiveness of coping, it is important to bear in mind that coping strategies are not universally beneficial or detrimental. There is an important difference between using a coping strategy and using it effectively (Suls and David, 1996). However, most research in the area of coping effectiveness suggests that a reliance on problem-focused coping strategies, as opposed to either emotion-focused or avoidance coping strategies is related to more beneficial outcomes (Aldwin, 2007; Compas, Connor-Smith, Saltzman, Harding Thomsen, and Wadsworth, 2001). A possible explanation for this observation is that problem-focused coping assists in transforming the situation or solving the problem, thereby facilitating goal attainment (e.g., Gaudreau and Blondin, 2002). In addition, active problem solving requires engagement and ownership of solutions, which in turn helps the person to cope better with similar problems in the future. Emotion-focused coping might help the performer to lower stress reactivity, but doesn't solve the problem whereas avoidance coping suggest that the person chooses not to deal with the problem and postpone problem solving to a later date. In both instances, it is less likely that goals will be achieved. However, it should be kept in mind that coping strategies that are beneficial for some individuals may be less effective, or even harmful, for someone with different personality traits (Bolger and Zuckerman, 1995; DeLongis and Holzman, 2005).

Daily report studies have provided evidence that people with high levels of neuroticism appear to be associated with poor coping outcomes (Holahan and Moos, 1987). In addition, individuals high on neuroticism are less likely to change their coping strategy in response to the needs of the situation (O'Brien and DeLongis, 1996). This lack of flexibility in coping strategies used by people high in neuroticism can also be a factor contributing to their unsuccessful outcomes. As suggested by Lazarus and Folkman (1984) being flexible in one's coping skills is a strong predictor of good coping skills. In addition, although those high on neuroticism might use coping strategies which are assumed to be effective like problem solving, the use of these strategies tend to be ineffective to the particular situation which they are coping with (Bolger and Zuckerman, 1995; DeLongis and Holtzman, 2005). Individuals high in neuroticism also tend to use more coping strategies overall. This might indicate that they have difficulty in finding the most appropriate coping strategy for particular stressful events (Suls and Martin, 2005). On the other hand, high levels of extraversion have been associated with less use of ineffective forms of emotion-focused coping such as self blame, wishful thinking, or avoidance coping (Hooker, Frazier, and Monahan, 1994). Extraverts are said to be flexible copers who are able to adapt their coping response based on the situation (Lee-Baggley, Preece, and DeLongis, 2005).

In summary, previous research in other life domains including health and relationships has suggested that personality influences coping either indirectly through differential experience of stress exposure (type, frequency), appraisal, reactivity, and coping effectiveness, or directly by influencing coping selection. As suggested by Suls and Martin (2005), and Semmer (2006) these mechanisms are not independent from one another and suggest that certain personalities will be more vulnerable or resistant to stress. Suls and Martin (2005) proposed the neurotic cascade. Neurotics experience different exposure (more stressful events), will react to these events with increased stress reactivity, appraise events as more harmful or threatening and fail to use the most appropriate coping strategies for particular stressful events. An additional problem which might strengthen this cascade is mood spillover. Because neurotics find it difficult to tackle a particular stressor they will still be in a negative mood state when they experience the next stressor thereby enhancing the negative cascade. By the same token, there will be other personality traits, like mental toughness, which can have the opposite effect. For example, mentally tough athletes might encounter less stressful situations, see stressful event as a challenge rather than a threat, will exhibit more emotional stability, and will have better coping strategies to tackle the stressful encounter effectively.

THE BIG FIVE

Although there is continuing debate on the structure of personality, at present time there is some consensus regarding a general taxonomy of personality. There is currently a significant body of evidence suggesting that the structure of personality consists of a five super-ordinate factor structure. The Big Five has been shown to capture much of the variance in personality trait ratings independent of cultures and languages (John and Srivastava, 1999). The Big Five provides a common framework in which the different and diverse systems of personality can be investigated. It represents personality at the broadest level of abstraction in which each dimension provides a number of more distinct personality characteristics (Carver and Scheier, 2008; John and Srivastava, 1999). These dimensions have a biological-heritable basis and transcend individual differences like age, gender, race, and culture (Costa and McCrae, 1992; Lee-Baggley et al., 2005; McCrae et al., 2000). There is still, however, some disagreement regarding the interpretation and naming of the five factors. The labels provided for the five personality dimensions have shortcomings and are easily misunderstood (John and Srivastava, 1999); therefore a brief description of each is provided below.

Searches on SPORTdiscus, PsychLIT, and PsychINFO did not yield any studies that have investigated the relationship between The Big Five and coping in the domain of sport. Therefore the following section of this chapter briefly outlines the findings between the Big Five and coping from other domains of psychology. Please note that most of this research has focused on the role of neuroticism and extraversion in relation to coping. Very few studies have investigated the role of agreeableness, conscientiousness, and openness to experience in relation to coping.

Extraversion. Extraversion implies an energetic approach towards the social and material world and is characterized by the tendency to experience positive emotions, being outgoing, warm, cheerful, active, and self-assured. When analyzing the relationship between extraversion and coping, it has been found that high levels of extraversion are associated with active coping and positive re-appraisal (Amirkahn, Risinger, and Swiscker, 1995; Costa, Summerfield, and McCrae, 1996; Watson and Hubbard, 1996), but less emotion-focused coping such as self-blame, wishful thinking, and avoidance coping (Hooker, Frazier, and Monahan, 1994). Individuals that score highly on extraversion are flexible copers who can adapt their coping response based on the situation (Lee-Baggley et al., 2005).

Neuroticism. Neuroticism (emotional stability), contrasts emotional constancy and even-temperedness with negative affectivity and include trait like experiencing negative emotional states (feeling anxious, nervous, and tense), generation of irrational ideas, and being impulsive and self-conscious. Individuals high in neuroticism use coping strategies that eliminate or minimize stressful feelings (Watson and Hubbard, 1996). Neurotics, in this respect, show a greater reliance on emotion-focused coping strategies and use less problem-focused coping strategies (Bolger and Zuckerman, 1995). As suggested earlier, individuals high in neuroticism might exhibit hyper-reactivity when encountering stressful events. In such situations, lowering of emotions would be required before the individual could engage in meaningful problem-focused coping attempts. High levels of neuroticism are also associated with poorer coping outcomes (Holahan and Moos, 1987).

Agreeableness. Agreeableness contrasts a pro-social and communal orientation towards others with antagonism and is associated with being unselfish, compliant, trusting, modest, and helpful. Individuals that score higher on agreeableness are likely to cope in ways that engage or protect social relationships such as seeking support and avoiding confrontation. They appear less likely to use emotion-focused coping such as self-blame, wishful thinking or avoidance and disengagement coping (Hooker et al., 1994; Watson and Hubbard, 1996).

Conscientiousness. Conscientiousness depicts socially prescribed impulse control and assists in task and goal directed behaviors. This includes characteristics like purposeful in cognition and behavior, organized, following rules and norms, delaying gratification, strong-minded, and being self-disciplined. High levels of conscientiousness have been associated with more planning and rational decision-making (Chartrand et al., 1993; Vollrath et al., 1994), but less use of avoidant or emotion-focused coping such as self-blame, distraction or disengagement (Hooker et al., 1994; O'Brien and DeLongis, 1996; Watson and Hubbard, 1996). Individuals high on conscientiousness have shown to be effective copers who adapt to the situation and respond efficiently (Lee-Baggley et al., 2005; O'Brien and DeLongis, 1996; Watson and Hubbard, 1996).

Openness to Experience. Openness to experience (vs. closed mindedness) refers to extensiveness, inventiveness, and complexity of an individual's mental and experiential life and includes traits like being creative, inquisitive, having unconventional values, and flexible in their way of thinking (John and Srivastava, 1999). High levels of openness have been positively associated with increased emotion (McCrae and Costa, 1986; Roesch, Wee, and Vaughn, 2006), and problem-focused coping (Watson and Hubbard, 1996; Roesch et al., 2006), whereas some studies have found no significant association between openness and coping (e.g. Hooker et al., 1994).

Taken together, it appears that the Big Five personality dimensions influence coping. However, it is unclear whether similar relationships exist in the domain of sport as has been found in other life domains. Sport has some unique characteristics. For example, physical activity or exercise is generally associated with positive psychological outcomes (e.g., Biddle, Fox, and Boutcher, 2000). It is unclear how such psychological outcomes are associated with stress reactivity or appraisal of events. Clearly, there is scope for further investigations in the relationship between the Big Five and coping in sport.

MENTAL TOUGHNESS

Approaches to Mental Toughness

Mental toughness is an important personality construct to consider when exploring coping in sport. Its intuitive appeal is clearly illustrated by Loehr's (1982) finding that coaches and athletes felt at least 50% of sporting success was due to mental toughness. However, mental toughness is perhaps one of the most overused but least understood terms within applied sport psychology (Jones, Hanton, and Connaughton, 2002). A number of major challenges remain in this field of research. Perhaps the most critical is to establish a clear definition of what this frequently used term really is, that is universally accepted among scholars. In order to try and operationalize the mental toughness concept, qualitative and psychometric approaches have been used.

Arguably, the most influential work within the qualitative perspective is that of Jones et al. (2002). They aimed to provide some degree of rigor in the investigation of the mental toughness concept, which had previously been lacking. Their aim was to define and identify key attributes of mental toughness. They selected qualitative methods because they, among others, argued that this would provide the opportunity to probe people's responses and establish detailed information, especially with regard to new research questions (Gould, Eklund, and Jackson, 1993; Fourie and Potgieter, 2001, Hanton and Connaughton, 2002; Hanton and Jones, 1999). Their study concentrated on the view of elite athletes in order to generate data for a profile of a mentally tough athlete, via interviews and focus groups.

The attributes developed by Jones et al. (2002) were, ranked in order of importance, as follows: (a) having an unshakable self-belief in your ability to achieve your competition goals, (b) bouncing back from performance set-backs as a result of increased determination to succeed (c) having an unshakable self-belief that you possess unique qualities and abilities that make you better than your opponents, (d) having an insatiable desire and internalized motives to succeed, (e) remaining fully focused on the task at hand in the face of competition-specific distractions, (f) regaining psychological control following unexpected, uncontrollable events, (g) pushing back the boundaries of physical and emotional pain, whilst maintaining technique and effort under distress in training and competition, (h) accepting that competition anxiety is inevitable and knowing that you can cope with it, (i) not being adversely affected by others' good and bad performances, (j) thriving on the pressure of competition, (k) remaining fully-focused in the face of personal life distractions, and (l) switching a sport focus on and off as required.

Crust (2008) suggested that recent qualitative studies have attempted to build upon this seminal study by Jones et al. (2002), but have in reality mainly replicated these previous findings (e.g., Connaughton, Wadey, Hanton, and Jones, 2008; Jones, Hanton and Connaughton, 2007; Gucciardi, Gordon, and Dimmock, 2008). The qualitative perspective has undoubtedly provided important information relating to the description of mental toughness. However, it has not explored how differences in mental toughness might impact on both practice and performance. The second major body of work, the psychometric approach, facilitates both a definition to be developed and also allows the vital comparisons between individuals who vary in their level of toughness.

Loehr (1982, 1986) had a pioneering role in the mental toughness scholarly activity. Taking a pragmatic standpoint, he developed the Psychological Performance Inventory (PPI). This measures seven broad areas: (a) self-confidence, (b) negative emotion, (c) attention control, (d) visualization and imagery control, (e) motivation, (f) positive energy, and (g) attitude control. The PPI has been used within the field of applied sport psychology. For example Golby and Sheard (2004) used the PPI in a study of rugby league players to measure toughness. Previous research had not found any significant differences in the tactical or physical attributes of the players (Brewer and Davis, 1995), which has lead to questions about the psychological profiles of the athletes as an explanation for performance differences. The study by Golby and Sheared revealed that international players scored higher on two scales, negative energy control and attention control, than other professional players. The study also showed a strong relationship between hardiness and mental toughness. Middleton, Marsh, Richards, and Perry (2004) criticized the research that used the PPI (e.g., Allen, 1988; Dongsung and Kang-Heon, 1994; Gould, Tuffey, and Loehr, 1996; Hanrahan, Grove, and Lockwood, 1990), because of the inadequate psychometric properties attributed to this instrument.

In an attempt to move the measurement issue forward Middleton et al (2004) married together qualitative and quantitative approaches to propose a new measure of mental toughness, called Mental Toughness Inventory (MTI; Middleton et al.). The MTI is a 67-item self-report questionnaire, which assesses 12 characteristics of mental toughness: (a) self efficacy, (b) potential, (c) mental self-concept, (d) task familiarity, (e) value, (f) personal bests, (g) goal commitment, (h) perseverance, (i) task focus, (j) positivity, (k) positive comparisons, and (l) stress minimization. This instrument has a clear factor structure and sound reliability, but further work on this instrument is necessary to examine the important aspect of predictive validity.

Additionally, Gucciardi, Gordon, and Dimmock (2009) recently developed an Australian football mental toughness inventory (afMTI). Based on their earlier work in Australian football they proposed that MT has 11 characteristics (Gucciardi et al., 2008). Their exploratory factor analysis only revealed four factors: Thrive through challenge, sport awareness, tough attitude, and desire success. Although there exploratory factor analysis only resulted in four factors the items within the afMTI were related to all 11 characteristics proposed previously. The development of this sport specific inventory is in its infancy and further studies are required to test its factor structure, psychometric properties, and predictive validity.

A significantly different approach has been adopted by Clough, Earle, and Sewell (2002). Rather than basing their model primarily on psychological skills, they attempted to build on the existing and well validated hardiness model (Kobasa, 1979). Kobasa proposed three components of hardiness (control, challenge, and commitment). Control is expressed as a tendency to feel and act as if one is influential (rather than helpful) in the face of the varied contingencies of life (Averill, 1973; Seligman, 1975; Kobasa, Maddi, and Kahn, 1982). Commitment is the tendency to involve oneself in (rather than experience alienation from) whatever one is doing or encounters. The final component of hardiness is challenge, which is expressed as the belief that change, rather than stability, is normal in life and that the anticipation of change provides incentives to grow rather than threats to security (Kobasa, Maddi, and Kahn, 1982). Crust (2008) has identified transferability as one of the key ways of judging the usefulness of concepts relating to mental toughness. Hardiness has been shown to demonstrate this, having been used in numerous settings, for example health care professionals (Topf, 1989), business executives (Kobasa, Maddi, and Kahn, 1982), public sector employees (Rush, Schoel, and Barnard, 1995) and the military (Westman, 1990).

Clough and colleagues, building on the work of Kobasa, identified a fourth component as being central to mental toughness - confidence. They therefore characterized mental toughness as having four interrelated but independent factors: (a) Control: individuals who score high on this scale feel that they are in control of their environment. Ongoing development of MTQ48 has enabled the identification of two sub-components to this scale; Emotional control and Life control. Individuals scoring highly on emotional control are better able to keep anxieties in check and are less likely to reveal their emotional state to other people. Individuals scoring higher on life control are more likely to believe that they control their lives; (b) Challenge: this describes the extent to which individuals see challenges as opportunities. Individuals who score highly on this scale will actively seek them out and will identify problems as ways for self-development; (c) Commitment: sometimes described as "stickability", this describes the ability for an individual to carry out tasks successfully despite any problems or obstacles that arise and (d) Confidence, individuals who are high in confidence have the self-belief to successfully complete tasks, which may be considered too difficult by individuals with similar abilities but with lower confidence. Again, this scale has two components; confidence in abilities and interpersonal confidence. Individuals scoring highly on confidence abilities are more likely to believe that they are a truly worthwhile person and individuals scoring higher on interpersonal confidence tend to be more assertive.

Clough et al. (2002), using their '4 C's' model, described the mental tough individual as *" tending to be sociable and outgoing as they are able to remain calm and relaxed, they are competitive in many situations and have lower anxiety levels than others. With a high sense of self-belief and an unshakeable faith that they control their own destiny, these individuals can remain relatively unaffected by competition or adversity"* (p. 38).

Clough et al. (2002) developed a 48-item, self-report questionnaire to assess the overall mental toughness of individuals; the MTQ48. It was designed to be used in sporting, occupational and educational settings. The MTQ48 has been shown to have both acceptable reliabilities (Clough et al., 2002; Nicholls, Polman, Levy, and Backhouse, 2008) and validity. Construct validity has been shown by Clough et al. (2002) and by Horsburgh, Schermer, Veselka, and Vernon (2009) who carried out both exploratory and confirmatory factor analyses on the scale. Horn (2002) has argued that validity is shown by an accumulation of evidence that the construct the questionnaire claims to measure is related to other theoretical constructs in the predicted direction. The MTQ48 has been shown to have excellent criterion related validity. It has been found to relate to pain tolerance (Crust and Clough, 2005), perceived exertion (Clough and Earle, 2001), rehabilitation adherence (Levy, Polman, Clough, Marchant, and Earle, 2006), and occurrence (Levy, Clough, Polman, Marchant, and Earle, 2005), managerial success (Marchant, Polman, Clough, Jackson, Levy, and Nicholls, 2009), leadership preferences of athletes (Crust and Azadi, in press), sporting experience (Nicholls, Polman, Levy, and Backhouse, 2009), recovery from setbacks (Clough et al., 2002), coping (Crust and Azadi, in press; Kaiseler, Polman, and Nicholls, in press; Nicholls et al., 2008 and 2009) and stressor appraisal/ coping effectiveness (Kaiseler et al., in press). Additionally, mental toughness, as operationalized by the MTQ48, has also been shown to be related to the 'Big Five' personality dimensions (Horsburgh et al., 2009), as well as more specific constructs such as optimism (Clough et al., 2002; Nicholls et al., 2009), life satisfaction, and self-efficacy (Clough et al., 2002).

Crust (2007) suggested that scholars state that mental toughness is a personality disposition. Although there is often an implicit assumption about this, it is rarely made explicit. Clough et al. (2002) do make it clear in their model that this construct is a personality trait. Support for this approach comes from a number of sources including its relationship with other personality factors (e.g. Clough et al., 2002; Horsburg et al., 2009), the finding that it does not vary from situation to situation (Crust and Azadi, in press), and the finding that it has a significant genetic component (Horsburgh et al., 2009).

Whilst it is clear that development of mental toughness can occur (e.g., Sheard and Golby, 2006), it is uncertain whether or not this a due to changes in mental toughness per se, or rather changes in individuals coping systems and techniques. The latter explanation is very similar to assertiveness training for introverts and anxiety management training for the trait anxious. It does not change the underlying nature of the individual; rather it allows them to cope more effectively with the interaction between themselves and the external environment.

Does Mental Toughness Impact on Coping?

Based on the findings from qualitative research (e.g. Jones et al., 2002; Jones et al., 2007; Bull, Shambrook, and Brooks, 2005; Thelwell, Weston, and Greenlees, 2005), which makes the implicit suggestion that coping and mental toughness are related constructs, Nicholls et al. (2008) explored the relationship between mental toughness, optimism, pessimism, and coping amongst a sample of 677 athletes. Coping was measured using the Coping Inventory for Competitive Sport (Gaudreau and Blondin, 2002). More mentally tough athletes were more likely to adopt more approach based coping strategies (mental imagery, effort expenditure, thought control, and logical analysis) and used fewer avoidance strategies (distancing, mental distraction, and resignation). They reported a differential pattern of relationships between the subscales of the MTQ48 and coping preferences. For example, lower levels of emotional control were associated with more venting of emotions, whereas higher levels of challenge was associated with greater use of mental imagery.

Crust and Azadi (in press) examined the relationship between mental toughness and athletes' use of psychological strategies, as measured by the Test of Performance Strategies (TOPS; Thomas, Murphy, and Hardy, 1999). They showed that mental toughness was related to greater use of some performance strategies in competition, namely activation, relaxation, self talk, emotional control, and goal setting. Williams and Krane (2006) identified this group of strategies as being key to peak performance. The single strongest inverse relationship was between mental toughness and negative thinking. Interestingly, Crust and Azadi also went on to consider the links between mental toughness and coping in practice contexts. Three strategies (relaxation, self talk, and emotional control) were related to mental toughness in both competition and practice environments. Clearly this shows that mental toughness does impact on which strategies are adopted, but this is not a simple relationship. It is clearly dependent on the context. Finally, Crust and Azadi investigated the relationships between the different subscales of the MTQ48 and coping. Again emotional control from the MTQ48 was linked to emotional control strategies, offering further validity evidence. The commitment component of the MTQ48 was the most clearly linked to the use of psychological performance strategies, correlating with 13 of the 16 TOPS scales. This shows that a committed individual will probably become a committed athlete, and they will have a far greater focus on the use of psychological skills. Crust and Azadi speculated that the magnitude of the relationships between the TOPS and the MTQ48 was strong evidence that the latter was not simply asset of context specific strategies.

A final study by Kaiseler et al. (in press) investigated the association between mental toughness appraisal, coping, and coping effectiveness in a sample of 482 athletes. Coping and coping effectiveness was measured using the MCOPE questionnaire. They showed that more mentally tough individuals experienced the same stressors, but that their intensity was lower. In addition, the mentally tough individual felt that they had higher levels of control over the self-reported stressful event. Similarly to the study by Nicholls et al. (2008) higher levels of mental toughness were associated with more problem-focused coping (planning, suppression of competing activities, and increasing effort), but less emotion-focused (humor, venting emotions, self-blame, and wishful thinking) and avoidance (denial and behavioral disengagement) coping. Finally, the results of this study suggest that athletes with higher mental toughness were more likely to perceive problem focused strategies to be effective and emotion focused coping to be less effective. This suggests that coping effectiveness is influenced by the coping strategy used by the mentally tough athlete. Again, this study showed the usefulness of the sub scales of the MTQ48, as they provided a much greater insight into the world of the athlete than a single measure would offer. For example, it was found that athletes with higher levels of commitment were less likely to use humor and disengagement. This chimes with the widely held view that mentally tough athletes do not easily give up and that they are unlikely to try to 'laugh things off.'

It is apparent that mental toughness has a major role to play in understanding coping. As such, it clearly demonstrates the usefulness and importance of understanding the personality of an athlete when trying to understand and improve their performance. The research on mental toughness shows that the tougher athlete will often adopt a different set of coping strategies when trying to deal with the stressors that impact on all individuals who operate in the sporting context. It is also clear that the relationship between mental toughness and coping is not a simple one. Different aspects of this broad concept influence coping in many, often subtle, ways. Additionally, observed relationships between mental toughness and coping appear to vary depending on the context.

CONCLUSION

Personality might influence either the emotional response to stressors (stress reactivity) or result in different baseline states of affectivity. It would also be important to establish whether personality influence the frequency of encountering stressful events as well as the type of event (differential exposure hypothesis; Suls, and Martin, 2005). The daily process method (DeLongis and Holtzman, 2005) might be a useful method for doing this. A significant limitation, however, is that it will be difficult to assess stressful encounters during actual competitive sporting events. The think aloud procedure (Nicholls and Polman, 2008) might be an alternative method to investigate this issue. On the whole, more sophisticated longitudinal studies are required using more advanced statistical techniques (e.g., multilevel modeling) to assess the influence of personality on the type of stressors encountered the frequency of such events, appraisal, coping, and coping effectiveness in the context of sport.

The mainstream psychological literature has suggested that higher levels of neuroticism might be associated with a negative cascade (Suls and Martin, 2005). However, as mentioned previously, it has been well reported that engagement in exercise or sport might have a number of positive psychological consequences for participants. For example, acute bouts of exercise participation are associated with improved mood, lower levels of state anxiety and lower levels of depression (e.g., Biddle and Mutrie, 2008; Biddle et al., 2000). Future research, therefore, should investigate whether such a negative cascade exists for neurotic individuals in the domain of sport or exercise participation or whether engagement in such activities might moderate affective states.

Although the MTQ48 has now been used in a number of published studies and a recent study by Horsburgh et al. (2009) suggested that the factorial structure of the instrument was acceptable, the psychometric properties of the instruments could probably be improved. Therefore studies should investigate the psychometric properties of the MTQ48 or alternative instruments that claim to measure mental toughness.

REFERENCES

Aldwin, C.M. (2007). *Stress, coping and development: An integrative perspective* (2nd ed.). New York: Guilford Press.

Allen, T.W. (1988). The cognitive bases of peak performance: A classroom intervention with student athletes. *Journal of Counselling and Development, 67*, 202-204.

Amirkham, J. H., Risinger, R. T., and Swickert, R. J. (1995). Personality and the problems of everyday life: The role of neuroticism in the exposure and reactivity to daily stressors. *Journal of Personality, 59,* 355-386.

Asendorpf, J.B., and Wilpers, S. (1998). Personality effects on social relationships. *Journal of Personality and Soical Psychology, 74*, 1531-1544.

Atkinson, J. W. (1974). The mainstream of achievement-oriented activity. In J.W. Atkinson and J.O. Raynor (Eds.), *Motivation and achievement* (pp. 13 – 41). New York: Halstead.

Averill, J.R. (1973). Personal control over aversive stimuli and its relationship to stress. *Psychological Bulletin, 80*, 286-303.

Biddle, S. J. H., and Mutrie, N. (2008). *Psychology of physical activity: Determinants, well-being and interventions* (2nd Ed.). London: Routledge.

Biddle, S.J.H., Fox, K.R., and Boutcher, S.H. (2000). *Physical activity and psychological well-being*. London: Routledge.

Bolger, N., and Zuckerman, A. (1995). A framework for studying personality in the stress process. *Journal of Personality and Social Psychology, 69*, 890-902.

Brewer, J., and Davis, J. (1995). Applied psychology of rugby league. *Sports Medicine, 13* 129-135.

Bull, S., Shambrook, C., James, W., and Brooks, J. (2005). Towards an understanding of mental toughness in elite English cricketers. *Journal of Applied Sport Psychology, 17*, 209-227.

Carver, C.S., and Scheier, M.F. (2008). *Perspectives on personality* (6th ed.). Boston: Pearson.

Carver, C. S., Scheier, M. F. and Weintraub, J. K. (1989). Assessing coping strategies: A theoretically based approach. *Journal of Personality and Social Psychology, 56,* 267-283.

Chartrand, J. M., Rose, M. L., Elliot, T. R., Marmaratosh, C., and Caldwell, S. (1993). Peeling back the onion: Personality, problem solving and career decision-making style correlates of career indecision. *Journal of Career Assessment, 1,* 66-82.

Clough, P. J., Earle, K., and Sewell, D. (2002) Mental toughness: the concept and its measurement. In I. Cockeril (ed.), *Solutions in sport psychology* (pp. 32-43). London: Thomson Publishing.

Compas, B. E., Connor-Smith, J. K., Saltzman, H., Harding Thomsen, H., and Wadsworth, M. E. (2001). Coping with stress during childhood and adolescence: Progress, problems, and potential in theory and research. *Psychological Bulletin, 127,* 87-127.

Connaughton, D., Wadey, R., Hanton, S., and Jones, G. (2008). The development and maintenance of mental toughness: Perceptions of elite performers. *Journal of Sport Sciences, 26,* 83-95.

Connor-Smith, J. K., and Flchsbart, C. (2007). Relations between Personality and Coping: A Meta-Analysis. *Journal of Personality and Social Psychology, 93,* (6), 1080-1107.

Costa, P. T., and McCrae, R. R. (1992). *Revised NEO Personality Inventory (NEO-PI-R) and NEO Five-Factor Inventory (NEO-FFI): Professional Manual.* Odessa, FL: Psychological Assessment Resources.

Costa, P. T., Somerfield, M. R., and McCrae, R. R. (1996). Personality and coping: A reconceptualization. In. M. Zeidner and N. S. Endler (Eds.), *Handbook of coping: Theory, research, applications* (pp.44-61). New York: Wiley.

Crust, L. (2008). A review and conceptual re-examination of mental toughness: Implications for future researchers. *Personality and Individual Differences, 45,* 576-583.

Crust, L. (2007). Mental toughness in sport: A review. *International Journal of Sport and Exercise Psychology, 5,* 270-290.

Crust, L., and Azadi, K. (in press) Mental toughness and athletes' use of psychological strategies. *European Journal of Sport Science.*

Crust, L., and Clough, P. J. (2005). Relationship between mental toughness and physical endurance. *Perceptual and Motor Skills, 100,* 192-194.

DeLongis, A., and Holtzman, S. (2005). Coping in context: The role of stress, social support, and personality in coping. *Journal of Personality, 73,* 1633-1656.

Derryberry, D., Reed, M.A., and Pilkenton-Taylor, C. (2003). Temperament and coping: Advantages of an individual differences perspective. *Development and Psychopathology, 15,* 1049-1066.

Dongsung, S.S., and Kang-Heon, L. (1994). A comparative study of mental toughness between elite and non-elite female athletes. *Korean Journal of Sport Science, 6,* 85-102.

Eysenck, M. (1988). Trait anxiety and stress. In S. Fisher and J. Reason (Eds.), *Handbook of life stress, cognition and health* (pp. 476 – 482). Chichester: John Wiley.

Fourie, S., and Potgieter, J. R. (2001). The nature of mental toughness in sport. *South African Journal for Research in Sport, Physical Education and Recreation, 23,* 63-72.

Gaudreau, P., and Blondin, J-P. (2002). Development of a questionnaire for the assessment of coping strategies employed by athletes in competitive sport settings. *Psychology of Sport and Exercise, 3,* 1-34.

Golby, J., and Sheard, M. (2004). Mental toughness and hardiness at different levels of rugby league. *Personality and Individual Differences, 37*, 933-942.

Gould, D., Eklund, R. C., and Jackson, S. A. (1993). Coping strategies used by US Olympic wrestlers. *Research Quarterly for Exercise and Sport, 64*, 83-93.

Gould, D., Tuffey, S., Udry, E., and Loehr, J. (1996). Burnout in competitive junior tennis players 1: A quantitative psychological assessment. *Sport Psychologist, 10*, 322-340.

Gucciardi, D.F., Gordon, S., and Dimmock, J.A. (2009). Development and preliminary validation of a mental toughness inventory for Australian football. *Psychology of Sport and Exercise, 10*, 201-209.

Gucciardi, D., Gordon, S., and Dimmock, J. (2008). Towards and understanding of mental toughness in Australian football. *Journal of Applied Sport Psychology, 20*, 261-281.

Gunthert, K. C., Cohen, L. H., and Armeli, S. (1999). The role of neuroticism in daily stress and coping. *Journal of Personality and Social Psychology, 77*, 1087-1100.

Hanrahan, S., Grove, J.R., and Lockwood, R.J. (1990). Psychological skills training for the blind athlete: A pilot program. *Adapted Physical Activity Quarterly, 7*, 143-155.

Hanton, S., and Connaughton, D. (2002). Perceived control of anxiety and its relationship to self-confidence and performance. *Research Quarterly for Exercise and Sport. 73*, 87-97.

Hanton, S., and Jones, G. (1999). The acquisition and development of cognitive skills and strategies I: Making the butterflies fly in formation. *The Sport Psychologist, 13*, 1-21.

Holahan, C.J., and Moos, R.H. (1987). Personal and contextual determinants of coping strategies. *Journal of Personality and Social Psychology, 52*, 946-955.

Hooker, K., Frazier, L. D., and Monaham, D. J. (1994). Personality and coping among caregivers of spouses with dementia. *The Gerontologist, 34*, 386-392.

Horn, T. (1992). *Advances in sport psychology*. Champaign: IL. Human Kinetics

Horsburgh, V. A., Schermer, J. A., Veselka, L., and Veron, P. A. (2009). A behavioural genetic study of mental toughness and personality. *Personality and Individual Differences, 46*, 100-105.

John, O. P. and Srivastava, S. (1999). The Big Five trait taxonomy: History, measurement, and theoretical perspective. In L.A. Pervin and O. P. John (Eds.), *Handbook of personality: Theory and research* (2nd ed., pp. 102-139). New York: Guilford Press.

Jones, G., Hanton, S., and Connaughton, D. (2007). A framework of mental toughness in the world's best performers. *The Sport Psychologist, 21*, 243-64.

Jones, G., Hanton, S. and Connaughton, D. (2002). What is this thing called mental toughness? An investigation of elite sport performers. *Journal of Applied Sport Psychology, 14*, 205-218.

Kaiseler, M., Polman, R.C.J., and Nicholls, A.R. (in press). Mental toughness, stress appraisal, coping and coping effectiveness in sport. *Personality and Individual Differences*.

Kobasa S. C. (1979). Stressful life events, personality, and health: An inquiry into hardiness. *Journal of Personality and Social Psychology, 37*, 1-11.

Kobasa, S.C., Maddi, S.R., and Kahn, S. (1982). Hardiness and health: A prospective study. *Journal of Personality and Social Psychology 42*:168-177.

Larsen, R.J., and Ketelaar, T. (1991). Personality and susceptibility to positive and negative emotional states. *Journal of Personality and Social Psychology, 61*, 132-140.

Lavallee, D., Thatcher, J., and Jones, M.V. (2004). *Coping and emotion in sport*. Hauppauge, NY: Nova Science Publishers.

Lazarus, R. S., and Folkman, S. (1984). *Stress, appraisal and coping.* New York: Springer.

Lee-Baggley, D., Preece, M., DeLongis, A. (2005). Coping with interpersonal stress: role of the big five traits. *Journal of Personality, 73,* 1141-1180.

Leventhal, E.A., Suls, J., and Leventhal, H. (1993). Hierarchical analysis of coping: Evidence from life-span studies. In H. Krohne (Ed.), *Attention and avoidance* (pp. 71-100). Seattle: Horgrefe and Huber.

Levy, A., Polman, R.C.J., Clough, P., Earle, K., and Marchant, D. (2006). Mental toughness as a determinant of beliefs, pain and adherence in sport injury rehabilitation. *Journal of Sport Rehabilitation, 15,* 246-254.

Levy, A.R., Clough, P., Polman, R., Marchant, D., and Earle, K. (2005). Mental toughness and injury occurrence in elite swimming. *Journal of Sport Sciences, 23,* 1256-1257.

Loehr, J.E. (1982). *Athletic excellence: Mental toughness training for sports.* New York: Plume.

Loehr, J. E. (1986). *Mental toughness training for sport: achieving athletic excellence.* Lexington, MA: Stephen Greene.

Marchant, D.C., Polman, R.C.J., Clough, P.J., Jackson, J.G., Levy, A.R., and Nicholls, A.R. (2009). Mental toughness: Managerial and age differences. *Journal of Managerial Psychology, 24,* 428-437.

McCrae, R. R., and Costa, P. T., (1986). Personality, coping and coping effectiveness in an adult sample. *Journal of Personality, 54,* 386-405.

McCrae, R. R., Costa, P.T., Jr., Ostendorf, F., Angleitner, A., Hrebickova, M., Avia, M. D., et al. (2000). Nature over nurture: Temperament, personality, and life span development. *Journal of Personality and Social Psychology, 78,* 173-186.

Middleton, S.C., Marsh, H.W., Martin,A.J. , Richards, G.E., Savis, J., Perry, C., et al. (2004). The Psychological Performance Inventory: Is the mental toughness test tough enough? *International Journal of Sport Psychology, 35,* 91-108.

Middleton, S.C., Marsh, H.W., Martin, A.J., Richards, G.E., and Perry, C. (2004). Developing the Mental Toughness Inventory. *Self Research Centre Biannual Conference, Berlin.*

Nicholls, A. R., and Polman, R. C. J. (2007). Coping in sport: A systematic review. *Journal of Sport Sciences, 25,* (1) 11-31.

Nicholls, A.R., and Polman, R.C.J. (2008).Think aloud: Acute stress and coping strategies during golf performances. *Anxiety Stress and Coping, 21,* 283-294.

Nicholls, A. R., and Polman, R. C.J., Levy, A. R., and Backhouse, S. (2009). Mental toughness in sport: Achievement level, gender, age, experience and sport type differences. *Personality and Individual Differences, 47,* 73-75.

Nicholls, A. R., and Polman, R. C.J., Levy, A. R., and Backhouse, S. (2008). Mental toughness, optimism, and coping among athletes. *Personality and Individual Differences, 44,* 1182-1192.

Nicholls, A., Polman, R., Levy, A., Taylor, J.A., and Cobley, S. (2007). Stressors, coping, and coping effectiveness: Gender, sport type, and level of ability differences. *Journal of Sports Sciences, 25(13),* 1521-1530.

O'Brien, T. B., and DeLongis, A. (1996). The interactional context of problem-, emotion-, and relationship-focused coping: The role of the Big Five personality types. *Journal of Personality, 64,* 775-813.

Roesch, S. C., Wee, C., and Vaughn, A. A. (2006). Relations between the Big Five personality traits and dispositional coping in Korean Americans: Acculturation as a moderating factor. *International Journal of Psychology, 41*, 85-96.

Rush, M.C., Schoel, W.A., and Barnard, S.M. (1995). Psychological resiliency in the public sector: Hardiness and pressure for change. *Journal of Vocational Behavior, 46*, 17-39.

Seligman, M.E.P. (1975). *Helplessness.* San Francisco: Freeman.

Semmer, S.K. (2006). Personality, stress, and coping. In M.E. Vollrath (Ed.), *Handbook of personality and health* (pp. 73-113). Chichester: John Wiley.

Sheard, M., and Goldby, J. (2006). Effect of psychological skills training program on swimming performance and positive psychological development. *International Journal of Sport and Exercise Psychology, 2,* 7-24

Suls, J., and David, J.P. (1996). Coping and personality: Third time's the charm? *Journal of Personality, 64*, 993-1005.

Suls, J., and Martin, R. (2005). The daily life of the garden-variety neurotic: Reactivity, stressor exposure, mood spillover, and maladaptive coping. *Journal of Personality, 73*, 1485-1509.

Thelwell, R., Weston, N., and Greenlees, I. (2005). Defining and understanding mental toughness within soccer. *Journal of Applied Sport Psychology, 17*, 326-332.

Topf, M. (1989). Personality hardiness, occupational stress, and burnout in critical care nurses. *Research in Nursing and Health, 12*, 179-186.

Vollrath, M., Banholzer, E., Caviezel, C., Fischli, C. and Jurgo, D. (1994). Coping as a mediator or moderator of personality in mental health? In. B. De Radd, W. K. B. Hofstee, and G. L. M. Van Heck (Eds.), *Personality Psychology in Europe, Vol. 5* (pp.262-273). Tilburg, The Netherlands: Tilburg University Press.

Watson, D., and Hubbard, B. (1996). Adaptional style and dispositional structure: Coping in the context of the Five-Factor model. *Journal of Personality, 64*, 737-774.

Westman, M. (1990). The relationship between stress and performance: The moderating effect of hardiness. *Human Performance, 3*, 141-155.

Williams, J., and Krane, V. (2006). Psychological characteristics of peak performance. In J. M. Williams (Ed.), *Applied sport psychology: Personal growth to peak performance* (5th ed., pp. 207-227). Mountain View, CA: Mayfield.

Zautra, A.J., Affleck, G.G., Tennen, H., Reich, J.W., and Davis, M.C. (2005). Dynamic approaches to emotion and stress in everyday life: Bolger and Zuckerman reloaded with positive as well as negative affects. *Journal of Personality, 73*, 1511-1538.

In: Coping in Sport: Theory, Methods, and Related Constructs   ISBN: 978-1-60876-488-4
Editor: Adam R. Nicholls   © 2010 Nova Science Publishers, Inc.

Chapter 9

COPING WITH ANXIETY IN SPORT

Yuri L. Hanin

KIHU-Research Institute for Olympic Sports, Finland

ABSTRACT

This chapter describes an individualized and evidence-based approach to coping with anxiety in high-achievement sport. The Individual Zones of Optimal Functioning (IZOF) model as applied to pre-competition anxiety (Hanin, 1978, 1995) and performance-related emotions (Hanin, 2000, 2004, 2007) is used as a framework to examine the relationship between *anxiety* and *emotion-focused* and *action-focused coping*. Anxiety is emotional experience (state-like, trait-like and meta-experience) and a component of *psychobiosocial* state which can be described along five basic dimensions: form, content, intensity, context and time. Individually optimal intensity of anxiety is used as criterion to evaluate if the current and anticipated anxiety should be reduced, increased, or maintained at a level that is optimal for the individual. Guidelines for *anxiety-centered* coping are proposed with the emphasis on emotion- and action-focused strategies that affect situational emotional experiences accompanying performance. The Identification-Control-Correction (ICC) program (Hanin and Hanina, 2009a,b) provides the step-wise procedures to optimize the process of task execution. Successful action-focused coping is reflected in emotion dynamics signaling a shift from the dysfunctional to functionally optimal person-environment (P-E) interactions. Both *reactive* and *anticipatory* coping strategies are relevant to achieve an optimal balance between current (or anticipated) task demands and personal resources. Future research should focus on coping with trait-like emotional experiences, meta-experiences, anticipatory coping, and the role of change and change management in coping.

INTRODUCTION

To understand coping and to evaluate its effectiveness, we need to know *what the person is coping with* (Lazarus and Folkman, 1984, p. 141) and how does the target of coping affect the process of coping. What is the interplay between emotion and coping as a critical factor in determining an athlete's potential success in competitive sport (Thatcher, Lavallee, and Jones,

2004, p. 5)? These questions are considered in this chapter from the perspective of the Individual Zones of Optimal Functioning (IZOF) model which was initially proposed to examine pre-competition anxiety (Hanin, 1978, 1995) and later elaborated for research of emotion-performance relationships in sport (Hanin, 1997, 2000, 2004, 2007).

I believe that effective coping requires individual-oriented idiographic approach and the process perspective (Lazarus and Folkman, 1984, see Nicholls and Polman, 2007 for a systematic review). Research shows that negatively-toned emotions are not always detrimental to athletic performance and positively-toned emotions (such as being self-confident or being pleased) are not always beneficial for all performers (see for reviews Hanin, 1997, 2000, 2004, 2007; Hanin and Syrjä, 1995, 1996; Harmison, 2006; Robazza, 2006; Ruiz, 2004a,b). Therefore, although state anxiety is the main focus in this chapter, coping with negatively-toned and positively-toned emotions that affect performance process are also examined. Emotion-performance relationships are bi-directional: pre-event emotions have either beneficial or detrimental impact on performance and on-going performance process affects mid-event and post-event emotional experiences. Accordingly, two groups of coping strategies are identified. *Emotion-focused* coping aims to manage (master, reduce, or tolerate – Folkman and Lazarus, 1985, p. 152) discrete emotions or global affect; whereas in *action-focused* coping, the athlete's focus is on the optimization of task execution process (Hanin and Hanina, 2009a, b). If the athlete is coping with a single emotion (anxiety, anger, or complacency), the term "centered" is appropriate for instance, *anxiety-centered* coping).

Change Management and Coping

High-achievement sport is a special setting with constant changes and the need for change management. That makes it a very special environment for the study of stress and stress-induced emotions like anxiety. In fact, "the essence of stress, coping, and adaptation is change… and unless we focus on change we cannot learn how people come to manage stressful events and conditions… (Folkman and Lazarus, 1985, p. 150).

Top-level athletes need to be ready for constant change and change management. Coping with anxiety is actually coping with change. Potential gain and loss are behind all stress-induced emotional experiences (Lazarus, 2000).

There are certain myths about change: all changes are quick, painless, cost nothing, and have the same meaning for all people involved. Actually the opposite is true: the change requires time; it is often very painful and may cost a lot; finally, change has different meaning for different people. Change is difficult for people because it requires individuals to find new ways of doing things; change creates uncertainty and requires additional work. Successful change is impossible without adjustment; behind almost all changes is additional demand on available resources leading to either loss or gain of an athlete's own resources.

A four-stage model of change proposed in organizational setting (Scott and Jaffe, 1989), which is relevant for anxiety-centered coping, is based on distinction between different emotions of people going through change process. These stages include *denial, resistance, exploration (or search), and active involvement*. Interestingly, anxiety can be observed in people not only in denial and resistance stages but also in exploration and commitment stages.

THE IZOF MODEL AS A FRAMEWORK FOR ANXIETY-CENTERED COPING

The IZOF model, developed in the naturalistic setting of elite sport, holds that emotion is a component of the psychobiosocial state conceptualized as a situational, multi-modal and dynamic manifestation of the total human functioning (Hanin, 1997, 2000). There are several empirically supported assumptions in the IZOF model that are relevant for emotion-focused and action-focused coping. For instance, each athlete has individually optimal anxiety level (high, moderate, or low; Hanin, 1978, 1986) and a constellation of individually optimal and dysfunctional emotion content, described by athlete-generated idiosyncratic markers (Hanin, 1997, 2000). The notion of optimal intensity zones reflects individual differences within athletes' ability to recruit and utilize efficiently available resources. Optimal pleasant and unpleasant emotions indicate availability of basic and emergency resources and their effective recruitment and utilization by producing energising and organising effects. In contrast, dysfunctional unpleasant and pleasant emotions reflect a lack of resources or their inefficient recruitment and utilization resulting in dis-energising and dis-organising effects of emotions upon performance.

Based on extensive studies of pre-competition anxiety and observations of elite athletes, a program for individualized intervention to optimize pre-competition anxiety was proposed and used in applied work with elite rowers and weightlifters (Hanin, 1980, 1986). Specifically, this intervention included: retrospectively establishing optimal anxiety level and zones; assessing actual and anticipated pre-start anxiety and attitudes towards competition 5-7 days prior to competition; comparing anticipated and actual (current) anxiety with pre-established optimal intensity; and managing (reducing, maintaining or increasing) anxiety level to help athletes enter and stay in the their optimal intensity zones. Annesi's (1998) intervention study with three skilled tennis players was one of the first well documented intervention investigations examining the efficacy of the selected principles of the IZOF model. Annesi identified the optimal zones using the Competitive State Anxiety Inventory-2 (CSAI-2; Martens, Burton, Vealey, Bump, and Smith, 1990) and taught athletes to enter their zones in order to enhance their performance during the season. However, his study was limited to the assessments of pre-competition anxiety using CSAI-2 and to the application of researcher-generated self-regulation strategies, which are sometimes ineffective or even inappropriate for individual performers. For instance, Murphy and Jowdy (1992) reported a case of an athlete who was requested to focus on a bright metal ball to concentrate better but when the athlete tried to use this cue the ball "exploded."

These concerns were addressed by assessing anxiety, positively-toned emotions, negatively-toned emotions, and somatic symptoms using athlete-generated idiosyncratic descriptors (Robazza, Pellizzari, and Hanin, 2004). These investigators also identified self-regulation strategies that the athletes used in their best performances and how they coped with difficult performance situations. Other studies also provided support of the effectiveness of individualized approach to emotion-focused coping (Minouchi, 2006; Robazza, Bortoli, and Nougier 2000, 2002).

Performance-Related Anxiety

State anxiety is defined as "a temporal cross-section in the conscious stream-of-life of a person consisting of subjective feelings of *worry, tension, nervousness, and apprehension* accompanied by the arousal of autonomic nervous system "(Spielberger, Gorsuch and Lushene, 1970). Similarly, Lazarus provides a detailed description of many faces of anxiety as unique existential emotion: "Synonyms for anxiety include *apprehension, unease, concern, and worry*... When we are anxious, we are *unable to relax*. We experience the sense that *something wrong* in the situation or in our lives. We are *uneasy, worry*, are *troubled* with *intrusive thoughts* that we cannot put to rest, and we want to *avoid or escape* from upcoming *confrontations* that are the concrete manifestations of our concern. Anxiety in many respects a unique emotion. Its dramatic plot is an *uncertain threat* (Lazarus and Lazarus, 1994, p. 46-47, italics added). These "feeling state" definitions of anxiety suggest that it is associated with person's ill-being poor wellbeing) with the implication that anxiety should be always reduced (Diener, 2000; Emmons and Diener, 1985). However, research shows that functionally high anxiety (Oatley and Jenkins, 1992) especially in top-level sport is often beneficial for athletic performance (Hanin, 1978; 1995; Mahoney and Avenir, 1977; Raglin, 1992; Raglin and Hanin, 2000).

Anxiety as Emotional Experience

The definition of anxiety as an emotional stress-induced reaction captures only one aspect of the person-environment (P-E) relationships. According to Vygotsky (1926/1984), to study something as an *indivisible whole (entirety),* it is necessary to use a construct that captures the characteristics of both interacting elements. In psychology, P-E interactions can be explored by examining the *experience* relating to a person's attitude towards their environment and exploring the meaning of environment for this person. Experience also has a biosocial orientation and is best represented as a unit of consciousness. Thus the analysis of any difficult situation should focus not so much on the situation or on person per se but on how *a particular* situation is *experienced* by *a particular* person.

Coping processes are centered on performance-related *experience* which is a component of the total human functioning that reflects the nature of past, on-going, or anticipated P-E interactions. The P-E interactions, as relationships between task demands (constraints) and a person's resources, include predominance of an organism over environment, the balance between person and environment, and the predominance of environment over an organism. Performance-related anxiety usually reflects disrupted P-E relationship when task demands are perceived as taxing or exceeding the person's resources (Lazarus, 1991, Vygotsky, 1926/1984). According to Vygotsky's suggestion, situational emotions are construed as reflecting the dynamics P-E interactions. From this perspective, coping as a goal-oriented activity involves "constantly changing cognitive and behavioral *efforts* to manage specific external and/or internal demands that are appraised as taxing or exceeding the resources of the person"... (Lazarus and Folkman, 1984, p. 141).

Anxiety as State-Like, Trait-Like and Meta-Experience

Three types of interrelated experiences include: *state-like, trait-like,* and *meta-experiences. State-like* experience of anxiety describes how tense, nervous, uncertain or worried the athlete was in a specific situation perceived as threatening. The intensity of this experience varies greatly across different athletes in the same situation and across different situations in the same athlete. *Trait-like* experiences of anxiety are relatively stable patterns of typical (habitual) emotional response by the athlete in similar situations. Trait anxiety indicates how often the athlete experiences elevated anxiety and feels nervous, tense or apprehensive prior to or during competition. *Meta-experiences* characterize the person's awareness of harmful or helpful effects of anxiety upon performance and his or her attitudes and preferences for high or low anxiety (Hanin, 2004, 2007; Mayer and Stevens, 1994). As lessons learned by athletes who will have experienced in different performance situations, meta-experiences determine appraisal and re-appraisal of performance situations and a choice of coping strategies that are deployed.

Implications for coping. The distinction between state-trait-meta experiences is helpful in selection of effective coping strategies. First, state-like anxiety levels (actual, optimal, dysfunctional, and anticipated) and intensity zones can be identified. Second, trait-like anxiety is assessed to estimate if the existing patterns can be potential barriers to anxiety management (old habits in emotional response). Finally, meta-anxiety as attitudes about experiencing anxiety ("worrying about worrying") determines the need to manage this response to avoid its potential detrimental effect on appraisals and re-appraisals.

Multidimensionality of Anxiety and Coping

Five basic dimensions posited in the IZOF model describe the defining characteristics of state-like experiences as a component of psychobiosocial (PBS) performance-related state (Hanin, 2000, 2003). Thus anxiety as emotional experience is always manifested in some *form* (subjectively perceived or observable); it has specific *content* (or quality); it is characterized quantitatively and qualitatively by its intensity; and as a process emotion unfolds over *time* (Folkman and Lazarus, 1985) in a particular *context* (in practices or competitions). The following sections examine how state-like anxiety can affect the coping process.

Form dimension. This suggests that state anxiety is manifested in affective modality related to several other components of psychobiosocial state. These component labels with selected descriptors include *cognitive* (alert, focused, confused, distracted), *affective* (worried, nervous, happy, angry, joyful, fearful), *motivational* (motivated, willing, desirous, interested), *volitional* (determined, brave, daring, persistent), *bodily* (tired, jittery, restless, sweaty, painless, breathless), *motor-behavioral* (sluggish, relaxed, sharp), *operational* (smooth, effortless, easy, clumsy actions), and *communicative* (connected, related, in touch) modalities. The validity of these assumptions regarding multimodal description of PBS states were tested empirically in different sports (Bortoli, Bertollo, and Robazza, 2009; Bortoli and Robazza, 2007; Hanin and Stambulova, 2002; Ruiz and Hanin, 2004 a, b; Würth and Hanin, 2005).

Implications for coping. A coping process can include different modalities of the PBS state and should not be limited to "cognitive and behavioral" efforts. Thus form-based coping efforts may include motivation-centered, volition-centered, bodily-centered, action-centered, and communication-centered strategies. Obviously, anxiety-centered coping will impact not only affective modality (other emotions) but also the concomitants of anxiety as a component of the PBS state. Therefore, in coping, it is useful to identify the target modality and how it interacts with other components of the PBS state.

Anxiety Content Dimension

Qualitatively, the content of anxiety as a negatively-toned emotional experience can be described either by researcher-generated labels from available anxiety scales or by using idiosyncratic (athlete-generated) markers. For instance, Spielberger et al., (1970) subscale of the State-Trait-Anxiety Inventory (STAI) includes the following "anxiety present" items as synonyms of anxiety: *tense, strained, upset, worrying, frightened, nervous, jittery, indecisive, worried,* and *confused*. Interestingly, "anxiety-absent" subscale was also used in assessments of anxiety and it included "self-confidence" and "complacency" items (*calm, secure, at ease, satisfied, comfortable, self-confident, relaxed, content, steady,* and *pleasant*).

In high achievement sport, the individual-oriented approach is especially relevant and the content of emotional experiences is categorized within the framework of two related factors: functioning (success-failure) and feeling (good-bad). The four derived categories include *success-related* functionally *optimal* pleasant (P+) and unpleasant (N+) emotions and *failure-related* dysfunctional unpleasant (N-) and pleasant (P-) emotions. These four categories help to identify the idiosyncratic labels of emotional experiences relevant for performance and reflecting the readiness to perform from an athlete's perspective (Hanin, 1997, 2000).

This emotion content categorization concurs well with Folkman and Lazarus's (1985) suggestion to group 15 discrete emotions into four appraisal categories. Anticipatory category includes *threat* emotions (worried, fearful, and anxious) and *challenge* emotions (confident, hopeful, and eager); whereas outcome category includes *harm* emotions (angry, sad, disappointed, guilty, and disgusted) and *benefit* emotions (exhilarated, pleased, happy, and relieved).

Apparently, pre-competitive anxiety falls mainly into anticipatory (threat emotion) category. The mid-event and post-event experiences include intermediate or final outcome emotion (harm or benefit emotions) category.

At different stages of performance process (preparation, task execution, evaluation) a constellation of different emotions is experienced. The anticipatory category (P+ challenge emotions and N+ threat emotions) is functionally optimal prior to and during performance. In contrast, the outcome-related category (N- harm emotions and P- benefit emotions), is apparently optimal in post-performance situations, but is dysfunctional (distracting attentional resources) prior to or during performance.

Implications for coping. Research could benefit from idiosyncratic description of anxiety content by compiling researcher-generated labels from existent anxiety scales and athlete-generated markers. In anxiety-centered coping, assessment of emotions other than anxiety is also recommended to capture the impact of different anticipatory and outcome emotions.

Anxiety Intensity Dimension

High inter-individual variability of optimal anxiety suggests that individual-oriented assessments and coping are preferable to group-oriented approaches. Research shows that about 65 percent of athletes perform well if their anxiety level is either high or low (see Hanin, 1980, 1995; Jokela and Hanin, 1999; Raglin and Hanin, 2000 for review). The "in-out of zone" notion describes anxiety-performance relationships at the individual level and suggests that optimal intensity of anxiety (high, moderate, or low) produces beneficial effect on individual performance (Hanin, 1978, 1995). Athletes perform up to their potential if their actual anxiety is within the earlier established optimal zones of intensity. If an athlete's actual anxiety state is out of her optimal zone, she is likely to perform below her potential.

Implications for coping. Anxiety as unpleasant emotional state seems to require reduction or minimization to enhance subjective well-being (Hammons and Diener, 1985). However, from the functioning perspective, in high-achievement sport, individually optimal intensity of anxiety can be high, moderate or low in different athletes. Thus current anxiety in athletes should be increased, decreased or maintained at individually optimal level. The direction of coping (intended impact) is based on the comparison between individually optimal zones and actual level of intensity. Individualized coping aims not only to help an athlete enter (or re-enter) the optimal zones (high, moderate, low), but also to stay away from the dysfunctional zones by keeping the intensity of performance-impairing emotions at a low level of intensity. Finally, research involving multi-event sports (Hanin, 1983) suggests that, for instance, the gymnast or decathlete may have different optimal anxiety within different events. More research is warranted to estimate if these differences are related to task demands, athlete's resources, or to the athlete's readiness for competition.

Time Dimension

Time dimension includes *topological* (phases, cycles, sequencing, and periodicity) and *metric* (duration, frequency) characteristics of anxiety and other emotional experiences. Short-term dynamics involves changes in emotion content and intensity across three stages of athletic performance: pre-event preparation, task execution, and post-event evaluation.

In pre-, mid-event situations the *anticipatory* pleasant (P+ challenge) and unpleasant (N+ threat) emotions are usually optimal for athletic performance, whereas *outcome* pleasant (P- complacency) and unpleasant (N- dejection) emotions are harmful and dysfunctional (Hanin, 2000). In post-performance situations outcome emotions are optimal unless they carry-over excessive complacency or disappointment as a spill-over effect to the forthcoming competition or competition-extraneous context (Cerin and Barnett, in press; Hanin, 2004). Similarly, high anxiety prior to and during performance can be beneficial for some athletes but detrimental in post-performance situations, if it disturbs recovery. On the other hand, there is a special need to cope with positively-toned emotions: pre-event complacency is usually detrimental; whereas elevated challenge emotions in post-performance situations may sometimes deplete available resources.

Implications for coping. The coping process should consider the role of temporal patterns in emotion-performance relationships. It is expected that the content and intensity of optimal and dysfunctional emotions change over time. Therefore, in emotion-focused coping one should be consider the patterns of emotions in pre-task, mid-task and post-task stages of performance process and also the transition patterns of appraisals between these three stages. In the case of anxiety-centered coping, the focus should be on anxiety and also on related emotional experiences. It is also important to distinguish between *reactive* (immediate) coping aiming to manage current emotions and actions and *anticipatory* coping focused on what can possibly happen.

Context Dimensions

Context dimension is an environmental characteristic of the impact of situational, interpersonal, intra-group, and organizational factors on emotion intensity and content (Hanin, 1989, 1992; Nicholls and Polman, 2007). Emotional experiences of varying form, content and intensity are usually observed in different settings (context). Situational impact is manifested in emotional experiences triggered in practices and competitions by athletes' anticipated or real contacts and interactions with significant others (a partner, a coach, and team-mates). Context dimension also includes culturally coded and culturally determined beliefs of participants about expected impact of specific emotions on their performance and about the rules of emotion display (expression or suppression) in a particular sub-culture.

Current research in sport psychology examines several contexts including successful and unsuccessful competitions of varying significance (local, national, or international), and different practice sessions. Additionally, a number of individually difficult situations or specific performance episodes may have a special meaning for athletes and the teams (weather conditions, competition sites, good and bad memories of past performances). These situations may also include qualifications, performance in the finals, play-offs, competing against a "weaker" opponent; and performing after repeated success or a series of slumps.

Implications for coping. Contrasting interpersonal and intra-group anxiety with individually optimal performance-related anxiety can be helpful in the selection of coping strategies. Based on this information, a focused supportive group environment or stressful situations could be created to reinforce required optimal regimens of communication in the group/team (see Hanin, 1978, 1989, 1992 for review). For instance, the stress caused by negative feedback from the coach may facilitate sometimes coping with the players' excessive complacency prior to or during important games. A target of emotion-focused coping is usually performance-related emotional experiences (state-like, trait-like or meta-experiences).

Individually optimal and dysfunctional feeling states are identified and contrasted with the anticipated and actual emotional states. Based on this comparison, emotion regulation is undertaken with two criteria to evaluate the effectiveness of coping: a change in the intensity and content of emotional state and its expected impact on performance. Obviously, coping targeted to optimize emotion-performance relationship involves both emotion-focused and action-focused coping strategies. In this approach, expert athletes' subjective experiences and their performance history are the main source of information for the selection of appropriate coping strategies (see, for instance, Appendix 1).

ACTION-FOCUSED COPING WITH ANXIETY

By definition, action-focused coping deals usually with a *task execution* or *performance process* involving the athlete's actions or a movement sequence ("chain") performed in competition. Inconsistency of athletic performance due to the unexpected technical difficulties is manifested in (a) *instability of technique* and a failure to consistently deliver expected results; (b) a sudden "*breakdown*" (or a "*loss*") of skill; and (c) "*habitual*" performance *errors* under competitive stress. Performance difficulties in top-level athletes are often related to changes in preparation, technique, coaching staff, etc. Athletes experience serious difficulties in dealing with these situations. For instance, the Olympic-level athlete was amazed and disappointed: "… my discus just did not fly, although my strength level is higher than ever. Everything should be OK but for some reasons the results are simply not there… ". Other quotes tell the same story: "I don't know how or why it happened", "something happened to my technique", "whatever I tried did not help", "I tried too much", "my focus was not clear", "I was distracted by irrelevant details", etc. These comments suggest that the athletes are not in control of performance and cannot manage the action process. Poor results, especially in competitions, trigger harm emotions (anger, disappointment, guilt, and sadness). These negatively-toned stress emotions shift to anticipatory threat emotions (anxiety, fear, and worry) about forthcoming competitions and this vicious circle goes on. Interestingly, athletes often complain about excessive pre-competition anxiety, fear, or a lack of self-confidence as a problem and a cause of their underperformance.

This is a typical situation when performance disruption is a primary problem leading to emotional distress (a secondary problem). Emotion-focused coping using conventional mental skills programs may temporally improve the situation, especially during practices but not during competitions. Action-focused coping would be the best option in this situation but, it is athletes and coaches as expert performers who traditionally are dealing with physical, technical, and tactical aspects of preparation.

A general framework for action-focused coping with performance difficulties and related emotions across different sports would be helpful to enhance a cooperation between sport psychologists, athletes, and coaches.

Such a framework was developed and tested in multiple case-studies in athletics (jumping, throwing, and running), swimming, diving, car racing, pistol shooting, volley-ball, and soccer. This new sports-specific research-based psycho-pedagogical program (termed *Identification-Control-Correction – ICC* program) is an extension of the IZOF model and deals mainly with performance difficulties in top-level athletes.

The ICC program includes identification of individually optimal performance, control and monitoring of performance in practices and competitions, and correction of habitual errors. In the sections that follow, a brief overview of the assessment procedures employed in the ICC program is provided. The entire approach is described in more details elsewhere (Hanin and Hanina, 2009a,b; Hanin and Hanina, 2006; Hanin, Korjus, Jouste, and Baxter, 2002).

Identification of Individually Optimal Performance

In the identification of individually optimal performance, the athlete constructs an image of the motor task in her sport as a chain of interrelated action components. For instance, the Olympic level diver described a forward dive in pike position with 2.5 somersaults (105B) as a sequence of eight action components: *forward approach, pre-jump (hurdle), take off, throw the arms forward, pike down, line up and water entry* (see Hanin and Hanina, 2009 b, pp. 89-91 for details).

A list of self-generated task components serves as a starting point for reflection to increase conceptual (self-knowledge) and physical (bodily) awareness of the optimal movement pattern. Optimal execution of each component in the chain (movement sequence) is then described with accompanying experiences. To identify and enhance an athlete's awareness of optimal and non-optimal movement patterns and to examine the differences between successful and unsuccessful task executions, athlete selects seven personally best and seven poor task executions in their specific event. Self-ratings help the athlete to learn the rating procedure and see if a draft of the initially selected components works well in self-descriptions. Usually self-ratings of 10-15 task executions are sufficient to make an athlete aware of effects of different components on performance outcomes and how these components affect each other. Athletes also begin to understand how their different foci affect performance (Rantanen, Hanin, and Hanina, 2007).

By the end of the action identification, athletes have a clear picture of the components of the chain and understand the role of optimal difference in intensity of effort (starting and final). Athletes are also aware of the variability ranges of each component in their good and poor performances. This analysis is complete when an athlete can report how he or she perceives the process of the task execution and thus the conceptual (self-knowledge) awareness of the skill is achieved. Additionally, an athlete acquires a new understanding of why he or she is successful or unsuccessful in the task execution.

In the previous example, the diver realized that the take off was the core component of the dive affecting the entire performance process and final results. However, if this new self-knowledge has been acquired without a learning trial session (see later), the athlete can suddenly "forget" his right focus under pressure. The diver's case illustrates this situation. His dive in the semi-finals was evaluated 10 points less than in the qualification and the athlete did not make it to the Olympic finals;

> I can do this dive quite well but I focused on wrong things. I can blame only myself. I focused on rotation but forgot to focus on the pre-jump which is the most important element for the good take off... In the air, I felt like I would fall in a tuck bomb on my neck. I did all that was possible to do in the air. But an error happened in the pre-jump and this disrupted the rhythm of my dive and water entry was spoiled (Hanin and Hanina, 2009 b, p.85)

Physical awareness of the most important components of the task is acquired in "vivo" practice where self-ratings follow immediately after an athlete's actual performance attempts. Following this procedure, self-ratings are performed during normal training session for 15 selected task executions (five series with three execution attempts in each series). In each of the four series, an athlete explores the impact of different foci which he or she used in previous successful performances. In the 5th series, the athlete attempts to achieve the best total results by deliberately using the focus that worked best in the four previous series.

In this enhancing awareness session, coach provides the feedback only after the self-ratings of the athlete who now attends to most essential aspects of performance and relies more on her own perceptions. In enhancing the athletes' conceptual and physical awareness of optimal movement pattern it is important that they focus on the entire movement sequence or a chain of components and their interaction. When the number of performance attempts is limited (as in pole-vaulting or ski-jumping), it is recommended to use imagery as a supplement or a substitute of physical performance attempts.

Control and Monitoring

Control and monitoring in the ICC-program are the natural extension of the identification of the individually optimal performance. The main goal here is to standardize the interactions between components within their optimal ranges. An athlete focuses more on the interaction between the key components of the task and consequently, the athlete's performance becomes more consistent and average results usually improve. Control and monitoring involve a deliberate and step-wise practice of the entire chain of optimal movement patterns from the first component to the last component of the chain. The goal of training is that an athlete deliberately *improves* only the first component in the chain. At the same time it is estimated how this improvement affects other components of the chain and the final results. It usually takes one practice per week for working on each chain component. Successful task execution helps to estimate the role of the first component and to identify most sensitive (variable) core components of the chain and their interaction during the deliberate control of the task execution. Control and monitoring are recommended to be used during the preparatory period and during competition season.

Standardization of between-Component Interaction

After the improvement of the first component in movement sequence, the next session is devoted to controlling the second component and then the subsequent components (one practice per each component). As a result, a movement pattern is constructed with improved control of the entire task execution. Control of each component affects the quality and the variability of each component and interaction between the chain components. Standardization of interaction between the components of the chain is manifested in the optimal effort intensity ratio (the difference between start and finish effort intensity) and in the right focus on 1-2 most important components of the chain. Under optimal conditions of practices, the standardization of movement pattern is reflected in the reduction of within-component and between-component variability. Deliberate control in this case is a series of shifts from the first component of the chain to the subsequent component. Control is exploratory in that the athlete performs and reflects on her experiences with a special reference to most effective focus and effort intensity. The main emphasis in control is on trying to influence a selected chain component and to enhance awareness of how it affects other components and the total outcomes of task execution. All this is expected to empower the athlete to influence the task execution process and the final results.

Competition Pattern and Skill Stabilization

Control and monitoring stage increases conceptual and physical self-awareness of skilled performances. It also demonstrates the athlete's action readiness to consistently perform up to her potential under optimal (and relatively stable) conditions of practices. Usually control and monitoring is completed when an athlete has created a competition pattern including effective focus, optimal ratio of effort intensity and 1-2 core chain components affecting the final results. This standardized pattern of individually optimal technique enables the athlete to free her attentional resources and to attend better to the external conditions. This information is necessary for the development of the concise *competition model* with a smaller number of movement components. Obviously, the *competition model* for effective control of individual performance is based on the image of optimal performances. However, it is also useful to examine ineffective performances to identify habitual errors and their causes usually including confusion, wrong or ineffective focus, inability to re-focus, or trying too much.

The identification and control aim to optimize performance under favorable conditions of practices with the minimum of external and internal distractions. The new or optimal skill pattern should be also stabilized under different conditions of competition which is an important and separate task. For this purpose, a shortened list of the task chain components including focus, optimal effort intensity, and 1-2 key components are used. Finally, during the control and monitoring, mastering each chain component is usually accompanied by the increase of the athlete's self-confidence, feeling of being more in control of own performance, and increased motivation. Anxiety originally triggered by uncertainty and low-self-awareness disappears. In other words, earlier inadequate emotions (anticipatory and outcome) become more optimal and reflect improvement in task execution process.

Correction of Habitual Performance Errors

The application of the Old Way-New Way for a rapid correction of habitual performance errors (Lyndon, 1989, 2000) with top-level athletes within the framework of the ICC program suggests that the method can also be effective in sport. However, several conceptual and practical aspects reflecting the specifics of expert performance in high-achievement setting should be considered. Firstly, in error analysis (Old Way), a concept of task components and the chain of components (Bernstein, 1947) are used to describe the athletes' subjective perceptions of their performance. Secondly, an error can be either a component of the chain or an interaction between the components and it is best identified under competitive stress or when an athlete deliberately tries too much in practices. Finally, an error analysis involves examination of personally best and worst performance to identify individually optimal and non-optimal performance (Identification stage of the ICC program).

An athlete's individual resources (strengths) are considered to identify an individually optimal movement pattern (New Way). In several cases, prior to change (pattern substitution), an athlete may need additional practice to learn this new movement pattern. New Way as the individually best pattern should be clearly identified by an athlete and a coach. It is not recommended to initiate a change in performance until both agree on why the selected New Way is the best available option. After a skill correction using the standard learning trial procedure to cope with proactive inhibition has been done, several practices should be conducted to make sure that this new skill is standardized in practices and stabilized (Bernstein, 1947) in competitions.

CONCLUSION

This chapter examined how anxiety-centered coping in sport is affected by the defining characteristics of state anxiety from the individualized perspective. However, in anxiety-centered coping, the athletes are dealing not only with competition anxiety but with other performance-related negatively-toned and positively-toned emotions, and actions. It is well known that emotion-focused coping affects not only emotions (anxiety, anger, self-confidence), but also the task execution, whereas action-focused coping produces a substantial change in the athlete's emotional state. Therefore, coping in sport should focus on emotion-performance relationship rather than separately on emotions and actions. Unfortunately, a large gap still exists between sport psychology practice that generally deals mainly with mental and emotional aspects of performance and athletes and coaches who focus exclusively on performance process. Action-focused coping using a framework of psycho-pedagogical ICC program offers an alternative approach for solving a host of performance-related and emotional problems faced by expert performers. Future research and practice should address several promising areas related to coping in sport. These may include coping with trait-like emotional experiences (habits in emotional behavior), meta-experiences, anticipatory coping, and the role of change and change management in coping.

APPENDIX 1.

Individualized emotion profiling for Coping and

1. How do you feel right now and why?
    a.   learning the assessment procedure
    b.   assessing the athlete's self-awareness

2. How did you feel prior to your best performance(s) (single or repeated - P+N+)?
    a.   re-activating positive experiences, strengths-based emphasis
    b.   predominant patterns – positive or negative or both (P+ N+)

3. Why did you feel this way? Thoughts and feelings at the moment?
    a.   ability for self-reflection and self-analysis
    b.   effective focus prior to competition

4. How did you feel prior to your worst performance(s) (single or repeated – N- P-)?

    a.   Minimizing significance and possible impact of negativity

    b.   re-activating negative experiences, weaknesses not important

    c.   predominant pattern – positive or negative or both (N- or P-)

5.   Why did you feel this way? Thoughts and feelings at the moment?

    a.   ability for self-reflection and self-analysis

    b.   ineffective pre-competition focus

6.   How do you feel about feeling nervous, tense prior to competition?

    a.   Meta-experiences: What does this feeling tell you?

    b.   How can you read your body signals?

7.   Anticipated and optimal emotion intensity (and content)

    a.   Direction of coping (decreasing or increasing emotion intensity)

    b.   A need to affect other form modalities (motivation, cognition, bodily)

REFERENCES

Annesi, J.J. (1998). Applications of the individual zones of optimal functioning model for the multimodal treatment of pre-competitve anxiety. *Sport Psychologist, 12*, 300-316.

Bernstein, N.A. (1947). *O postroyenii dvizheniy* (On Construction of Movements). Moscow, USSR: MEDGIZ Publishers. (In Russian).

Bortoli, L, Bertollo, M., Robazza, C. (2009). Dispositional goal orientations, motivational climate, and psychobiosocial states in youth sport. *Personality and Individual Differences, 47*, 18-24.

Bortoli, L., and Robazza, C. (2007). Dispositional goal orientations, motivational climate, and psychobiosocial states in physical education. In L. A. Chiang (Ed.), Motivation of exercise and physical activity (pp. 119-133). New York: Nova Science Publishers.

Cerin, E. and Barnett, A. (In press). Mechanisms Linking Affective Reactions to Competition-Related and Competition-Extraneous Concerns in Martial Artists. *Scandinavian Journal of Sports Sciences and Medicine.*

Diener, E. (2000). Subjective Well-Being. *American Psychologist, 55 (1),* 34-43.

Emmons R. A. and Diener E. (1985). Personality correlates of subjective well-being. *Personality and Social Psychology Bulletin, 11*, 89-97.

Folkman, S. and Lazarus, R.S. (1985). If it changes it must be a process: study of emotion and coping during three stages of a college examination. *Journal Personality and Social Psychology, 48*, 150-170.

Hanin, Y. (1978) A study of anxiety in sports. In W.F. Straub (Ed.), *Sport Psychology: An analysis of athlete behavior.* (pp. 236 - 249).Movement Publications: Ithaca, NY.

Hanin, Y.L. (1986). The state-trait anxiety research on sports in the USSR. In: C.D. Spielberger and R. Diaz-Guerrero (Eds.) *Cross-cultural Anxiety.* (Vol.3, pp.45-64). Washington: Hemisphere Publishing Corporation.

Hanin, Y. (1989). Interpersonal and intragroup anxiety in sports. In D. Hackfort and C.D. Spielberger (Eds.), *Anxiety in sports* (pp. 19 - 28). Washington, DC: Hemisphere.

Hanin, Y. L. (1992) Social Psychology and Sport: Communication Processes in Top Performance Teams. *Sports Science Review* , 1, 13-28.

Hanin, Y. L. (1995). Individual Zones of Optimal Functioning (IZOF) Model: An Idiographic Approach to Performance Anxiety. In K. Henschen and W. Straub (Eds.). *Sport Psychology: an Analysis of Athlete Behavior.* (pp.103-119). Longmeadow, MA: Movement Publications.

Hanin, Y. L. (1997). Emotions and Athletic Performance: Individual Zones of Optimal Functioning Model. *European Yearbook of Sport Psychology, 1*, pp. 29-72.

Hanin, Y. L. (Ed.). (2000). *Emotions in sport.* Champaign, Illinois: Human Kinetics.

Hanin, Yuri L. (2003, February). Performance Related Emotional States in Sport: A Qualitative Analysis [48 paragraphs]. *Forum Qualitative Sozialforschung / Forum: Qualitative Social Research* [On-line Journal], *4* (1). See at: http://www.qualitative-research.net/fqs-texte/1-03/1-03hanin-e.htm

Hanin, Y.L. (2004). Emotions in Sport: An Individualized Approach. In: C. D. Spielberger (Ed.), *Encyclopedia of Applied Psychology.* Vol. 1 (pp. 739-750). Oxford, UK: Elsevier Academic Press.

Hanin Y. (2007). Emotions in Sport: Current issues and perspectives. In G. Tenenbaum and R.C. Eklund (Eds.). *Handbook of Sport Psychology* 3rd ed. (pp. 31-58). Hoboken, NJ: John Wiley and Sons.

Hanin, J., and Hanina, M. (2006). Correction of Habitual Performance Errors in Expert Athletes: Theory and Practice. In: K. Thomson, J. Liukkonen, and T. Jaakkola (Eds.). *Promotion of Motor Skills in Sport and Physical Education.* (pp. 89-97) Jyväskylä University, Department of Sport Sciences: Jyväskylä, Finland.

Hanin, J, and Hanina, M., (2009a). Optimization of performance in top-level athletes: An Action-Focused Coping. *International Journal of Sport Sciences and Coaching, 4,* pp. 47-58.

Hanin, J, and Hanina, M., (2009b). Optimization of performance in top-level athletes: An Action-Focused Coping. Authors' Response to the commentaries. *International Journal of Sport Sciences and Coaching, 4,* pp.83-91.

Hanin, Y., Korjus, T., Jouste, P., and Baxter, P. (2002). Rapid technique correction using old way / new way: two case studies with Olympic athletes. *The Sport Psychologist, 16,* 79-99.

Hanin Y. L., and Stambulova, N. B. (2002). Metaphoric description of performance states: An application of the IZOF model. *The Sport Psychologist, 16,* 396-415.

Hanin,Y.L. and Syrjä, P. (1995). Performance affect in junior ice hockey players: an application of the individual zones of optimal functioning model. *The Sport Psychologist, 9,* 169-187.

Hanin,Y.L. and Syrjä, P. (1996). Predicted, actual and recalled affect in Olympic-level soccer players: idiographic assessments on individualized scales. *Journal of Sport and Exercise Psychology, 18,* 325-335.

Jokela, M., and Hanin, Y. (1999). Does Individual Zones of Optimal Functioning Model discriminate between successful and less successful athletes? A meta-analysis. *Journal of Sport Sciences, 17,* 873-887.

Lazarus, R. S. and Folkman, S. (1984). *Stress, appraisal, and coping.* Springer Publishing Company, New York.

Lazarus R.S. and Lazarus, B.N. (1994). *Passion and Reason: making sense of our emotions.* Oxford University Press, New York

Lyndon, E. H. (1989). I did it my way! An introduction to Old way/new way. *Australasian Journal of Special Education, 13*, 32-37.

Lyndon, E. H. (2000). *Conceptual mediation: A new theory and new method of conceptual change.* Australia: University of Adelaide. Unpublished doctoral dissertation.

Mahoney, M.J. and Avener, M. (1977). Psychology of the elite athlete: an exploratory study. *Cognitive Therapy and Research, 1*, 135-141.

Martens, R., Vealey, R.S., and Burton, D. (1990). *Competitive Anxiety in Sport.* Champaign, IL.: Human Kinetics.

Mayer, J.D., and Stevens, A.A. (1994). An emerging understanding of the reflective (meta) experience of mood. *Journal of Research in Personality, 28*, 351-373.

Minouchi, Y. (2006). Relationships Between Emotions and Sport performance: Emotion Control Based on IZOF Model. *Japanese Journal of Sport Psychology, 33*, 15-26.

Nicholls, A.R., and Polman, R.C.I. (2007). Coping in sport: A systematic review. *Journal of Sports Sciences, 25*, 11-31.

Oatley, K., and Jenkins, J.M. (1992). Human emotions: function and dysfunction. *Annual Review of Psychology, 43*, 55-85.

Raglin, J.S. (1992). Anxiety and sport performance. In: J.O. Holloszy (Ed.), *Exercise and sports sciences reviews,* (Vol. 20, pp.243 - 274). Baltimore, MD: Williams and Wilkins.

Raglin J. and Hanin, Y. (2000) Competitive anxiety and athletic performance. In: Hanin, Y. L. (Ed.). *Emotions in Sport.* (pp. 93-112). Champaign, Illinois: Human Kinetics.

Rantanen, V., Hanin, J., and Hanina, M. (2007). Käytännön malli lajitekniikan parantamiseksi. (Practical model for improvement of sports technique). *HUU: Huippu-Urheilu-Uutiset, 3*, 34-35.

Robazza, C. (2006). Emotion in sport: An IZOF perspective. In S. Hanton and S.D. Mellalieu (Eds.). *Literature Reviews in Sport Psychology.* Hauppage, N.Y.: Nova Science.

Robazza, C., Pellizzari, M., and Hanin, Y. (2004). Emotion Self-regulation and Athletic Performance: An Application of the IZOF Model. *Psychology of Sport and Exercise*, 5, 379-404.

Ruiz, M. C., and Hanin, Y. L. (2004a). Metaphoric description and individualized emotion profiling of performance related states in high-level karate athletes. *Journal of Applied Sport Psychology*, 16, 1-16.

Ruiz, M. C., and Hanin, Y. L. (2004b). Idiosyncratic Description of Anger States in Skilled Spanish Karate Athletes: An application of the IZOF model. *Revista de Psicologia del Deporte, 13*, 75-93.

Spielberger, C. D, Gorsuch, R. L., and Lushene, R. E. (1970). *Manual for the State-Trait Anxiety Inventory (STAI).* Palo Alto: Consulting Psychologist Press.

Thatcher, J., Lavallee, and Jones, M.V. (2004). Coping and Emotion in Sport: An Introduction. In: D. Lavallee, J. Thatcher, and M.V. Jones (Eds.) Coping and Emotion in Sport. Nova Science Publishers, Inc. New York, pp. 3-8.

Vygotsky, L.S. (1926/1984). *Sobranie sochinenii,* [The complete works], v. 4 Moscow: Pedagogika.

Würth, S. and Hanin, Y.L. (2005). Der emotionale Vorstartzustand im Zusammenhang mit Sportververletzungen.(Pre-performance Emotional State related to Sport Injuries).

Leipziger Sportwissenschaftliche Beitrage (LSB),46 (1), 117-143. Academia Verlag. Sankt Augustin.

In: Coping in Sport: Theory, Methods, and Related Constructs   ISBN: 978-1-60876-488-4
Editor: Adam R. Nicholls   © 2010 Nova Science Publishers, Inc.

Chapter 10

COPING AND SELF-DETERMINATION IN SPORT: UNDERLYING MECHANISMS AND EMPIRICAL EVIDENCE

Catherine E. Amiot[1] and Patrick Gaudreau[2]
[1]Université du Québec à Montréal, Canada
[2]University of Ottawa, Canada

ABSTRACT

Research on coping has traditionally focused on the situational, cognitive, and personality antecedents of coping utilization. However, Lazarus (1999) argued that coping is also influenced by motivational processes as goals and motives provide meaning to the person-situation transaction. This chapter explores the relationship between motivation and coping within the confines of self-determination theory (Deci and Ryan, 2000, 2002). To this end, the underlying tenets of self-determination theory are presented to distinguish between self-determined and nonself-determined types of motivational orientations. Empirical evidences showing the cognitive, emotional, and behavioral advantages of self-determined motivation are briefly reviewed before delineating the adaptive processes through which coping and self-determination are linked. Then, sport and social psychology studies that investigated the associations between self-determination and coping are described. Researchers have recently questioned the directionality of this association as motivation and coping could influence each other in a complex reciprocal manner. Longitudinal studies are reviewed to explore the possibility that motivation influences coping which, in turn, produces meaningful changes in one's level of self-determined motivation. The chapter concludes by presenting future research directions aimed at further investigating the associations between coping and self-determination.

Coping and Self-Determination in Sport: Underlying Mechanisms and Empirical Evidence

The present chapter explores the association between self-determination and coping. To illustrate this association, imagine an athlete who engages freely in his favorite sport, for example ultimate Frisbee. For him, ultimate Frisbee is an extremely pleasant activity and he fully enjoys the excitement felt when playing this sport and learning new plays and moves. Within his team, a cohesive and supportive climate is also established. He feels he can really be ''himself'' in this context and make suggestions as to what strategies the team should adopt (Bettencourt and Sheldon, 2001). At an even deeper level, this ultimate Frisbee player not only feels that this sport is important and allows him to reach valued goals (e.g., being in shape), he also feels that being an ultimate Frisbee player is part of who he is and what his core values are (respect for other players; doing one's best).

Now imagine that this athlete is selected to take part, with a selected group of athletes, in a very competitive ultimate Frisbee tournament. After joining his new team, he takes part in preparatory practices and adjusts his game to this level of competition in order to meet the team's objectives. Which coping and adaptation strategies is this player likely to use in this new and stressful context? Some strategies that aim at focusing on the challenge at hand and at investing efforts in meeting the new demands of this level of competition? Or his he likely to disengage from this stressful situation and avoid being involved in developing the team strategy?

The aim of this chapter is to present self-determination theory and link some of its basic tenets to the coping process. To this end, the underlying processes through which coping and self-determination are linked will first be discussed. Then, research that investigates the associations between self-determination and coping will be reviewed. The recursive and reciprocal associations between self-determination and coping will next be presented. Finally, future research directions aimed at further investigating the associations between coping and self-determination will be proposed.

Self-Determination Theory

Self-determination theory (SDT) is an established, empirically supported, and useful motivational theory that has been applied in a variety of life domains including sport, work, leisure, and interpersonal relations (Deci and Ryan, 2000, 2002, 2008). Its goal is to explain how we can optimize the design of social environments so as to maximize people's development, performance, and well-being (Deci and Ryan, 1985; Ryan, 1995). SDT is grounded in humanistic principles. One of its main tenets suggests that humans are active, and are geared toward greater development and increased levels of choice, authenticity, and self-determination (Deci and Ryan, 2000). To allow for such development, the necessary nutriments must be supplied by the social environment, namely through the satisfaction of the needs for autonomy (de Charms, 1968; Deci, 1975), competence, and relatedness (Deci and Ryan, 2000). While the need for autonomy refers to the desire for volition and freedom (de Charms, 1968), the need for competence refers to the propensity to have an effect on the environment and to attain valued outcomes within it (Harter, 1978; White, 1963), and the need for relatedness to the need to feel belongingness and connectedness with others (Baumeister and Leary, 1995). When satisfied, these needs should lead to a more authentic, self-determined, and integrated functioning (Deci and Ryan, 2000).

Another fundamental tenet of SDT assumes that people are moved to act by very different types of factors – different types of motivations. Some individuals may act out of choice and pleasure while others act out of internal or external pressure. By supplying this differentiated approach to motivation, SDT allows to identify distinct types of motivation, which all have specific consequences for learning, performance, and well-being (Deci and Ryan, 2000, 2002). These types of motivation can be organized along a continuum, ranging from less to more self-determined motivations. Figure 1 provides an illustration of this motivational continuum. Nonself-determined forms of motivations include *amotivation*, which refers to the feeling that one's actions will not bring about the desired outcomes and results from not valuing the activity, *external regulation*, which underlies actions that are performed in order to obtain rewards and recognition or to avoid punishment from other people, as well as *introjected regulation*, which represents actions that are emitted out of the pressure one imposes on him or herself.

It is only when the behavior is emitted out of an identified regulation that it is considered self-determined. *Identified regulation* is the motivation by which individuals perform an action because it is important for oneself. *Integrated regulation* underlies behaviors emitted to allow the expression of one's deepest values and beliefs. Finally, the most self-determined form of motivation is *intrinsic motivation*, by which the behavior is emitted out of choice and pleasure, and for its own sake (Deci and Ryan, 1985, 2002). Some studies have combined the identified, integrated, and intrinsic motivations to form a self-determined motivation composite, whereas the amotivation, external, and introjected regulated motivations can be combined to form a nonself-determination composite (e.g., Knee and Zuckerman, 1998; Knee et al., 2002; see Amiot et al., 2004; Gaudreau and Antl, 2008 for examples in sport).

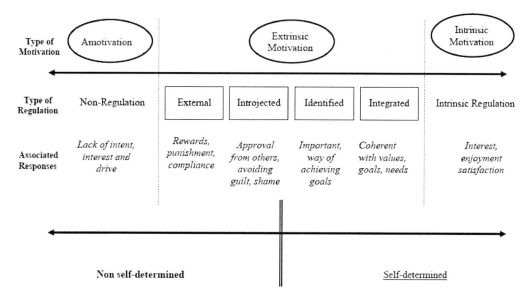

Figure 1. Continuum of Motivations Proposed by Self-Determination Theory (Deci and Ryan, 2000, 2002, 2008).

The more self-determined the motivation, the more it is endorsed by an individual, and hence, the more it represents the individual's "true" self (Ryan and Deci, 1995).

A large and rich literature based on SDT has confirmed these central propositions (e.g., Deci and Ryan, 2000, 2008). In the realm of sports more specifically, the satisfaction of the basic psychological needs have been found to predict positively self-determined motivation toward sports (e.g., Blanchard, Amiot, Perreault, Vallerand, and Provencher, 2009; Kowal and Fortier, 2000; Ntoumanis, 2001). As well, the six types of motivation proposed on the SDT continuum have been identified through factor analyses in different instruments designed specifically to assess motivation toward sports (Brière et al., 1995; Markland and Tobin, 2004; Pelletier et al., 1995, 2007; Longsdale, Hodge, and Rose, 2008; Mallett, Kawabata, Newcombe, Otero-Forero, and Jackson, 2007).

Another series of studies conducted in the sport context have confirmed that the more a behavior is emitted for self-determined reasons, the more positive its consequences (see Vallerand, 2007, for a review). For instance, studies conducted with master swimmers (Kowal and Fortier, 1999), gymnasts (Gagné, Ryan, and Bargmann, 2003), and basketball players (Blanchard et al., 2009) revealed that the self-determined forms of motivation were associated with positive affective consequences such as flow, positive affect, and vitality, whereas the nonself-determined forms of motivation predicted these consequences negatively. At the cognitive level, self-determined sport motivation has been positively associated with more concentration (Kowal and Fortier, 1999). Importantly, self-determined forms of motivation also predict actual behavioral outcomes such as objective perseverance and engagement in sports (e.g., Ferrer-Caja and Weiss, 2000; Standage, Sebin, and Loney, 2008).

This positive effect of self-determined motivation emerges even in the context of stress and change. In a study conducted during important academic transitions, intrinsic motivation predicted short-term persistence in university studies (6 months later), whereas identified regulation predicted more academic satisfaction, less psychological distress, and both short-term and long-term (18 months) persistence in university studies. In contrast, introjected regulation was associated with more psychological distress in the longer-term (Koestner, Fichman, and Mallet, 2002, as cited in Koestner and Losier, 2002). Self-determined individuals have also been shown to react more adaptively to failure. For instance, self-determined children confronted with failure at a task displayed more adaptive reactions as they increased the time spent on the task and improved their subsequent performance (Boggiano, 1998). Thus, not only can self-determination lead to more positive consequences in general, but it also predicts such positive consequences during stressful and changing events.

Self-Determination and Coping with Stress

One may wonder through exactly which mechanisms does self-determination have its positive impact on different outcomes even in stressful contexts. Given the importance of coping strategies and their usefulness in understanding people's various reactions to stress (e.g., Aldwin, 1994; Lazarus and Folkman, 1994; Nicholls and Polman, 2007, in the sport context), coping could represent such a mediating process. Linking self-determination and coping is also consonant with classic theoretical propositions. In fact, according to Lazarus (1991), coping research needs to consider the motivational antecedents leading to the selection of particular modes of coping. Given the broadness of SDT and its utility in different life contexts including sport (Deci and Ryan, 2000; Vallerand, 2007), it appears relevant to conceptually link self-determination to coping. To establish the conceptual links between self-determination and coping, we briefly review the coping definition and categories retained for our review.

Coping processes. Coping aims at dealing with external demands and requirements, at developing new responses and behaviors, and at reducing the discrepancy between the person and the environment (Costa, Somerfield, and McCrae, 1996). Coping has been specifically defined as the person's behavioral and cognitive efforts to manage the internal and external demands of a troubled person-environment transaction (Folkman, 1984; see Skinner, Edge, Altman, and Sherwood, 2003).

In order to determine the adaptiveness of various coping strategies, distinctions have been made between different dimensions of coping (e.g., Compas et al., 2001; Endler and Parker, 1994; Lazarus and Folkman, 1984; Rudolf, Dennig, and Weisz, 1995). In this chapter we focus on two broad dimensions of coping strategies. *Task-oriented coping*, also labeled primary control coping or assimilation coping, refers to the strategies aimed at doing something concrete in altering the source of the stress, and includes the coping actions used to change or to act directly on some aspects of the stressful situation (i.e., problem-focused coping). This coping dimension also includes coping strategies aimed at changing the meaning of a stressful situation as well as at regulating negative emotions arising from this situation (i.e., emotion-focused coping). Overall, this task-oriented coping dimension subsumes coping strategies that promote a constructive engagement with stressors, or with the self's reactions to them, and that are organized, flexible, and constructive (Skinner et al., 2003). Another coping dimension, *disengagement-oriented coping* (Compas et al., 2001; Endler and Parker, 1994), refers to strategies that are employed in order to disengage oneself from the task and to focus on task-irrelevant cues. This higher-order coping dimension has been conceptualized as being less adaptive given that it involves dealing harshly with the self or with the stressful situation, and that it is characterized by rigid, disorganized, or derogatory ways of coping (Skinner et al., 2003).

These two higher-order dimensions of coping have been proposed to be useful in accounting for how coping mediates the relationship between stress and outcomes such as well-being (Skinner et al., 2003). Generally, task-oriented coping responses have been proposed to improve the fit between an organism and its environment as well as to alleviate the negative impact of stress, whereas disengagement-oriented coping responses exacerbate the effect of stress (Zeidner and Saklofske, 1996).

Conceptual links between self-determination and coping. A number of underlying processes help to explain why self-determination is conceptually related to coping and how this motivational antecedent can trigger the use of more adaptive coping strategies.

First, one's motivational orientation shapes the subjective experience of stress and influences the appraisal process. According to Skinner and Edge (2002), self-determination acts like a source of energy and direction for cognitions, emotions, and behaviors during stressful situations. Self-determination allows for a less reactive and externally-driven reaction to stress. A self-determined orientation should thus reduce the perception of objective environmental demands, which should then trigger adaptive coping actions. Inversely, during stressful events, non self-determined forms of motivation have been proposed to undermine coping by increasing the perception of objective external demands and pressures, and by triggering maladaptive action tendencies (Skinner and Edge, 2002). With respect to appraisals specifically, a self-determined motivation has been proposed to lead people to appraise stressful situations as challenges rather than as threats, whereas a nonself-determined orientation should make the self more defensive and susceptible to appraising the situation as threatening and ego-relevant (Skinner and Edge, 2002; Skinner et al., 2003; Hodgins and Knee, 2002). While appraisals of challenge should then lead to more adaptive coping, appraisals of threat should trigger the use of less adaptive forms of coping.

Second, a self-determined motivation allows a direct access to one's personal goals and values. Theoretically, self-determination has been characterized by a greater awareness of one's inner needs (Deci and Ryan, 1985), as well as by an enhanced access to one's genuine preferences, desires, and goals (Ryan and Connell, 1989; Skinner and Edge, 2002). Empirically, self-determination has been associated with greater self-consistency (Koestner, Bernieri, and Zuckerman, 1992). These characteristics should be particularly useful when coping with stress given that this enhanced access to personal needs and goals allows the individual not to become overly destabilized by external events. Such an access also facilitates the use of more personally suited and efficient coping strategies. Along these lines, Skinner and Edge (2002) proposed that when negotiating the environmental demands involved in stressful situations, these characteristics should enable self-determined individuals to maintain access to their goals and to display open and flexible actions allowing them to "stay in touch with" the hierarchy of their genuine priorities. These authors add that when people have access to motivational resources, the regulation of their actions should be more adaptive, that is, more organized and coherent, more flexible and open to internal and external information, and more constructive. Non self-determined motivation, however, should be associated with difficulty accessing one's genuine goals, with a greater responsiveness to external cues and demands, and with expectations that the social context is intentionally coercive, thus making the stressful situation appear more stressful.

In stressful contexts, such as when taking part in a competitive sporting event, a self-determined orientation could thus allow individuals to stay in touch with their own goals and priorities, choose the coping strategies that suit them best, and prevent them from becoming overly destabilized by demanding external contingencies (Koestner et al., 1992). From a SDT point of view, individuals also have an inherent tendency to approach optimally challenging tasks and assimilable situations, and to engage with new stimuli and situations that are optimally discrepant from their current cognitive structure (Deci and Ryan, 2000). It could be that when undertaking a new challenge (i.e., taking part in a highly competitive ultimate frisbee tournament), a self-determined orientation allows individuals to choose optimal and self-fitting goals even in such a stressful situation, which facilitates the negotiation of the challenges emerging in this new context.

Empirical Evidence in Social and Sport Psychology

Empirical evidence supporting the association between self-determination and coping is just emerging. This section of the chapter aims to review such evidence. Knee and Zuckerman (1998) were the first, to our knowledge, to investigate the association between self-determination and coping. In their one-semester prospective study among university students, they assessed *global motivation* (e.g., Deci and Ryan, 1985). In fact, motivation can be assessed at different levels of generality (Vallerand, 1997), including a dispositional or *global level* (why people do what they do in a variety of life contexts), the *contextual level* (why people do what they do in specific life domains, such as sports, studies, leisure, work), and the *situational level* (why people do what they do in a specific situation). Coping was also assessed at the global level to capture participants' general ways of dealing with stressors (Zuckerman and Gagné, 2003). Their results revealed significant and meaningful associations between global motivation and coping styles. Whereas self-determined motivation was negatively associated with disengagement-oriented coping (i.e., denial, behavioral and mental disengagement) and marginally positively associated with task-oriented coping strategies (planning and seeking of social support for instrumental reasons), non self-determined motivation was associated to a greater use of disengagement-oriented coping (denial, behavioral and mental disengagement).

Knee, Patrick, Vietor, Nanayakkara, and Neighbors (2002) replicated these results when investigating the associations between global self-determination and coping strategies used in the more specific context of a stressful argument with one's romantic partner. In this study, a self-determined orientation was positively associated with task-oriented coping and with accommodation-oriented coping (seeking emotional support, positive reappraisal, and acceptance of the event), whereas a nonself-determined orientation was positively associated with disengagement-oriented coping.

Similar results were obtained in studies conducted in the context of a stressful sport competition (Amiot, Gaudreau, and Blanchard, 2004; Perreault and Vallerand, 2007). In the Amiot, Gaudreau and Blanchard (2004) study, athletes completed two questionnaires. The Time 1 questionnaire was completed just before an important competition. This questionnaire assessed motivation toward sport (a contextual motivation; Brière et al., 1995) and baseline positive and negative affect (PANAS; Watson, Clark, and Tellegen, 1997). The Time 2 questionnaire was completed during the first practice following this competition and it assessed positive and negative affect, situational coping strategies (i.e., used during the competition; Gaudreau and Blondin, 2002), and goal attainment (Gaudreau and Amiot, 2009). Assessing coping just a few days after the sport competition allowed to minimize retrospective biases in the measurement of coping, an issue of concern in the coping literature (Nicholls and Polman, 2007).

A path model was tested. We anticipated that while self-determination toward sport should predict the use of task-oriented coping strategies during the competition, nonself-determined sport motivation should predict the use of disengagement-oriented coping strategies. Then, whereas task-oriented coping strategies were expected to predict higher goal attainment in the competition, disengagement-oriented coping should predict lower goal attainment. Finally, goal attainment was hypothesized to predict an increase in positive affect from pre- to post-competition and a drop in negative affect. Results confirmed these associations. Tests of mediation also confirmed that the relationships between motivation and outcomes (i.e., goal attainment and change in affective states) and between coping and change in affective states were fully mediated by the intervening variables included in the model.

More recently, Gaudreau and Antl (2008) further investigated the antecedents leading athletes to endorse a self-determined vs. a non self-determined sport motivation in this sequence of variables, namely, perfectionism. An important distinction was also made between two forms of perfectionism: evaluative concerns perfectionism (ECP) and personal standards perfectionism (PSP). Whereas ECP entails a socially prescribed tendency to evaluate oneself harshly, to doubt one's capacities, and to perceive that others require perfection from oneself, PSP involves a self-oriented tendency to set highly demanding standards and to strive for their attainment (Dunley and Blankstein, 2000). Results confirmed that while ECP predicted a nonself-determined sport motivation, SPS predicted self-determined sport motivation. Whereas self-determined sport motivation predicted task-oriented coping (as in previous studies), this study revealed that nonself-determined sport motivation predicted not only disengagement-oriented coping, but also distraction-oriented coping – a coping family comprising the strategies used to momentarily focus on stimuli unrelated to the stressful situation (e.g., distancing; mental distraction). Then, while task-oriented coping predicted higher goal attainment, disengagement-oriented coping predicted lower goal attainment. In this study, goal attainment even had an impact on well-being at the global level of generality, namely, on global life satisfaction. Mediation analyses also confirmed that motivation styles partially mediated the associations between perfectionism and coping, and that goal attainment fully mediated the associations between coping and life satisfaction.

Planning can also be considered a specific form of coping (Carver and Scheier, 1989; Lazarus and Folkman, 1984). Carraro and Gaudreau (a, in press) found significant associations between goal motivation or self-concordance (i.e., reasons underlying the pursuit of goals), planning as a specific form of coping strategy, and goal progress (see also D'Angelo, Reid, and Pelletier, 2007). In this study, participants listed goals they had in two life contexts: physical activity and academic studies. They also indicated the planning strategies employed to attain these goals (i.e., their spontaneous implementation intentions), and their actual progress on these goals. Findings revealed that goal concordance predicted more planning, which in turn predicted increased goal progress. Interestingly, these effects were contained within their respective life context. For instance, academic self-concordance predicted planning strategies used specifically in the context of academic studies and academic goal progress. This sequence was also observed (in parallel) in the physical activity context.

Reciprocal Associations between Self-Determination and Coping

These past studies confirm the fact that a self-determined orientation predicts the use of more adaptive coping strategies whereas a nonself-determined orientation predicts less adaptive forms of coping. Let us now question the directionality of this association and explore the possibility that coping could also predict individuals' motivational orientations. More specifically, can the coping strategies used to deal with stress also come to have an impact on one's motivation?

Some commentators have proposed that coping efforts can be conceptualized as developmental mechanisms (e.g., Brandtstadter, 1998; Heckhausen and Schulz, 1995; Skinner and Zimmer-Gembeck, 2007). Skinner and Edge (2002) have proposed that constructive coping is the key locus of self-development and that prolonged negotiations with environmental demands characterize the very process of integration, through which originally extrinsic goals and behaviors become integrated in the true self and hence autonomously regulated (see also Deci and Ryan, 1991; Ryan, 1993). Based on these theoretical propositions, adaptive coping strategies could hence predict an *increase* in self-determined motivation over time.

This process whereby self-determination increases over time is fundamental in SDT. As stated earlier, the goal of SDT is to understand how we can optimize human potential and develop strategies to enhance self-determination. SDT theorists also propose that the self possesses an inherent tendency to develop and to become increasingly self-determined (Ryan and Deci, 1995; Ryan, 1991). In SDT, the process through which one's motivation becomes increasingly self-determined over time is called integration (Deci and Ryan, 2000; Ryan and Deci, 2003). More specifically, from a SDT point of view, integration is a process by which individuals transform socially sanctioned requests into personally endorsed values and self-regulations (Deci and Ryan, 1991). Integration takes place when individuals assimilate and reconstitute formerly external regulations so that they can take them into their self and be self-determined while enacting them. It represents the organism's acquisition of internal regulations to replace external ones. According to Deci and Ryan (1991, 2000), when the integration process functions optimally, people will identify with the importance of new behaviors and social regulations, assimilate them into their self, and fully accept them as their own. When behaviors emerge from the self, they are considered as self-regulated or autonomous, which means that they are relatively consistent with and are enacted from the self (Ryan, 1993). Thus, the more fully a regulation becomes integrated, the more it becomes part of the self and the more it is the basis for self-determined behavior.

To illustrate this process in the context of sport, let's go back to our ultimate frisbee player. When entering his new competitive team, this player might feel unease with certain aspects of the team functioning – certain specific rules or norms for instance (e.g., a norm that discourages players to talk to other players just before the game so as not to break their concentration). At first, our new player might obey these norms and rules out of *external regulation* – to avoid being sanctioned or socially rejected by his teammates and to gain interpersonal acceptance. However, with time, this player might come to see the inherent utility of the team's norms (i.e., it helps him concentrate too; he sees the value of calmness in keeping quiet) and to accept them as his own. At this point, the ultimate frisbee player would display this behavior out of *identified regulation*. This passage from an external regulation to an identified regulation represents the integration process.

Few investigations have examined changes in self-determination over time (e.g., Otis, Grouzet, and Pelletier, 2005; Ratelle, Guay, Larose, and Senécal, 2004). In a cross-sectional study, Chandler and Connell (1987) showed that, with increasing age, children display greater internalized reasons for performing different behaviors, thus suggesting an increase in self-determination over time, as children become older. In longitudinal studies conducted among medical students throughout their training (Williams and Deci, 1996), it was found that when instructors were more supportive of their students' need for autonomy in the context of the course, students showed a greater increase over time in self-determined motivation for learning the course material. In the context of sports, Guay, Vallerand, and Blanchard (2000, Study 4) showed that the satisfaction of the needs for autonomy, collective (or team) competence, and relatedness predicted an increase in intrinsic motivation for playing basketball over time. Increases in identified regulation were predicted by the satisfaction of the need for autonomy and relatedness, whereas decreases in amotivation were predicted by relatedness. Changes in external regulation were not predicted by any of the needs.

To account for these changes in self-determination, we proposed that adaptive coping could also represent a process promoting integration over time (Amiot, 2004; Amiot, Blanchard, and Gaudreau, 2008; Amiot, de la Sablonnière, Terry, and Smith, 2007; see Carraro and Gaudreau, b, in press, for an example in sports). In a longitudinal study conducted among university students undergoing the stressful transition to university, Amiot, Blanchard, and Gaudreau (2008) found empirical evidence for the role played by coping strategies in the process of becoming increasingly self-determined toward university studies (i.e., a contextual motivation likely to change over time). This three-wave longitudinal study was conducted among new students during their first semester at university. The Time 1 questionnaire, completed at the very beginning of the semester, included measures of global motivation (Guay, Mageau, and Vallerand, 2003), baseline academic motivation (Vallerand et al., 1992, 1993), and well-being (Ryff and Keyes, 1995). The Time 2 questionnaire was completed just after mid-term examinations (i.e., after students had the opportunity to learn the demands of their new life context) and included a measure of coping with the transition to university (Carver, Scheier, and Weintraub, 1989). The Time 3 questionnaire was completed at the end of the semester (i.e., just before final examinations) and included measures of academic motivation and well-being. In line with the self-determination continuum, self-determination indices were computed for the global motivation and the academic motivation scales using the following formula: [(3 x intrinsic motivation + 2 x integrated regulation + identified regulation) – (introjected regulation + 2 x external regulation + 3 x amotivation)].

It was hypothesized that one's global motivation, assessed at the beginning of the semester (Time 1), would predict a greater use of task-oriented coping strategies (assessed after mid-semester – Time 2) when dealing with the transition, and a lesser use of disengagement-oriented forms of coping. Then, task-oriented coping should positively predict changes in well-being from the beginning to the end of the term (i.e., from Time 1 to Time 3), while disengagement-oriented coping should negatively predict these changes in well-being. We also anticipated that the use of task-oriented coping would lead to an increase in academic self-determination from the beginning to the end of the semester (hence capturing the integration process). Inversely, the use of disengagement-oriented coping was expected to predict a decrease in academic self-determination. In line with the transactional model of stress and coping, we also assessed the mediating role of coping in the relation between global self-determination and the consequences (Lazarus and Folkman, 1984; Lazarus, 1991). To capture the integration process proposed by SDT, special statistical techniques were employed to tap into the changes taking place in academic self-determination over time (i.e., true intraindividual change techniques: Raykov, 1992; Steyer, Partchev, and Shanahan, 2000).

Results obtained from structural equation modeling confirmed our hypotheses. Support was found for the role played by global self-determination in the prediction of more task-oriented coping and less disengagement-oriented coping, as in previous studies (Amiot et al., 2004; Gaudreau and Antl, 2008; Knee and Zuckerman, 1998; Knee et al., 2002). Moreover, results revealed that task-oriented coping predicted an increase in academic self-determination across the semester and more positive well-being. Inversely, disengagement-oriented coping predicted a decrease in academic self-determination over time and lower well-being. Together, these results confirm the role played by coping in the integration process.

Future Research Directions on Coping and Self-Determination in Sport

While theoretical and empirical links between self-determination and coping have been established, a lot of work remains to be conducted to further investigate the association between these constructs. Given that sport is a highly relevant and involving life domain, future investigations should be conducted in this context. Doing so would not only inform interventions aimed at optimizing athletes' experience of the sport context, but it would also allow for a better understanding of the theoretical links between self-determination and coping.

A first avenue for future research involves investigating the mechanisms through which self-determination predicts the specific coping strategies that are used by athletes. As mentioned above, self-determination shapes the experience of stress and it should influence cognitive appraisals of the stressful situation. Furthermore, self-determined individuals have, by definition, a greater access to their own goals, priorities, and feelings (e.g., Hodgins and Knee, 2002). Could appraisals (i.e., challenge, threat) and self-knowledge (Campbell et al., 1996; Kernis et al., 2000) mediate the associations between self-determination and coping?

According to the transactional model of stress (Lazarus and Folkman, 1984), appraisals, which precede coping, constitute the set of conscious and unconscious processes of evaluating the subjective importance of the stressful event, as well as one's ability to cope with it. While appraisals of challenge and of possessing adequate resources have been linked to the use of more adaptive coping strategies, appraisals of threat and lack of resources have been associated with the use of less adaptive forms of coping (Skinner et al., 2003). Because self-determination has been associated with lesser amounts of anxiety (see Vallerand, 1997), it could be through the subjective interpretation of the stressful situation that self-determination would lead to an assessment of this situation as being more challenging than threatening and hence to the establishment of a more adaptive plan of action to deal with stress (Skinner and Edge, 2002). Future research should test to role of these finer mechanisms.

Another mediator that could be interesting to investigate to better understand the association between self-determination and coping pertains to mindfulness. In fact, a stressful situation such as an important sport competition requires that athletes keep track of external demands, challenges, and constraints likely to arise throughout the competition, while at the same time keeping contact with their own internal states (i.e., physiological activation, affective states, objectives and goals). This process of simultaneous awareness of one's internal states and external requirements can be related to the concept of mindfulness, which can be defined as "the clear and single-minded awareness of what actually happens to us and in us at the successive moments of perception" (Nyanaponika Thera, 1972, p. 5). This state has also been associated with enhanced self-determination (e.g., Brown and Ryan, 2003). Mindfulness could thus represent a concrete process through which athletes stay in touch with both the external demands existing in the competitive setting (doing so is necessary to stay in the game!) as well as their own emotions, cognitions, and actions in this situation, and establish a balance between these internal and external circumstances.

A second avenue for future research could be to test systematically if a self-determined motivational orientation has a more beneficial effect in the context of greater stress. For instance, a study could compare whether the association between self-determination and coping is stronger in a highly demanding sport competition than in a less demanding and stressful competition. Doing so would not only help identify the processes most likely to come into play when athletes experience high levels of stress but it would also further our knowledge about how the impact of individual differences (i.e., global motivational orientation) can be accentuated in times of stress (e.g., Caspi and Moffit, 1991).

CONCLUSION

Future research could further investigate the reciprocal associations between self-determination and coping. To this aim, long-term longitudinal studies could be conducted, where the effects of baseline self-determination are controlled for and where coping strategies assessed throughout a sports season are then measured at each sport competition. It could be found that the repeated use of task-oriented coping strategies over time across different sport competitions shape athletes' self-determined sport motivation. Such findings, which would confirm that coping can represent an integration mechanism, could also pave the way to interesting stress management interventions that would also have a positive impact on athletes' motivation.

AUTHOR NOTE

The writing of this chapter was facilitated thanks to grants from the Fonds québécois pour la recherche sur la société et la culture (FQRSC) and from the Social Sciences and Humanities Research Council of Canada (SSHRC) to Catherine E. Amiot. We thank Natasha Carraro for her feedback on an earlier version of this chapter.

REFERENCES

Aldwin, C. M. (1994). Stress, coping and development: An integrative perspective. New York: Guilford Press.

Amiot, C. E. (2004). The self in the process of coping with change. Unpublished doctoral dissertation, University of Ottawa.

Amiot, C. E., Blanchard, C. M., and Gaudreau, P. (2008). The self in change: A longitudinal investigation of coping and self-determination processes. *Self and Identity, 7(2)*, 204-224.

Amiot, C. E., de la Sablonnière, R., Terry, D. J., and Smith, J. R. (2007). Integration of social identities in the self: Toward a cognitive-developmental model. *Personality and Social Psychology Review, 11(4)*, 364-388.

Amiot, C. E., Gaudreau, P., and Blanchard, C. M. (2004). Self-determination, coping, and goal attainment in sport. *Journal of Sport and Exercise Psychology, 26,* 396-411.

Baumeister, R. F., and Leary, M. R. (1995). The need to belong: Desire for interpersonal attachments as a fundamental human motivation. *Psychological Bulletin, 117(3)*, 497-529.

Bettencourt, B. A., and Sheldon, K. (2001). Social roles as mechanism for psychological need satisfaction within social groups. *Journal of Personality and Social Psychology, 81(06)*, 1131-1143.

Blanchard, C. M., Amiot, C. E., Perreault, S., Vallerand, R. J., and Provencher, P. J. (in press). Cohesiveness and Psychological Needs: Their Effects on Self-Determination and Athletes' Subjective Well-being. Psychology of Sport and Exercise.

Boggiano, A. K. (1998). Maladaptive achievement patterns: A test of a diathesis-stress analysis of helplessness. *Journal of Personality and Social Psychology, 69,* 1681-1695.

Brandtstädter, J. (1998). Handbook of child psychology. In W. Damon and R. M. Lerner (Eds). *Theoretical models of human development* (pp. 807-863). Hoboken, NJ: John Wiley and Sons Inc.

Brière, N. M., Vallerand, R. J., Blais, M. R., and Pelletier, L. G. (1995). Développement et validation d'une mesure de motivation intrinsèque, extrinsèque et d'amotivation en contexte sportif : L'échelle de motivation dans les sports (ÉMS). *International Journal of Sports Psychology, 26*, 465-489.

Brown, K. W., and Ryan, R. M. (2003). The benefits of being present: Mindfulness and its role in psychological well-being. *Journal of Personality and Social Psychology, 84(4)*, 822-848.

Campbell, J. D., Trapnell, P. D., Heine, S. J., Katz, I. M., Lavallee, L. F., and Lehman, D. R. (1996). Self-concept clarity: Measurement, personality correlates, and cultural boundaries. *Journal of Personality and Social Psychology, 70,* 141-156.

Carraro, N., and Gaudreau, P. (a, in press). Implementation planning as a pathway between goal motivation and goal progress for academic and physical activity goals. *Journal of Applied Social Psychology.*

Carraro, N., and Gaudreau, P. (b, in press). The role of self-regulation in promoting the integration of physical activity into the self. *American Journal of Health Behavior.*

Carver, C. S., Scheier, M. F., and Weintraub, J. K. (1989). Assessing coping strategies: A theoretically based approach. *Journal of Personality and Social Psychology, 56,* 267-283.

Caspi, A., and Moffit, T. E. (1991). Individual differences are accentuated during periods of social change: The case of puberty. *Journal of Personality and Social Psychology, 61, 157-168.*

Chandler, C. L., and Connell, J. P. (1987). Children's intrinsic interest, extrinsic, and internalized motivation: A developmental study of children's reasons for liked and disliked behaviors. *British Journal of Developmental Psychology, 5,* 357-365.

Compas, B. E., Connor-Smith, J. K., Saltzman, H., Thomsen, A. H., and Wadsworth, M. E. (2001). Coping with stress during childhood and adolescence: Problems, progress, and potential in theory and research. *Psychological Bulletin, 127,* 27-127.

Costa, P. T., Somerfield, M. R., and McCrae, R. R. (1996). Personality and coping: A reconceptualization. In M. Zeidner and N. S. Endler (Eds.), *Handbook of coping: Theory, research, applications* (pp. 44-61). New York: Wiley.

D'Angelo, M. S., Reid, R. D., and Pelletier, L. G. (2007). A model for exercise behavior change regulation in patients with heart disease. *Journal of Sport and Exercise Psychology, 29*, 208-224.

de Charms, R. (1968). *Personal causation: The internal affective determinants of behavior.* New York: Academic Press.

Deci, E. L. (1975). Intrinsic motivation. New York: Plenum Press.

Deci, E. L. and Ryan, R. M. (1985). Intrinsic motivation and self-determination in human behavior. New York: Plenum Press.

Deci, E. L., and Ryan, R. M. (1991). A motivational approach to self: Integration in personality. In R. Dienstbier (Ed.), *Nebraska symposium on motivation, Vol. 38, Perspectives on motivation* (pp. 237-288). Lincoln, NE: University of Nebraska Press.

Deci, E. L., and Ryan, R. M. (1995). Human autonomy: The basis for true self-esteem. In M. H. Kernis (Ed.), *Efficacy, agency, and self-esteem.* New York, NY: Plenum Press.

Deci, E. L., and Ryan, R. M. (2000). The ''what'' and ''why'' of goal pursuits: Human needs and the self-determination of behavior. *Psychological Inquiry, 11,* 227-268.

Deci, E. L., and Ryan, R. M. (2002). *Handbook of self-determination research.* Rochester, NY: University of Rochester Press.

Deci, E. L., and Ryan, R. M. (2008). Self-determination theory: A macrotheory on human motivation, development, and health. *Canadian Psychology, 49,* 182-185.

Endler, N. S., and Parker, J. D. A. (1994). Multidimensional assessment of coping: A critical evaluation. *Journal of Personality and Social Psychology, 58,* 844-854.

Ferrer-Caja, E., and Weiss, M. R. (2000). Predictors of intrinsic motivation among adolescent students in physical education. *Research Quarterly for Exercise and Sport, 71(3)*, 267-279.

Folkman, S. (1984). Personal control and stress in the coping process: A theoretical analysis. *Journal of Personality and Social Psychology, 46,* 839-852.

Gagné, M., Ryan, R. M., and Bargmann, K. (2003). Autonomy support and need satisfaction in the motivation and well-being of gymnasts. *Journal of Applied Sport Psychology, 15(4)*, 372-390.

Gaudreau, P., and Antl, S. (2008). Athletes' broad dimensions of dispositional perfectionism: Examining changes in life satisfaction and the mediating role of sports-related motivation and coping. *Journal of Sports and Exercise Psychology, 30(3)*, 356-382.

Gaudreau, P., and Blondin, J.-P. (2002). Development of a questionnaire for the assessment of coping strategies employed by athletes in competitive sport settings. *Psychology of Sport and Exercise, 3(1)*, 1-34.

Guay, F., Mageau, G. A., and Vallerand, R. J. (2003). On the hierarchical structure of self-determined motivation: A test of top-down, bottom-up, reciprocal, and horizontal effects. *Personality and Social Psychology Bulletin, 29(8)*, 992-1004.

Guay, F., Vallerand, R. J., and Blanchard, C. (2000). On the assessment of situational intrinsic and extrinsic motivation: The Situational Motivation Scale (SIMS). *Motivation and Emotion, 24(3)*, 175-213.

Harter, S. (1978). Effectance motivation reconsidered: Toward a developmental model. *Human Development, 21(1)*, 34-64.

Heckhausen, J., and Schulz, R. (1995). A life-span theory of control. *Psychological Review, 102(2)*, 284-304.

Hodgins, H. S., and Knee, C. R. (2002). The integrating self and the conscious experience. In E. L. Deci and R. M. Ryan (Eds.), *Handbook of self-determination research* (pp. 87-99). Rochester, NY: The University of Rochester Press.

Kernis, M. H., Paradise, A. W., Whitaker, D. J., Wheatman, S. R., and Goldman, B. N. (2000). Master of one's psychological domain? Not likely of one's self-esteem is unstable. *Personality and Social Psychology Bulletin, 26,* 1297-1305.

Knee, C. R., Patrick, H., Vietor, N. A., Nanayakkara, A., and Neighbors, C. (2002). Self-determination as growth motivation in romantic relationships. *Personality and Social Psychology Bulletin, 28,* 609-619.

Knee, C. R., and Zuckerman, M. (1998). A nondefensive personality: Autonomy and control as moderators of defensive coping and self-handicapping. *Journal of Research in Personality, 32,* 115-130.

Koestner, R., Bernieri, F., and Zuckerman, M. (1992). Self-determination and consistency between attitudes, traits, and behaviors. *Personality and Social Psychology Bulletin, 18,* 52-59.

Koestner, R., and Losier, G. F. (2002). Distinguishing three ways of being internally motivated: A closer look at introjection, identification, and intrinsic motivation. In E. L. Deci and R. M. Ryan (Eds), *Handbook of self-determination research* (pp. 101-121). Rochester, NY: University of Rochester Press.

Kowal, J., and Fortier, M. S. (1999). Motivational determinants of flow: Contributions from self-determination theory. *Journal of Social Psychology, 139(3)*, 355-368.

Kowal, J., and Fortier, M. S. (2000). Physical activity behavior change in middle-aged and older women: The role of barriers and of environmental characteristics. *Journal of Behavioral Medicine, 30(3)*, 233-242.

Lazarus, R. S., and Folkman, S. (1984). *Stress, appraisal, and coping.* New York: Springer.

Lazarus, R. S. (1991). *Emotion and adaptation.* New York: Oxford University Press.

Mallett, C., Kawabata, M., Newcombe, P., Otero-Forero, A, and Jackson, S. (2007). Sport motivation scale-6 (SMS-6): A revised six-factor sport motivation scale. *Psychology of Sport and Exercise. Special Issue: Advances in self-determination theory research in sport and exercise, 8(5)*, 600-614.

Markland, D., and Tobin, V. (2004). A modification to the Behavioural Regulation in Exercise Questionnaire to include an assessment of amotivation. *Journal of Sports and Exercise Psychology, 26(2)*, 191-196.

Nicholls, A. R., and Polman, R. C. J. (2007). Coping in sport: A systematic review. *Journal of Sports Sciences, 25(1)*, 11-31.

Ntoumanis, N. (2001). Empirical links between achievement goal theory and self-determination theory in sport. *Journal of Sport Sciences, 19*, 397-409.

Nyanaponika Thera. (1972). *The power of mindfulness.* San Francisco, CA: Unity Press.

Otis, N., Grouzet, F. M. E., and Pelletier, L. G. (2005). Latent motivational change in an academic setting: A 3-year longitudinal study. *Journal of Educational Psychology, 97*, 170-183.

Pelletier, L. G., Fortier, M. S., Vallerand, R. J., Tuson, K. M., Brière, N. M., and Blais, M. R. (1995). Toward a new measure of intrinsic motivation, extrinsic motivation, and amotivation in sports : The Sport Motivation Scale (SMS). *Journal of Sport and Exercise Psychology, 17(1)*, 35-53.

Perreault, S., and Vallerand, R. J. (2007). A test of self-determination theory with wheelchair basketball players with and without disability. *Adapted Physical Activity Quarterly, 24*, 305-316.

Ratelle, C. F., Guay, F., Larose, S., and Senecal, C. (2004). Family correlates of trajectories of academic motivation during a school transition: A semiparametric group-based approach. *Journal of Educational Psychology, 96*, 743-754.

Raykov, T. (1992). Structural models for studying correlates and predictors of change. *Australian Journal of Psychology, 44(2)*, 101-112.

Rudolf, K. D., Dennig, M. D., and Weisz, J. R. (1995). Determinants and consequences of children's coping in the medical setting: Conceptualization, review, and critique. *Psychological Bulletin, 118,* 328-357.

Ryan, R. M. (1993). Agency and organization: Intrinsic motivation, autonomy and the self in psychological development. In J. Jacobs (Ed.), *Nebraska symposium on motivation: Developmental perspectives on motivation* (Vol. 40, pp. 1-56). Lincoln: University of Nebraska Press.

Ryan, R. M. (1995). Psychological needs and the facilitation of integrative processes. *Journal of Personality, 63,* 397-427.

Ryan, R. M. and Connell, J. P. (1989). Perceived locus of causality and internalization: Examining reasons for acting in two domains. *Journal of Personality and Social Psychology, 57,* 749-761.

Ryan, R. M. (1993). Agency and organization: Intrinsic motivation, autonomy and the self in psychological development. In J. Jacobs (Ed.), *Nebraska symposium on motivation: Developmental perspectives on motivation* (Vol. 40, pp. 1-56). Lincoln: University of Nebraska Press.

Ryan, R. M., and Deci, E. L. (2003). On assimilating identities to the self: A self-determination theory perspective on internalization and integrity within cultures. In M. R. Leary and J. P. Tangney (Eds.), *Handbook of self and identity* (pp. 253-272). New York: Guilford.

Ryff, C. D., and Keyes, C. L. M. (1995). The structure of psychological well-being revisited. *Journal of Personality and Social Psychology, 69,* 719-727.

Skinner, E., and Edge, K. (2002). Self-determination, coping, and development. In E. L. Deci and R. M. Ryan (Eds), *Handbook of self-determination research* (pp. 297-337). Rochester, NY: University of Rochester Press.

Skinner, E. A., Edge, K., Altman, J., and Sherwood, H. (2003). Searching for the structure of coping: A review and critique of category systems for classifying ways of coping. *Psychological Bulletin, 129,* 216-269.

Skinner, E., and Zimmer-Gembeck, M. J. (2007). The development of coping. *Annual Review of Psychology, 58,* 119-144.

Standage, M., Sebin, S. J., and Loney, T. (2008). Does exercise motivation predict engagement in objectively-assessed bouts of moderate-intensity exercise? *Journal of Sport and Exercise Psychology, 30,* 337-352.

Steyer, R., Partchev, I., and Shanahan, M.J. (2000). Modeling true intraindividual change in structural equation models: The case of poverty and children's psychosocial adjustment. In T. D. Little, K. U. Schnabel, and J. Baumert (Eds), *Modeling longitudinal and multilevel data: Practical issues, applied approaches, and specific examples* (pp. 109-126). Mahwah, NJ: Lawrence Erlbaum.

Vallerand, R. J. (1997). Toward a hierarchical model of intrinsic and extrinsic motivation. In M. Zanna (Ed.), *Advances in experimental social psychology, Vol. 29* (pp. 271-360). New York: Academic Press.

Vallerand, R. J., Pelletier, L. G., Blais, M. R., Brière, N. M., Senécal, C., and Vallières, E. F. (1992). The Academic Motivation Scale: A measure of intrinsic, extrinsic, and motivation in education. *Educational and Psychological Measurement, 52,* 1003-1019.

Vallerand, R. J., Pelletier, L. G., Blais, M. R., Brière, N. M., Senécal, C., and Vallières, E. F. (1993). On the assessment of intrinsic, extrinsic, and motivation in education: Evidence on the concurrent and construct validity of the Academic Motivation Scale. *Educational and Psychological Measurement, 53,* 159-172.

Watson, D., and Clark, L. (1997). Measurement and mismeasurement of mood: Recurrent and emergent issues. *Journal of Personality Assessment, 38(2)*, 267-296.

White, R. W. (1959). Motivation reconsidered: The concept of competence. *Psychological Review, 66,* 297-333.

Williams, G. C., and Deci, E. L. (1996). Internalization of biopsychosocial values by medical students: A test of self-determination theory. *Journal of Personality and Social Psychology, 70,* 767-779.

Zeidner, M., and Saklofske, D. (1996). Adaptive and maladaptive coping. In M. Zeidner and N. S. Endler (Eds.), *Handbook of coping: Theory, research, applications* (pp. 505-531). New York: Wiley.

Zuckerman, M., and Gagné, M. (2003). The COPE revised: Proposing a 5-factor model of coping strategies. *Journal of Research in Personality, 37,* 169-204.

In: Coping in Sport: Theory, Methods, and Related Constructs   ISBN: 978-1-60876-488-4
Editor: Adam R. Nicholls   © 2010 Nova Science Publishers, Inc.

Chapter 11

ACHIEVEMENT GOALS AND COPING IN SPORT

Chris Harwood and Derwin Chan
Loughborough University, UK

ABSTRACT

The purpose of this chapter is to discuss the role that achievement motivation plays in our understanding of coping responses and strategies in sport. First, we outline the tenets of achievement goal theory by focusing on the original approaches championed by Nicholls (1984) and Dweck (1986), as well as the role of motivational climate (Ames, 1992) as a key situational factor. The body of academic knowledge illustrating the potential relationships between task and ego goals and coping is then reviewed. As an antecedent of coping-related behavior, a high task goal has been consistently associated with adaptive forms of coping, whereas an ego goal has been related to less adaptive coping responses. However, the methodological sophistication of past studies, the lack of understanding of the combined effects of task/ego goals, and the scarcity of studies at a situational level leaves many questions unanswered. A number of relevant future directions for this research area are therefore presented.

INTRODUCTION

As one of the most publically-focused, and therefore socially-evaluated, achievement contexts, competitive sport imposes a wide range of physical, psychological, social-environmental and organizational demands upon an athlete (Fletcher, Hanton, and Mellalieu, 2006). The ability to cope with these demands represents a critical, complex, and often dynamic process within the on going goal of ensuring effective performance, psychological well being, and personal development. A great deal of research has primarily targeted the coping strategies that both reflect and explain athletes' behavior in these demanding circumstances (e.g., Nicholls, Polman, Levy, Taylor, and Cobley, 2007; Nicholls and Polman, 2007; Pensgaard and Duda, 2003). It is widely accepted that athletes who use more direct strategies to deal with the source of problems, and actively seek solutions to overcome them, demonstrate better behavioral adaptations towards stress than those who adopt indirect or avoidance styles to cope with stress. Comparatively, however, we still know little about the antecedents or individual difference factors that may contribute to the endorsement of adaptive or maladaptive coping styles in sport settings.

From the mid-1980's, social cognitive theories of motivation (mainly originating from educational psychology) dominated with respect to the explanation of motivated behaviours in sport (see Harwood, Spray and Keegan, 2008 for a review). Achievement goal theory (AGT; Ames, 1984; Dweck, 1986; Maehr and Nicholls, 1980; Nicholls, 1984) emerged as a central framework focused on how individual differences in achievement goals and situational/environmental factors explained both positive and negative patterns of cognition, affect and behavior in achievement tasks. Naturally, one of the areas targeted by achievement goal researchers was coping, and a steady amount of research has subsequently focused on how an athlete's achievement goals may underpin or influence the coping strategies and experiences of athletes (e.g., Kristiansen, Roberts, and Abrahamsen, 2008; Ntoumanis, Biddle, and Haddock, 1999; Pensgaard and Roberts, 2003).

The purpose of this chapter is therefore to outline achievement goal theory and introduce the reader to some of the key studies that have advanced our understanding of the relationship between achievement motivation and coping strategies and responses. In addition, we will identify where future research possibilities exist in this salient area so that academics may target their resources towards relevant, needed and practically engaging questions.

ACHIEVEMENT GOAL THEORY

Achievement goal theory proposes that it is the 'quality' of an individual's motivation (at any one point in time) as opposed to the 'quantity' of motivation that determines the cognitions, emotions, and behaviours of people in and around an achievement task such as sport. Achievement goal theorists believe that individuals assign a certain meaning to achievement situations that is related to their personal definitions of success and failure, and that this in turn basically affects how they think, feel, act, behave, and cope in that context. In the late 1970's and early 1980's, the work in classroom settings of John Nicholls, Carol Dweck, and Martin Maehr provided the foundation for our understanding of achievement goals in sport (Dweck, 1986; Maehr and Nicholls, 1980; Nicholls, 1984, 1989). In sport settings, through the early work of Glyn Roberts (1984, 1992) and Joan Duda (1987), it has been Nicholls' theoretical approach to achievement goals that has acted as the conduit for the vast majority of research. However, Dweck's approach and latterly Elliot's model (Elliot, 1997; Elliot and Church, 1997; Elliot and McGregor, 2001) has featured in a growing number of studies related to coping. In this chapter, we will focus heavily on Nicholls' model as well as clarifying Dweck's approach with its largely similar features.

According to both Nicholls and Dweck, the demonstration of competence (or ability) in an achievement context serves as a central achievement motive. People engage in achievement tasks to gain a sense of competence. However, Nicholls believed that competence (cf: ability) could be construed by individuals in two different manners. First, ability can be judged high or low with reference to the individual's own past performance or knowledge, and in this context, gains in mastery indicate competence. Second, ability can be judged as a current capacity relative to that of others, where a gain in personal mastery alone does not indicate high ability. To demonstrate high capacity, one must achieve more than others with equal effort or show less effort than others to achieve an equal performance (Nicholls, 1984).

Essentially, these two contrasting conceptions or 'definitions' of regarding what 'ability' can mean, underpins two very contrasting achievement goals. When an individual gains a sense of competence through personally mastering or improving upon a task, they are said to be *task involved*. For an individual pursuing a *task involved goal*, perceived self-improvement is sufficient to generate a sense of personal achievement. However, an individual is said to be *ego involved* when they gain a sense of competence by either demonstrating superior performance to others, or via an equal performance to others but with less effort exhibited. Both achievement goals revolve around the nature of the self. When an athlete is in a state of task involvement, his/her main focus is on the development of the self, regardless of others. They are focused on, and inherently value, *improving* their own competence or ability. In contrast, when athletes are in a state of ego involvement, the perceived ability of the self normatively compared to others is most valuable. The primary concern is therefore not improving, but rather *proving* the ability or competence that one has at the task in relation to other competitors.

Individual Differences in Achievement Goals

The motivational state of the athlete (i.e., task or ego involved) in a given situation is clearly important to a variety of subsequent factors in that situation (e.g., effort; attention; and coping responses), but Nicholls (1984, 1989) argued that individual differences also exist in terms of the tendency to adopt and pursue certain achievement goals. Developed through the processes of socialization during childhood and adolescence, Nicholls believed that individuals develop a pre-disposition or dispositional proneness towards one or indeed both achievement goals. He labeled these as achievement goal orientations, whereby a task goal orientation (task oriented) refers to the dispositional proneness to become task involved, and an ego goal orientation (ego oriented) refers to the personal propensity to be ego involved.

Dweck (1986) offered an alternative view of how these two achievement goals might be adopted, and the individual differences that underpin such goals. She proposed that individuals judge the nature of competence in similar ways to which they view the *malleability* of attributes, such as the world, the self, and the personality of other people. She argued that individuals possess *implicit theories* pertaining to whether people and constructs have the capacity to grow, change, and develop versus staying naturally fixed and unchangeable. She proposed that *Entity theorists* believe that ability is fixed (gifted), uncontrollable, and relatively stable over time, whereas *Incremental theorists* believe that ability is unstable, malleable through learning, improvable, and open to development. She believed that those individuals oriented towards an entity theory would be likely to carry entity beliefs about achievement in a task, and would therefore pursue a *performance goal* (cf: ego goal) which focused on proving their fixed capacity of ability by beating others. In contrast, those incremental theorists would be likely to possess incremental beliefs about a task, and adopt a *learning goal* (cf: task goal) focused on improvement and self-mastery in that task.

In short, individual differences in the endorsement of goal orientations and implicit theories of ability, can vary the way people act, think, and feel in an achievement setting. Different belief systems subjectively underpin what competence is and how it is demonstrated. It is easy to see the similarities in Nicholls and Dweck's approaches - incremental theorists align with a task orientation (learning goal) and define success as personal growth and development, as they believe that ability is modifiable through practice and learning. They focus on improving their ability. Entity theorists align with an ego orientation (performance goal) and feed their competence needs by outperforming others and proving their ability, as they believe that ability is fixed, unchangeable, and important to show! (Biddle, Wang, Chatzisarantis, and Spray, 2003; Sarrazin, et al., 1996; Wang, Liu, Biddle, and Spray, 2005).

Situational Factors and Motivational Climate

Individual differences in achievement goals and implicit theories, however, do not guarantee that an athlete will adopt commensurate task (learning) or ego (performance) goals in a particular achievement situation. AGT further proposes that these pre-dispositions will interact with social-environmental cues to determine our goal adoption (states of task/ego involvement) and achievement behaviours in a given situation (Ames, 1992a; Ames and Archer, 1988; Nicholls, 1984, 1989). For instance, an athlete with a high task orientation and moderate ego orientation may be exposed to a situation where the social and personal consequences of winning are strongly emphasized and the importance of personal development is relatively less salient. This may promote a more intensive state of ego involvement due to the power of these situational cues. Carole Ames (Ames, 1992a; Ames and Archer, 1988) is credited with achievement goal theory's focus on situational and environmental cues. Over the years, the term 'motivational climate' has become synonymous with the psychosocial atmosphere that promotes or triggers the adoption of a particular achievement goal. Significant others and important social agents such as coaches, parents, teachers, and peers may exert substantial influence on an athlete's personal definition of ability through their explicit expectations, reward systems, and behaviours. In other words, an athlete's achievement goal state might be heavily socially influenced due to what they perceive from significant others as important to demonstrate in terms of competence. A perceived task involving climate exists when the perceived social environment emphasizes, values and respects effort, improvement, cooperation and self-referenced learning; in contrast, an ego involving climate exists when the perceived social environment promotes comparisons with other competitors, emphasizes competitive outcomes and rewards winning (Ames, 1992a, 1992b; Ames and Archer, 1988).

Research into Achievement Goal Theory

Over the past two decades, an immense amount of research has investigated task and ego goals at dispositional and situational levels, including research into perceived motivational climate as an antecedent of task and ego involvement.

By 2003, a systematic review, of 98 published studies (accumulated sample size = 21,076) about dispositional goal orientation in sport/ PE (Biddle, Wang, Kavussanu, and Spray, 2003), concluded that a task orientation predicted more positive cognitive and behavioral outcomes (e.g., effort, positive affect, perceptions of competence, and efficient information processing) than did an ego orientation. Similarly, research on implicit theories of ability in physical education (PE) contexts showed that PE students with higher incremental beliefs, as opposed to entity beliefs, experienced greater enjoyment (Biddle, Wang, Chatzisarantis, et al., 2003), and reported higher motivation, self-efficacy, and reduced negative affect in the face of difficulty (Kasimatis, Miller, and Marcussen, 1996).

With respect to environmental influences, an ego-involving climate in PE/sport, as opposed to a task-involving climate, was associated with less positive affect (e.g., Boixados, Cruz, Torregrosa, and Valiente, 2004; Whitehead, Andree, and Lee, 2004), higher psychological distress (e.g., Ntoumanis and Biddle, 1998; Pensgaard and Roberts, 2000), and lower perceived competence (e.g., Kavussanu and Roberts, 1996; Standage, Duda, and Ntoumanis, 2003a, 2003b).

These research findings are highly consistent with the hypotheses proposed by Nicholls (1984), that task-involvement is more likely to result in adaptive patterns of cognitive, affective, and behavioral responses. Although a number of adaptive responses may also be experienced in a state of high-ego involvement, Nicholls suggested that this situation is limited to individuals with a high perception of ability (i.e., confident of achieving superiority).

However, because an ego involved athlete's sense of competence depends upon outcomes that are less reliable, controllable, and predictable, his or her perceived competence is more vulnerable in the face of challenges, difficulties, and normative failure. In summary, when ego-involved athletes are confident in winning, they are likely to engage the task in a positive manner.

However, when they perceive threats to their demonstration of ability, their uncertainty about success can lead them towards negative and maladaptive response patterns, including effort withdrawal, low persistence, avoidance of moderately-challenging tasks, and greater stress and anxiety. Athletes high in task involvement do not perceive such threats and tend to embrace challenges and adversity with a focus upon effort, problem solving and self-mastery.

Research into Achievement Goals and Coping

With empirical findings in broad support of these theoretical assumptions, researchers began to speculate if the perception of a task involving climate, a task orientation and incremental beliefs about ability served as antecedents of adaptive coping strategies in sport. They were equally interested in whether ego orientation, an ego involving climate or an entity view of ability was more likely to precipitate maladaptive coping responses. (See Table 1 for a summary of the key findings)

Table 1. A summary of studies within Achievement Goal Theory and Coping

Author	Purpose	Methodology	Results				Conclusion
			Task Goal	Ego Goal	Task Climate	Ego Climate	
Kim and Duda (1998)	Investigate the relationship between dispositional goal orientations and perceived motivational climate to athletes' perceived controllability over and ways of coping	Design: Cross-sectional Participants: 404 college level athletes Measures: TEOSQ[1] (task and ego orientation), PMCSQ-2[2] (task and ego involving climates), ACSQ[3] (active planning/cognitive restructuring, emotional calming, mental withdrawal, seeking social support, turning to religion, and behavioural risk), self reported psychological difficulties, and the controllability and performance debilitation during negative psychological state Analysis: Multiple regression	No significant association	No significant association	Psychological difficulties (-ve), performance impairment (-ve), perceived controllability over negative psychological states (+ve),	Psychological difficulties (+ve), maladaptive coping strategies (behavioural disengagement, venting/negative emotion, denial, wishful thinking, and blaming self/others; +ve)	Motivational climate created by coaches was a better predictor of coping strategies than achievement goal orientation.
Kaplan and Midgley (1999)	Investigate the relationships between classroom goal structure and self-report coping strategies and affect among students	Design: Two-year longitudinal Participants: 880 fifth grade elementary school students in United States Measures: PALS[4] (task and ego involving climate), ACI[5] (positive, projective, denial, non-coping), ASS[6] (positive and negative affect) Analysis: Structural equation modeling	N/A	N/A	Positive coping (+ve)	Projective coping (-ve), denial coping (-ve),	Coping strategies completely mediate the relationship between classroom goal structure and affect.
Ntoumanis, Biddle and Haddock (1999)	Examine the relationships between motivational factors, types of coping, affect, and situational perception of control	Design: Cross-sectional Participants: 356 British university athletes Measures: TEOSQ[1], PMCSQ-2[2], items for coping strategies derived from COPE[7], WCQ[8] and PANAS[9] (problem-focused: effort, suppression of competitive activities; emotion-focused: behavioural	Suppression of competitive activities (+ve)	Venting of emotions (+ve)	Suppression of competitive activities (+ve), Effort (+ve), seeking social support (+ve)	Behavioural disengagement (-ve), venting of emotions (-ve), seeking social support (+ve)	Task-involving climate and task goal orientation predicted problem-focused coping. Ego-involving climate and ego goal orientation predicted emotion-focused coping. Coping strategies were more related to motivational climates than

		disengagement, venting of emotions, distancing), seeking social support for emotional and instrumental reason) Analysis: Structural equation modeling					goal orientations. Coping strategies mediated the relationship between motivational climate, achievement goal and affect.
Pensgaard, Roberts, and Ursin (1999)	Compare the motivational factors and the use of coping strategies among elite athletes with or without physical disability	Design: Cross-sectional Participants 99 Norwegian athletes from the winter Olympics and Paralympics Measures: POSQ[10] (task and ego orientation), PMCSQ[11] (task and ego-involving climate), COPE[7], Expectation and Satisfactions[12], qualitative interviews Analysis: MANOVA (quantitative data) and phenomenological descriptive approach (qualitative data)	No significant difference	No significant difference	Paralympics athletes > Olympic athletes	No significant difference	Paralympics athletes perceived more task-involving climate, adopted more redefinition and growth strategies for coping, and felt more satisfied with effort and results
Grant and Dweck (2003)	Investigate the structure and impacts of achievement goal orientation	Design: Cross-sectional (study 4) Participants: 92 participants from university community Measures: AGI[13] (learning, ability, outcome, normative), COPE[7], psychological concomitants of goals[14] (loss of intrinsic motivation, withdrawal of time and effort, planning, help-seeking, effort-based attribution of failure, ability based attribution of failure, rumination, loss of self worth) Analysis: Multiple regression	Learning goal: Active coping (+ve), planning[7] (+ve), positive reinterpretation (+ve), denial (-ve), behavioural disengagement (-ve), mental disengagement (-ve), loss of intrinsic motivation (-ve), withdrawal of time and effort (-ve), planning (-ve), effort-based attribution of failure (+ve), ability-based attribution of failure (-ve)	Ability goal: positive reinterpretation (-ve), loss of self worth (+ve), loss of intrinsic motivation (-ve), withdrawal of time and effort (-ve), rumination (-ve), ability-based attribution of failure (+ve); Outcome goal: loss of intrinsic motivation (+ve), help seeking (+ve); Normative goal: denial (-ve), behavioural disengagement (-ve), ability-based attribution of failure (-ve)	N/A	N/A	Learning goals predicted active coping and sustained motivation, and higher achievement in the face of challenge. Ability goal heightened performance after success achieved but was linked to poorer performance and withdrawal after setbacks. Normative goal was associated with avoidance coping (e.g., denial and behavioural disengagement).

Table 1. (Continued)

Study	Aim	Design/Method				Conclusion
Pensgaard and Roberts (2003)	Investigate the relationship between task goal and ego goal orientations and the use of stress-coping strategies among athletes participating in the 1994 Winter Olympic Games	Design: Cross-sectional. Participants: 69 Norwegian athletes who participated in the 1994 Winter Olympics. Measures: POSQ[10], COPE[7]. Analysis: median split (high/low profiles of task/ego orientation), ANOVA	4 profiles: High task high ego (HH); high task low ego (HL); low task high ego (LH); low task low ego (LL). Active: HL > HH, LH, LL; Social emotional: HL > HH, LH, LL; Redefinition and growth: HL, LH > HH, LL; Active coping, planning, and denial between high and low ego orientation groups were significant different for female, but not for male. High ego male employed higher active coping than high ego female	N/A	N/A	High task/low ego oriented athlete employed more active coping strategies than high task/high ego, low task/high ego, and the low task/low ego groups. High ego orientation was associated with less active coping and planning, and more denial as a coping strategies among female athletes, but not among male athletes.
Kristiansen, Roberts, and Abrahamsen (2008)	To explore the relationship between task involvement and coping with stress in competition among elite wrestlers	Design: Cross-sectional. Participants: 82 elite wrestlers in Northern Europe. Measures: POSQ[10], PMCSQ[11], Brief COPE[15], interview. Analysis: Pearson correlation, canonical correlation, content analysis	**Pearson correlation** — Adaptive coping (-ve), emotional support (+ve), instrumental support (+ve), self-distraction (+ve) / Active coping (-ve) / Adaptive coping (-ve), emotional support (+ve), instrumental support (+ve), positive reframe (+ve) / Active coping (-ve), religion (+ve), positive reframe (-ve), denial (+ve)	**Canonical correlation** — N/A / N/A / High task/low ego involving climate: self distraction (+ve), active coping (+ve), emotional support (+ve), instrumental support (+ve), positive reframe (+ve), planning (+ve), religion (+ve). Low task/high ego involving climate: denial (+ve), religion (+ve), positive reframe (-ve), acceptance (-ve)	**Content analysis** — Task orientation and task involving climate are associated with adaptive coping (e.g. team support, practice routine, concentration)	High task involved wrestlers (high task oriented, and perceived high task-involved climate) use more adaptive coping strategies.
Lau and Nie (2008)	Investigate the cross-level interactions between personal goals and classroom goal structure,	Design: Cross-sectional. Participants: 3943 grade 5 students from 38 different schools (130 different classrooms). Measures: PALS[4], (motivational climates,	Achievement (-ve), engagement (+ve), interests (+ve), effort withdrawal (-ve), avoidance	Approach performance: engagement (+ve); Avoidance performance: achievement (-e), engagement (+ve),	Achievement (+ve), effort withdrawal (-ve), avoidance coping (+ve) / Achievement (-ve), engagement (-ve), effort withdrawal (-ve). Exacerbated the impacts of performance-	Personal performance-approach goals were related to engagement, thus it seemed beneficial Task-involving climate, task goal, and performance-approach goal are

					Entity		
and their impacts on math achievement, engagement, interest, effort withdrawal, and avoidance coping	approach-avoidance goal orientation), avoidance coping scale[16], interest/intrinsic motivation[17], effort withdrawal scale[18], engagement[19], math test. Analysis: Hierarchical linear model	coping (-ve),	effort withdrawal (-ve), avoidance coping (+ve)		avoidance goal on engagement (-ve), effort withdrawal (-ve), and avoidance coping (-ve).		associated with maladaptive behavioural and motivational outcomes. The impacts of achievement motivation and classroom goal structure interacted in a multilevel manner.

		Incremental/ learning	Gift	General	Stable	
Ommundsen (2003)	Investigate the relationship between implicit theory of ability and self-regulation of learning in PE among secondary school students	Design: Cross-sectional. Participants: 343 secondary school student at ninth grade. Measures: CNAAQ[20] (incremental belief, entity belief, MSLQ[21] (elaboration strategies, metacognitive of self-regulation, regulation of effort, help seeking). Analysis: MANOVA, multiple regression	Metacognitive-elaboration (+ve), effort regulation (+ve), help seeking (+ve)	help seeking (-ve)	Metacognitive-elaboration (-ve), effort regulation (-ve), help seeking (-ve)	PE students with incremental conceptions of ability, as opposed to those whose conceptions are predominantly fixed, make more use of metacognitive/elaboration strategies, regulate their effort better and seem more prepared to request help from teachers and classmates when needed.

MANOVA for profiles

Metacognitive-elaboration: High incremental-low entity group> Low incremental-low entity group, high incremental-high entity group> Low incremental-low entity group, low incremental-high entity group

Help seeking: High incremental-low entity group, high incremental-high entity group> Low incremental-low entity group, low incremental-high entity group

Regulation of effort: High incremental-low entity group > low incremental-low entity group

(1) TEOSQ= Task and Ego Orientation in Sport Questionnaire (Duda & Nicholls, 1992); (2) PMCSQ-2= Perceived Motivational Climate in Sport Questionnaire (Newton, Duda, & Yin, 2000); (3) ACSQ= Korean Approach to Coping in Sport Questionnaire (Kim, Duda, & Ntoumanis, 2003); (4) PALS= Patterns of Adaptive Learning Survey (Midgley, et al., 1996); (5) ACI= Academic Coping Inventory (Tero & Connell, 1984); (6) ASS= Affect-in-School Scale (Wolters, Garcia, & Pintrich, 1992); (7) COPE= COPE Inventory (Carver, et al., 1989); (8) WCQ= Ways of Coping Questionnaire (Folkman, 1984); (9) PANAS= Positive and Negative Affect Schedule (Watson, Clark, & Tellegen, 1988); (10) POSQ= Perception of Success Questionnaire (Roberts & Ommundsen, 1996); (11) PMCSQ= (Seifriz, Duda, & Chi, 1992); (12) Expectation and Satisfaction (Pensgaard, et al., 1999); (13) AGI= Achievement Goal Inventory (Grant & Dweck, 2003); (14) Psychological concomitants of goals (Molden & Dweck, 2000); (15) Brief COPE (Carver, 1997); (16) Avoidance coping scale was adapted from the Motivated Strategies for Learning Questionnaire (Pintrich, Smith, Garcia, & Mckeachie, 1993); (17) Items for intrinsic motivation and enjoyment was adopted from Elliot and Church (1997); (18) Effort Withdrawal Scale (Meece, Blumenfeld, & Hoyle, 1988; Nicholls, Patashnick, & Nolen, 1985) (19) Engagement was based on students' report of their attention, effort, and participation in their math classes (Steinberg, Lamborn, Dornbusch, & Darling, 1992; Wellborn & Connell, 1987); (20) CNAAQ= Conception of the Nature of Sport Ability Questionnaire (Sarrazin, et al., 1996); (21) MSLQ=Motivated Strategies for Learning Questionnaire (Pintrich, et al., 1993).

Early Investigations in Sport

Kim and Duda (1998) conducted the first study to look at the relationships between achievement goal orientation, motivational climate, and coping strategies in competitive sport. They found that perceived motivational climate was associated with various forms of adaptive and maladaptive coping strategies, among 404 college-level Korean athletes. A task-involving climate was positively associated with perceived controllability over a negative psychological state, and was negatively associated with self-reported psychological difficulties and performance debilitation during negative psychological states. Conversely, an ego-involving climate positively predicted psychological difficulties and maladaptive coping strategies, including behavioral disengagement, venting of emotion, denial, wishful thinking, and self/other blaming. Interestingly, self-reported achievement goal orientations showed no significant relationship with coping.

In a similar study with 356 college level athletes in Britain (Ntoumanis, Biddle, and Haddock, 1999), canonical correlations demonstrated that high task-involving climates and high task orientation were linked to problem-focused coping (i.e., suppression of competing activities, effort), whereas a high ego-involving climate and ego orientation predicted emotional (avoidance) coping (i.e., behavioral disengagement, venting of emotion). In addition, mediation analyses within the structural equation model confirmed the hypothesized mediating effect of coping strategies between the motivational variables (i.e., goal orientation and motivational climate) and affect, with problem-focused coping serving as the mediator between task goals (goal orientation and motivational climate) and positive affect, and emotion-focused coping serving as the mediator between ego goals and negative affect. These results were in line with Lazarus's suggestions about the importance of motivational processes on coping (Lazarus, 1991).

Lazarus noted that "how the person copes depends not only on the coping possibilities and how they are appraised but also on what a person wants to accomplish in the encounter" (p. 115). In his model of coping, goals/motives in a given situation form antecedents of cognitive appraisal, coping choices, and subsequent emotional outcomes, where motivational antecedents consist of both dispositional and situational components. AGT appears to embed neatly into this model. Task goal orientation and the perception of task-involving climate promote self-referenced goals with self-improvement as a valued indicator of success. Mistakes are viewed as part of the learning process, and there is a clear inclination towards the use of active and effortful coping strategies to deal with challenges. An ego goal orientation and an ego-involving climate reflect the importance of normative adequacy, increasing the tendency to depreciate effort and persistence when faced with a threat (and particularly when perceived ability is low). Direct actions to tackle the source of stress are less likely, and individuals may either diminish the importance of the threat or distance themselves from stressors (Grant and Dweck, 2003; Ntoumanis, et al., 1999).

The Exacerbating Effects of Motivational Climates

These early studies offered some insight into how the interaction between dispositional goal orientation and the perceived motivational climate would lead to certain coping behaviours. Kim and Duda (1998) argued that motivational climate is a better predictor of coping strategies than achievement goal orientation. Ntoumanis and colleagues (1999) held a similar perspective due to the fact that motivational climates were associated with more forms of coping in the structural equation model.

A more recent study from the education domain, using more advanced statistical analysis, offers insight for this line of inquiry. Lau and Nie (2008) employed hierarchical linear modeling (multilevel analysis) to examine the effects of goal orientation and motivational climate on coping amongst 3943 grade 5 elementary school students (from 38 different schools, 130 different classrooms). Similar to previous studies in this area, a task goal and task involving climate were deemed to be more adaptive than an ego goal or ego involving climates, in that they were positively associated with active coping, and negatively associated with avoidance coping. An ego-involving climate exacerbated the negative impact of performance-avoidance goals (i.e., an ego goal focused avoiding the demonstration of low ability; Elliot and Church, 1997) on coping. In other words, students with high performance-avoidance goals showed stronger connections with maladaptive coping (i.e., reduction of behavioral engagement, effort withdrawal, and avoidance coping) in highly ego-involving classrooms (i.e., the motivational climate created by teachers) than those in low ego-involving classrooms.

Papaioannou, Marsh, and Theodorakis (2004) argued that multilevel modeling should be used to resolve the confounding issue of within-group similarity and between-group dissimilarity in motivational climate research. However, there have not been any studies (as yet) using a multilevel approach to examine the impacts of motivational climate and goal orientation on coping in competitive sport or PE contexts.

Achievement Goal Profiling Research

In the previous sections, we presented several studies which used correlational approaches such as multiple regression and structural equation modeling to examine the relative impact of goal orientation on coping with respect to that of motivational climate (Kim and Duda, 1998; Lau and Nie, 2008; Ntoumanis, et al., 1999). However, it is important to note that task and ego goals are theoretically independent of each other (i.e., the principle of orthogonality; see Harwood and Hardy, 2001; Harwood, Hardy, and Swain, 2000). In other words, an athlete may possess a high task and high ego goal orientation, or be low in one or both dispositional goals. This presents a complex problem since predictions for a task and ego orientation vis a vis coping responses are potentially different. What coping strategies are likely to be used when an athlete reports that s/he is high in both goal orientations (i.e., the high-high goal profile)?

To further this line of enquiry, Pensgaard and Roberts (2003) employed a median split technique to cluster 69 Winter Olympic competitors into the four goal profiles and examined differences regarding their use of coping strategies. This person-centred approach in achievement goal research is termed 'goal profiling', and a number of researchers believe this to be more effective in understanding the practical interaction between task and ego goal orientation (Harwood, Spray, and Keegan, 2008). The results of the Pensgaard and Roberts (2003) study showed that high task/low ego (HL) oriented athletes employed more problem-focused coping (i.e., active coping) as well as emotion-focused coping (i.e., social emotional support) strategies than the athletes in the other three goal profiles. However, amongst high task/ high ego (HH), low task/low ego (LL), and low task/high ego (LH) groups, no significant differences were found in their coping strategies, except that the LH group reported higher redefinition and growth (emotion-focused coping) than the HH and LL groups.

It is worth noting that a lack of significance might be due to the fact that low sample size in each goal profile limited the statistical power to detect the differences in coping strategies between groups. Moreover, the study consisted only of Olympic level athletes, so the results may not generalize well to junior level athletes or competitive amateurs. The application of goal profiling research in understanding coping behaviour remains scarce, yet it is critical to unravel the interplay between task and ego orientations and the mechanisms that may lead to adaptive coping being facilitated over maladaptive coping (or vice versa) within a high-high profile.

At the situational level, some studies have acknowledged that the motivational climate can be both task and ego involving because individuals may perceive conflicting cues from significant others within the same environment. As Harwood and colleagues (2008) noted, effort, improvement, and social comparison might equally be emphasized in a sport team, given that a number of significant others could promote different values upon the athlete. For example, the coach of a team may create a task-involving climate by emphasizing process goals and improvement, but players (i.e. peers) in the team may foster an ego-involving climate by promoting rivalry and intra-team member competition. Moreover, a coach or a PE teacher may give equally positive reinforcement to winning as well as to improvement, so a sporting context with high task involving climate and ego involving climate is practically possible.

With these observations in mind, Kristiansen, Roberts, and Abrahamsen (2008) used canonical correlation analyses to examine the multivariate relationship between the two motivational climates and various forms of coping. Two combinations of motivational climates emerged significantly from the functions of canonical correlation. A high task/ low ego (HL) climate was associated with higher active coping, emotional support, instrumental support, positive reframing, planning, religion, and lower self-distraction. Secondly, a low task/ high ego (LH) climate was associated with higher denial and religion, and lower positive reframing and acceptance. As expected, the HL climate was linked to more adaptive coping than LH climate, however, as LL and HH climates did not emerge in the results, we are still uncertain about the combined effects of perceived task and ego involving climates on coping, and the underpinning mechanisms at work. More studies that use person-centered approaches, including qualitative investigations to engage a richer understanding, are recommended for this area.

Research on Implicit Theories and Coping

Implicit theories have received less attention within achievement goal research in sport, and particularly with respect to coping research. However, the concepts of implicit theory do share a notable similarity with one of the mainstream theories of coping. The goodness-of-fit model of coping effectiveness proposed by Folkman (1991, 1992) suggests that the coping options, and their related effectiveness, not only depend upon the coherence between the person-environmental threats and the appraisal of the individual, but also account for the match between the perceived controllability of the stressor and the endorsed coping strategies associated with the stressor. While the initial stress and coping model proposed that problem-focused coping was more adaptive than emotion-focused coping (see Folkman, 1984), the goodness-of-fit model argued that the relative effectiveness of coping would depend on the appraisal of control over the stress. When the perceived encounter is under personal control, problem-focused coping is believed to be more appropriate, thus it is more likely to be adopted. Whereas when the perceived difficulty is beyond our control, emotion-focused coping is deemed more relevant, thus it is more likely to be applied.

This concept of controllability in goodness-of-fit model shares some degree of congruence with the implicit theory of ability. Specifically, implicit theory could plausibly be a moderator of an individual's preference or effectiveness in using certain coping strategies, as the two contrasting implicit views alter the degree to which one appraises the controllability of environmental stress. Incremental theorists perceive a stressful situation as malleable to change, so they might engage in more problem-focused/ active coping strategies (e.g., planning, exerting more effort). Entity theorists recognize a stressful situation as fixed and uncontrollable, and thus would possibly adopt more emotion-focused/avoidance coping (e.g., acceptance, denial, distancing) options. Nonetheless, no single study has formally examined the relationship between implicit theory of ability and the preference/effectiveness of coping strategies in sport. A number of studies, however, have offered some indications about what might be expected.

In sport and PE contexts, research regarding implicit theory of ability has shown consistent findings with respect to the suggestions of Dweck and coworkers (Dweck, 1999; Dweck, Chiu, and Hong, 1995). Incremental beliefs and entity beliefs have been positively associated with task and ego orientation respectively and they have both demonstrated direct effects on a variety of cognitive, behavioural, and affective patterns in PE and sport (Biddle, Soos, and Chatzisarantis, 1999; Biddle, Wang, Chatzisarantis, et al., 2003; Lintunen, Valkonen, Leskinen, and Biddle, 1999; Ommundsen, 2001a, 2001b; Sarrazin, et al., 1996). In line with Dweck's theoretical model, incremental beliefs were shown to be a positive predictor of a variety of adaptive responses, such as perceived competence, intention, enjoyment and satisfaction in PE and sport. Entity beliefs were found to be maladaptive, and associated with self-handicapping, anxiety, and reduced satisfaction in PE (Ommundsen, 2001a, 2001b). Given that entity theorists do not consider achievement drawbacks as a consequence of inadequate effort, and even believe that exerting more effort indicates a further lack of ability, they are more reluctant to take remedial actions for their perceived inadequacy than incremental theorists (Hong, Chiu, Dweck, Lin, and Wan, 1999).

A recent study by Ommundsen (2003) investigated the self-regulatory styles and implicit beliefs of grade nine PE students. Students who reported higher incremental beliefs were more likely to use metacognitive-elaboration (i.e., planning, monitoring, regulating), regulation of effort, and help-seeking to learn different tasks in PE than those with low incremental beliefs. In contrast, students who held higher entity beliefs, in general, reported less use of metacognitive-elaboration, regulation of effort, and help-seeking when engaging in different tasks in PE.

Overall therefore, research favours the proposition that incremental theorists use more problem-focused/ active coping to deal with difficulties in sport settings than entity theorists do. Nevertheless, further investigations are clearly required to address these arguments.

Future Research Directions

Although the existing literature on AGT has drawn out a general picture regarding how achievement goals may be related to adaptive and maladaptive coping, it is clear that there are far more questions unanswered than answered. In the previous sections, we have highlighted certain limitations of the current research, and in this section we aim to further reinforce the key areas of interest and present unexplored areas in an attempt to stimulate future research.

More goal profiling research. As noted previously, task and ego goals are supposedly related to adaptive and maladaptive coping patterns, but their combined effects on coping is still a debatable topic in sport. A growing number of goal profiling studies have suggested that a moderate-to-high task combined with a corresponding level of ego orientation, compared to other goal profiles, is associated with more adaptive behavioural patterns in sport, such as higher perceptions of physical ability (Hodge and Petlichkoff, 2000), higher sport motivation (Sit and Lindner, 2007; Wang, Chatzisarantis, Spray, and Biddle, 2002), greater use of mental skills (Cumming, Hall, Harwood, and Gammage, 2002; Harwood, Cumming, and Fletcher, 2004; Harwood, Cumming, and Hall, 2003), and higher mental toughness (Kuan and Roy, 2007). All of these correlates are potentially helpful for sport participants to maintain long term sport involvement and persistence in the face of threats. Therefore is a high ego orientation an advantage in terms of an athlete's menu of coping responses provided that it exists with a high task orientation? What mechanisms are at work here and how do the two dispositions function together? Does perceived competence matter within a high-high profile given that a high ego orientation can be a curse for those with low perceived competence? These are very relevant and topical questions that remain uninvestigated.

In a similar vein, the interactions between incremental belief and entity belief have not been fully examined thoroughly in the context of coping in sport. Ommundsen's (2003) study showed that students with implicit beliefs of high incremental-low entity or high incremental-high entity reported more metacognitive-elaboration and help seeking than those with implicit beliefs of the low incremental-low entity or low incremental-high entity. Therefore, athletes who adopt a balanced combination of both implicit theories potentially cope as effectively as those who adopt high incremental belief and low entity belief. Yet, the self regulation constructs of Ommundsen (2003) were limited to only some aspects of active coping. Future research should target a wider range of coping strategies.

Examining goal involvement and coping. Most studies in AGT applying Nicholls' model have measured achievement goals at a dispositional level (i.e., goal orientation). However, given the role of motivational climate in predicting coping as a situational factor, it might be fair to assume that the most important construct to measure is the achievement goal in a specific situation (i.e., the goal state of task and ego involvement). Task and ego involvement may in fact fluctuate across different contexts (e.g., training, competitions) and change from moment to moment according to situational/environmental cues (see Harwood and Hardy, 2001; Harwood, Hardy and Swain, 2000). The presence of environmental threats and challenges in sport are usually sudden, unpredictable, and unique across different time points and situations. Therefore only by investigating the actual goal involvement of an athlete at given time point or context will we understand how this actually translates to the nature/type of coping responses demonstrated by athletes at these particular moments (e.g., pre-race; during performance). It is worth noting that the level of measurement of achievement goals should match the level of measurement of coping strategy/response. For example, the COPE inventory (Carver, Scheier, and Weintraub, 1989) aims to measure situational level coping strategies (i.e., in the most recent competition) but by a retrospective approach. Measures of achievement goal orientation (measured at dispositional level) would not necessarily give an accurate picture of what the achievement goals actually were in that context. Nor is a retrospective measure of coping, that fails to account for the dynamical changes can occur in situ, that useful either. Future studies may seek to experimentally induce a state of task or ego involvement and assess how sport participants with differing primary achievement goal states respond to particular adversities by assessing 'real time' coping strategies at a situational level. This would present a challenge in terms of measurement, but is nevertheless what is required to advance the field beyond its currently superficial understanding.

In addition, a greater focus may be placed on the temporal effects of achievement motivation on coping. Task goals and incremental theories of ability may promote problem focused coping responses when other forms of coping may be more effective and relevant for that situation. For example, problem-focused coping is deemed more adaptive in the long term, whereas avoidance coping could also be helpful when dealing with immediate threats (Anshel and Kaissidis, 1997; Kim and Duda, 2003). Would the task involved performer cope in the most efficient manner for the demands of the situation, or exert greater resources when the situation didn't necessarily warrant such an approach? This 'fit' between achievement goal, coping response and task demands would be interesting to investigate.

Acknowledging other conceptualizations of achievement goals. In this chapter, we have focused on Nicholls' and Dweck's approaches to AGT. However, an alternative model of AGT has emerged in recent years. Elliot and colleagues have argued that individuals strive to achieve in competitive contexts not only to demonstrate their competence, but also to avoid demonstrating incompetence (Elliot, 1997; Elliot and Church, 1997). Therefore, they introduced a valence dimension by bi-furcating ego goals into performance-approach goals and performance-avoidance goals. These two ego/performance goals represent an individual's aim of action to outperform others or to avoid being outplayed by others, respectively. A recent study by Lau and Nie (2008) in education revealed that a performance-approach goal was associated positively with engagement in a math class whereas a performance-avoidance goal was related negatively to engagement, and positively to effort withdrawal and avoidance coping. In recent years, this trichotomous model has been extended to a 2x2 quadratic model, as valence was incorporated into the task/mastery dimension leading to the constructs of mastery-approach and mastery avoidance goals (Elliot and Conroy, 2005; Elliot and McGregor, 2001; Wang, Biddle, and Elliot, 2007). There is limited research to the authors' knowledge that has specifically applied Elliot's trichotomous or 2 x 2 model to coping in sport, but the literature would suggest that both mastery- and performance-approach goals are likely to the far more adaptive vis a vis coping responses than both avoidance goals.

Considering further individual differences. The nature of coping and coping effectiveness could vary across gender, type of sport, and skill levels of individuals (Nicholls, et al., 2007). Similarly, these individual differences can also affect the relationship between achievement motivation and coping. Pensgaard and Roberts (2003) reported a moderating effect of gender between ego orientation and coping, revealing that the negative coping responses associated with ego orientation were found only in female athletes compared to male athletes. Pensgaard also examined the individual differences in terms of able bodied vs. disabled athletes by comparing athletes in the Olympic and Paralympic Games (Pensgaard, Roberts, and Ursin,

1999). Athletes in the Paralympics reported higher perceptions of task-involving climate, more frequent use of more redefinition and growth strategies for coping (a form of emotion focused coping), and higher satisfaction with their effort and results in the competition. Further, the qualitative investigation of Kristiansen and colleagues (2008) revealed that wrestlers frequently endorsed a high task-involvement, and use both problem-focused and emotion-focused coping during the race-preparation period and competitions.

Collectively, this small sample of studies suggests that we should be mindful that links between achievement motivation and coping may not necessarily be generalized across all sport participants. The impact of such individual differences on the relationship between achievement goals and coping should be scrutinized by studies with a greater variety of samples (e.g., cross-cultural sampling), and use of more stringent analytical approaches (e.g., multi-group structural equation modeling).

CONCLUSION

Coping is a crucial element of successful athletic performance and long term athlete development. Research that attempts to explain how adaptive coping in sport might be maximized, and maladaptive coping minimized, is therefore important both on humanistic and also commercial grounds. Achievement goal theories offer one lens for researchers and practitioners to look through and consider when investigating the antecedents of coping. Research in this area would suggest that an individuals' dispositional goal orientation, their personal beliefs about competence, and the psychosocial environment play relevant roles in how athletes come to deal with the environmental demands and personal adversities that they face in sport.

Research suggests that a task goal orientation, an incremental belief of ability, and a perceived environment emphasizing task involvement is associated with more adaptive coping responses in the face of threats, challenges, and setbacks. However, investigations of the AG/coping link are still at an early stage in sport, and research has been dominated by quantitative, cross-sectional, and correlational studies, which weaken the conclusions about the causal relationship between achievement motivation and coping responses. It would serve us well to be cautious about the level of evidence and external validity of the findings. Further research within the areas noted and improved designs such as randomized controlled trials and interventions may assist in scrutinizing the unanswered research questions in this field.

REFERENCES

Ames, C. (1992a). Achievement goals, motivational climate, and motivational processes. In G. C. Roberts (Ed.), *Motivation in sport and exercise* (pp. 161-176). Champaign, IL: Human Kinetics.

Ames, C. (1992b). Classrooms: Goals, structures, and student motivation. *Journal of Educational Psychology, 84*, 261-271.

Ames, C., and Archer, J. (1988). Achievement goals in the classroom: Students' learning strategies and motivation processes. *Journal of Educational Psychology, 80*, 260-267.

Ames, C. A. (1984). Achievement attributions and self instruction under competitive and individualistic goal structures. *Journal of Educational Psychology, 76*, 478-487.

Anshel, M. H., and Kaissidis, A. N. (1997). Coping style and situational appraisals as predictors of coping strategies following stressful events in sport as a function of gender and skill level. *British Journal of Psychology, 88*, 263-276.

Biddle, S. J. H., Soos, I., and Chatzisarantis, N. (1999). Predicting physical activity intentions using a goal perspectives approach: a study of Hungarian youth. *Scandinavian Journal of Medicine and Science in Sports, 9*(6), 353-357.

Biddle, S. J. H., Wang, C. J. K., Chatzisarantis, N. L. D., and Spray, C. M. (2003). Motivation for physical activity in young people: entity and incremental beliefs about athletic ability. *Journal of Sports Sciences, 21*(12), 973-989.

Biddle, S. J. H., Wang, C. K., Kavussanu, M., and Spray, C. (2003). Correlates of achievement goal orientations in physical activity: A systematic review of research. *European Journal of Sport Sciences, 3*, 1-20.

Boixados, M., Cruz, J., Torregrosa, M., and Valiente, L. (2004). Relationships among motivational climate, satisfaction, perceived ability, and fair play attitudes in young soccer players. *Journal of Applied Sport Psychology, 16*(4), 301-317.

Carver, C. S. (1997). You want to measure coping but your protocol's too long: Consider the brief COPE. *International Journal of Behavioral Medicine, 4*(1), 92-100.

Carver, C. S., Scheier, M. F., and Weintraub, J. K. (1989). Assessing coping strategies - A theoretically based approach. *Journal of Personality and Social Psychology, 56*(2), 267-283.

Cumming, J., Hall, C., Harwood, C., and Gammage, K. (2002). Motivational orientations and imagery use: a goal profiling analysis. *Journal of Sports Sciences, 20*(2), 127-136.

Duda, J. L. (1987). Toward a developmental theory of children's motivation in sport. *Journal of Sport Psychology, 9*, 130-145.

Duda, J. L., and Nicholls, J. G. (1992). Dimensions of achievement-motivation in schoolwork and sport. *Journal of Educational Psychology, 84*(3), 290-299.

Dweck, C. S. (1986). Motivational processes affecting learning. *American Psychologist, 41*, 1041-1048.

Dweck, C. S. (1999). *Self-Theories: Their Role in Motivation, Personality, and Development.* Philadelphia, PA: Taylor and Francis.

Dweck, C. S., Chiu, C. Y., and Hong, Y. Y. (1995). Implicit Theories and Their Role in Judgments and Reactions - a World from 2 Perspectives. *Psychological Inquiry, 6*(4), 267-285.

Elliot, A. J. (1997). Integrating the "classic" and "contemporary" approaches to achievement motivation: A hierarchical model of approach and avoidance achievement motivation. . In M. L. Maehr and P. R. Pintrich (Eds.), *Advances in motivation and achievement* (Vol. 10, pp. 143-179). Greenwich, CT: JAI Press.

Elliot, A. J., and Church, M. A. (1997). A hierarchical model of approach and avoidance achievement motivation. *Journal of Personality and Social Psychology, 72*(1), 218-232.

Elliot, A. J., and Conroy, D. E. (2005). Beyond the dichotomous model of achievement goals in sport and exercise psychology. *Sport and Exercise Psychology Review, 1*, 17-25.

Elliot, A. J., and McGregor, H. A. (2001). A 2 x 2 achievement goal framework. *Journal of Personality and Social Psychology, 80*(3), 501-519.

Fletcher, D., Hanton, S., and Mellalieu, S. D. (2006). An organizational stress review: Conceptual and theoretical issues in competitive sport. In S. Hanton and S. D. Mellalieu (Eds.), *Literature Reviews in Sport Psychology* (Vol. 321-373). Hauppauge, NY: Nova Science.

Folkman, S. (1984). Personal Control and Stress and Coping Processes - a Theoretical-Analysis. *Journal of Personality and Social Psychology, 46*(4), 839-852.

Folkman, S. (1991). Coping across the life span: Theoretical issues. In E. M. Cumming, A. L. Greene and K. H. Karraker (Eds.), *Life-span developmental psychology: Perspectives on stress and coping* (pp. 3-19). Hillsdale, NJ: Lawrence Erlbaum Associates.

Folkman, S. (1992). Making the case for coping. In C. B. N. (Ed.), *Personal coping: Theory, research and application* (pp. 31-46). Westport, CT: Praeger.

Grant, H., and Dweck, C. S. (2003). Clarifying achievement goals and their impact. *Journal of Personality and Social Psychology, 85*(3), 541-553.

Harwood, C. G., Cumming, J., and Fletcher, D. (2004). Motivational profiles and psychological skills use within elite youth sport. *Journal of Applied Sport Psychology, 16*(4), 318-332.

Harwood, C. G., Cumming, J., and Hall, C. (2003). Imagery use in elite youth sport participants: Reinforcing the applied significance of achievement goal theory. *Research Quarterly for Exercise and Sport, 74*(3), 292-300.

Harwood, C. G., and Hardy, L. (2001). Persistence and effort in moving achievement goal research forward: A response to treasure and colleagues. *Journal of Sport and Exercise Psychology, 23*(4), 330-345.

Harwood, C. G., Hardy, L., and Swain, A. (2000). Achievement goals in sport: A critique of conceptual and measurement issues. *Journal of Sport and Exercise Psychology, 22*(3), 235-255.

Harwood, C. G., Spray, C. M., and Keegan, R. (2008). Achievement goal theories in sport. In T. S. Horn (Ed.), *Advances in Sport Psychology* (3 ed., pp. 157-185). Champaign, IL: Human Kinetics.

Hodge, K., and Petlichkoff, L. (2000). Goal profiles in sport motivation: A cluster analysis. *Journal of Sport and Exercise Psychology, 22*(3), 256-272.

Hong, Y. Y., Chiu, C. Y., Dweck, C. S., Lin, D. M. S., and Wan, W. (1999). Implicit theories, attributions, and coping: A meaning system approach. *Journal of Personality and Social Psychology, 77*(3), 588-599.

Kaplan, A., and Midgley, C. (1999). The relationship between perceptions of the classroom goal structure and early adolescents' affect in school: The mediating role of coping strategies. *Learning and Individual Differences, 11*, 187-212.

Kasimatis, M., Miller, M., and Marcussen, L. (1996). The effects of implicit theories on exercise motivation. *Journal of Research in Personality, 30*(4), 510-516.

Kavussanu, M., and Roberts, G. C. (1996). Motivation in physical activity contexts: The relationship of perceived motivational climate to intrinsic motivation and self-efficacy. *Journal of Sport and Exercise Psychology, 18*(3), 264-280.

Kim, M. S., and Duda, J. L. (1998). Achievement goals, motivational climates and occurrence of and responses to psychological difficulties and performance debilitation among Korean athletes. *Journal of Sport and Exercise Psychology, 20*, S124-S124.

Kim, M. S., and Duda, J. L. (2003). The coping process: Cognitive appraisals of stress, coping strategies, and coping effectiveness. *Sport Psychologist, 17*(4), 406-425.

Kim, M. S., Duda, J. L., and Ntoumanis, N. (2003). Examination of the validity and reliability of the Korean Approach to Coping in Sport Questionnaire (ACSQ-Korean). *International Journal of Applied Sports Sciences, 14*(2), 35-55.

Kristiansen, E., Roberts, G. C., and Abrahamsen, F. E. (2008). Achievement involvement and stress coping in elite wrestling. *Scandinavian Journal of Medicine and Science in Sports, 18*(4), 526-538.

Kuan, G., and Roy, J. (2007). Goal profiles, mental toughness and its influence on performance outcomes among Wushu athletes. *Journal of Sports Science and Medicine, 6*, 28-33.

Lau, S., and Nie, Y. Y. (2008). Interplay between personal goals and classroom goal structures in predicting student outcomes: A multilevel analysis of person-context interactions. *Journal of Educational Psychology, 100*(1), 15-29.

Lazarus, R. S. (1991). *Emotion and adaptation*. New York: Oxford University Press.

Lintunen, T., Valkonen, A., Leskinen, E., and Biddle, S. J. H. (1999). Predicting physical activity intentions using a goal perspectives approach: a study of Finnish youth. *Scandinavian Journal of Medicine and Science in Sports, 9*(6), 344-352.

Maehr, M. L., and Nicholls, J. G. (1980). Culture and achievement motivation: A second look. In N. Warren (Ed.), *Studies in cross-cultural psychology* (Vol. 3, pp. 221-267). New York: Academic Press.

Meece, J. L., Blumenfeld, P. C., and Hoyle, R. H. (1988). Students Goal Orientations and Cognitive Engagement in Classroom Activities. *Journal of Educational Psychology, 80*(4), 514-523.

Midgley, C., Maehr, M. L., Hicks, L. H., Roeser, R., Urdan, T., Anderman, E., et al. (1996). *Patterns of adaptive learning survey (PALS)*: University of Michigan.

Molden, and Dweck, C. S. (2000). Intrinsic and extrinsic motivation: The search for optimal motivation and performance. In C. Sansone and J. M. Harackiewicz (Eds.), *Meaning and motivation* (pp. 131-159). San Diego, CA: Academic Press.

Newton, M., Duda, J. L., and Yin, Z. N. (2000). Examination of the psychometric properties of the Perceived Motivational Climate in Sport Questionnaire-2 in a sample of female athletes. *Journal of Sports Sciences, 18*(4), 275-290.

Nicholls, A. R., Polman, R., Levy, A. R., Taylor, J., and Cobley, S. (2007). Stressors, coping, and coping effectiveness: Gender, type of sport, and skill differences. *Journal of Sports Sciences, 25*(13), 1521-1530.

Nicholls, A. R., and Polman, R. C. J. (2007). Coping in sport: A systematic review. *Journal of Sports Sciences, 25*(1), 11-31.

Nicholls, J. G. (1984). Achievement motivation: Conceptions of ability, subjective experience, task choice, and performance. *Psychological Review, 91*, 328-346.

Nicholls, J. G. (1989). *The competitive ethos and democratic education*. Cambridge, MA: Harvard University Press.

Nicholls, J. G., Patashnick, M., and Nolen, S. B. (1985). Adolescents' theories of education. *Journal of Educational Psychology, 77*, 683-692.

Ntoumanis, N., and Biddle, S. (1998). The relationship between competitive anxiety, achievement goals, and motivational climates. *Research Quarterly for Exercise and Sport, 69*(2), 176-187.

Ntoumanis, N., Biddle, S. J. H., and Haddock, G. (1999). The mediating role of coping strategies on the relationship between achievement motivation and affect in sport. *Anxiety Stress and Coping, 12*(3), 299-327.

Ommundsen, Y. (2001a). Pupils' affective responses in PE: The influence of implicit theories of the nature of ability. *European Physical Education Review, 7*, 219-242.

Ommundsen, Y. (2001b). Self-handicapping strategies in physical education classes: The influence of implicit theories of the nature of ability and achievement goals. *Psychology of Sport and Exercise, 2*, 139-156.

Ommundsen, Y. (2003). Implicit Theories of Ability and Self-regulation Strategies in Physical Education Classes. *Educational Psychology, 23*(2), 141-157.

Papaioannou, A., Marsh, H. W., and Theodorakis, Y. (2004). A multilevel approach to motivational climate in physical education and sport settings: An individual or a group level construct? *Journal of Sport and Exercise Psychology, 26*(1), 90-118.

Pensgaard, A. M., and Duda, J. L. (2003). Sydney 2000: The interplay between emotions, coping, and the performance of Olympic-level athletes. *Sport Psychologist, 17*(3), 253-267.

Pensgaard, A. M., and Roberts, G. C. (2000). The relationship between motivational climate, perceived ability and sources of distress among elite athletes. *Journal of Sports Sciences, 18*(3), 191-200.

Pensgaard, A. M., and Roberts, G. C. (2003). Achievement goal orientations and the use of coping strategies among Winter Olympians. *Psychology of Sport and Exercise, 4*(2), 101-116.

Pensgaard, A. M., Roberts, G. C., and Ursin, H. (1999). Motivational factors and coping strategies of Norwegian Paralympic and Olympic winter sport athletes. *Adapted Physical Activity Quarterly, 16*(3), 238-250.

Pintrich, P. R., Smith, D. A. F., Garcia, T., and Mckeachie, W. J. (1993). Reliability and Predictive-Validity of the Motivated Strategies for Learning Questionnaire (Mslq). *Educational and Psychological Measurement, 53*(3), 801-813.

Roberts, G. C. (1984). Achievement motivation in children's sport. In J. G. Nicholls (Ed.), *Advances in motivation and achievement, Vol. 3: The development of achievement* (pp. 251-281). Greenwich, CT: JAI Press.

Roberts, G. C. (1992). *Motivation in Sport and Exercise*. Champaign, IL: Human Kinetics.

Roberts, G. C., and Ommundsen, Y. (1996). Effect of goal orientation on achievement beliefs, cognition and strategies in team sport. *Scandinavian Journal of Medicine and Science in Sports, 6*(1), 46-56.

Sarrazin, P., Biddle, S., Famose, J. P., Cury, F., Fox, K., and Durand, M. (1996). Goal orientations and conceptions of the nature of sport ability in children: A social cognitive approach. *British Journal of Social Psychology, 35*, 399-414.

Seifriz, J. J., Duda, J. L., and Chi, L. K. (1992). The Relationship of Perceived Motivational Climate to Intrinsic Motivation and Beliefs About Success in Basketball. *Journal of Sport and Exercise Psychology, 14*(4), 375-391.

Sit, C. H. P., and Lindner, K. J. (2007). Achievement goal profiles, perceived ability and participation motivation for sport and physical activity. *International Journal of Sport Psychology, 38*(3), 283-303.

Standage, M., Duda, J. L., and Ntoumanis, N. (2003a). A model of contextual motivation in physical education: Using constructs from self-determination and achievement goal theories to predict physical activity intentions. *Journal of Educational Psychology, 95*(1), 97-110.

Standage, M., Duda, J. L., and Ntoumanis, N. (2003b). Predicting motivational regulations in physical education: the interplay between dispositional goal orientations, motivational climate and perceived competence. *Journal of Sports Sciences, 21*(8), 631-647.

Steinberg, L., Lamborn, S. D., Dornbusch, S. M., and Darling, N. (1992). Impact of parenting practices on adolescent achievement: Authoritative parenting, school involvement, and encouragement to succeed. *Child Development, 63,* 1266–1281.

Tero, P. F., and Connell, J. P. (1984). When children think they've failed: An academic coping inventory. Unpublished manuscript, University of Rochester.

Wang, C. K. J., Biddle, S. J. H., and Elliot, A. J. (2007). The 2x2 achievement goal framework in a physical education context. *Psychology of Sport and Exercise, 8*(2), 147-168.

Wang, C. K. J., Chatzisarantis, N. L. D., Spray, C. M., and Biddle, S. J. H. (2002). Achievement goal profiles in school physical education: Differences in self-determination, sport ability beliefs, and physical activity. *British Journal of Educational Psychology, 72,* 433-445.

Wang, C. K. J., Liu, W. C., Biddle, S. J. H., and Spray, C. M. (2005). Cross-cultural validation of the Conceptions of the Nature of Athletic Ability Questionnaire Version 2. *Personality and Individual Differences, 38*(6), 1245-1256.

Watson, D., Clark, L. A., and Tellegen, A. (1988). Development and validation of brief measures of positive and negative affect - the Panas scales. *Journal of Personality and Social Psychology, 54*(6), 1063-1070.

Wellborn, J. G., and Connell, J. P. (1987). Manual for the Rochester Assessment Package for Schools. Rochester, NY: University of Rochester.

Whitehead, J., Andree, K. V., and Lee, M. J. (2004). Achievement perspectives and perceived ability: how far do interactions generalize in youth sport? *Psychology of Sport and Exercise, 5*(3), 291-317.

Wolters, C., Garcia, T., and Pintrich, P. R. (1992). Assessing early adolescents' school competence and commitment. Unpublished manuscript, University of Michigan.

In: Coping in Sport: Theory, Methods, and Related Constructs   ISBN: 978-1-60876-488-4
Editor: Adam R. Nicholls   © 2010 Nova Science Publishers, Inc.

Chapter 12

COPING, SELF-CONCEPT AND SELF-ESTEEM IN SPORT

J. Robert Grove and Ben Jackson
University of Western Australia, Australia

ABSTRACT

Relationships among appraisal, coping responses, and identity-related constructs such as self-concept and self-esteem are examined. Emphasis is placed on the way in which selected coping strategies may invoke affect regulation, self-protection, and self-enhancement mechanisms to help athletes maintain a positive sense of self in threatening circumstances. The specific threatening circumstances considered are impending competition, performance slumps, injury, and transitional experiences. A conceptual model of identity-maintenance coping at the individual level is presented, and a parallel model is proposed for identity-maintenance at the group-level.

INTRODUCTION

Coping responses serve a variety of purposes. Although the regulation of distress is generally seen as the primary function of coping efforts (Lazarus and Folkman, 1984), other important outcomes are also evident. These outcomes include the generation of positive affect as well as the development of resilience, self-reliance, and self-confidence (Folkman and Moskowitz, 2000; Holahan, Moos, and Schaefer, 1996). In this chapter, we focus more broadly on these self-related outcomes of the coping process. Specifically, we present a conceptual model of the relationship between coping responses, self-concept, and self-esteem, and we discuss selected areas of research that illustrate the key elements of this model within the sport domain.

A Conceptual Model

A detailed analysis of the self-concept and self-esteem constructs is beyond the scope of our discussion. However, we view them as positively correlated yet qualitatively distinct psychological constructs reflecting an individual's perception and evaluation of themselves. Self-concept is both hierarchical and multidimensional, with domain-specific perceptions of the self influencing general self-concept at a more global level (Marsh, 2008; Shavelson, Hubner, and Stanton, 1976). As such, self-concept is closely linked to personal identity (Cross and Cross, 2008). Although self-esteem is sometimes analysed at a domain-specific level, it is more typically viewed as a global construct reflecting overall judgments of personal self-worth (Crocker and Wolfe, 2001; Rosenberg, 1965). Importantly, both self-concept and self-esteem are malleable, and they therefore can be influenced by external events and personal actions (Kernis and Goldman, 2003; Marsh, 2008). Moreover, because a positive self-concept and positive self-esteem are valued personal resources, people will seek to protect them when threatened and enhance them when threatened and enhance them when it is feasible to do so (Baumeister, 1998; Crocker and Park, 2003; Greve and Wentura, 2003).

With these considerations in mind, Figure 1 shows the general framework that will guide our discussion of the relationships between coping, self-concept, and self-esteem in sport. This model acknowledges the importance of appraisal processes as well as the notion that negative affect is experienced when appraisal suggests a potential threat or loss (Lazarus and Folkman, 1984).

These threats or losses can be either physically-oriented or ego-oriented (Krohne et al., 2000), but, regardless of their nature, they prompt cognitive and/or behavioural coping responses (Krohne, 1993; Schwarzer and Schwarzer, 1996). Although Issues of intentionality and awareness remain controversial within the coping literature (Tennen, Affleck, Armeli, and Carney, 2000), we believe that coping responses can be undertaken either consciously or unconsciously. Indeed, a definition of coping that excludes unconscious processes strikes us as unrealistic and overly restrictive, especially when potential threats to identity are involved (cf. Coyne and Gottlieb, 1996).

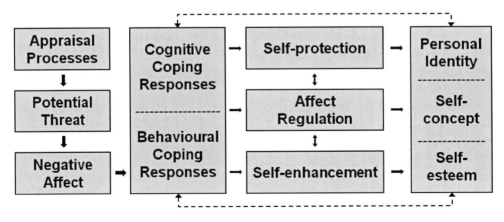

Figure 1. Conceptual model of the relationships between appraisal, coping, self-concept and self-esteem.

Self-protection, self-enhancement, and affect regulation are the key psychological mechanisms that connect coping with self-concept and self-esteem in our model. Self-protection occurs when cognitive and/or behavioural coping strategies are used to reduce the negative impact of real or imagined threats to these core self-perceptions. Self-enhancement occurs when cognitive and/or behavioural coping strategies are used to amplify positive aspects of the self in response to real or imagined threats (Alicke and Sedikides, 2009). Because of the central importance of identity, self-concept, and self-esteem to the individual, these two processes are deeply ingrained in human behaviour. Indeed, their prevalence in both individualistic and collectivist cultures suggests that they may have evolutionary significance because they provide important mental health benefits (Sedikides, Skowronski, and Gaertner, 2004). Affect regulation (i.e., reduction of negative affect and promotion of positive affect) is one of these mental health benefits (Alicke and Sedikides, 2009). Affect regulation can also be a direct result of using particular coping strategies rather than an indirect result of strategies that involve self-protection or self-enhancement (Folkman and Moskowitz, 2000), and our model acknowledges this possibility. It also acknowledges the possibility that there are relationships between coping, identity, self-concept, and self-esteem which are based on mechanisms other than self-protection, self-enhancement, and affect regulation.

Appraisal processes and coping responses are strongly influenced by the context in which potential stressors are encountered (Lazarus, 1993; Holahan, Moos, and Schaeffer, 1996). Likewise, the motivation to preserve, protect, or enhance valued self-perceptions is also influenced by contextual factors. More specifically, these motives are strongest when: (a) potential threats or losses impinge on issues or characteristics that are central to the individual's identity and (b) an evaluative audience is capable of providing social or tangible feedback (Alicke and Sedikides, 2009; Leary, 1995). Because these are precisely the circumstances surrounding sport performance, there are numerous ways in which coping might influence identity, self-concept, and self-esteem among athletes. We explore some of these possibilities in the sections that follow.

Coping in Advance of Performance

Positive reappraisal. This cognitive coping strategy involves reframing a stressor so that it is viewed in a positive rather than negative way. Positive reappraisal is acknowledged as an important element of coping in numerous measurement models (Schwarzer and Schwarzer, 1996), and it has also been shown to be a viable dimension of sport-related coping (Crocker, 1992; Eklund, Grove, and Heard, 1998). Indeed, interviews with elite athletes reveal that they frequently employ reappraisal strategies to cope with preperformance anxiety symptoms (Hanton and Jones, 1999). Consistent with the model presented in Figure 1, there is also evidence that reappraisal has beneficial consequences for self-esteem which are mediated by positive affect (Nezlek and Kuppens, 2008).

The extent to which a potential stressor is interpreted as a threat or a challenge is a fundamental aspect of the appraisal process, and these two interpretations produce distinct emotional reactions (Lazarus and Folkman, 1984). Negative affect is experienced when the stressor is viewed as a threat to the physical or psychological self, but positive affect is experienced when the stressor is viewed as a challenge (Maes, Leventhal, and de Ridder,

1996). There also appear to be distinctly different patterns of sympathetic arousal and endocrine response associated with threat and challenge appraisals (Olff, Langeland, and Gersons, 2005). Sport-specific research by Cerin (2003) indicates that a combination of threat and challenge interpretations is common during the precompetitive period, and that the level of perceived threat correlates positively with state anxiety and fear. The level of perceived challenge, on the other hand, correlates positively with interest and excitement. These relationships are reinforced by the findings of an experimental study conducted by Hale and Whitehouse (1998). In that study, manipulation of challenge versus threat orientations among soccer players produced lower levels of anxiety and higher levels of self-confidence in the challenge condition.

Additional research within the sport domain indicates that athletes frequently employ positive reappraisal as a coping strategy prior to competition, and that doing so has beneficial consequences for self-esteem. More specifically, Holt and Hogg (2002) identified reappraisal as a primary theme surrounding the coping efforts of international competitors prior to the Women's World Cup finals. Among youth soccer players aged 9 to 15 years, Lewthwaite (1990) found that perceived threat was significantly and negatively correlated with self-esteem. Findings obtained by Adie, Duda, and Ntoumanis (2009) reinforce this conclusion and provide strong evidence for the relationships between reappraisal, affect regulation, and self-esteem. Adie et al. asked team sport athletes to imagine an important future competition against an evenly-matched opponent and then assessed challenge-related versus threat-related thinking about the confrontation. Their findings indicated that threat appraisals increased negative affect and reduced self-esteem. On the other hand, challenge appraisals increased positive affect and also increased self-esteem.

Mental imagery. Visualization is an important element of cognitive-behavioural treatments for a variety of stressful conditions and circumstances including illness, chronic pain, phobias, and anxiety disorders (Borkovec, 2006; Singer, 2006). Coping-focused imagery and mastery-focused imagery are two forms of visualization that are frequently used in these treatment programs. Coping imagery emphasizes the visualization of anxiety-provoking situations as well as the thoughts and sensations that typically accompany them. These anxiety cues then serve as a trigger for the use of relaxation techniques and the mental rehearsal of coping strategies (Borkovec and Ruscio, 2001). Mastery imagery emphasizes visualization of successful task performance and/or performing in a confident, focused, and in-control manner (e.g., Cumming, Olphin, and Law, 2007; Feltz and Reissinger, 1990; Spencer and Norem, 1996).

Research conducted within the sport domain generally supports the use of these two forms of mental imagery as effective precompetition coping strategies. For example, Cumming et al. (2007) had athletes imagine a precompetition scene using several different scripts. One of these scripts had a mastery emphasis, and another script had a coping emphasis. State anxiety and self-confidence measures were then taken immediately following the imagery sessions. Results indicated that self-confidence was enhanced by both the mastery and coping rehearsals. Importantly, however, the coping protocol produced these increases in self-confidence despite concomitant increases in state anxiety levels. It was therefore recommended as particularly relevant for stress management during the pre-competitive period (Cumming et al., 2007). This recommendation was reinforced by the work of Mellalieu, Hanton, and Thomas (2009) who employed a coping-focused imagery intervention prior to actual competition. Their protocol emphasized the reappraisal of tension and anxiety symptoms as facilitative rather than debilitative. Findings indicated that the intervention increased pre-competition positive affect and decreased pre-competition negative affect despite the continued presence of state anxiety symptoms.

Sport-related studies of mastery-focused imagery have shown that it is positively related to a number of self-referent qualities. In one of the first studies along these lines, Feltz and Reissinger (1990) examined the impact of successful performance imagery on self-efficacy for a muscular endurance task. They found that the mastery-focused imagery intervention led to improvements in both the level and strength of self-efficacy beliefs when participants were confronted with the prospect of poor competitive performance. Correlational studies of both players and coaches also support a positive relationship between the use of mastery-focused imagery and self-efficacy (Mills, Munroe, and Hall, 2000/2001; Short, Smiley, and Ross-Stewart, 2005). Other correlational studies have demonstrated a positive relationship between the use of mastery imagery and self-confidence during the pre-competitive period (Callow and Hardy, 2001; Moritz, Hall, Martin, and Vodocz, 1996).

The direct connection between imagery, self-concept, and self-esteem has not been thoroughly examined. However, Suinn (1996) argues that one important reason for using mental imagery is to produce desirable changes in self-image, self-schemas, and self-perceptions. In addition, Hodges and colleagues (1979) showed that coping imagery was capable of reducing discrepancies between current self-concept and ideal self-concept. As noted above, there is also evidence that mastery-oriented imagery is positively related to self-referent psychological constructs such as self-efficacy and self-confidence (e.g., Callow and Hardy, 2001; Feltz and Reissinger, 1990; Moritz et al., 1996). It is likely that imagery-induced benefits for these lower-level self-referent constructs will have spin-off benefits for higher-level self-referent constructs such as self-concept and self-esteem (cf. Sonstroem and Morgan, 1989).

Self-handicapping. People sometimes employ proactive coping strategies in an attempt to reduce threats to self-esteem. One such strategy is self-handicapping, which refers to actions taken in advance of performance that provide a believable excuse for failure but also allow personal credit to be taken for success (Jones and Berglas, 1978). At times, these proactive threat-reduction tactics take the form of verbal statements about temporary obstacles (e.g., illness, injury, or lack of preparation), and at other times they take the form of actual behaviours that might interfere with performance (e.g., ingesting drugs or alcohol, withholding practice effort, or choosing to perform under sub-optimal conditions) (Hirt, Deppe, and Gordon, 1991; Snyder, 1990). Analyses of the conditions surrounding the use of self-handicapping strategies have shown that they are especially likely to occur in situations involving public displays of performance and that are: (a) evaluative in nature; (b) perceived as important by those involved; (c) high in outcome uncertainty; and (d) potentially threatening to self-esteem or public esteem if failure occurs (Arkin and Oleson, 1998; Self, 1990). Interestingly, all of these characteristics are inherent to competitive sport.

Self-handicapping is an intriguingly subtle-yet-powerful coping strategy because it not only reduces negative affect prior to performance (Snyder, 1990) but also allows for either self-protection or self-enhancement to be used as needed. More specifically, once a potential handicap is identified (either publicly or privately), the individual is in a position to augment the role of their personal contributions when the subsequent performance is good or, alternatively, to discount the role of their personal contributions when the performance is bad (cf. Kelly, 1971). The golfer who stands on the first tee and comments on how little they have been playing in recent weeks has effectively said "If I play well, I deserve credit for doing it without much practice; if I play poorly, it has more to do with the circumstances than with me". Thus, even before any shots have been hit, the threat potential of the situation has been reduced because a self-perception (or public image) of good golfing ability can be protected or enhanced as needed (cf. Snyder, 1990; Leary and Kowalski, 1990). Field studies in real-world performance settings have demonstrated that self-handicapping does indeed serve the dual purpose of protecting self-perceptions of ability and enhancing self-esteem (Feick and Rhodewalt, 1997; McCrea and Hirt, 2001).

The literature on self-handicapping within competition and sport was first reviewed by Prapavessis, Grove, and Eklund (2004). A subsequent publication by Maddison and Prapavessis (2007) drew heavily on the initial review but also provided updated coverage of the literature. In this chapter, we restrict our attention to self-handicapping studies that have particular relevance to the coping model shown in Figure 1. In that regard, studies of pre-competitive mood states have clearly shown that negative affect during the pre-competitive period is associated with a dispositional tendency to make use of self-handicapping strategies (Prapavessis and Grove, 1994; Prapavessis, Grove, Maddison, and Zillmann, 2003). Moreover, studies in which state measures of anxiety and self-handicapping have been simultaneously administered indicate that competitive situations increase anxiety levels as well as increasing the use of self-handicapping tactics (Ryska, Yin, and Cooley, 1998; Thill and Cury, 2000). Although the use of these tactics may not reduce the intensity of pre-competitive anxiety symptoms, it does appear capable of stimulating a reappraisal of these symptoms as facilitative rather than debilitative (Coudevylle, Martin Ginis, Famose, and Gernigon, 2008).

Sport-related studies have also examined the relationship between self-handicapping and a number of self-referent constructs. One of the most consistent findings across these studies has been that global self-esteem is negatively related to the use of self-handicapping (i.e., lower self-esteem is associated with more self-handicapping). This finding has been obtained in studies of recalled past performances (Martin and Brawley, 2002, Study 1), anticipated future performances (Prapavessis and Grove, 1998), and actual performances (Coudevylle, Martin Ginis, and Famose, 2008; Martin and Brawley, 2002, Study 2). Studies of task-specific self-efficacy have produced similar findings. For example, Kuczka and Treasure (2005) found that golfers with lower levels of golf self-efficacy identified more disruptive events prior to tournament play than those with higher levels of golf self-efficacy. Similarly, Coudevylle, Martin Ginis, and Famose (2008) observed that basketball players with low basketball self-efficacy opted-out of voluntary practice more than those with high levels of basketball self-efficacy. Since individuals with low self-esteem often doubt their abilities (Snyder and Higgins, 1988), these findings are consistent with the view that an important motivation behind self-handicapping is the desire to bolster perceptions of domain-specific ability which, in turn, maintains global self-esteem (McCrea and Hirt, 2001). Findings from a study of judo competitors by Greenlees, Jones, Holder, and Thelwell (2006) reinforce this view and also provide evidence that self-handicapping enables self-protection and self-enhancement mechanisms to unfold as needed. Specifically, they found that citing a large number of situational handicaps prior to competition was associated with increases in perceived judo ability following successful performances as well as resistance to decreases in perceived judo ability following unsuccessful performances.

Coping with Performance Slumps

Athletes devote considerable time and effort to refining their physical skills, and their identity is often closely tied to beliefs about physical prowess (Brewer, Van Raalte, and Linder, 1993; Lavallee, Grove, Gordon, and Ford, 1998). Poor performances are therefore a source of concern, and prolonged periods of poor performance (i.e., "slumps") can be highly stressful (Madden, Summers, and Brown, 1990). Negative emotions such as confusion, frustration, anger, anxiety, helplessness, and self-doubt are part of this stress response, and these negative emotions are exacerbated because the causes of performance slumps are often indeterminate (Grove, 2004; Taylor, 1988). Appraisal processes and the availability of support networks also influence the level of negative affect experienced in response to a slump. Specifically, stressful reactions are most extreme when a slump is interpreted as a loss or a threat, when there is a lack of perceived control over the cause of the slump, and when support networks are weak or absent (Grove, 2004; Grove and Stoll, 1999).

The prevailing ethos in sport strongly encourages hard work, commitment, dedication, and sacrifice (Howe, 2004; Hughes and Coakley, 1991). It is therefore not surprising to find that active, task-oriented coping strategies are cited most often when athletes report how they cope with performance slumps. This preference for task-oriented coping can be seen clearly in Table 1, which shows summary data from three studies ($N = 278$) where slump-referenced versions of the Coping Inventory for Stressful Situations (CISS; Endler and Parker, 1990) were administered to athletes from a variety of sports. A large-scale study of slump-related coping involving 630 athletes reinforced these findings by showing a clear preference for effort/resolve strategies over wishful thinking and denial/avoidance strategies for coping with performance slumps (Grove, Eklund, and Heard, 1997).

Table 1. Use of task-oriented, emotion-oriented, and avoidance-oriented coping strategies by athletes in response to performance slumps

Data Source	N	Task-oriented Coping		Emotion-oriented Coping		Avoidance-oriented Coping	
		Mean	SD	Mean	SD	Mean	SD
Grove and Heard (1997), LOT Group	90	59.83	7.39	41.43	9.11	40.40	9.59
Grove and Heard (1997), TSCI Group	123	53.91	7.78	42.69	10.78	41.92	10.71
Prapavessis et al. (2003), Study 1	65	58.20	10.10	43.34	10.90	45.65	17.20
Weighted Averages	278	56.83	8.20	42.43	10.27	42.30	11.86
		Task vs. Emotion		Task vs. Avoidance		Emotion vs. Avoidance	
Effect Sizes (d)	278	1.55		1.42		0.01	

Unfortunately, a persistent tendency to "attack the problem" may only exacerbate the frustration, negative affect, and self-doubt that accompanies a performance slump. Taylor (1988) therefore advocates time-out and emotional disclosure as important elements of effective slump-related coping because they assist in the regulation of negative affect. Selected thought management strategies have also been recommended as useful strategies for regulating affect and protecting or enhancing self-efficacy when faced with a slump. These thought management strategies include affirmative self-talk, thought stoppage, and reappraisal of causal attributions (Grove, 2004). Self-protection or self-enhancement processes might also be stimulated by mastery rehearsal. By recalling an excellent performance from the past, reliving it in detail, and projecting it onto an upcoming encounter, athletes may be able to maintain positive self-perceptions despite current performance difficulties (Grove, 2004).

Coping with Injury

The occurrence of injury has the potential to create a marked discrepancy between ideal and actual conceptions of self (Alicke and Sedikides, 2009; Higgins, 1996), and it may therefore have negative psychological consequences for athletes. Indeed, injury has been shown to be associated with decreased self-esteem (e.g., Leddy, Lambert, and Ogles, 1994; Tracey, 2003), loss of identity (e.g., Petitpas and Danish, 1995) and diminished self-concept (e.g., Rose and Jevne, 1993; Ford and Gordon, 1999; Vergeer, 2006). As a result, it is possible that injured athletes may implement coping strategies that seek to: (a) limit or reverse any negative effects upon their athletic self-perceptions, and (b) guard against detrimental affective and self-esteem consequences. In the following section, we consider some of the strategies that may be important for successfully protecting or enhancing one's sense of self in the face of injury.

Mental imagery. Research indicates that individuals utilise various context-specific imagery strategies during rehabilitation, designed to target healing, pain management, and future injury prevention (Driediger, Hall, and Callow, 2006; Gould, Udry, Bridges, and Beck, 1997; Green and Bonura, 2007; Vergeer, 2006). The use of healing imagery (e.g., imaging physiological improvements in the body, feeling stronger, being fully recovered, etc.) has been shown, for example, to be associated with faster recovery rates in athletes (Driediger et al., 2006; Ievleva and Orlick, 1991). Indeed, Dreidiger and colleagues proposed that this form of imagery may contain a powerful motivational component for those undergoing rehabilitation. In addition, pain management imagery strategies (e.g., focusing on dealing with, blocking, and dispersing expected and actual pain) may improve pain management ability and adherence during rehabilitation (cf. Driediger et al., 2006; Hall, 2001).

The use of these context-specific imagery techniques may protect against lowered self-esteem by reducing self-concept discrepancies brought about by injury. More specifically, Alicke and Sedikides (2009) suggest that self-perceptions in important areas of involvement include a perceived level of functioning as well as an aspirational (i.e., desired) level of functioning. When the gap between perceived capabilities and desired capabilities increases substantially, self-protection motives are served by cognitive and behavioural processes that shift the perceived level of functioning back towards the aspiration level. The use of injury-related imagery techniques may serve this function for athletes because of the positive effects it has on motivation, pain tolerance, adherence, and recovery.

Reframing. Although injury has negative physical and psychosocial consequences, the process of *reframing* (i.e., reappraising) one's situation and exploring potential benefits may be another mechanism by which individuals can protect and/or enhance their sense of self. Indeed, the appraisals that people make regarding their injury may actually supersede the injury itself in terms of shaping their rehabilitation progress (Brewer, 1994). Several authors have acknowledged the role of seeking out positive aspects associated with the injury experience (e.g., Ievleva and Orlick, 1991; Rose and Jevne, 1993; Tracey, 2003; Udry, Gould, Bridges, and Beck, 1997).

More specifically, by appraising one's injury as an opportunity for both personal and sporting development, athletes may experience significantly improved adjustment to rehabilitation. With respect to personal growth, periods of injury may be appraised as a vehicle for character development, and research in sport has indicated that athletes who adopt this perspective report enhanced maturity and independence as a result of their injury (e.g., Udry et al., 1997; Tracey, 2003). This approach also provides opportunities for athletes to improve their capabilities and conceptions of self in important domains outside of sport, including academic, social, and close relationship settings (Ford and Gordon, 1999; Gould et al., 1997; Udry et al., 1997). Alicke and Sedikides (2009) contend that the way in which individuals view themselves on each of these lower-level "interests" (e.g., sport, school, relationships, social interactions) plays a key role in shaping their global self-esteem. Thus, despite diminished conceptions of self in relation to sporting endeavours, by approaching injury as a means for personal development (and enhancing one's standing on these other dimensions) athletes may protect, and even advance, their general self-concept and global self-esteem during a period of injury.

The adaptive consequences of reframing one's injury, however, may not be limited to non-athletic aspects of the self (e.g., social, relationship, academic improvements). For example, in Udry et al.'s (1997) investigation, injured athletes discussed reframing in terms of the ways their experience may also lead to enhanced performance, via increased motivation as well as improved technical and tactical knowledge about their sport. Bearing this in mind, reappraisal processes such as taking the opportunity to become more knowledgeable about one's sport (e.g., by speaking with one's coach, studying strategy, etc.) may also be directly responsible for bringing about a positive shift back towards one's sport-specific aspiration level. Together, these character-related and performance-based benefits suggest that reframing may be particularly suited to preventing decreases in self-concept and self-esteem as a result of athletic injury.

Attributions. In addition to imagery and reframing, the causal attributions that athletes make during rehabilitation may provide further insight into self-protective/enhancing processes associated with injury. Studies in this area have explored attributions about the causes of injury (e.g., Brewer, 1999; Hagger, Chatzisarantis, Griffin, and Thatcher, 2005; Tedder and Biddle, 1997) as well as attributions about progress during rehabilitation (Brewer et al., 2000; Evans and Hardy, 2002; Grove, Hanrahan, and Stewart, 1990; Laubach, Brewer, Van Raalte, and Petitpas, 1996). Despite some inconsistencies due to the specific types of injuries examined, findings suggest that attributing rehabilitation progress to internal, controllable factors is associated with faster recovery, as rated by practitioners (Laubach et al., 1996) and the injured athletes themselves (Brewer et al., 2000). At the same time, attributing progress to external, uncontrollable factors is associated with increases in negative affect and poorer rehabilitation adherence (Evans and Hardy, 2002). Vulnerability-oriented attributions have also been associated with higher levels of negative affect, lower levels of positive affect, and reduced physical functioning following a sports injury (Hagger et al., 2005). Thus, it is apparent that strategic use of attribution processes can serve to regulate affect during injury rehabilitation. If the attribution of rehabilitation progress to controllable factors (e.g., effort, determination, attitude) also enhances recovery (Brewer et al., 2000; Hagger et al., 2005; Laubach et al., 1996), then the restoration of functional capacities may reduce the impact of injury on physical self-concept, general self-concept, and self-esteem.

Coping with Transitions

Significant theoretical and empirical attention has been devoted to understanding the psychological processes surrounding transitional experiences in sport (e.g., Alfermann and Stambulova, 2007; Lavallee and Wylleman, 2000). Broadly speaking, these transitions can occur in response to positive or negative events that are either expected or unexpected (Wylleman, De Knop, Ewing, and Cumming, 2000). If they are negative and/or unexpected, transitional experiences can threaten important self-perceptions, generate negative affect, and stimulate coping efforts designed to protect self-concept, self-esteem, and identity. For sport performers, the protection of athletic identity appears to be especially important. Athletic identity is the extent to which the individual defines themself in terms of their athletic role (Baillie and Danish, 1992; Brewer et al., 1993), and transition-relevant threats to this salient self-concept dimension can stimulate self-protective coping. For example, in a study of athletes who were either selected or not selected for a state team, Grove, Fish, and Eklund (2004) found that players who missed out on selection displayed reductions in self-reported athletic identity in the period immediately following team selection decisions. Grove and colleagues proposed that these reductions in athletic identity may have served to protect general self-concept and self-esteem by temporarily reducing the perceived importance of the domain in which the negative outcome occurred.

Retirement has been a particularly strong area of emphasis within the transitions literature, with numerous researchers exploring the emotional reactions, coping processes, and identity-related correlates of withdrawal from sport (e.g., Alfermann, Stambulova, and Zemaityte, 2004; Petitpas, 2009; Sinclair and Orlick, 1993). Whilst retirement is not uniformly associated with negative consequences (e.g., Lally, 2007), it is widely acknowledged that sports career termination can have serious negative repercussions in relation to one's sense of self (Grove, Lavallee, Gordon, and Harvey, 1998; Werthner and Orlick, 1986). Indeed, Taylor and Ogilvie's (1994, 2001) athletic career termination model emphasizes that this process is associated with substantial fluctuations in one's core self-perceptions (e.g., self-esteem). Thus, transitions to retirement represent a particularly salient context for examining how coping processes invoke self-protection, self-enhancement, and/or affect regulation mechanisms in order to maintain a positive self-concept and self-esteem. Moreover, given that "the impact of a transition is moderated by its effect on the individual's assumptions about the self" (Warriner and Lavallee, 2008, p.302), athletes who are able to successfully invoke these mechanisms are likely to experience a more positive adjustment to post-athletic life (cf. Alicke and Sedikides, 2009).

Several factors have been shown to exacerbate the potential negative experiences associated with sport career termination, including being forced (rather than choosing) to retire because of factors outside one's control, such as injury and de-selection (e.g., Bußmann and Alfermann, 1994). However, regardless of the precipitating event, coping effectiveness plays a crucial role in determining psychosocial adjustment (e.g., Grove, Lavallee, and Gordon, 1997; Taylor and Ogilvie, 2001). The purpose of this section is to discuss how selected coping strategies may (or may not) allow for effective self-protection during the transition to retirement and the associated benefits (or costs) for self-concept and self-esteem. To do so, we will focus on two separate issues: athletic identity and physical self-concept.

Developing a broader self-identity. It has been shown that athletes who develop a strong athletic identity whilst neglecting other aspects of the self may have inhibited decision-making skills (e.g., Pearson and Petitpas, 1990), use inefficient coping strategies during career termination (e.g., Sinclair and Orlick, 1993), and display maladaptive adjustment to retirement (e.g., Kerr and Dacyshyn, 2000). Importantly, individuals with strong or exclusive athletic identities also exhibit low levels of post-career preparation (e.g., self-reflection, planning for alternative careers) and tend not to reflect upon, or create, alternate constructions of 'self' in order to protect themselves against leaving the athletic domain (e.g., Adler and Adler, 1989; Sparkes, 1998). That is, highly identified athletes may not recognise or internalize dimensions of their self-concept outside those which relate to their sporting pursuits, and, as a result, they may experience a damaging loss of identity upon withdrawal from competition (e.g., Grove et al., 2004; Kerr and Dacyshyn, 2000). Accordingly, it is important to consider the possible ways in which coping strategies may function to maintain self-concept and self-esteem in this context.

The extant literature highlights a number of instances where self-protective coping processes have been effective in guarding against adverse self-concept effects associated with sport retirement. For instance, in Sinclair and Orlick's (1993) study of career termination, "finding another focus of interest" away from sport was the most commonly cited beneficial coping method. The authors concluded that exploring other interests and potential activities (e.g., future career, academic possibilities) is a key mechanism that can be used to *broaden one's self-identity*, thus providing a buffer against the negative psychological effects of athletic retirement (cf. Lavallee and Andersen, 2000). Alfermann and Stambulova (2007) also noted that using mental rehearsal and goal setting relating to a potential future career in the period leading up to one's retirement may serve an identity-protective role as one makes the transition out of sport. Similarly, in discussing this notion of management (or redirection) of identity as a method of coping prior to retirement, Lally (2007) stated that "athletes who decrease the prominence of the athletic role as self-protection... before their actual sport withdrawal and actively foster other identity dimensions may successfully avoid identity issues following athletic retirement." Thus, with respect to the framework presented earlier, cognitive and behavioural coping strategies that encourage identity diversification (e.g., devoting time to discovering and internalising a non-athletic self-identity, mentally rehearsing involvements outside of sport, and goal setting in relation to non-sport activities) appear to invoke self-protection mechanisms and thereby reduce the adverse effects of career termination on self-concept and self-esteem. If these coping strategies lead to success in non-sport activities, it could be argued that they also invoke self-enhancement mechanisms.

Protecting physical self-perceptions. Physical changes that athletes experience as a result of discontinuing their training regime represent another potential threat associated with retirement. Previous research has documented decreases in physical self-concept and global self-esteem upon withdrawal from sport (e.g., Stephan, Bilard, Ninot, and Delignières, 2003; Stephan, Torregrosa, and Sanchez, 2007). Indeed, general self-concept and self-esteem are shaped, in part, by physical self-perceptions (Fox, 1997), and this influence may be magnified for athletes who hold a particularly strong athletic identity (cf. Lally, 2007). As a result, an athlete's global self-perceptions may decline when they begin to appraise their physique or physical capabilities in a less favourable manner due to reductions in vigorous physical activity. Therefore, a simple and practical coping mechanism in this instance may be to continue engagement in physical training and sports activities during retirement in order to protect against threats to self-concept and self-esteem. Indeed, Sinclair and Orlick (1993) noted that athletes attributed adaptive psychosocial adjustment after retirement to the continuation of training and exercise during the transition period. It is worth noting, however, that although continuing to train after retirement represents a viable mechanism for self-protection, some degree of physical deterioration will in most cases be unavoidable (especially if career termination is brought about by injury). In such instances, the use of coping strategies designed to broaden identity beyond the 'athletic self' may be particularly important for regulating affect and protecting against decrements in self-concept and self-esteem. That is, by developing an identity away from sport, former competitors may become less reliant upon their physical competencies for defining the self and maintaining self-esteem.

CONCLUSION

Throughout this chapter, we have focused on the intrapersonal (i.e., within-person) coping responses that might help athletes to protect or enhance their self-views in response to perceived threats. It is important to note, however, that coping efforts are not exclusively intrapersonal in nature (Nicholls, Polman, Levy, Taylor, and Cobley, 2007). Indeed, significant others such as coaches, physiotherapists, sport psychologists, and team-mates play an important role in shaping the effectiveness of coping strategies. For example, the quality of relationships with rehabilitation service providers can bolster or undermine personal coping efforts during injury recovery (Holt and Hoar, 2006). Similarly, the way in which self-handicapping processes operate has been shown to differ when perceptions of team cohesion are either high or low (Carron, Prapavessis, and Grove, 1994; Hausenblas and Carron, 1996). The existence of these social influences suggests that coping processes could serve protection, regulation, and enhancement purposes at the level of the collective in much the same way that they serve these purposes at the level of the individual. In Figure 2, we suggest some of the group-level processes that might be involved and some of the group outcomes that might be achieved. An elaboration on selected elements follows.

Social identity theorists assert that "identity" includes both a personal and a social or collective component (e.g., Tajfel and Turner, 1986). With respect to team settings, perceptions of collective identity reflect beliefs about whether one's group or team is valued and compares favourably with other teams (Luhtanen and Crocker, 1992).

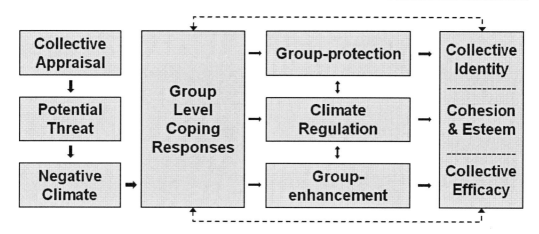

Figure 2. Conceptual model of the relationships between collective appraisal, coping and group outcomes.

Luhtanen and Crocker (1992) proposed that collective identity beliefs may be an important factor in shaping group members' cognitions and behaviour (e.g., their collective self-esteem), and they operationalized this construct with the Collective Self-Esteem Scale (CSES). In the CSES, individuals are asked to respond to questions such as "overall, my social group is considered good by others" and "in general, others respect the social group I am a member of." Although these items are couched in a broader social context, the application of such statements to sport settings is readily apparent (e.g., "overall, my team is considered good by others"). Importantly, Luhtanen and Crocker also noted that collective self-esteem may "moderate the extent to which individuals will attempt to protect or enhance their collective identities." That is, when faced with threats to collective self-esteem, individuals may implement strategies that seek to maintain their group's identity. In interdependent sporting contexts, threats to team identity can take many forms, but they undoubtedly include many of the same events that we have previously discussed as potential threats at the individual level. Some examples are extended periods of poor team performance, the loss of key players through injury, the dismissal of a coach, or a significant turnover in playing personnel. It is possible that the way in which teams attempt to cope with these threats will be stimulated by needs for group-protection and/or group-enhancement.

Luhtanen and Crocker (1992) detailed an array of potential coping strategies in the face of such stressors. These coping strategies included seeking out favourable comparisons between one's own group and other groups as well as derogating other groups. With particular relevance to sporting pursuits, they also outlined how attributional processes might be used to cope with perceived threats to a group's collective identity. Recently, these types of team-referent attributions have received attention in the sport science literature (e.g., Green and Holeman, 2004; Greenlees et al., 2007; Shapcott, Carron, Greenlees, and El-Hakim, 2008). Drawing from previous investigations (e.g., Taylor and Doria, 1981), these studies have tested and provided support for the notion of team-serving attributional biases in sport. This phenomenon occurs when group success is attributed to internal, stable, and controllable factors (e.g., team ability), or when group failure is attributed to external, unstable, and uncontrollable factors (e.g., bad luck, poor officials). Following successful performance, these attributional patterns are believed to arise from a desire to maximize the group's perceived "value" (Greenlees et al., 2007), whereas following failure these attributional patterns allow team members to protect their group image. With this in mind, it would be interesting to explore further the way in which team-based attributions are used as a form of collective identity protection and enhancement within various interdependent sporting contexts. It would also be interesting to explore the ways in which coaches use attributional strategies to cope with threats to their team's collective esteem and collective identity.

Communication processes also deserve scrutiny as a group-level coping strategy because of their potential to regulate the climate surrounding team activities and thereby influence collective identity. The content and effectiveness of intra-team communication has been shown to be associated with various adaptive outcomes, including enhanced efficacy perceptions, cohesion, and satisfaction in sports teams (e.g., Holt and Sparkes, 2001; Sullivan and Feltz, 2003; Sullivan and Gee, 2007). It is possible that communication processes are also important in coping with events that threaten team members' perceptions of their group. Sullivan and Feltz (2003) recently presented an instrument designed to assess communication processes in team sports (i.e., the Scale for Effective Communication in Team Sports; SECTS). Interestingly, the SECTS contains a "distinctiveness" subscale which taps into the "messages that serve to promote a shared and inclusive team identity" (Sullivan and Callow, 2005, p.88), as well as an "acceptance" subscale measuring the supportive messages that occur between team members. By using this measurement tool, it might be possible to determine: (a) if, and how, these aspects of communication are activated in situations that pose a danger to group identity; and (b) the specific types of identity-supportive communications that are used to cope with group-related stressors.

REFERENCES

Adie, J. W., Duda, J. L., and Ntoumanis, N. (2009). Achievement goals, competition appraisals, and the psychological and emotional welfare of sport participants. *Journal of Sport and Exercise Psychology, 30*, 302-322.

Adler, P. A., and Adler, P. (1989). The glorified self: The aggrandizement and the construction of self. *Social Psychology Quarterly, 52*, 299-310.

Alfermann, D., and Stambulova, N. (2007). Career transitions and career termination. In G. Tenenbaum and R. C. Eklund (Eds.) *Handbook of sport psychology (3rd ed.)* (pp. 712-733). New York: Wiley.

Alfermann, D., Stambulova, N., and Zemaityte, A. (2004). Reactions to sports career termination: A cross-national comparison of German, Lithuanian, and Russian athletes. *Psychology of Sport and Exercise, 5*, 61-75.

Alicke, M. D., and Sedikides, C. (2009). Self-enhancement and self-protection: What they are and what they do. *European Review of Social Psychology, 20*, 1-48.

Arkin, R. M., and Oleson, K. L. (1998). Self-handicapping. In J. M. Darley and J Cooper (Eds.), *Attribution and social interaction: The legacy of Edward E. Jones* (pp. 313-347). Washington, DC: American Psychological Association.

Baillie, P. H. F., and Danish, S. J. (1992). Understanding career transition of athletes. *The Sport Psychologist, 6*, 77-98.

Baumeister, R. F. (1998). The self. In D. T. Gilbert, S. T. Fiske, and G. Lindzey (Eds.), *Handbook of social psychology (4th ed., Vol. 2)* (pp. 680-740). New York: McGraw-Hill.

Borkovec, T. D. (2006). Applied relaxation and cognitive therapy for pathological worry and generalized anxiety disorder. In G. L. Davey and A. Wells (Eds.). *Worry and its psychological disorders: Theory, assessment and treatment* (pp. 273-287). Hoboken, NJ: Wiley.

Borkovec, T. D., and Ruscio, A. M. (2001). Psychotherapy for generalized anxiety disorder. *Journal of Clinical Psychiatry, 62 (Suppl 11)*, 37-42.

Brewer, B. W. (1994). Review and critique of models of psychological adjustment to athletic injury. *Journal of Applied Sport Psychology, 6*, 87-100.

Brewer, B. W. (1999). Causal attribution dimensions and adjustment to sport injury. *Journal of Personal and Interpersonal Loss, 4*, 215-224.

Brewer, B. W., Cornelius, A. E., Van Raalte, J. L., Petitpas, A. J., Sklar, J. H., Pohlman, M. H., Krushell, R. J., and Ditmar, T. D. (2000). Attributions for recovery and adherence to rehabilitation following anterior cruciate ligament reconstruction: A prospective analysis. *Psychology and Health, 15*, 283-291.

Brewer, B. W., Van Raalte, J. L., and Linder, D. E. (1993). Athletic identity: Hercules' muscles or Achilles heel? *International Journal of Sport Psychology, 24*, 237-254.

Bußmann, G., and Alfermann, D. (1994). Drop-out and the female athlete. In D. Hackfort (Ed.), *Psycho-social issues and interventions in elite sport* (pp.90-128). Frankfurt, Germany: Lang.

Callow, N., and Hardy, L. (2001). Types of imagery associated with sport confidence in netball players of varying skill levels. *Journal of Applied Sport Psychology, 13*, 1-17.

Carron, A. V., Prapavessis, H., and Grove, J. R. (1994). Group effects and self-handicapping. *Journal of Sport and Exercise Psychology, 16*, 246-257.

Cerin, E. (2003). Anxiety versus fundamental emotions as predictors of perceived functionality of pre-competitive emotional states, threat, and challenge in individual sports. *Journal of Applied Sport Psychology, 15*, 223-238.

Coudevylle, G. R., Martin Ginis, K. A., and Famose, J-P. (2008). Determinants of self-handicapping strategies in sport and their effects on athletic performance. *Social Behavior and Personality, 36*, 391-398.

Coudevylle, G. R., Martin Ginis, K. A., Famose, J-P. and Gernigon, C. (2008). Effects of self-handicapping strategies on anxiety before athletic competition. *The Sport Psychologist, 22*, 304-315.

Coyne, J. C., and Gottlieb, B. H. (1996). The mismeasure of coping by checklist. *Journal of Personality, 64*, 959-991.

Crocker, P. R. (1992). Managing stress by competitive athletes: Ways of coping. *International Journal of Sport Psychology, 23*, 161-175.

Crocker, J., and Park, L. E. (2003). Seeking self-esteem: Construction, maintenance, and protection of self-worth. In M. R. Leary and J. P. Tangney (Eds.). *Handbook of self and identity* (pp. 291-313). New York: Guilford Press.

Crocker, J., and Wolfe, C. T. (2001). Contingencies of self-worth. *Psychological Review, 108*, 593-623.

Cross, W. E., and Cross, T. B., (2008). The big picture: Theorizing self-concept structure and construal. In P. B. Pedersen, J. G. Draguns, Lonner, W. J., and Trimble, J. E. (Eds.). *Counseling across cultures (6th ed.)* (pp. 73-88). Thousand Oaks, CA: Sage Publications.

Cumming, J., Olphin, T., and Law, M. (2007). Self-reported psychological states and physiological responses to different types of motivational general imagery. *Journal of Sport and Exercise Psychology, 29*, 629-644.

Driediger, M., Hall, C., and Callow, N. (2006). Imagery use by injured athletes: A qualitative analysis. *Journal of Sports Sciences, 24*, 261-271.

Eklund, R. C., Grove, J. R., and Heard, N. P. (1998). The measurement of slump-related coping: Factorial validity of the COPE and Modified-COPE inventories. *Journal of Sport and Exercise Psychology, 20*, 157-175.

Endler, N. S., and Parker, J. D. A. (1990). *Coping Inventory for Stressful Situations (CISS): Manual.* Toronto: Multi Health Systems.

Evans, L., and Hardy, L. (2002). Injury rehabilitation: A qualitative follow-up study. *Research Quarterly for Exercise and Sport, 73*, 320-329.

Feick, D. L., and Rhodewalt, F. (1997). The double-edged sword of self-handicapping: Discounting, augmentation, and the protection and enhancement of self-esteem. *Motivation and Emotion, 21*, 147-163.

Feltz, D. L., and Reissinger, C. A. (1990). Effects of in vivo emotive imagery and performance feedback on self-efficacy and muscular endurance. *Journal of Sport and Exercise Psychology, 12*, 132-143.

Folkman, S., and Moskowitz, J. T. (2000). Positive affect and the other side of coping. *American Psychologist, 55*, 647-654.

Ford, I. W., Gordon, S. (1999). Coping with sport injury: Resource loss and the role of social support. *Journal of Personal and Interpersonal Loss, 4*, 243-256.

Fox, K. R. (1997). *The physical self: From motivation to well being.* Champaign, IL: Human Kinetics.

Gould, D., Udry E., Bridges, D., and Beck, L. (1997). Coping with season-ending injuries. *The Sport Psychologist, 11*, 379-399.

Green, L. B., and Bonura, K. B. (2007). The use of imagery in the rehabilitation of injured athletes. In D. Pargman (Ed.), *Psychological bases of sport injuries* (3rd ed., pp. 131-147). Morgantown, WV: Fitness Information Technology.

Green, T. D., and Holeman, S. (2004). Athletes' attributions for team performance: A theoretical test across sports and genders. *Social Behavior and Personality, 32*, 199-206.

Green, S. L., and Weinberg, R. S. (2001). Relationships among athletic identity, coping skills, social support, and the psychological impact of injury in recreational participants. *Journal of Applied Sport Psychology, 13*, 40-59.

Greenlees, I., Jones, S., Holder, T., and Thelwell, R. (2006). The effects of self-handicapping on attributions and perceived judo competence. *Journal of Sports Sciences, 24*, 273-280.

Greenlees, I., Stopforth, M., Graydon, J., Thelwell, R., Filby, W., and El-Hakim, Y. (2007). The impact of match importance and gender on the team-serving attributional bias among interdependent sports team players. *Group Dynamics: Theory, Research, and Practice, 11*, 54-65.

Greve, W., and Wentura, D. (2003). Immunizing the self: Self-concept stabilization through reality-adaptive self-definitions. *Personality and Social Psychology Bulletin, 29*, 39-50.

Grove, J.R. (2004). Performance slumps in sport: Prevention and coping. In C.D. Spielberger (Ed.), *Encyclopedia of applied psychology – Volume 3* (pp. 833-842). New York: Academic Press.

Grove, J. R., Eklund, R. C., and Heard, N. P. (1997). Coping with performance slumps: Factor analysis of the Ways of Coping in Sport Scale. *The Australian Journal of Science and Medicine in Sport, 29*, 99-105.

Grove, J. R., Fish, M., and Eklund, R. C. (2004). Changes in athletic identity following team selection: Self-protection versus self-enhancement. *Journal of Applied Sport Psychology, 16*, 75-81.

Grove, J. R., Hanrahan, S. J., and Stewart, R. M. L. (1990). Attributions for rapid or slow recovery from sports injuries. *Canadian Journal of Sport Sciences, 15*, 107-114.

Grove, J. R., Lavallee, D., and Gordon, S. (1997). Coping with retirement from sport: The influence of athletic identity. *Journal of Applied Sport Psychology, 9*, 191-203.

Grove, J. R., Lavallee, D., Gordon, S., and Harvey, J. H. (1998). Account-making: A model for understanding and resolving distressful reactions to retirement from sport. *The Sport Psychologist, 12*, 52-67.

Grove, J. R., and Stoll, O. (1999). Performance slumps in sport: Personal resources and perceived stress. *Journal of Personal and Interpersonal Loss, 4*, 203-214.

Hagger, M. S., Chatzisarantis, N. L. D., Griffin, M., and Thatcher, J. (2005). Injury representations, coping, emotions, and functional outcomes in athletes with sports-related injuries: A test of self-regulation theory. *Journal of Applied Social Psychology, 35*, 2345-2374.

Hale, B. D., and Whitehouse, A. (1998). The effects of imagery-manipulated appraisal on intensity and direction of competitive anxiety. *The Sport Psychologist, 12*, 40-51.

Hall, C. (2001). Imagery in sport and exercise. In R. Singer, H. Hausenblas, and C. Janelle (Eds.), *Handbook of sport psychology (2nd ed.)* (pp. 529-549). New York: Wiley.

Hanton, S., and Jones, G. (1999). The acquisition and development of cognitive skills and strategies: I. Making the butterflies fly in formation. *The Sport Psychologist, 13*, 1-22.

Hausenblas, H., and Carron, A. V. (1996). Group cohesion and self-handicapping in female and male athletes. *Journal of Sport and Exercise Psychology, 18*, 132-143.

Higgins, E. T. (1996). Ideals, oughts, and regulatory focus: Affect and motivation from distinct pains and pleasures. In P.M. Gollwitzer, and J.A. Bargh (Eds.), *The psychology of action: Linking cognition and motivation to behaviour* (pp. 91-114). New York: Guilford.

Hirt, E. R., Deppe, R. K., and Gordon, L. J. (1991). Self-reported versus behavioral self-handicapping: Empirical evidence for a theoretical distinction. *Journal of Personality and Social Psychology, 61*, 981-991.

Hodges, W. F., McCaulay, M., Ryan, V. L., and Strosahl, K. (1979). Coping imagery, systematic desensitization, and self-concept change. *Cognitive Therapy and Research, 3*, 181-192.

Holahan, C. J., Moos, R. H., and Schaefer, J. A. (1996). Coping, stress resistance, and growth: Conceptualizing adaptive functioning. In M. Zeidner and N. S. Endler (Eds.), *Handbook of coping: Theory, research, applications* (pp. 24-43). New York: Wiley.

Holt, N. L., and Hoar, S. D. (2006). The multidimensional construct of social support. In S. Hanton and S.D. Mellalieu (Eds.), *Literature reviews in sport psychology* (pp. 199-225). Hauppauge, NY: Nova Science Publishers.

Holt, N. L., and Hogg, J. M. (2002). Perceptions of stress and coping during preparations for the 1999 women's soccer World Cup finals. *The Sport Psychologist, 16*, 251-271.

Holt, N. L., and Sparkes, A. C. (2001). An ethnographic study of cohesiveness in a college soccer team over a season. *The Sport Psychologist, 15*, 237-259.

Howe, D. P. (2004). *Sport, professionalism, and pain: Ethnographies of injury and risk.* London: Routledge.

Hughes, R., and Coakley, J. (1991). Positive deviance among athletes: The implications of overconformity to the sport ethic. *Sociology of Sport Journal, 8,* 307-325.

Ievleva, L., and Orlick, T. (1991). Mental links to enhanced healing: An exploratory study. *The Sport Psychologist, 5,* 25-40.

Jones, E. E., and Berglas, S. (1978). Control of attributions about the self through self-handicapping strategies: The appeal of alcohol and the role of underachievement. *Personality and Social Psychology, Bulletin, 4,* 200-206.

Kelly, H. H. (1971). *Attribution in social interaction.* New York: General Learning Press.

Kernis, M. H., and Goldman, B. M. (2003). Stability and variability in self-concept and self-esteem. In M. R. Leary and J. P. Tangney (Eds.). *Handbook of self and identity* (pp. 106-127). New York: Guilford Press.

Kerr, G., and Dacyshyn, A. (2000). The retirement experience of elite female gymnasts. *Journal of Applied Sport Psychology, 12,* 115-133.

Krohne, H. W. (1993). Vigilance and cognitive avoidance as concepts in coping research. In H. W. Krohne (Ed.), *Attention and avoidance* (pp. 19-50). Seattle: Hogrefe and Huber.

Krohne, H. W., Egloff, B., Varner, L. J.; Burns, L. R.; Weidner, G., and Ellis, H. C. (2000). The assessment of dispositional vigilance and cognitive avoidance: Factorial structure, psychometric properties, and validity of the Mainz Coping Inventory. *Cognitive Therapy and Research, 24,* 297-311.

Kuczka, K. K., and Treasure, D. C. (2005). Self-handicapping in competitive sport: Influence of the motivational climate, self-efficacy, and perceived importance. *Psychology of Sport and Exercise, 6,* 539-550.

Lally, P. (2007). Identity and athletic retirement: A prospective study. *Psychology of Sport and Exercise, 8,* 85-99.

Laubach, W. J., Brewer, B. W., Van Raalte, J. L., and Petitpas, A. J. (1996). Attributions for recovery and adherence to sport injury rehabilitation. *The Australian Journal of Science and Medicine in Sport, 28,* 30-34.

Lavallee, D., and Andersen, M. (2000). Leaving sport: Easing career transitions. In M. Andersen (Ed.), *Doing sport psychology,* (pp. 223-236). Champaign, IL: Human Kinetics.

Lavallee, D., Grove, J. R., Gordon, S., and Ford, I. W. (1998). The experience of loss in sport. In J. H. Harvey (Ed.), *Perspective on loss: A sourcebook* (pp. 241-252). Philadelphia: Brunner/Mazel.

Lavallee, D., and Wylleman, P. (2000). *Career transitions in sport: International perspectives.* Morgantown, WV: Fitness Information Technology.

Lazarus, R. S. (1993). Coping theory and research: past, present, and future. *Psychosomatic Medicine, 55,* 234-247.

Lazarus, R. S., and Folkman, S. (1984). *Stress, appraisal, and coping.* New York: Springer.

Leary, M. R. (1995). *Self-presentation: Impression management and interpersonal behaviour.* Madison, WI: Brown and Benchmark.

Leary, M. R., and Kowalski, R. M. (1990). Impression management: A literature review and two-component model. *Psychological Bulletin, 107,* 34-47.

Leddy, M. H., Lambert, M. J., Ogles, B. M. (1994). Psychological consequences of athletic injury among high level competitors. *Research Quarterly for Exercise and Sport, 65,* 347-354.

Lewthwaite, R. (1990). Threat perception in competitive trait anxiety: The endangerment of important goals. *Journal of Sport and Exercise Psychology, 12,* 280-300.

Luhtanen, R., and Crocker, J. (1992). A collective self-esteem scale: Self-evaluation of one's social identity. *Personality and Social Psychology Bulletin, 18,* 302-318.

Madden, C. C., Summers, J. J., and Brown, D. F. (1990). The influence of perceived stress on coping with competitive basketball. *International Journal of Sport Psychology, 21,* 21-35.

Maddison, R., and Prapavessis, H. (2007). Self-handicapping in sport: A self-presentation strategy. In S. Jowett and D. Lavallee (Eds.), *Social psychology in sport* (pp. 209-220). Champaign, IL: Human Kinetics.

Maes, S., Leventhal, H., and de Ridder, D. T. D. (1996). Coping with chronic diseases. In M. Zeidner and N. S. Endler (Eds.), *Handbook of coping: Theory, research, applications* (pp. 221-251). New York: Wiley.

Manuel, J. C., Shilt, J. S., Curl, W. W., Smith, J. A., Durant, R. H., Lester, L., and Sinal, S. H. (2002). Coping with sports injuries: An examination of the adolescent athlete. *Journal of Adolescent Health, 31,* 391-393.

Marsh, H. W. (2008). A multidimensional, hierarchical model of self-concept: An important facet of personality. In G. J. Boyle, G. Matthews, and D. H. Saklofske (Eds.). *The SAGE handbook of personality theory and assessment, Volume 1: Personality theories and models* (pp. 447-469). Thousand Oaks, CA: Sage Publications.

Martin, K. A., and Brawley, L. R. (2002). Self-handicapping in physical achievement settings: The contribution of self-esteem and self-efficacy. *Self and Identity, 1,* 337-351.

McCrea, S. M., and Hirt, E. R. (2001). The role of ability judgments in self-handicapping. *Personality and Social Psychology Bulletin, 27,* 1378-1389.

Mellalieu, S. D., Hanton, S., and Thomas, O. (2009). The effects of a motivational general-arousal imagery intervention upon preperformance symptoms in male rugby union players. *Psychology of Sport and Exercise, 10,* 175-185.

Mills, K. D., Munroe, K. J., and Hall, C. R. (2000/2001). The relationship between imagery and self-efficacy in competitive athletes. *Imagination, Cognition and Personality, 20,* 33-39.

Moritz, S. E., Hall, C. R., Martin, K. A., and Vodocz, E. (1996). What are confident athletes imaging? An examination of image content. *The Sport Psychologist, 10,* 171-179.

Nezlek, J. B., and Kuppens, P. (2008). Regulating positive and negative emotions in daily life. *Journal of Personality, 76,* 561-579.

Nicholls, A. R., Polman, R., Levy, A. R., Taylor, J., and Cobley, S. (2007). Stressors, coping, and coping effectiveness: Gender, type of sport, and skill differences. *Journal of Sports Sciences, 25,* 1521-1530.

Olff, M., Langeland, W., and Gersons, B. P. R. (2005). Effects of appraisal and coping on the neuroendocrine response to extreme stress. *Neuroscience and Biobehavioral Reviews, 29,* 457-467.

Pearson, R. E., and Petitpas, A. J. (1990). Transitions of athletes: Developmental and preventive perspectives. *Journal of Counseling and Development, 69,* 7-10.

Petitpas, A. J. (2009). Sport career termination. In B. Brewer (Ed.), *Sport psychology* (pp. 113-120). London: Wiley-Blackwell.

Petitpas, A. J., and Danish, S. (1995). Caring for injured athletes. In S. Murphy (Ed.), *Sport psychology interventions* (pp. 255-281). Champaign, IL: Human Kinetics.

Prapavessis, H., and Grove, J. R. (1994). Personality variables as antecedents of precompetitive mood state temporal patterning. *International Journal of Sport Psychology, 25*, 347-365.

Prapavessis, H., and Grove, J. R. (1998). Self-handicapping and self-esteem. *Journal of Applied Sport Psychology, 10*, 175-184.

Prapavessis, H., Grove, J. R., and Eklund, R. C. (1994). Self-presentation issues in competition and sport. *Journal of Applied Sport Psychology, 16*, 19-40.

Prapavessis, H., Grove, J. R., Maddison, R., and Zillmann, N. (2003). Self-handicapping tendencies, coping, and anxiety responses among athletes. *Psychology of Sport and Exercise, 4*, 357-375.

Rose, J., and Jevne, R. F. J. (1993). Psychological processes associated with athletic injuries. *The Sport Psychologist, 7*, 309-328.

Rosenberg, M. (1965). *Society and adolescent self-image*. Princeton: Princeton University Press.

Ryska, T. A., Yin, Z. N., and Cooley, D. (1998). Effects of trait and situational self-handicapping on competitive anxiety among athletes. *Current Psychology, 17*, 48-56.

Schwarzer, R., and Schwarzer, C. (1996). A critical survey of coping instruments. In M. Zeidner and N. S. Endler (Eds.), *Handbook of coping: Theory, research, applications* (pp. 107-132). New York: Wiley.

Sedikides, C., Skowronski, J. J., and Gaertner, L. (2004). Self-enhancement and self-protection motivation: From the laboratory to an evolutionary context. *Journal of Cultural and Evolutionary Psychology, 2*, 61-79.

Self, E. A. (1990). Situational influences on self-handicapping. In R. L. Higgins, C. R. Snyder, and S. Berglas (Eds.), *Self-handicapping: The paradox that isn't* (pp. 37-68). New York: Plenum Press.

Shapcott, K. M., Carron, A. V., Greenlees, I., and El-Hakim, Y. (2008). Do member attributions for team outcomes represent a collective belief? *Psychology of Sport and Exercise, 9*, 487-492.

Shavelson, R. J., Hubner, J. J., and Stanton, G. C. (1976). Validation of construct interpretations. *Review of Educational Research, 46*, 404-441.

Short, S. E., Smiley, M., and Ross-Stewart, L. (2005). The relationship between efficacy beliefs and imagery use in coaches. *The Sport Psychologist, 19*, 380-394.

Sinclair, D. A., and Orlick, T. (1993). Positive transitions from high-performance sport. *The Sport Psychologist, 7*, 138-150.

Singer, J. (2006). *Imagery in psychotherapy*. Washington, DC: American Psychological Association.

Snyder, C. R. (1990). Self-handicapping processes and sequelae: On the taking of a psychological dive. In R. L. Higgins, C. R. Snyder, and S. Berglas (Eds.), *Self-handicapping: The paradox that isn't* (pp. 107-150). New York: Plenum Press.

Snyder, C. R., and Higgins, R. L. (1988). Excuses: Their effective role in the negotiation of reality. *Psychological Bulletin, 104*, 23-45.

Sonstroem, R. J., and Morgan, W. P. (1989). Exercise and self-esteem: Rationale and model. *Medicine and Science in Sports and Exercise, 21*, 329-337.

Sparkes, A. C. (1998). Athletic identity: An Achilles' heel to the survival of self. *Qualitative Health Research, 8*, 644-664.

Spencer, S. M., and Norem, J. K. (1996). Reflection and distraction: Defensive pessimism, strategic optimism, and performance. *Personality and Social Psychology Bulletin, 22*, 354-365.

Stephan, Y., Bilard, J., Ninot, G., Delignières, D. (2003). Bodily transitions out of elite sport: A one-year study of physical self and global self-esteem among transitional athletes. *International Journal of Sport and Exercise Psychology, 1*, 192-207.

Stephan, Y., Torregrosa, M., and Sanchez, X. (2007). The body matters: Psychophysical impact of retiring from elite sport. *Psychology of Sport and Exercise, 8*, 73-83.

Suinn, R. M. (1996). Imagery rehearsal: A tool for clinical practice. *Psychotherapy in Private Practice, 15(3)*, 27-31.

Sullivan, P. J., and Callow, N. (2005). A cross-cultural examination of the factor structure of the scale for effective communication in team sports. *Group Dynamics: Theory, Research, and Practice, 9*, 87-92.

Sullivan, P. J., and Feltz, D. L. (2003). The preliminary development of the scale for effective communication in team sports (SECTS). *Journal of Applied Social Psychology, 33*, 1693-1715.

Sullivan, P. J., and Gee, C. G. (2007). The relationship between athletic satisfaction and intrateam communication. *Group Dynamics: Theory, Research, and Practice, 11*, 107-116.

Tajfel, H., and Turner, J. C. (1986). The social identity theory of intergroup behaviour. In S. Worchel and W. Austin (Eds.), *Psychology of intergroup relations* (2nd ed., pp. 7-24). Chicago: Nelson-Hall.

Taylor, J. (1988). Slumpbusting: A systematic analysis of slumps in sport. *The Sport Psychologist, 2*, 39-48.

Taylor, D. M., and Doria, J. R. (1981). Self-serving and group-serving bias in attribution. *The Journal of Social Psychology, 113*, 201-211.

Taylor, J., and Ogilvie, B. C. (1994). A conceptual model of adaptation to retirement among athletes. *Journal of Applied Sport Psychology, 6*, 1-20.

Taylor, J., and Ogilvie, B. C. (2001). Career termination among athletes. In R. N. Singer, H. A. Hausenblas, and C. M. Janelle (Eds.), *Handbook of sport psychology* (2nd ed., pp. 672-691). New York: Wiley.

Tedder, S., and Biddle, S. J. H. (1997). Psychological processes involved during sports injury rehabilitation: An attribution-emotion investigation. *Journal of Sports Sciences, 16*, 106-107.

Tennen, H., Affleck, G., Armeli, S., and Carney, M. A. (2000). A daily process approach to coping: Linking theory, research, and practice. *American Psychologist, 55*, 626-636.

Thill, E. E., and Cury, F. (2000). Learning to play golf under different goal conditions: Their effects on irrelevant thoughts and on subsequent control strategies. *European Journal of Social Psychology, 30*, 101-122.

Tracey, J. (2003). The emotional response to the injury and rehabilitation process. *Journal of Applied Sport Psychology, 15*, 279-293.

Udry, E., Gould, D., Bridges, D., and Beck, L. (1997). Down but not out: Athlete responses to season-ending injuries. *Journal of Sport and Exercise Psychology, 19*, 229-248.

Vergeer, I. (2006). Exploring the mental representation of athletic injury: A longitudinal case study. *Psychology of Sport and Exercise, 7*, 99-114.

Warriner, K., and Lavallee, D. (2008). The retirement experiences of elite female gymnasts: Self identity and the physical self. *Journal of Applied Sport Psychology, 20*, 301-317.

Werthner, P., and Orlick, T. (1986). Retirement experiences of successful Olympic athletes. *International Journal of Sport Psychology, 17*, 337-363.

Wylleman, P., De Knop, P., Ewing, M., and Cumming, S. (2000). Transitions in youth sport: A developmental perspective on parental involvement. In D. Lavallee and P. Wylleman (Eds.), *Career transitions in sport: International perspectives* (pp. 143-160). Morgantown, WV: Fitness Information Technology.

In: Coping in Sport: Theory, Methods, and Related Constructs   ISBN: 978-1-60876-488-4
Editor: Adam R. Nicholls   © 2010 Nova Science Publishers, Inc.

Chapter 13

CHOKING UNDER PRESSURE AS SELF-DESTRUCTIVE BEHAVIOR

Geir Jordet

Norwegian School of Sport Sciences, Norway

ABSTRACT

This chapter discusses choking under pressure, which is presented as a case of self-destructive behavior that involves: ego threat, emotional distress, and self-regulation failure. When high levels of egotism are threatened, emotional distress often occurs. Athletes choke when they self-regulate to escape these unpleasant emotions (tradeoffs) or when they engage in mis-guided self-regulation strategies, which are also referred to as counterproductive strategies. The attempts to cope may backfire and cause performance failure (self-destruction). Empirical evidence, primarily from real-world research, is presented for each of these steps. Recommendations to prevent choking (reduce ego threat, normalize emotional distress, and optimize self-regulation) are based on this model and inspired by lessons learned from high-reliability organizations such as airlines and hospitals.

INTRODUCTION

"If I am also the favorite, it can become difficult to cope with the expectations. Pressure increases both tension and fear of failure." (Kjetil Andre Aamodt, four-time alpine skiing Olympic champion, in Gangdal, 2006, p. 58). Athletes often cite performance pressure as a major source of stress in competitive sport (e.g., Gould, Jackson, and Finch, 1993; McKay, Niven, Lavallee, and White, 2008). Thus, it is important for athletes to effectively cope with pressure and its consequences. In this chapter, I will introduce a new conceptual framework and review evidence that hopefully enhances the understanding of why and how athletes sometimes fail to cope successfully with this pressure and end up choking. It is argued that choking is a case of self-destructive behavior, where the very attempts that athletes engage in to cope with pressure can backfire and cause performance failure. Please note that the focus of this chapter is on choking under pressure and on coping with the processes that lead to choking, and not on coping with choking once it has happened.

Terminology

Performance pressure refers to an aspect of the situation, which may be caused by the importance of an athlete wanting to do well on a particular occasion. Choking under pressure has typically been defined as performing worse than expected in situations with a high degree of perceived importance (Baumeister, 1984; Beilock and Gray, 2007). In their recent review of research on choking, Beilock and Gray (2007) emphasize that choking is a discrete phenomenon, meaning that it has a discernable beginning and end. This, they argue, distinguishes choking from related states such as slumps (usually conceived as more enduring states). Similarly, Jackson and Beilock (2007) insinuate that choking is "relatively short or acute instances of poor performance." Describing choking as discrete, short, and acute is logical and suited to experimental laboratory studies, which typically take place within a relatively small space (i.e., the lab) and within a confined time period (an hour or two). However, it is important that the concept of choking is open for mechanisms that extend beyond limits set by laboratories. Thus, although it seems reasonable to have some boundaries on choking (i.e., a situation, a competition/game, or perhaps a tournament), performance failures under pressure may not always be isolated instances. What is observed by viewers as a discrete performance failure (e.g., a failed golf putt or a missed penalty shot) may sometimes merely be the ultimate outcome of many small accumulated failures. Also, as will be discussed in more detail later within this chapter, the very self-regulatory attempts an athlete initiates to cope with pressure can be responsible for the ultimate failure to perform. Thus, athletes may experience a series of failed responses to pressure, none of them big enough to alone activate a major performance failure, but together they trigger an escalating negative spiral of poor performances, which can be viewed as choking.

Laboratory Studies

Several recent reviews have addressed choking under pressure in some depth (e.g., Beilock and Gray, 2007; Jackson and Beilock, 2007). Much of the research on this topic consists of laboratory studies published in leading psychology journals, designed to test cognitive or attentional mechanisms involved in choking (e.g., Beilock and Carr, 2005; Gray, 2004; Masters, 1992). Two distinct theoretical processes have been given the most weight, which are called the distraction hypothesis and the explicit monitoring hypothesis.

The distraction hypothesis suggests that pressure induces worry, which then distracts the working memory resources and attention from the task. Performance suffers as a result of the distraction and decreased attention on the task (Beilock and Gray, 2007). Studies have shown that tasks that heavily rely on working memory (such as mathematical problem solving) are particularly susceptible to this type of performance failure (e.g., Beilock, Kulp, Holt, and Carr, 2004). In other studies, only people with highly effective working memories were negatively affected under pressure (Beilock and Carr, 2005). Thus, these studies suggest that distraction is responsible for choking under pressure on tasks that put high demands on working memory, which in sport may be tasks that require complex strategizing and decision making.

The explicit monitoring hypothesis suggests that pressure induces athletes to consciously monitor and control movements, which are normally executed without conscious control (Beilock and Gray, 2007). This was first studied by Baumeister (1984). Over six experiments, he found support for the links between pressure, self-consciousness, and low performance (choking). Later studies have elaborated on these findings. For example, in an experiment with soccer dribbling, it was shown that experts' performance is harmed when they attentionally monitor step-by-step performance, while on the contrary, less experienced performers benefitted from such skill-focus (Beilock, Carr, MacMahon, and Starkes, 2002). These experiments were replicated and extended in field hockey and soccer-dribbling, with a skill focus and pressure having a negative effect on performance (Jackson, Ashford, and Norsworthy, 2006). This suggests that expert athletes who choke on motor tasks, which are normally executed automatically, may do so because they explicitly, and excessively, monitor their actions.

Laboratory choking experiments have typically induced pressure on participants through monetary incentives, peer pressure, and/or social evaluations (Beilock and Gray, 2007). For example, in some studies (e.g., Beilock and Carr, 2001), participants are told that they will receive a money prize if they perform up to a certain standard on a task, but because it is a two-person team effort they will only receive the prize if both participants are successful. Then they are told that the other participant already has successfully performed and that it is up to the present participant to perform as well, in order for both participants to get the prize. Such experimental setups have allowed researchers to control and observe their variables in order to study cognitive and attentive processes. However, these benefits are accompanied by low ecological validity – the extent to which the laboratory situation is representative of situations in the real-world (Beilock and Gray, 2007). This is a serious shortcoming, because there is evidence to suggest that choking may occur differently in real-world settings compared to laboratory settings. A recent study among competitive ballroom dancers revealed that the participants had substantially higher stress (measured from levels of salivary cortisol) in real-world dance tournaments compared to when they were exposed to laboratory-induced stress (Rohleder, Beulen, Chen, Wolf, and Kirschbaum, 2007). The researchers argued that threats that are relevant and central in a person's life will evoke a larger stress response than the less relevant laboratory threats. What is more, some researchers have argued that lab experiments cannot fully replicate major real-world threat magnitudes, as the levels of stress that participants would encounter would be so high that these experiments would be considered unethical (Campbell, Baumeister, Dhavale, and Tice, 2003).

If indeed the pressure created in laboratories is lower, or different, than that experienced in real-world settings, it is not inconceivable that the mechanisms underlying choking also are different. One possible example of different mechanisms can be observed on self-paced task completion times. In laboratory tasks performers spend more time completing a task under pressure than under no pressure (e.g., Masters, 1992; Pijpers, Oudejans, Holsheimer, and Bakker, 2003) and in tasks where performers are instructed to act as quickly as possible, experts perform better and novices worse (Beilock, Bertenthal, McCoy, and Carr, 2004). This is consistent with the explicit monitoring hypothesis, suggesting that experts benefit from conditions that reduce attention to step-by-step execution. However, in another study, elite biathletes shot better with short external focus times only with moderate physiological arousal, whereas with maximum levels of physiological arousal, longer focus times gave better performances (Vickers and Williams, 2007). It was concluded that under extreme distress, maintaining attention to external task information prevented the athletes from choking. Similarly, in my own research on performance during international soccer penalty shootouts, players who took a shot under the most severe pressure conditions exhibited the shortest preparation times (Jordet, 2009a, 2009b; Jordet and Hartman, 2008) and the players with the shortest times performed worse than the players with the longest times (Jordet, Hartman, and Sigmundstad, in press). Thus, it is possible that the levels of perceived threat and distress experienced by performers in field situations are considerably higher than the levels that researchers have been able to induce in laboratories, and that this affects the mechanisms that have been identified to explain choking under pressure. To clarify these questions, there is an urgent need to supplement the vast knowledge base we have from laboratory studies with high ecological-validity field studies.

Field Studies

Much field research on choking has focused on the so-called home choke phenomenon. At first, it was found that despite a robust general home advantage in American professional baseball and basketball, teams performed significantly worse when playing at home in decisive playoff games (Baumeister and Steinhilber, 1984). The proposed explanation for this was that athletes under pressure experienced an increased self-focus in front of a supportive audience, which resulted in choking. However, later field investigations showed that the home-choke could only be found in baseball for the period 1950 – 1968 (Schlenker, Phillips, Boniecki, and Schlenker, 1995). Furthermore, recent research has failed to find evidence for the home-choke in ice-hockey (Loignon, Gayton, Brown, Steinroeder, and Johnson, 2007) or basketball (Tauer, Guenther, and Rozek, 2009). Some of these researchers unconditionally reject the existence of the home-choke, suggesting that we should "remove mention of the home choke and give it the same exit that most home teams give road teams in the playoffs." (Tauer et al., 2009, p. 160).

This seems to be a premature conclusion, given that support for the home choke has been gained in a handful of studies since the original investigation in the 1980s (e.g., Baumeister, 1995; Benjafield, Liddell, and Benjafield, 1989; Dohmen, 2008; Wright, Jackson, Christie, McGuire, and Wright, 1991; Wright, Voyer, Wright, and Roney, 1995). For example, in a study of golf players from the British Open, the British "home players" performed worse in the last round than in the first round, when compared to the non-British "away players" (Wright et al., 1991). Further, soccer players taking regular penalties in German soccer league games were more likely to choke (defined in the study as shooting the ball in the posts or wide of the goal) at home than when playing away, and this effect was largest in tied games (Dohmen, 2008). These processes have also been convincingly documented in laboratory studies, where participants objectively performed better in front of a hostile crowd than before a friendly crowd (Butler and Baumeister, 1998).

Thus, perhaps choking scholars could move their focus from whether the home-choke exists or not to identifying the conditions under which the home-choke might, or might not occur. One such study addressed the home-choke in relation to team status in professional American basketball, baseball, and ice-hockey (Benjafield et al., 1989). It was found that the only three teams who played significantly worse at home in decisive playoff games, compared to the first games in the playoff, happened to be the three most-winning teams in the history of those three sports, the Boston Celtics, New York Yankees, and Montreal Canadians, respectively. This suggests that team status and home-crowd expectations should be considered when studying the home-choke phenomenon. An anecdote from international soccer hints at something similar. England's team has a unique and high position to its fans (Corbett, 2006; Winner, 2005) and in the soccer world (Jordet, 2009b) that may bring about enormous expectations. Possibly as a result of this, the English soccer team has underperformed in a series of important home games, including the decisive qualification game prior to the 2008 European Championships, where they lost 2-3 to Croatia at home, after some brutal defensive blunders. When Fabio Capello took over as the coach and had just led his first home game, he commented: "They were nervous at the start because there is pressure playing at Wembley (the home stadium) and we need to take that off them." (BBC, 2007).

One of the major aims of this book chapter is to stimulate to more field research on choking under pressure. This aim will be pursued by introducing a relatively new conceptual framework that may lend itself well to explain ecologically valid data, as it addresses choking in a wider social psychological context. Also, throughout the chapter, the various parts of this conceptual model will be illustrated with results from our own field research on the international soccer penalty shootout.

CHOKING AS SELF-DESTRUCTIVE BEHAVIOR

Performance failures can come in many forms. French soccer player Zinedine Zidane made nearly all the newspaper covers in the world after he was sent off with a red card for head butting his Italian opponent, Marco Materazzi, only 10 minutes before the final whistle in the 2006 World Cup final. Zidane was arguably the most profiled player of this World Cup and this was the last game of his career, thus the game that would seal his legacy. How could this happen to him, the brightest superstar of the tournament, at this most critical moment?

One answer may be found in theories about self-destructive behavior. When favorable or proud views about oneself are questioned, contradicted, mocked or challenged, people often aggress, and this can be described as a self-regulatory breakdown under ego threat (Baumeister, Smart, and Boden, 1996). Specifically, when there is a discrepancy between two views of self: a favorable self-appraisal and a much less favorable appraisal, people who refuse to lower their self-appraisals may aggress against the source of the threat, thus the person conveying the less favorable appraisal. In the case of Zidane, he later indicated that the words that were said badly wounded his pride: "I am a man before anything else. I'd rather have been punched in the face than to hear these things." (Canal plus, 2006).

By directing anger outward, a downward revision of the self-concept is avoided (Baumeister et al., 1996). In this light, it is possible to explain Zidane's head butting action as a case of self-regulatory breakdown by a performer whose high self-image (from being the best player in the world, with a high masculine ego) is threatened (by Materazzi's insults) in a critical situation (10 minutes left in a World Cup final, the last game of his career), with the ultimate result being self-destruction (with red card and a lost game).

Baumeister (1997) refers to choking under pressure as one specific type of self-defeating behaviors. Self-defeating behavior, or simply self-destruction, is viewed as "the quintessential example of irrationality" (Baumeister and Scher, 1988, p. 3), given that it encompasses people in different ways conducting bad or harmful acts to themselves. A series of other behaviors can be categorized as self-destructive behaviors, including procrastination, self-handicapping, binge eating, alcohol abuse, violence, and suicide. In this chapter, I intend to elaborate on this view and show that choking under pressure also can be viewed as a general form of self-destructive behavior. This view expands upon Baumeister's (1997) presentation of choking under pressure as self-defeating behavior. Interestingly, Baumeister categorized choking as merely one specific sub-type of self-defeating behavior (a counterproductive strategy) and did not discuss it in relation to other subtypes.

Baumeister (1997) presents much evidence for two factors being involved in self-defeating behaviors: threatened egotism (when people's favorable views about themselves are questioned by other people or events); and self-regulation failure (when people's systems for regulating and controlling their behavior systematically break down). In addition, he argues that emotional distress often seem to function as a mediator. Based on this, a simple model can be drawn up to illustrate how these steps together can explain choking under pressure (see Figure 1). In what follows, I will go through each of these steps. Following Baumeister (1997), the two first steps, egotism and threat, will be presented together as ego threat.

Figure 1. The steps involved in choking under pressure (based on Baumeister, 1997).

Ego Threat

"I had to get used to being famous, if you define famous as receiving constant attention. After the World Cup, interest in me grew by the day. There was an intense spotlight focused on my every move." (Michael Owen, 2004, p. 105, about the months after his 1998 World Cup breakthrough as an England soccer player).

Egotism is used by Baumeister (1997) as a generic term representing all favorable self views and is synonymous with prestige, public esteem, respect, self-esteem, self-confidence, pride, and narcissism. The "threat" in "ego threat" is defined here as some event that can possibly lower one's self-appraisal (Baumeister, 1997). Essentially, ego threats offer people a choice (Baumeister, 1997). People can accept the possible bad evaluation (thus lowering one's self-appraisal) or reject it (and maintain their original self-appraisal). Most people would not readily accept a decrease in self-appraisal, thus faced with this choice they stick to their original view. For example, Michael Owen (from the quote introducing this section) scored a fantastic goal in the 1998 World Cup quarterfinal and he had an incredibly high public status (and arguably high self-appraisal) when starting the next season in England. The first games he then played carried the risk of not performing up to those high standards and expectations (i.e., a possible bad evaluation). Owen could accept this possibility, lower his self-appraisal and say to himself that "It's ok if I don't perform in these games, I don't mind if people assess my abilities as inferior to what I showed them in the World Cup". However, like probably most athletes would, Owen (2004, p. 107) rejected the possible bad evaluation: "I felt I needed to achieve something fresh to convince people I was here to stay." The discrepancy that then arises between one's high self-appraisal and the threat involving a possible reduction in appraisal elicits emotions that are perceived as unpleasant. This state can be quite intense, and it can be experienced as a crisis where the self-focused emotional distress takes over. Michael Owen (2004, p. 106-107) appeared to go through a similar process: "It may seem odd to imagine me being so tortured so soon after that night in St Etienne, but I just wanted to kill the idea that I was a precocious boy who would fade." Fortunately for him, he was able perform well in those first games and ultimately expressed feeling: "so relieved that nobody would be able to point to the World Cup and describe it as a fleeting moment for a lucky kid."

People with favorable self-appraisals are shown to have higher desire for self-enhancement and self-protection (particularly under threat) than those with less favorable appraisals of themselves (Baumeister, 1997). Given also that performance situations carry an implicit threat, the opportunity to lose esteem in the case of a negative outcome, performers with high egotism may be more vulnerable to ego threats than performers with lower egotism. People with high self-appraisals simply have more to lose.

Although there is some evidence in the choking literature to suggest that people with the highest working memory capacity fail under conditions of high pressure (Beilock and Carr, 2005; Gimmig, Huguet, Caverni, and Cury, 2006), the perils of high egotism have received very little explicit attention in theories on choking under pressure. However, in organizational psychology, the vulnerabilities of high egotism are frequently portrayed (e.g., Cohan, 2009; Collins, 2009). For example, in his latest book, management guru Jim Collins documents that hubris born of success is the first stage (of five) to explain how some of the world's greatest business companies have failed. Similarly, in research on high-reliability organizations such as airlines and hospitals, there is evidence that the best pilots and physicians display hazardous over-confidence (Brown and Moren, 2003), often make the worst mistakes (Reason, 2000), and are least likely to participate in systematic programs of error management (Helmreich, Merrit, and Wilhelm, 1999). Further, in laboratory studies, it has been shown that participants with high self-esteem perform well on tasks with low pressure, but when ego threat is added, they set too risky goals and choke (Baumeister, Heatherton, and Tice, 1993). This was replicated in a military field situation (grenade toss), where high self-esteem cadets receiving ego-threatening feedback picked more difficult targets than low self-esteem cadets, which ultimately reduced performance (Smith, Norrell, and Saint, 1996).

In sport, Taylor and Cuave (1994) examined the so called "sophomore slump" among American professional baseball players. They found a significant decline in some aspects of performance during the second year of competition following an outstanding first season, although other evidence suggested that some of the performances the second year could be explained as a statistical regress towards the mean. Furthermore, interviews with athletes who have won major sport competitions have documented that winning enhanced the pressure to deliver future performances, an expectation that many struggled to cope with (Jackson, Dover, and Mayocchi, 1998; Jackson, Mayocchi, and Dover, 1998; Kreiner-Phillips and Orlick, 1993). For example, in interviews of 18 Australian gold medallists about the post-Olympic experience (Jackson, Dover, and Mayocchi, 1998), the most frequently found dimension was "experiencing expectations and pressure from others", cited by 72% of the athletes. In addition, relevant research based on achievement goal theory reveals that ego-oriented athletes (whose goals are related to demonstrating higher abilities than others; Nicholls, 1989) have higher levels of anxiety than others (e.g., Roberts, 1986, Newton and Duda, 1992) and employ denial more as a coping strategy (females only, Pensgaard and Roberts, 2003). Finally, students who receive praise for ability (thus increasing egotism) display lower motivation and poorer performance than those who are praised for effort (Mueller and Dweck, 1998).

I conducted research on the phenomenon of high egotism under threat, using the soccer penalty shootout as case. The most internationally esteemed players (defined as those who took a shot after they had received one or more prestigious international awards, such as "FIFA player of the year") performed worse than players with lower public status (Jordet, 2009a). In yet another study, players from the national teams with the highest status performed worse than players from the teams with less status (Jordet, 2009b). Similar effects were indicated in a study of penalty shootouts held in the cup competition in Germany, where players from the top league teams seemed to miss more decisive shots than players from the lower league teams (Kocher, Lenz, and Sutter, 2008). These studies clearly suggest that athletes with high egotism and thus, high expectations to live up to, are more likely to choke (or flop) under pressure in elite sport situations.

The more important it is for an athlete to perform during high pressure situations, the higher the ego threat. Two statisticians (Berry and Wood, 2005) conducted a study of 2,003 field goal attempts in the National Football League (NFL). The results showed that success rate dropped from regular kicks to high-pressure kicks. Similarly, in an archival data study I conducted with all kicks ever taken in penalty shootouts in the World Cup, European Championships and Copa America, shot performance was significantly lower on the relatively more important shots, such as those taken in the World Cup (the most important tournament; Jordet, Hartman, Visscher, and Lemmink, 2007) in addition to penalties taken closer to the final decision (e.g., McGarry and Franks, 2000). In a follow-up we differentiated the important kicks, according to the potential direct implications of each shot (e.g., shot valence; Jordet and Hartman, 2008). Positively valenced shots were defined as those where a goal would instantly secure a win and negatively valenced shots as those where a miss instantly would produce a loss. The results showed that players scored on 92% of the positive valence shots compared to only 62% of the negative valence shots, which is a large and functionally meaningful difference in outcome. This is equivalent to the finding that more individual errors are made in decisive baseball World Series games when the team is behind in the score, as compared to when they are ahead (Schlenker et al., 1995).

Interestingly, the performance drop in the NFL-study (Berry and Woods, 2005) was larger in situations where the opposing teams called a timeout immediately before the kick (i.e., "iced the kickers"). The researchers argued that having time to dwell on the kick could cause the kickers to choke under pressure, which was replicated in soccer penalty shootouts. Waiting for the referee to signal that the shot could be initiated, typically because the goalkeeper took time to get in the goal (equivalent to "icing" the American football kicker), was associated with missing more shots (Jordet, Hartman, and Sigmundstad, in press). This can be explained from several theoretical perspectives. It is possible that performers in these situations miss their shots because they take more time to think about their actions (i.e., following the explicit monitoring view). It is also possible that players who were "iced" simply had to endure the ego threat and emotional distress for longer periods of time, which could either distract them from the task at hand (i.e., the distraction view) and/or increase the chance of the players engaging in maladaptive self-regulation strategies (i.e., the self-destructive behavior view).

In sum, there is much data showing that high egotism under threat makes performers more vulnerable to choking under pressure. However, more research is needed on the different types of egotism. For example, in one study it was found that only people with defensive high self-esteem are vulnerable to self-regulation failure under pressure (Lampird and Mann, 2006).

Emotional Distress

"When we were in the mid circle I became incredibly nervous. I thought it showed on TV that my legs were shaking, that is how nervous I was." (Participant in penalty shootout at the 2004 European Championships, Jordet and Elferink-Gemser, 2009).

Emotional distress will here be defined, following Baumeister (1997), as negative or unpleasant affect, spanning from anxiety and aggression to depression, guilt and shame. This type of affect has been thoroughly addressed by sport psychology researchers, although mostly limited to competitive anxiety (for reviews, see Hardy, Jones, and Gould, 1996; Mellalieu, Hanton, and Fletcher, 2006) and it has also been directly linked to choking under pressure (Hill, Hanton, Fleming, and Matthews, 2009; Wang, Marchant, and Morris, 2004). Given this topic's extensive coverage in the literature, I will simply outline some of the ways in which emotional distress features in the model of choking as self-destructive behavior.

In Baumeister's (1997) theory of self-defeating behavior, the role of emotional distress is hypothesized to mediate between ego threat and self-regulation failure. Thus, an athlete with a threatened self-image may experience intense emotional distress, which in turn may undermine self-regulation and this ultimately leads to choking. Specifically, when experiencing intense distress, people typically think about immediate issues and less on history or long-term implications. In this process, emotional distress may be so salient and dominant that people accord top priority toward ending the distress, and the steps to end the distress may take precedence over other more adaptive patterns of self-regulation (Baumeister, 1997). This has also been referred to in the sport psychology literature as "experiential avoidance" (Gardner and Moore, 2006).

Some non-sport studies support this pattern. For example, people who are upset, angry or scared have been shown to act more impulsively and take more risks (Leith and Baumeister, 1996). In the highly pressure-filled soccer penalty shootout, retrospective evidence points to anxiety being a central emotion. In an interview study we conducted with 10 players who took part in one of the 2004 European Championship soccer penalty shootouts (Jordet, Elferink-Gemser, Lemmink, and Visscher, 2008), anxiety was the only emotion reported by all 10 players. Furthermore, high anxiety symptom intensity and debilitative symptom direction were significantly related to low perceptions of control (Jordet, Elferink-Gemser, Lemmink, and Visscher, 2006).

In sum, emotional distress seems to be an important part of the choking process in that anxiety may mediate between threat and faulty self-regulation. The processes that ultimately make performers choke in pressure situations, the way they self-regulate when their egos are threatened, and the levels of emotional distress are high will now be discussed.

Self-Regulation Failure

You don't want to ruin it all. You don't want to *not* go through to the next round because *you* missed. So, you just hope that you will *not* miss your penalty, and you think: 'don't miss, don't miss, don't miss'! '*Don't* miss!' That is all I am thinking. (Participant in penalty shootout at the 2005 World Cup for U20 teams; italics added to express his emphasis; Jordet and Elferink-Gemser, 2009)

Self-regulation refers to the ability to change oneself and exert control over inner processes (Baumeister and Vohs, 2004). The relationship between self-regulation and coping is close, with the construct of coping falling somewhere within self-regulation (Hoar, Kowalski, Gaudreau, and Crocker, 2006). However, following the terminology in Baumeister's (1997) model, this chapter will primarily stick to the word "self-regulation," even when "coping" could also be used.

The most extreme response to pressure is arguably "ego shock" (Campbell et al., 2003). Retrospective accounts show that people's responses to major blows to self-esteem were characterized by feeling frozen, unable to act, emotionally numb, feeling distant from self, and experiencing the world as strange (Campbell et al., 2003). The researchers argue that these processes are involuntary, automatic and temporary, thus they happen before self-regulation or coping is set in. Although similar descriptions have been offered by people surviving large disasters (Ripley, 2008), this concept has received little explicit attention by sport researchers. Identifying ego shock in sport, as well as its possible causes and implications, is an interesting avenue for future research.

According to Baumeister (1997), self-regulation can fail because: (a) the performer underregulates, which means that the self fails to make the necessary effort to adaptively change its response towards achieving the desirable outcome; and (b) the performer can fail because he or she mis-regulates, which means that some effort is put in towards changing one's response, which may be both concerted and effective, but it is misdirected or in other ways wrongly applied.

Self-regulation failures can be linked to tradeoffs. This is when people engage in a self-regulation strategy that produces short term gains, but with delayed costs that ultimately far outweigh the initial short term gains (Baumeister, 1997). Specifically, people under ego threat who experience high levels of emotional distress may prioritize temporary escape from the distress. Several non-sport studies have highlighted how people systematically pursue such tradeoffs, but end up systematically self-destructing. For example, people with high self-esteem who under-perform in laboratory pressure situations sometimes favor speed over accuracy (Baumeister et al., 1993). In another study, about 12% of prison inmates claim that at some point during police interrogation have made a false confession. Fifty-one percent of these inmates reported 'escape from police pressure' as the primary reason (Kassin and Gudjonsson, 2004). Thus, the short term benefit of confession (escape from the aversive emotional state) is perceived to outweigh the long term costs (spending time in prison). This illustrates a self-destructive tradeoff, where people under pressure aim for a short term goal, without proper consideration of the more important long term goal.

Our studies on soccer penalty shootouts illustrate the same tradeoffs in elite sport. Video analyses of penalty shooters consistently showed that players under particularly high ego threat, that is, players who took a shot in negative valence conditions (Jordet and Hartman, 2008), who had high individual status (Jordet, 2009a) or who represented countries with high team status (Jordet, 2009b), exhibited faster preparation times than the players who performed under less threat. Many of the high ego threat players displayed a body language suggesting that they could not get their shots done and over with quickly enough. Quotes from players, who have missed some of these shots, support that this could be a tradeoff self-regulation strategy, where short time relief is given the highest priority. Steven Gerrard (2006), an English international soccer player, spoke about a penalty he missed during the 2006 World Cup: "Why do I have to wait for the bloody whistle? Those extra couple of seconds seemed like an eternity, and they definitely put me off." Gareth Southgate, who failed to score in a penalty shootout in the 1996 European Championships said "All I wanted was the ball: put it on the spot, get it over and done with." (Southgate and Woodman, 2003, p. 191). Unfortunately for these players, preparing or responding fast in these situations is associated with lower performance and thus, more missed penalties (Jordet, Hartman, and Sigmundstad, in press). Country analyses also showed that players from England (the country with the highest number of penalty shootout losses, five losses in six attempts) were faster than players from all the other nations, and significantly faster than players from most other large soccer nations in Europe (Czech Republic/Czechoslovakia, France, Germany, Italy, and the Netherlands; Jordet, 2009b). Interestingly, a study of international level golfers gave results in line with these findings (Nicholls, Holt, and Polman, 2005). Speeding up ("I just started rushing shots.") was associated with ineffective coping. This all suggests that rushing one's preparation in high pressure sport situations indeed can be a self-destructive strategy linked to choking.

Self-regulation failures can also lead to self-destructive behavior by use of counterproductive strategies, where people pursue a positive performance end, but the means that are chosen are not properly suited to bring about the desired outcome and the result is self-destruction. For example, in the first three months following 9/11, more Americans lost their lives while driving to avoid the risk of flying than the total number of passengers that were killed in the four original lethal flights (Gigerenzer, 2004). The best example of a counter productive self-regulation strategy associated with choking under pressure is explicit monitoring. People invest extra effort to do well in situations where it is important to do well and they start consciously monitoring and controlling their movements, which paradoxically reduces performance (for more, see earlier in this chapter or review by Beilock and Gray,

2007). Another type of counter productive strategy is ironic self-instruction, such as that exhibited in the quote by the Dutch soccer player introducing the sub-section of this chapter where he tells himself "don't miss" (the penalty shot). Although this strategy is logical (it *is* indeed important not to miss), it is also counter productive. Much research has documented that instructing oneself to not do something (e.g., "don't miss") will under physical or cognitive load (e.g., performance pressure) ironically increase the probability of doing the act that one wanted to avoid (e.g., Bakker, Oudejans, Binsch, and van der Kamp, 2006; Wegner, Ansfield, and Pilloff, 1998).

Among the other potentially counterproductive strategies that sport performers sometimes engage in to protect one's ego against threat are self-handicapping (putting obstacles in the way of one's own performance, so that anticipated or possible failure can be blamed on the obstacle instead of on lack of ability; Tice and Baumeister, 1990) and sandbagging (the false claim or demonstration of inability to create artificially low expectations; Gibson, Sachau, Doll, and Shumate, 2002). More research is needed to determine the exact roles these strategies can have for athletes performing under pressure.

PREVENTING CHOKING UNDER PRESSURE

The night before the game we took penalties. Obviously, you can't really practice this, but I still had each of them take one shot. One! No second chance. In front of all the other players, they had to walk over the entire field to take a penalty in the other end. When you walk a hundred meters to take a shot, you get a lot of thoughts in your head (Guus Hiddink, about preparing his South Korea team for a possible penalty shootout in the 2002 World Cup quarterfinal; van den Nieuwenhof, 2006, p. 145).

In this section I will very briefly review some of the evidence that various types of practice can help athletes prevent choking under pressure, as well as some exploratory ideas for how to prevent the processes that are associated with choking as self-destructive behavior.

Alleviating the Effects of Explicit Monitoring

One approach to preventing explicit monitoring of movements under pressure is implicit learning. Skills that are independent of explicit instructions are less likely to fall apart from excessive explicit monitoring under pressure (Masters, 2000). The effect of several methods have been supported in research, such as learning through analogies (table tennis players told to "move the bat as if it is traveling up the side of a mountain" to achieve top spin; Poolton, Maxwell, and Masters, 2006) and initial error-less learning (golf players initially conduct repetitions from very short distances where no errors are made, then progressively increase to the target distance; Poolton, Masters, and Maxwell, 2005).

It is also possible to limit the opportunities athletes have for explicit monitoring during pressure. This has been documented with the addition of an external distraction (Mesagno, Marhcant, and Morris, 2009), with pre-performance routines (Mesagno, Marchant, and Morris, 2008) and by simply attending away from the internal production of movements and towards the environment or the effects of one's actions (Wulf and Prinz, 2001). The benefits of an external focus has recently been supported for skilled golfers performing 20 meter chips under anxiety conditions, with particular good effects for distal attention towards the flight of the ball and its intended direction (Bell and Hardy, 2009). Finally, it has been recommended to perform as fast as possible to prevent too much thinking about the performance (Beilock, Bertenthal et al., 2004). Please note that although this strategy might alleviate explicit monitoring and thus potentially facilitate performance, other evidence indicate that short preparation times are associated with poor performance (Jordet and Hartman, 2008; Jordet et al., in press) and ineffective coping (Nicholls et al., 2005). Thus, performers should be cautious if trying to speed up their performance to avoid excessive thinking.

Acclimatizing Performers to Pressure

Another approach to prevent choking under pressure is to acclimatize performers to the processes that are believed to occur during pressure. Based on the explicit monitoring hypothesis, some researchers have suggested training under self-conscious conditions, thus making athletes more used to those mechanisms that are hypothesized to occur under pressure (Beilock and Carr, 2001). A recent intervention study documented the effect of this kind of training on high-pressure soccer penalty taking (Reeves, Tenenbaum, and Lidor, 2007). Other experiments have revealed that training with mild anxiety has a positive effect on performing under pressure conditions (Oudejans and Pijpers, 2009; Oudejans and Pijpers, in press). In a non-sport experiment, police officers training with pressure showed no deterioration in performance under pressure conditions, as compared to a non-pressure training control group who showed clear signs of choking under pressure (Oudejans, 2008). This supports classical psychological interventions such as simulation training and suggests that coaches should consider adding pressure in training to prepare for high-pressure competitions.

Reducing Ego Threat

In his book, 'the curse of the self', social psychologist Mark Leary (2004) discusses a series of ideas for overcoming this curse. Among his recommendations is to foster ego compassion. This involves accepting that one is not perfect and that failures, losses, and adversity invariably will occur. It essentially involves being kind and forgiving with ourselves, recognizing that we, as humans, have shortcomings and will make occasional mistakes. Leary's ideas can be transferred into pragmatic recommendations by borrowing insights from other, non-sport high-performance settings. Given that the imminent threat in pressure situations often signal the possibility of making a mistake (e.g., Holt and Mandigo, 2004; Nicholls et al., 2005; Reeves, Nicholls, and KcKenna, 2009), it makes sense to learn from organizations where making a mistake not "only" costs a lost spot on the team, a lost game or a lost championship, but where mistakes easily can cost human lives. Examples of such organizations are airlines, hospitals, nuclear power plants, and aircraft carriers. Research shows that 70% of aircraft accidents involve human errors, and causes of errors include fatigue, fear, cognitive workload, poor communication and flawed decision making (Helmreich, 2000). Thus, these show clear parallels to performance demands in sport competitions, pointing to a potential for positive transfer between these fields. Many studies have been conducted on the characteristics of effective high-reliability organizations (e.g., Weick and Sutcliffe, 2007). First of all, these organizations are not flawless – people there make as many errors as others; the difference is that they do not let errors disable and ruin them. The best of these organizations focus on quickly and mindfully reacting and coping with errors and on learning from errors (instead of totally avoiding them). Furthermore, for many of these organizations, error control is proactive, non-punitive and directed at the system, culture and communication, not just the erroneous acts of individuals (Reason, 2000).

Thus, translated to sport settings, coaches could communicate to their athletes that mistakes under pressure indeed *will* occur and rather than to attempt avoiding making individual mistakes altogether, the focus can be on collectively coping with the consequences of these mistakes. This involves having in place both individual and collective systems for coping with small failures, for example derived from the large variety of coping strategies that have been unveiled in studies on athletes (for review, see Nicholls and Polman, 2007). Such proactive and system based approach to making mistakes in sport has the potential to reduce the athletes' experiences of ego threat, which in turn may reduce the chances of choking under pressure to occur (see Chapter 16, by Tamminen and Holt, for a discussion of pro-active coping).

It may also be helpful to specifically target athletes with particularly high status and public image, as they seem extra vulnerable to high ego threat. Consistent with the system based approach to errors just reviewed, an accepting and mindful approach to high status may facilitate adaptive responses. This could include educating athletes about the processes associated with high status and expectations and discuss the positive and negative sides of being the favorite (Haberl, 2007).

Normalizing Emotional Distress

A natural follow up to reducing ego threat by accepting one's imperfections and weaknesses is to learn to accept emotional distress. Unpleasant emotions are natural and human when performing under high levels of ego threat, and athletes will cope better with pressure situations when they understand and internalize this philosophy: "They have to learn to respond to the feelings that come from uncertainty as exciting, beneficial and welcome. This is an honest and natural response." (Rotella and Lerner, 1993, p. 536)

Accepting unpleasant emotions will decrease the chance of engaging in short term affect regulation that so easily can take focus away from regulating those processes that are necessary for bringing about performance (for more details on a similar type of intervention, see the Mindfulness-Acceptance-Commitment approach described by Gardner and Moore, 2006).

Optimizing Self-Regulation

Athletes should be made aware of the possible self-destructive effects of certain self-regulatory behaviors, such as some of the tradeoffs and counterproductive strategies that were shown earlier in this chapter. Trying to change or control oneself can create more problems than it solves if such changes are not pursued carefully (Leary, 2004). Furthermore, athletes should replace misguided self-regulation strategies with more adaptive behaviors. For example, in high-pressure situations where some athletes may be tempted to hurry to get the situation over with (such as the penalty shootout, see Jordet and Hartman, 2008; Jordet et al., in press; and international golf-tournaments, see Nicholls et al., 2005), athletes could be educated to resist this urge and rather take a few extra seconds to make sure the preparatory steps are carefully taken. Interventions with the Dutch national soccer teams performing in international tournaments have tentatively supported the effect of this approach (Jordet, 2008).

An alternative general principle that can serve optimal self-regulation is to respond to threats mindfully, flexibly, and dynamically, rather than automatically, habitually, and rigidly (Weick and Sutcliffe, 2007). This might seem contrary to prescriptions by the explicit monitoring hypothesis. However, being mindful of circumstances and events does not necessarily involve monitoring and controlling one's own movements, it is rather about being aware of the situation without evaluating, deliberating or exerting excessive effort. Many competent coaches have perfected this type of approach, from Timothy Gallwey's awareness exercises in tennis (1974) and golf (1979) to NBA basketball coach Phil Jackson's "Being aware is more important than being smart" (Jackson and Delehanty, 2005). Given that choking under pressure often seems to take place through some type of self-regulatory behavior that instinctively is initiated in order to escape unpleasant emotions (tradeoff) or in order to excessively ensure successful performance (counterproductive strategies), it is logical to suggest that athletes should not just mechanically and mindlessly self-regulate. Rather, it is hypothesized that working with athletes to mindfully be aware of task, context, thoughts and emotions will equip them with a better basis to engage in optimal self-regulation strategies that effectively can prevent choking.

CONCLUSION

In this chapter, I have presented a new way to conceptualize choking under pressure in sport. In short, performers choke under pressure when they experience high levels of ego threat and emotional distress, which they then respond to with misguided self-regulation strategies. Thus, coping plays a major role for this model of choking.

Several directions can be suggested for future research. Above all, there is a large need for more real-world research on choking under pressure. Our series of studies on international soccer penalty shootouts will hopefully inspire future field researchers to similarly address this phenomenon by systematically combining data from game archives, videos, interviews, questionnaires and interventions. Conducting research on real-world choking may also have conceptual implications. The model presented in this chapter is believed to capture well some of the complexity that may characterize choking in real-world competitions (i.e., choking as a cumulative, dynamic, interactive, and cyclical process). However, these macroscopic features need to be closely examined and empirically tested. In addition, the model provides specific descriptions of the mechanisms through which choking is believed to occur. Researchers should test each of the facets of the model directly – in the field (different sports and different levels of performance), but also under more controlled conditions in the laboratory. Particularly pertinent questions are, to what extent is there a causal relationship between egotism, escapist self-regulation, and choking? And, what is the specific role of emotional distress (e.g., competitive anxiety) for choking? Finally, it would be interesting to see the effects of various types of interventions for preventing choking under pressure. Will interventions that reduce ego threat and/or stimulate athletes to optimize their self-regulation decrease the probability of athletes choking? And, is an approach based on ego compassion, acceptance of threat/emotional distress, and/or flexible and mindful self-regulation an effective way to work with these processes in sport?

REFERENCES

Bakker, F. C., Oudejans, R. R. D., Binsch, O., and van der Kamp, J. (2006). Penalty shooting and gaze behavior: Unwanted effects of the wish not to miss. *International Journal of Sport Psychology, 37*, 265-280.

Baumeister, R. F. (1984). Choking under pressure: Self-consciousness and paradoxical effects of incentives on skillful performance. *Journal of Personality and Social Psychology, 46*, 610-620.

Baumeister, R. F. (1995). Disputing the effects of championship pressures and home audiences. *Journal of Personality and Social Psychology, 68*, 644-648.

Baumeister, R. F. (1997). Esteem threat, self-regulatory breakdown, and emotional distress as factors in self-defeating behavior. *Review of General Psychology, 1*, 145-174.

Baumeister, R. F., Heatherton, T. F., and Tice, D. M. (1993). When ego threats lead to self-regulation failure: Negative consequences of high self-esteem. *Journal of Personality and Social Psychology, 64*, 141-156.

Baumeister, R. F., and Scher, S. J. (1988). Self-defeating behavior patterns among normal individuals: Review and analysis of common self-destructive tendencies. *Psychological Bulletin, 104*, 3-22.

Baumeister, R. F., Smart, L., and Boden, J. M. (1996). Relation of threatened egotism to violence and aggression: The dark side of high self-esteem. *Psychological Review, 103*, 5-33.

Baumeister, R. F., and Steinhilber, A. (1984). Paradoxical effects of supportive audiences on performance under pressure: The home field disadvantage in sports championships. *Journal of Personality and Social Psychology, 47*, 85-93.

Baumeister, R. F., and Vohs, K. D. (Eds.) (2004). *Handbook of self-regulation: Research, theory, and applications*. New York: Guilford Press.

BBC (2007). *Capello buoyed by England promise*. Retrieved July 5, 2009, from http://news.bbc.co.uk/sport2/hi/football/internationals/7229548.stm.

Beilock, S. L., Bertenthal, B. I., McCoy, A. M., and Carr, T. H. (2004). Haste does not always make waste: Expertise, direction of attention, and speed versus accuracy in performing sensorimotor skills. *Psychonomic Bulletin and Review, 11*, 373-379.

Beilock, S. L., and Carr, T. H. (2001). On the fragility of skilled performance: What governs choking under pressure? *Journal of Experimental Psychology: General, 130*, 701-725.

Beilock, S. L., and Carr, T. H. (2005). When high-powered people fail: Working memory and "choking under pressure" in math. *Psychological Science, 16*, 101-105.

Beilock, S. L., Carr, T. H., MacMahon, C., and Starkes, J. L. (2002). When paying attention becomes counterproductive: Impact of divided versus skill-focused attention on novice and experienced performance of sensorimotor skills. *Journal of Experimental Psychology: Applied, 8*, 6-16.

Beilock, S. L., and Gray, R. (2007). Why do athletes choke under pressure? In G. Tenenbaum, and R.C. Eklund (Eds.), *Handbook of sport psychology* (3rd ed., pp. 425-444). Hoboken, NJ: John Wiley and Sons.

Beilock, S. L., Kulp, C. A., Holt, L. E., and Carr, T. H. (2004). More on the fragility of performance: Choking under pressure in mathematical problem solving. *Journal of Experimental Psychology: General, 133*, 584-600.

Bell, J. J., and Hardy, J. (2009). Effects of attentional focus on skilled performance in golf. *Journal of Applied Sport Psychology, 21*, 163-177.

Benjafield, J., Liddel, W. W., and Benjafield, I. (1989). Is there a home field disadvantage in professional sports championships? *Social Behavior and Personality, 17*, 45-50.

Berry, S., and Wood, C. (2004). The cold-foot effect. *Chance, 17*, 47-51.

Brown, N. M., and Moren, C. R. (2003). Background emotional dynamics of crew resource management: Shame emotions and coping responses. *International Journal of Aviation Psychology, 13*, 269-286.

Butler, J. L., and Baumeister, R. F. (1998). The trouble with friendly faces: Skilled performance with a supportive audience. *Journal of Personality and Social Psychology, 75*, 1213-1230.

Campbell, W. K., Baumeister, R. F., Dhvale, D., and Tice, D. M. (2003). Responding to major threats to self-esteem: A preliminary, narrative study of ego-shock. *Journal of Social and Clinical Psychology, 22*, 79-96.

Canal plus (2006). *Interview with Zinedine Zidane, July 12, 2006*. Retrieved July 5, 2009, from http://www.youtube.com/watch?v=fESPK2cmjpY.

Cohan, W. D. (2009). *House of cards: A tale of hubris and wretched excess on Wall street*. New York: Random House.

Collins, J. (2009). *How the mighty fall: And why some companies never give in*. New York: HarperCollins.

Corbett, J. (2006). *England expects: A history of the England football team*. London: Aurum Press.

Dohmen, T. J. (2008). Do professionals choke under pressure? *Journal of Economic Behavior and Organization, 65*, 636-653.

Gallwey, W. T. (1974). *The inner game of tennis*. New York: Random House.

Gallwey, W. T. (1979). *The inner game of golf*. New York: Random House.

Gangdal, J. (2006). *Kjetil Andre Aamodt. Den neste er den beste* [The next one is the best one]. Oslo, Norway: Aschehoug.

Gardner, F. L., and Moore, Z. E. (2006). *Clinical sport psychology*. Champaign, IL: Human Kinetics.

Gerrard, S. (2006). *Gerrard: My autobiography*. London: Transworld publishers.

Gibson, B., Sachau, D., Doll, B., and Shumate, R. (2002). Sandbagging in competition: Responding to the pressure of being the favorite. *Personality and Social Psychology Bulletin, 28*, 1119-1130.

Gigerenzer, G. (2004). Dread risk, September 11, and fatal traffic accidents. *Psychological Science, 15*, 286-287.

Gimmig, D., Huguet, P., Caverni, J-P., and Cury, F. (2006). Choking under pressure and working memory capacity: When performance pressure reduces fluid intelligence. *Psychonomic Bulletin and Review, 13*, 1005-1010.

Gould, D., Jackson, S., and Finch, L. (1993). Sources of stress in national champion figure skaters. *Journal of Sport and Exercise Psychology, 15*, 124-159.

Gray, R. (2004). Attending to the execution of a complex sensorimotor skill: Expertise differences, choking, and slumps. *Journal of Experimental Psychology: Applied, 10*, 42-54.

Haberl, P. (2007). The psychology of being an Olympic favorite. *Athletic Insight: The Online Journal of Sport Psychology*, 9. Retrieved July 15, 2009, from http://www.athleticinsight.com/Vol9Iss4/Favorite.htm.

Hardy, L., Jones, G., and Gould, D. (1996). *Understanding psychological preparation for sport: Theory and practice of elite performers*. Chichester, UK: Wiley and Sons.

Helmreich, R. L. (2000). On error management: Lessons from aviation. *British Medical Journal, 320*, 781-785.

Helmreich, R. L., Merrit, A. C., and Wilhelm, J. A. (1999). The evolution of crew resource management training in commercial aviation. *The International Journal of Aviation Psychology, 9*, 19-32.

Hill, D. M., Hanton, S., Fleming, S., and Matthews, N. (2009). A re-examination of choking in sport. *European Journal of Sport Science, 9*, 203-212.

Hoar, S. D., Kowalski, K. C., Gaureau, P., and Crocker, P. R. E. (2006). A review of coping in sport. In S. Hanton, and S. D. Mellalieu (Eds.), *Literature Reviews in Sport Psychology* (pp. 47-90). London: Nova Science.

Holt, N. L., and Mandigo, J. L. (2004). Coping with performance worries among male youth cricket players. *Journal of Sport Behavior, 27*, 39-57.

Jackson, R. C., Ashford, K. J., and Norsworthy, G. (2006). Attentional focus, dispositional reinvestment, and skilled motor performance under pressure. *Journal of Sport and Exercise Psychology, 28*, 49-68.

Jackson, R. C., and Beilock, S. L. (2007). Performance pressure and paralysis by analysis: Research and implications. In D. Farrow, J. Baker, and C. MacMahon (Eds.), *Developing sport expertise: Researchers and coaches put theory into practice* (pp. 104-114). London: Routledge.

Jackson, P., and Delehanty, H. (1995). *Sacred hoops: Spiritual lessons of a hardwood warrior*. New York: Hyperion.

Jackson, S. A., Dover, J., and Mayocchi, L. (1998). Life after winning gold: I. Experiences of Australian Olympic gold medalists. *The Sport Psychologist, 12*, 137-155.

Jackson, S. A., Mayocchi, L., and Dover, J. (1998). Life after winning gold: II. Coping with change as an Olympic gold medalists. *The Sport Psychologist, 12*, 137-155.

Jordet, G. (2008). Performing under pressure: Preparing the Netherlands U21 soccer team for the 2007 European Championships. *Proceedings of the Annual Conference for Association for Applied Sport Psychology (AASP), USA*, 50.

Jordet, G. (2009a). When superstars flop: Public status and "choking under pressure" in international soccer penalty shootouts. *Journal of Applied Sport Psychology, 21*, 125-130.

Jordet, G. (2009b). Why do English players fail in soccer penalty shootouts? A study of team status, self-regulation, and choking under pressure. *Journal of Sports Sciences, 27*, 97-106.

Jordet, G., and Elferink-Gemser, M. T. (2009). *Interviews with participants in international soccer penalty shootouts.* Unpublished manuscript.

Jordet, G., Elferink-Gemser, M. T., Lemmink, K. A. P. M., and Visscher, C. (2006). The "Russian roulette" of soccer?: Perceived control and anxiety in a major tournament penalty shootout. *International Journal of Sport Psychology, 37*, 281-298.

Jordet, G., Elferink-Gemser, M. T., Lemmink, K. A. P. M., and Visscher, C. (2008). Emotions at the penalty mark: an analysis of elite players performing in an international penalty shootout. In T. Reilly, and A. M. Williams (Eds.), *Science and Football VI* (pp. 409–414). Oxford: Routledge.

Jordet, G., and Hartman, E. (2008). Avoidance motivation and choking under pressure in soccer penalty shootouts. *Journal of Sport and Exercise Psychology, 30*, 452-459.

Jordet, G., Hartman, E., and Sigmundstad, E. (in press). Temporal links to performing under pressure in international soccer penalty shootouts. *Psychology of Sport and Exercise.*

Jordet, G., Hartman, E., Visscher, C., and Lemmink, K. A. P. M. (2007). Kicks from the penalty mark in soccer: The roles of stress, skill, and fatigue for kick outcomes. *Journal of Sports Sciences, 25*, 121-129

Kassin, S. M., and Gudjonsson, G. H. (2004). The psychology of confessions: A review of the literature and issues. *Psychological Science in the Public Interest, 5*, 33-67.

Kocher, M. G., Lenz, M. V., and Sutter, M. (2008). Performance under pressure: The case of penalty shootouts in football. In P. Andersson, P. Ayton, and C. Schmidt (Eds.), *Myths and facts about football: The economy and psychology of the world's greatest sport* (pp. 61-72). Newcastle, UK: Cambridge Scholars Publishing.

Kreiner-Phillips, K., and Orlick, T. (1993). Winning after winning: The psychology of ongoing excellence. *The Sport Psychologist, 7*, 31-48.

Lampird, K. H., and Mann, T. (2006). When do ego threats lead to self-regulation failure? Negative consequences of defensive high self-esteem. *Personality and Social Psychology Bulletin, 32*, 1177-1187.

Leary, M. R. (2004). *The curse of the self: Self-awareness, egotism, and the quality of human life.* New York: Oxford University Press.

Leith, K. P., and Baumeister, R. F (1996). Why do bad moods increase self-defeating behavior? Emotion, risk-taking, and self-regulation. *Journal of Personality and Social Psychology, 71*, 1250-1267.

Loignon, A., Gayton, W. F., Brown, M., Steinroeder, W., and Johnson, C. (2007). Home disadvantage in professional ice hockey. *Perceptual and Motor Skills, 104*, 1262-1264.

Masters, R. S. W. (1992). Knowledge, knerves and know-how: The role of explicit versus implicit knowledge in the breakdown of a complex motor skill under pressure. *British Journal of Psychology, 83*, 343-358.

Masters, R. S. W. (2000). Theoretical aspects of implicit learning in sport. *International Journal of Sport Psychology, 31*, 530-541.

McGarry, T., and Franks, I. M. (2000). On winning the penalty shoot-out in soccer. *Journal of Sports Sciences, 18*, 401 – 409.

McKay, J., Niven, A. G., Lavallee, D., and White, A. (2008). Sources of strain among elite UK track athletes. *The Sport Psychologist, 22*, 143-163.

Mellalieu, S. D., Hanton, S., and Fletcher, D. (2006). A competitive anxiety review: Recent directions in sport psychology research. In S. Hanton, and S. D. Mellalieu (Eds.), *Literature Reviews in Sport Psychology* (pp. 1-46). London: Nova Science.

Mesagno, C., Marchant, D., and Morris, T. (2008). A pre-performance routine to alleviate choking in "choking-susceptible" athletes. *The Sport Psychologist, 22*, 439-457.

Mesagno, C., Marchant, D., and Morris, T. (2009). Alleviating choking: The sounds of distraction. *Journal of Applied Sport Psychology, 21*, 131-147.

Mueller, C. M., and Dweck, C. S. (1998). Praise for intelligence can undermine children's motivation and performance. *Journal of Personality and Social Psychology, 75*, 33-52.

Newton, M., and Duda, J. L. (1992). The relationship of task and ego orientation to performance-cognitive content, affect, and attributions in bowling. *Journal of Sport Behavior, 16*, 209-220.

Nicholls, J.G. (1989). *The competitive ethos and democratic education*. Cambridge, MA: Harvard University Press.

Nicholls, A. R., Holt, N. L., and Polman, R. C. J. (2005). A phenomenological analysis of coping effectiveness in golf. *The Sport Psychologist, 19*, 111-130.

Nicholls, A. R., and Polman, R. C. J. (2007). Coping in sport: A systematic review. *Journal of Sports Sciences, 25*, 11-31.

van den Nieuwenhof, F. (2006). *Hiddink: Dit is mijn wereld* [Hiddink: This is my world]. Eindhoven, the Netherlands: De Boekenmakers.

Oudejans, R. R. D (2008). Reality-based practice under pressure improves handgun shooting performance of police officers. *Ergonomics, 51*, 261-273.

Oudejans, R. R. D., and Pijpers, J. R. (2009). Training with anxiety has a positive effect on expert perceptual-motor performance under pressure. *The Quarterly Journal of Experimental Psychology, 62*, 1631-1647.

Oudejans, R. R. D., and Pijpers, J. R. (in press). Training with mild anxiety may prevent choking under high levels of anxiety. *Psychology of Sport and Exercise*.

Owen, M. (2005). *Off the record: My autobiography*. London: CollinsWillow.

Pensgaard, A. M., and Roberts, G. C. (2003). Achievement goal orientations and the use of coping strategies among winter Olympians. *Psychology of Sport and Exercise, 4*, 101-116.

Pijpers, J. R., Oudejans, R. R. D., Holsheimer, F., and Bakker, F. C. (2003). Anxiety-performance relationships in climbing: A process-oriented approach. *Psychology of Sport and Exercise, 4*, 283-304.

Poolton, J. M., Masters, R. S. W., and Maxwell, J. P. (2005). The relationship between initial errorless learning conditions and subsequent performance. *Human Movement Science, 24*, 362-378.

Poolton, J. M., Maxwell, J. P., and Masters, R. S. W. (2006). The influence of analogy learning on decision-making in table tennis: Evidence from behavioural data. *Psychology of Sport and Exercise, 7*, 677-688.

Reason, J. (2000). Human error: Models and management. *British Medical Journal, 320*, 768-770.

Reeves, C. W., Nicholls, A. R., and KcKenna, J. (2009). Stressors and coping strategies among early and middle adolescent premier league academy soccer players: Differences according to age. *Journal of Applied Sport Psychology, 21*, 31-48.

Reeves, J. L., Tenenbaum, G., and Lidor, R. (2007). Choking in front of the goal: The effects of self-consciousness training. *International Journal of Sport and Exercise Psychology, 5*, 240-254.

Ripley, A. (2008). *The unthinkable: Who survives when disaster strikes – and why*. New York: Crown Publishers.

Roberts, G. C. (1986). The perception of stress: A potential source and its development. In R. Weiss, and D. Gould (Eds.), *Sport for children and youths* (pp. 119-126). Champaign, IL: Human Kinetics.

Rohleder, N., Beulen, S. E., Chen, E., Wolf, J. M., and Kirschbaum, C. (2007). Stress on the dance floor: The cortisol stress response to social-evaluative threat in competitive ballroom dancers. *Personality and Social Psychology Bulletin, 33*, 69-84.

Rotella, R. J., and Lerner, J. D. (1993). Responding to competitive pressure. In R. N. Singer, M. Murphey, and L. K. Tennant (Eds.), *Handbook of Research on Sport Psychology* (pp. 528-541), New York: Macmillan.

Schlenker, B. R., Phillips, S. T., Boniecki, K. A., and Schlenker, D. R. (1995). Championship pressures: Choking or triumphing in one's own territory? *Journal of Personality and Social Psychology, 68*, 632-643.

Southgate, G., and Woodman, A. (2003). *Woody and Nord: A football friendship*. London: Penguin books.

Smith, S. M., Norrell, J. H., and Saint, J. L. (1996). Self-esteem and reactions to ego threat: A (battle)field investigation. *Basic and Applied Social Psychology, 18*, 395-404.

Tauer, J. M., Guenther, C. L., and Rozek, C. (2009). Is there a home choke in decisive playoff basketball games? *Journal of Applied Sport Psychology, 21*, 148-162.

Taylor, J., and Cuave, K. L. (1994). The Sophomore slump among professional baseball players: Real or imagined? *International Journal of Sport Psychology, 25*, 230-239.

Tice, D. M., and Baumeister, R. F. (1990). Self-esteem, self-handicapping, and self-presentation: The strategy of inadequate practice. *Journal of Personality, 58*, 443-464.

Vickers, J. A., and Williams, A. M. (2007). Performing under pressure: The effects of physiological arousal, cognitive anxiety, and gaze control in biathlon. *Journal of Motor Behavior, 39*, 381–394.

Wang, J., Marchant, D., and Morris, T. (2004). Coping style and susceptibility to choking. *Journal of Sport Behavior, 27*, 75-92.

Wegner, D. M., Ansfield, M., and Pilloff, D. (1998). The putt and the pendulum: Ironic effects of the mental control of action. *Psychological Science, 9*, 196-1999.

Weick, K. E., and Sutcliffe, K. M. (2007). *Managing the unexpected: Resilient Performance in an age of uncertainty*. San Fransisco, CA: John Wiley and Sons.

Winner, D. (2005). *Those feet: An intimate history of English football*. London: Bloomsbury.

Wright, E. F., Jackson, W., Christie, S. D., McGuire, G. R., and Wright, R. D. (1991). The home-course disadvantage in golf championships: Further evidence for the undermining effect of supportive audiences on performance under pressure. *Journal of Sport Behavior, 14*, 51-60.

Wright, E. F., Voyer, D., Wright, R. D., and Roney, C. (1995). Supporting audiences and performance under pressure: The home-ice disadvantage in hockey championships. *Journal of Sport Behavior, 18*, 21-28.

Wulf, G., and Prinz, W. (2001). Directing attention to movement effects enhances learning: A review. *Psychonomic Bulletin and Review, 8*, 648-660.

PART V: COPING EFFECTIVENESS

In: Coping in Sport: Theory, Methods, and Related Constructs   ISBN: 978-1-60876-488-4
Editor: Adam R. Nicholls   © 2010 Nova Science Publishers, Inc.

Chapter 14

EFFECTIVE VERSUS INEFFECTIVE COPING IN SPORT

Adam R. Nicholls
University of Hull, UK

ABSTRACT

It is essential that athletes cope effectively with stress in order to maintain emotional well-being during competitive sports events. This chapter identifies which coping effectiveness model/theory/ approach/explanation is the most appropriate for researchers and applied practitioners in sport settings. The outcome model, goodness-of-fit approach, the automaticity explanation of coping effectiveness, choice of coping strategy explanation of coping effectiveness, the path analysis of coping effectiveness model, and the research associated with these models is critically evaluated. Based on the current literature, it appears that the choice of coping strategy explanation is the most accurate and practical theory of coping effectiveness, as coping strategies appear to be predominantly effective or ineffective. Assessment issues, applied implications, and future research directions in the area of coping effectiveness are also considered.

INTRODUCTION

To perform successfully in sport, especially when experiencing immense stress, it is essential that athletes cope effectively (e.g., Haney and Long, 1995; Lazarus, 2000). Indeed, Folkman and Moskowitz (2004) suggested that the underlying reason for studying coping is that some forms of coping will be more effective than others. They also recommended that this information should be used by researchers to develop coping interventions to enhance emotional well-being, which is drastically reduced when stress is experienced and not managed effectively. Coping effectiveness is an attractive concept to sport psychology researchers and coaches alike, because if an athlete is coping effectively with stress, they are likely to perform to a greater level (e.g., Haney and Long, 1995). However, the issue of "determining" coping effectiveness remains extremely difficult, due to two specific reasons (Somerfield and McRae, 2000). Firstly, researchers have debated the effectiveness of particular strategies. Lazarus (1999), alongside Lazarus and Folkman (1984), suggested that coping strategies are neither inherently effective nor ineffective and that a particular coping strategy or combination of coping strategies may be effective in one situation, but not another. Conversely, Carver, Scheier, and Weintraub (1989), suggested that coping strategies are either pre-dominantly effective or ineffective, although they suggested that a strategy will not be effective or ineffective all of the time and that this may vary across individuals. Secondly, a coping strategy could be effective during one part of a stressful situation (Folkman and Moskowitz, 2004), but as the stressful situation progresses it could become ineffective, indicating that both short- and long-term coping effectiveness could be considered. As such, our understanding of coping effectiveness is limited, especially in sport settings (e.g., Nicholls and Polman, 2007a; Ntoumanis and Biddle, 1998).

Coping effectiveness has recently been defined as the "degree in which a coping strategy or combination of strategies is or are successful in alleviating the negative emotions caused by stress" (Nicholls and Polman, 2007a, p. 15). On reflection, I feel this definition could perhaps be refined slightly to encapsulate the majority of research that has explored coping effectiveness. I believe removing "the negative emotions caused by" from the Nicholls and Polman definition would be more aligned to the conceptualizations of Lazarus (1999) who stated that when a person copes effectively they will experience less stress. As such, I believe that coping effectiveness refers to the *degree in which a coping strategy or combination of strategies is or are successful in alleviating stress.*

The review by Nicholls and Polman (2007a) included a section on coping effectiveness, but coping effectiveness is complex and requires much more attention than it was given by that review. Moreover, they did not explore two of the five models which attempted to account for coping effectiveness (e.g., the outcome model and the path analysis model), nor did they comment upon which coping effectiveness model was the most accurate. Accordingly, the purpose of this chapter paper was to identify which coping effectiveness model is the most appropriate for researchers and applied practitioners in the sport domain. The five models, theories, approaches, or explanations that have attempted to understand the notion of effective versus ineffective and their associated research were critically evaluated. Researchers such as Folkman (1991, 1992) have used the terms approaches, models, and theories interchangeably, so this chapter has followed that format.

OUTCOME MODEL

The outcome model of coping effectiveness, proposed by Folkman (1984, 1991, 1992), judges the effectiveness of coping in relation to a pre-determined outcome. Applied to a sport setting, a coping strategy or strategies that promote a favorable outcome in a stressful situation such as holing a putt in golf, making a conversion in rugby union, or scoring a penalty in soccer would be classified as being effective coping strategies. A coping strategy or series of strategies that result in an unfavorable outcome such as missing free throw shot in basketball or having a double fault in tennis would be classified as being ineffective, if these were the pre-determined outcome variables.

Folkman (1991, 1992) suggested that the ability of the outcome model of coping effectiveness to gauge the effects of coping depends on the choice of outcome, because the selection of an inappropriate outcome could induce inaccurate estimations of coping. To prevent coping being either underestimated or over estimated, Folkman (1991) suggested that scholars could consider two important constructs: relevance and proximity. The selected outcome should be relevant to the stressful situation and something that coping can affect (Folkman, 1991). In a sporting situation, coping is thought to influence a range of factors such as injury occurrence (e.g., Smith, Ptacek, and Smoll, 1992), satisfaction (e.g., Scanlan and Lewthwaite, 1992), and performance (e.g., Haney and Long, 1995), which could all be used as outcome variables. Additionally, Folkman (1991) also stated that in order to evaluate the effects of coping on an outcome, coping has to be independent of the outcome variable. Proximity refers to the nearness in time between the outcome and the coping strategies that are thought to be causally related. Folkman (1992) suggested that the more proximal an outcome is in relation to a specific coping strategy or strategies, the higher our certainty that there is a causal relationship. The more distal an outcome is from the coping process, the harder it is to be certain that coping influenced the outcome. For instance, if a tennis player used visualization to prepare himself or herself to hit a serve in the first game of a match when experiencing stress, this coping strategy could be attributed to the outcome of player hitting their first serve in. However, it would be much more difficult to attribute whether a coping strategy used in the first game of a match had an effect on an unsuccessful serve in the last set of a tennis match. This is because there are a number of factors that may have contributed to the failure of achieving the outcome towards the end of a sporting event such as fatigue, dehydration, or technical problems rather than an ineffective coping strategy, used much earlier. Folkman (1992) recommended that if distal outcomes are used, it is essential that selected outcomes have the potential for change over the period studied. In sport settings percentage or frequency statistics could be used, such as the percentage of successful free throw shots in basketball, injury incidence, or state anxiety levels as opposed to the outcome variables that are not likely to change such as running speed or personality, because these are relatively fixed.

The outcome model of coping effectiveness was not featured in the review by Nicholls and Polman (2007a). Literature searches in SPORTdiscus, PSYClit, and PSYCinfo, revealed that only one study in the sport domain has measured coping effectiveness in relation to the outcome of a stressful episode. With a sample of 318 U.S. and 404 Korean athletes, Kim and Duda (2003) explored this model using "satisfaction," "enjoyment," and "desire to continue" as the outcome variables among athletes from diverse sports including soccer, golf, volleyball, and track and field. Their findings provided support for the outcome model as coping was associated with the pre-selected outcomes. However, the pre-selected outcomes of enjoyment and desire to continue in sport are questionable, because there is no evidence to suggest that coping in sport is related to the desire to continue or enjoyment in sport. There are a variety of sport specific outcomes that Kim and Duda could have used to assess this model, such as the number of tackles made in soccer, percentage of putts holed from within five feet, or the percentage of successful spikes in volleyball, given the relationship between coping and performance (e.g., Haney and Long, 2005). Although, it acknowledged that performance statistics could be influenced by a multitude of factors such as opponents, weather, and the amount of game time a player has, which has to be taken into consideration when using objective measurements of performance.

A potential limitation, and my overriding concern with the outcome model, is that coping is considered to be effective when there is a successful outcome (e.g., holes a putt or wins a match in a stressful situation) and ineffective when the reverse occurs. However, Crocker,

Kowalski, and Graham (1998) stated that just because an athlete is failing to perform, it is not a formality that they are failing to cope. An individual might be losing because their opponent has played very well, he or she has encountered technical difficulties, or the athlete is in a situation that simply cannot be mastered. This is supported by an effective coping quote from Nicholls, Holt, and Polman (2005, p. 123):

> [I] walked slowly and took my time and it ended up a loss but it wasn't . . . I made a big putt on the 18th but it was the way I went through my mannerisms just the same if I am going to play nine holes with my friend. That is the way I controlled it and I was very pleased even though I lost my match. I was very pleased how I controlled everything with my pre shot routine going through it and keeping it going.

In this quotation, the golfer felt that he coped effectively with the stress he was experiencing, but he still lost the match. In order to overcome such limitations, Folkman (1991) advocated that multiple outcomes are used, which are both short- and long-term, when longitudinal research is conducted.

Goodness-of-Fit Approach

The goodness-of-fit approach (Folkman, 1984; 1991; 1992; Menaghan, 1982) is the most tested model of coping effectiveness in the sport psychology literature. The goodness-of-fit approach postulates that effective coping depends on two fits, (a) the fit between reality (i.e., what is actually going on in the person-environment transaction made by the person) and appraisal, and (b) the fit between appraisal and coping (Folkman, 1984; 1992; Lazarus and Folkman, 1984; Menaghan, 1982). Appraisal is an evaluative focused process in which one attempts to explore meaning or the significance of a situation and was categorized into primary and secondary appraisal (Lazarus and Folkman). During primary appraisal the individual makes an evaluation about the encounter in relation to his or her well-being. If an encounter has been appraised as stressful the individual evaluates the coping options available to them, the likelihood that a coping option will achieve what it is meant to do, and whether the person feels they can deploy the strategies effectively, which is known as secondary appraisal (Lazarus, 1999; Lazarus and Folkman).

The fit between reality and appraisal relates to the congruence between what is actually occurring in the stressful episode and the person's appraisal regarding the significance of the event and the options for coping available to them (Folkman, 1991, 1992). A mis-match between reality and appraisal may lead to ineffective coping. For example, an athlete may fail to appraise a match as being threatening and will therefore not deploy any coping strategies, but with the benefit of hindsight he or she may have realized it was a threatening event and that he or she should have attempted to cope. Likewise, if an athlete appraises a match as being threatening, when it was not actually threatening to him or her, it will have lead to unnecessary coping. Conversely, an athlete may have accurately appraised a stressful sporting event as being threatening, harmful, challenging, or beneficial, but be unrealistic in the coping resources required to cope with the stressful event. An underestimation of the coping resources available to the athlete will result in an athlete deploying only restricted coping efforts. An overestimation of coping resources will often lead to feelings of disappointment when the athlete fails to manage a stressful situation (Folkman, 1992).

The fit between appraisal and coping relates to the match between the appraisal an individual makes about the controllability of the stressor and the actual coping processes that they use to manage the stressor (Folkman, 1992). It has been hypothesized that problem-focused coping (e.g., strategies directed towards managing the stressor such as planning, information seeking, and goal setting) will be effective in situations that an athlete perceives they can control. Emotion-focused coping (e.g., strategies directed towards managing emotional distress; See Chapter 1 for explanation of problem- and emotion-focused coping dimensions), on the other hand, was theorized as being more effective in stressful situations that were perceived as being uncontrollable to the athlete (Folkman, 1984). There is evidence from the sport psychology literature, which suggests that high perceived control of a stressor has been associated with problem-focused coping strategies (e.g., Anshel, 1996; Anshel and Kaissidis, 1997; Haney and Long, 1995; Kim and Duda, 2003) and emotion-focused coping strategies are more frequently deployed in response to uncontrollable stressors (e.g., Anshel, 1996; Anshel and Kaissidis, 1997). However, these research attempts have only focused on the fit between appraisal and coping and not the fit between reality and appraisal, which influences the fit between appraisal and coping (Folkman, 1991; 1992). A second limitation of these studies is that they have not actually reported whether athletes perceive their coping as being more effective when there is a match between appraisal and coping. This is required in order to help establish whether the goodness-of-fit approach may help explain coping effectiveness among athletic populations.

Although the goodness-of-fit approach has received some support (e.g., Kim and Duda, 2003), there are a number of limitations to this model that may be difficult or even impossible to overcome. The most important aspect of the goodness-of-fit approach is that there is a match between the controllability of the stressors and coping responses. Recent research by Nicholls and colleagues (e.g., Nicholls, Holt, and Polman, 2005; Nicholls, Holt, Polman, and James, 2005; Nicholls and Polman, 2008) has reported that stress is a multifaceted experience, with athletes often reporting more than one stressor simultaneously. It is entirely possible that an athlete may experience one stressor that is controllable, but another stressor that is uncontrollable whilst playing sport. If an athlete has to cope with two stressors simultaneously, with one stressor being controllable (e.g., technical problems) and the other uncontrollable (e.g., opponents playing well), it is impossible for there to be a fit between appraisal and coping, as conceived by Folkman (1984), because an athlete may feel they can control one stressor, but not the other.

If an athlete does experience only one stressor at a time and deploys coping strategies from the same dimension, it is possible for there to be a match between appraisal and coping. However, recent research (e.g., Nicholls, 2007a; Nicholls, Holt, and Polman, 2005; Nicholls, Jones, Polman, and Borkoles, in press; Nicholls, Holt, Polman, and Bloomfield, 2006; Nicholls and Polman, 2008) suggests that coping is very complex, as athletes use coping strategies in combinations from different dimensions. This makes it very difficult for the proposed fit between stressor controllability and coping to be measured for research purposes. This was previously acknowledged by Folkman (1992), who stated that there is often "interplay" between problem- and emotion-focused strategies. As such, Folkman suggested that in situations perceived as being controllable the majority of coping strategies deployed should be problem-focused, whereas coping should be predominantly emotion-focused in uncontrollable situations. This would suggest that there is seldom, if ever, a perfect fit between coping and appraisals as conceived by Folkman (1991, 1992).

Another limitation of the goodness-of-fit approach is the difficulty surrounding the classification of coping. This approach requires the categorization of coping strategies into the problem- or emotion-focused dimension. However, it has been suggested that it is virtually impossible to accurately classify a coping strategy within a dimension, because a single strategy may have more than one function (e.g., Compas, Worsham, Ey, and Howell, 1996; Lazarus, 1999; Skinner, Edge, Altman, and Sherwood, 2003; See Chapter 1 for an extended discussion of this debate). Indeed, Eklund, Grove, and Heard (1998) reported that the coping strategy seeking social support can be used for instrumental or emotional reasons. When social support is used for instrumental reasons it is a problem-focused coping strategy, but when it used for emotional reasons it is an emotion-focused coping strategy. The are a number of difficulties in testing the goodness-of-fit approach, which raises questions regarding its suitability in sporting contexts.

AUTOMATICITY

Gould, Eklund, and Jackson (1993) found evidence to suggest that coping effectiveness is related to the automaticity of a coping strategy. They proposed that involuntarily or subconscious strategies are more effective and associated with superior performance than strategies that require conscious effort. The automaticity explanation of coping effectiveness has received additional support from Dugdale, Eklund, and Gordon (2002), who also found that automatic strategies were reported as being more effective than less automatic coping strategies. The main issue regarding this explanation of coping effectiveness relates to whether automatic strategies, which require no conscious effort, can actually be classified as coping strategies (see Chapter 1, for a discussion of whether involuntary responses to stress can be classified as coping).

CHOICE OF COPING STRATEGY EXPLANATION OF COPING EFFECTIVENESS

The notion that the effectiveness of a coping strategy is related to the type of strategy an athlete deploys was first mentioned in a sport setting by Eubank and Collins (2000). Coping strategies such as thinking ahead and positive self-talk were reported as being effective coping strategies, whereas strategies such as thinking about thoughts that are irrelevant to the task at hand and negative self-talk were ineffective among a sample of regional gymnasts and tennis players. Support for this theory was provided by Nicholls et al., (2005) who examined coping effectiveness among a sample of Irish international golfers. Strategies such as the golfers blocking negative thoughts, rationalizing, and breathing exercises were effective, whereas strategies such as making routine changes, speeding up shots, and trying too hard were found to be ineffective. The argument that coping effectiveness is related to the choice of a coping strategy is partially supported by recent diary studies that have examined the effectiveness of coping strategies among international adolescent and professional rugby union players (e.g., Nicholls et al., 2006; Nicholls, Jones et al., 2009; Nicholls and Polman, 2007b). Strategies that were deemed to be more effective overall were blocking negative thoughts, increased effort, and increased concentration, although the effectiveness of these strategies did vary.

In an additional study, Nicholls (2007a) examined coping effectiveness among a sample of five international adolescent golfers over a period of 28-days in order to assess fluctuations via open ended diary responses. The findings of this study provided tentative support for the notion that some strategies may be predominantly more effective than others. For instance, increased focus was only reported as an effective coping strategy, whereas making technical adjustments was only cited as an ineffective strategy. In response to managing opponent stressors, blocking negative thoughts was cited as an effective coping strategy on five occasions and an ineffective coping strategy three times. However, the effectiveness of a coping strategy or combination of coping strategies also fluctuated from day to day and even in the same round. That is, certain strategies were effective during one round, but not on a different day, or even at the start of the round but not towards the end of a round. Based on the research of Nicholls and colleagues (e.g., Nicholls et al., 2006; Nicholls, Jones et al., 2009; Nicholls and Polman, 2007b) it appears that over a prolonged period of time some coping strategies will be pre-dominantly more effective than others, but these strategies will not be effective all of the time.

PATH ANALYSIS MODEL OF COPING EFFECTIVENESS

Haney and Long (1995) developed a model of coping effectiveness based on Lazarus and Folkman's (1984) transactional model of stress and coping and Bandura's (1986) social cognitive theory, which is concerned with the belief one has in his or her ability to execute specific behaviors. The model was tested over two sporting trials in basketball, hockey, or soccer. The model of Haney and Long contained six factors that were thought to define coping effectiveness, based upon Lazarus and Folkman and Bandura. These factors were: (1) self-efficacy appraisals, which refer to the beliefs an individual has in his or her ability to successfully execute specific behaviors (Bandura, 1977), (2) control, which refers to appraisals of controlling stressful situations including, behavioral, and/or cognitive control, (3) somatic anxiety (e.g., physiological arousal), (4) engagement coping, which included efforts to manage a stressful event, (5) disengagement coping, which included coping attempts that focused the attention of the individual away from the stressful event, and (6) sporting performance in one of the three sports tested.

The level of fit for this model was relatively poor for the two rounds of the competitive events, so Haney and Long (1995) revised their model and freed the path between somatic anxiety and control. This resulted in a Goodness-of-fit-index (GFI) of .95. The ratio for chi-square to degrees of freedom (Q) was 4.3:1, and was deemed acceptable. In addition to the overall fit of the model, there were a number of specific relationships that are noteworthy. Athletes who felt more in control of the situation, emotions, and performance used less disengagement coping and performed better. Additionally, athletes who performed better in Trial 1 were more self-efficacious, more in control, and were less anxious than the athletes who performed poorly.

ASSESSING COPING EFFECTIVENESS

An important issue to consider when assessing coping effectiveness is who is the most suitable person to measure coping effectiveness? Is it the athlete, the coach, or team mates of an athlete? I firmly believe that the only person that can judge the effectiveness of a coping strategy or strategies is the athlete himself or herself. As cited previously within this chapter, Crocker et al. (1998) made an excellent point on this issue and I am in complete agreement with them. Failure in performance could be due to a number of reasons other than coping. Therefore, if other people such as coaches or teammates judged coping effectiveness they would not necessarily be aware of this information and could rate that an athlete has coped ineffectively just because they performed poorly. Furthermore, scholars have utilized self-reports to measure coping, so it seems sensible that if we rely on athletes to self-report how they coped, then we can rely on athletes to report the effectiveness of such strategies themselves.

Researchers have used a variety of Likert-type scales to measure coping effectiveness including 10-point (e.g., Nicholls, Polman, Levy, Taylor, and Cobley, 2007), 7-point (e.g., Ntoumanis and Biddle, 1998), and 4-point scales (e.g., Nicholls, Jones et al., 2009), which makes it difficult to compare studies. In order for comparisons to be made across studies, it would be more appropriate for researchers to agree on the number of points within their Likert-type scale. Alternatively, visual analogue scales could also be used to measure coping effectiveness, because they do not limit participants' responses and could yield more varied results (e.g., Polman, Nicholls, Cohen, and Borkoles, 2007).

Likert-type and analogue scales are useful for measuring short-term coping effectiveness and in particular the effectiveness of specific coping strategies, because the data obtained could be used to compare the effectiveness of different strategies. If coping effectiveness is measured using these scales on repeated occasions it would be possible to monitor the effectiveness of different coping strategies longitudinally allowing comparisons to be made. Finally, measuring the effectiveness of coping strategies using Likert-type scales enables researchers to explore the relationship between other variables such as affect (e.g., Ntoumanis and Biddle, 1998) or emotional intensity (e.g., Nicholls, Jones et al., 2009). Although these scales generate the effectiveness scores of particular coping strategies over different time periods, they do not provide insights into the experiences of athletes in relation to effective versus ineffective coping.

Researchers have employed two qualitative techniques to assess coping effectiveness: interviews (e.g., Nicholls, Holt, and Polman, 2005) and open-ended diaries (e.g., Nicholls, 2007a). Using interviews and diaries can generate detailed accounts of coping effectiveness, which is important when little is known about a particular phenomenon (Crocker et al., 1998). This type of data could potentially allow researchers to tap into the underlying reasons regarding why certain strategies were effective or why athletes coped effectively or ineffectively on different occasions. Interviews allow for some retrospection, which is particularly useful for assessing overall coping effectiveness in a stressful situation (Folkman and Moskowitz, 2004). This may yield information on how individual strategies interact with one another to provide a global understanding of the coping effectiveness experience.

An alternative method of assessing coping effectiveness is to monitor stress levels. Lazarus (1999) indicated that when coping is effective, lower levels of stress will be experienced by the individual. With the exception of Haney and Long (1995), it appears researchers within the sport domain have not measured stress levels in order to ascertain coping effectiveness. The stress thermometer (e.g., Kowalski and Crocker, 2001) could be suitable tool for this and it could be used in addition to coping effectiveness Liker-type scale measures of coping effectiveness.

APPLIED IMPLICATIONS

It is essential that athletes are taught and then encouraged to deploy coping strategies, because it appears that not attempting to cope has been associated with frustration (e.g., Nicholls et al., 2005) and performance inefficiencies (Haney and Long, 1995). However, research concerning the application of coping effectiveness data among athletes is scant, but it is essential that researchers develop theory guided interventions to teach people to manage stress more effectively (Folkman and Moskowitz, 2004). Based on the critiques of the five models of coping effectiveness, applied consultants may wonder exactly how to teach their clients to cope effectively with stress.

A coping effectiveness training program with an international golfer, based on the premise that certain strategies would be more effective than other strategies (e.g., Bolger and Zuckerman, 1995; Eubank and Collins, 2000) and previous research supporting this theory (e.g., Nicholls et al., 2005) was devised by Nicholls (2007b). As such, the purpose of the intervention was to increase behaviors that had been identified as being related to effective coping (e.g., committing to all shots, trusting his swing, and maintaining a routine) and minimize strategies associated with ineffective coping experiences (e.g., trying to hit the ball greater distances, making technical adjustments, and focusing on opponents too much), with a 16-year-old international adolescent golfer. Overall, the participant increased the number of effective coping strategies he used and reduced the number of ineffective coping strategies employed across the 21 day study. The participant reported that the training program was beneficial, although no performance data was collected.

The notion of teaching an athlete to use effective strategies and refrain from using ineffective strategies may appear a contradiction, as Lazarus (1999) suggested that there are no coping strategies that are either effective or ineffective at all times. However, it is feasible to suggest that in certain sports a number of strategies could be predominantly effective or ineffective, depending on the nature of the sport. Longitudinal research with golfers (e.g., Nicholls, 2007a) and professional rugby union players (e.g., Nicholls et al., 2006; Nicholls, Jones et al., 2009) suggests that strategies are differentially effective at various times, but certain strategies have been found to be much more effective than others over a prolonged period. For instance, in Nicholls, Jones et al.'s study blocking negative thoughts had a higher mean effectiveness score than acceptance during matches. This supports Carver et al. (1989) who stipulated that strategies are either pre-dominantly effective or ineffective. Furthermore, athletes could be encouraged to practice the pre-dominantly effective coping strategies they are taught on a repeated basis to enhance familiarity. Gould et al. (1993) indicated that learning coping strategies could be the key to enhancing coping effectiveness, so athletes should be familiar with a range of strategies.

Applied consultants could also encourage their clients to assess the controllability of the stressful situation they are in and deploy strategies directed towards the stressor when they feel in control of the overall stress. Athletes could also be taught and encouraged to use strategies that are directed towards controlling their emotional distress in relation uncontrollable stressors. Despite my concerns regarding the goodness-of-fit approach, interventions based on coping effectiveness approach by Chesney and colleagues among patients diagnosed with HIV (e.g., Chambers, Taylor, Johnson, and Folkman, 2003; Chesney, Folkman, and Chambers, 1996), have yielded positive results.

Future Research Directions

Although our knowledge of coping effectiveness has increased, additional research is required in order to cement our understanding further. This is vital for both theory development and then applied practice. With regard to the former, more work is required in testing the theories of coping effectiveness to either refine them or disregard them for sport. Research could be conducted to explore coping in relation to sport specific outcomes (e.g., performance statistics), which appear to be a useful way of classifying effective versus ineffective coping. It is essential that pre-selected outcomes are relevant and proximal to coping. Folkman (1992) also suggested that multiple outcomes should be used. The recent paper by Kim and Duda (2003) used three different outcomes, which seems a suitable guide for future research. However, scholars could consider a number of variables that may influence the success of an athlete in achieving their outcomes. These include the standard of an opponent, weather conditions, and task difficulty.

This review has proposed some practical limitations of the goodness-of-fit approach, which needs to be addressed by future research. For this model of coping effectiveness to be assessed accurately, researchers need to consider the fit between both reality and appraisal, and appraisal and coping. Assessing the fit between reality and appraisal represents a daunting task for coping scholars. This could involve a period of reflection allowing the athlete to recall what was actually occurring in a stressful episode after a time delay, as reflection is thought to be important in helping people find meaning and understand situations better (e.g., Folkman and Moskowitz, 2004). Future research could also assess the impact of a coping intervention based on the goodness-of-fit approach among athletes, to see if the results are as positive for athletes as they are for HIV patients.

To avoid confusion among both researchers and athletes taking part in research, it is essential that athletes are asked to recall coping strategies rather than cognitive styles, thus future research should distinguish between cognitive styles and coping and exclude cognitive styles from coping analyses, before measuring the effectiveness of any strategies. Indeed, a focus on secondary appraisal and how people evaluate the coping options available to them before deploying these strategies, could be important. The time or the amount of thought it takes to identify and then deploy a coping strategy, which could be rated on a Likert-type scale, could be a more suitable option and may enhance our understanding of coping effectiveness. This proposal relates to the work of Gould et al. (1993), who suggested that the wrestlers had learned their coping strategies more efficiently, so one could deduct that it would take these athletes less time to evaluate the strategies they could use and which strategies would be more effective, before attempting to cope. Experimental research designs could clarify this issue. It would also be interesting to see if teaching athletes to evaluate stressful situations and deploy coping strategies quicker, through designing programs to accelerate secondary appraisal would enhance coping effectiveness.

The majority of research from the sport psychology literature suggests that certain strategies are more effective than other strategies (e.g., Eubank and Collins, 2000; Nicholls, Holt, and Polman, 2005; Nicholls et al., 2006; Nicholls, Jones, et al., in press; Nicholls et al., 2007). Based on the recommendations by Carver et al. (1989), future research could also explore the underlying factors that may determine whether a coping strategy is predominantly effective of ineffective. Coping scholars have suggested the match between the coping strategy and control is a key issue (e.g., Folkman, 1992), but other research has suggested that a coping strategy can be effective or ineffective even when it is used to manage the same stressor (e.g., Nicholls, 2007a). This would indicate that there could be other variables that might determine whether a coping strategy is effective or not. Findings from the mainstream literature by Bolger and Zuckerman (1995) suggest that personality may be a worthwhile construct to explore. Researchers could also explore the effectiveness of different strategies in a plethora of sports, to identify effective versus ineffective strategies to provide an underpinning to the work of applied practitioners.

A limitation of the model proposed by Haney and Long (1995) relates to the classification of coping. They categorized all of the coping strategies used by athletes into either engagement or disengagement dimensions, which is problematic (e.g., Compas et al., 1996; Lazarus, 1999; Skinner et al., 2003). Future research could adapt the model proposed by Haney and Long, by categorizing coping at the strategy level, such as using the 10-subscales of the Coping Inventory for Competitive Sports (e.g., Gaudreau and Blondin, 2002). However, with an increased number of coping parameters, it would mean a larger participant sample would be required (e.g., Biddle, Markland, Gilbourne, Chatzisarantis, and Sparkes, 2001). This model could be further refined by including emotions, because scholars have suggested that stressors, coping, and emotions occur as one conceptual unit (e.g., Lazarus, 1999). Additionally, the path analysis model could be examined over multiple rounds of competition. Haney and Long acknowledged that there could have been a better fit had a third round of competition been included in the data collection.

In the extant literature there has been a pre-occupation with short-term assessments of coping effectiveness during sport performance, but in order to maximize our understanding of this construct, researchers could assess coping effectiveness over periods such as a season and examine inter- and intra-individual differences in relation to coping. This will allow researchers to assess the effectiveness of certain coping strategies over a prolonged period and identify factors that may contribute to effective coping. Holistic approaches that take into account both within-event stressors and stressors occurring outside of competition (e.g., Nicholls, Backhouse, Polman, and McKenna, 2009) will allow researchers to look at coping effectiveness in relation to all stressors an athlete experiences.

CONCLUSION

It is important we understand more about coping effectiveness, as this research has the potential to inform both theory and applied practice. It appears that there are flaws in all of the models, theories, approaches, or explanations of coping effectiveness. The sport literature provides more support for the choice explanation of coping effectiveness. Although strategies are neither effective nor ineffective at all times, research in sports suggests that certain strategies will be predominantly effective or ineffective. However, it should be noted that the outcome and path analysis model of coping effectiveness require more attention and the goodness-of-fit approach has been useful in coping effectiveness training in non-sport domains, so may be useful for underpinning interventions. Refining existing or developing new models that enable researchers to explain why certain strategies are effective in certain situations, but not others, may advance our understanding of coping effectiveness.

REFERENCES

Anshel, M. H. (1996). Coping styles among adolescent competitive athletes. *Journal of Social Psychology, 136,* 311-324.

Anshel, M. H., and Kaissidis, A. N. (1997). Coping style and situational appraisals as predictors of coping strategies following stressful events in sport as a function of gender and skill level. *British journal of psychology, 88,* 263-276.

Bandura, A. (1977). Self-efficacy: Toward a unifying theory of behavioral change. *Psychological Review, 84,* 191-215.

Bandura, A. (1986). *Social foundations of thought and action.* Englewood Cliffs, NJ: Prentice Hall.

Biddle, S. J. H., Markland, D., Gilbourne, D., Chatzisarantis, N. L. D., Sparkes, A. C. (2001). Research methods in sport and exercise psychology: Quantitative and qualitative issues. *Journal of Sports Sciences, 19,* 777-809.

Bolger, N., and Zuckerman, A. (1995). A framework for studying personality in the stress process. *Journal of Personality and Social Psychology, 69,* 890-902.

Carver, C. S., Scheier, M. F., and Weintraub, J. K. (1989). Assessing coping strategies: A theoretically based approach. *Journal of Personality and Social Psychology, 56,* 267-283.

Chesney, M. A., Chambers, D. B., Taylor, J. M., Johnson, L. M., and Folkman, S. (2003). Coping effectiveness training for men living with HIV: Results from a randomized clinical trial testing a group-based intervention. *Psychosomatic Medicine, 65,* 1038-1046.

Chesney, M. A., Folkman, S., and Chambers, D., B. (1996). Coping effectiveness training for men living with HIV: preliminary findings. *International Journal of STD and AIDS, 7,* 75-82.

Compas, B. E., Worsham, N., Ey, S., and Howell, D. C. (1996). When mom or dad has cancer: II Coping, cognitive appraisals, and psychological distress in children of cancer patients. *Health Psychology, 15,* 167-175.

Cramer, P. (2000). Defense mechanisms in psychology today: Further processes for adaptation. *American Psychologist, 55,* 637-646.

Crocker, P. R. E., Kowalski, K. C., and Graham, T. R. (1998). Measurement of coping strategies in sport. In J. L. Duda (Ed.), *Advances in sport and exercise psychology measurement* (pp. 149-161). Morgantown, WV: Fitness Information Technology.

Dugdale, J. R., Eklund, R. C., and Gordon, S. (2002). Expected and unexpected stressors in major international competition: Appraisal, coping, and performance. *The Sport Psychologist, 16,* 20-33.

Eklund, R. C., Grove, J. R., and Heard, N. P. (1998). The measurement of slump-related coping: Factorial validity of the COPE and Modified-COPE inventories. *Journal of Sport and Exercise Psychology, 20,* 157-175.

Eubank, M., and Collins D. (2000). Coping with pre- and in-event fluctuations in competitive state anxiety: A longitudinal approach. *Journal of Sports Sciences, 18,* 121-131.

Folkman, S. (1984). Personal control and stress and coping processes: A theoretical analysis. *Journal of Personality and Social Psychology, 46,* 839-852.

Folkman, S. (1991). Coping across the life span: Theoretical Issues. In E. M. Cummings, A. L. Greene, and K. H. Karraker (Eds.) *Life-span developmental psychology: Perspectives on stress and coping* (pp. 3-19). Hillsdale, NJ: Erlbaum.

Folkman, S. (1992). Making the case for coping. In B. N. Carpenter (Ed.), *Personal coping: Theory, research and application* (pp. 31-46). Westport, CT: Praeger.

Folkman, S., and Moskowitz, J. T. (2004). Coping: Pitfalls and promise. *Annual Review of Psychology, 55,* 745-774.

Gaudreau, P., and Blondin, J.-P. (2002). Development of a questionnaire for the assessment of coping strategies employed by athletes in competitive sport settings. *Psychology of Sport and Exercise, 3,* 1-34.

Gould, D., Eklund, R. C., and Jackson, S. A. (1993). Coping strategies used by US Olympic wrestlers. *Research Quarterly for Exercise and Sport, 64,* 83-93.

Haney, C. J., and Long, B. C. (1995). Coping effectiveness: A path analysis of self-efficacy, control, coping and performance in sport competitions. *Journal of Applied Social Psychology, 25,* 1726-1746.

Kim, M. S., and Duda, J. L. (2003). The coping process: Cognitive appraisals of stress, coping strategies, and coping effectiveness. *The Sport Psychologist, 17,* 406-425.

Kowalski, K. C., and Crocker, P. R. (2001). Development and validation of the coping function questionnaire for adolescents in sport. *Journal of Sport and Exercise Psychology, 23,* 136–155.

Lazarus, R. S. (1999). *Stress and emotion: A new synthesis.* New York: Springer.

Lazarus, R. S. (2000). How emotions influence performance in competitive sports. *The Sport Psychologist, 14,* 229-252.

Lazarus, R. S., and Folkman, S. (1984). *Stress, appraisal and coping.* New York: Springer.

Menaghan E. (1982). Measuring coping effectiveness: A panel analysis of marital problems and coping efforts. *Journal of Health and Social Behavior, 23,* 220–34

Nicholls, A. R. (2007a). A longitudinal phenomenological analysis of coping effectiveness among Scottish international adolescent golfers. *European Journal of Sport Science, 7,* 169–178.

Nicholls, A. R. (2007b). Can an athlete be taught to cope more effectively? The experiences of an international level adolescent golfer during a training program for coping. *Perceptual and Motor Skills, 104,* 494-500.

Nicholls, A. R., Backhouse, S. H., Polman R.C. J., and McKenna, J. (2009). Stressors and affective states among professional rugby union players. *Scandinavian Journal of Medicine and Science in Sports, 19,* 121-128.

Nicholls, A. R., Holt, N. L., and Polman, R. C. J. (2005). A phenomenological analysis of coping effectiveness in golf. *The Sport Psychologist, 19,* 111-130.

Nicholls, A. R., Holt, N. L., Polman, R. J. C., and Bloomfield, J. (2006). Stressors, Coping, and Coping Effectiveness Among Professional Rugby Union Players. *The Sport Psychologist, 20,* 314-329.

Nicholls, A. R., Holt, N. L., Polman, R. C. J., and James, D. W. G. (2005). Stress and coping among international adolescent golfers. *Journal of Applied Sport Psychology, 17,* 333-340.

Nicholls, A.R., Jones, C. R., Polman, R. C. J., and Borkoles, E. (2009). Stressors, coping, and emotion among professional rugby union players during training and matches. *Scandinavian Journal of Medicine and Science in Sports, 19,* 113-120.

Nicholls, A. R., and Polman, R. C. J. (2007a). Coping in sport: A systematic review. *Journal of Sport Sciences.*

Nicholls, A. R. and Polman, R. C. J. (2007b). Stressors, coping and coping effectiveness among players from the England under-18 rugby union team. *Journal of Sport Behavior, 30,* 119-218.

Nicholls, A. R., and Polman, R. C. J. (2008). Think aloud: Stress and coping during golf performances. *Anxiety, Stress, and Coping, 21,* 283-294.

Nicholls, A. R., Polman, R.C. J., Levy, A., Taylor, J. A., and Cobley, S. P. (2007). Stressors, coping, and coping effectiveness: Gender, sport type, and skill differences. *Journal of Sports Sciences, 25,* 1521-1530.

Ntoumanis, N., and Biddle, S. J. H. (1998). The relationship of coping and its perceived effectiveness to positive and negative affect in sport. *Personality and Individual Differences, 24,* 773-778.

Polman, R. C. J., Nicholls, A. R., Cohen, J. and Borkoles, E. (2007). The influence of game location and outcome on behaviour and mood states among professional rugby league players. *Journal of Sports Sciences, 25,* 1491-1500.

Scanlan, T. K., and Lewthwaite, R. (1984). Social psychological aspect of competition for male you sport participants: I. Predictors of competitive stress. *Journal of Sport Psychology, 6,* 208-226.

Skinner, E.A., Edge, K., Altman, J., and Sherwood, H. (2003). Searching for the structure of coping: A review and critique of category systems for classifying ways of coping. *Psychological Bulletin, 129,* 216-269.

Smith, R. E., Ptacek, J. T., and Smoll, F. L. (1992). Sensation seeking, stress, and adolescent injuries: A test of stress-buffering, risk-taking, and coping skills hypotheses. *Journal of Personality and Social Psychology, 62,* 1016-1024.

Somerfield, M. R., and McCrae, R. R. (2000). Stress and coping research: Methodological challenges, theoretical advances, and clinical applications. *American Psychologist, 55,* 620-625.

PART VI: FUTURE ORIENTATED ASPECTS OF COPING

In: Coping in Sport: Theory, Methods, and Related Constructs   ISBN: 978-1-60876-488-4
Editor: Adam R. Nicholls   © 2010 Nova Science Publishers, Inc.

Chapter 15

COPING SELF-EFFICACY IN SPORT

Jennifer A. Scorniaenchi and Deborah L. Feltz
Michigan State University, U.S.

ABSTRACT

An athlete's ability to cope with the environmental demands of stress in competition is important to successful performance. Coping self-efficacy (CSE), defined as the belief regarding one's ability to cope with diverse threats (e.g., stress, unwanted thoughts, difficult situations, or pain), is regarded as an important variable affecting an athlete's coping effectiveness (Bandura, 1997; Feltz, Short, and Sullivan, 2008). This chapter provides an overview of self-efficacy, the concept of CSE and its measurement, and a review of relevant research. The chapter ends with recommendations for researchers and practitioners on future directions in this area to prompt further research and inquiry.

INTRODUCTION

All athletes and coaches need coping skills to manage the stress and pressures they face in competition. Those who deal with their adversity and develop successful coping strategies are more likely to be able to focus on their performance than those who dwell on competitive stressors (Gould, Guinan, Greenleaf, Medberry, and Peterson, 1999). As described in previous chapters, coping refers to all conscious cognitive and behavioral efforts used in order to manage a stressful situation (Lazarus and Folkman, 1984). Readers might recall that researchers, such as Gaudreau and Blondin (2002), have categorized coping into three higher-order dimensions: (a) task-orientated, (b) distraction-orientated, and (c) disengagement-orientated coping. Task-orientated coping refers to the use of strategies aimed directly at managing stress (e.g., mental imagery, effort expenditure, and relaxation). Distraction-orientated coping strategies are those that direct the attention to unrelated aspects of the sport competition or context. Lastly, disengagement-orientated coping refers to strategies where athletes disengage themselves from attempts to achieve their personal goals.

Regardless of the type of coping that an athlete might employ, one of the most important psychological constructs thought to affect successful coping in sport is CSE (Bandura, 1997; Feltz, Short, and Sullivan, 2008). Empirical evidence suggests that CSE is critical in understanding whether or not a person will respond to potentially threatening or stressful situations effectively (Bandura, 1997; Cieslak, Benight, and Lehman 2008; Gyurcsik and Bray, Brittain, 2004; Gyurcsik, Brawley, and Langhout, 2002; Ozer and Bandura, 1990; Milne, Hall, and Forwell, 2005). CSE is a type of efficacy belief within Bandura's (1986, 1997) theory of self-efficacy that refers to one's perceived ability to manage perceived threats Before describing CSE and its relationship to effective coping and performance, we provide an overview of self-efficacy theory and its relationship to CSE.

THEORETICAL FRAMEWORK AND CONSTRUCT DEFINITIONS

In order to understand CSE, it is important to first understand the construct in which it is rooted; self-efficacy. Bandura (1977, 1997) proposed the theory of self-efficacy as a cognitive explanation for differences in the abilities of individuals to carry out challenging tasks. Self-efficacy beliefs are judgments of what people can accomplish with their skills; they are not judgments about the skills they have or do not have (Bandura). The skills that we are referring to include the physical skills of the task, coping skills, learning skills, and self-regulatory skills. Efficacy judgments about the physical skills of the task is often referred to as task self-efficacy (Kirsch, 1982). All efficacy judgments are produced through a complex process of self-appraisal and self-persuasion that relies on cognitive processing of diverse sources of efficacy information (Bandura). Bandura categorized these sources as past performance accomplishments, vicarious experiences, verbal persuasion, and physiological states. These sources are further explained in the next section as they related to CSE.

People's efficacy judgments about a certain skill affect their functioning through four major psychological processes: cognitive, motivational, affective, and selection (Bandura, 1997). Thus, efficacy beliefs influence people's thought patterns (e.g., the perceived threat of environmental events, worries, goals) and levels of motivation as reflected in the effort they expend in the activity and their perseverance in the face of difficulties (Bandura 1977, 1997). People's self-efficacy to cope influences emotional reactions (e.g., joy or anxiety) and stress experience. For instance, low efficacy beliefs about being able to cope with competitive pressure can create feelings of anxiety. People also select activities and environments based on their efficacy judgments to be successful.

In relating self-efficacy theory to coping skills, Bandura (1997) defined CSE (also referred to as ameliorative efficacy) as the belief regarding one's ability to cope with diverse threats (e.g., stress, unwanted thoughts, difficult situations, or pain). People's beliefs in their coping capabilities affect how much stress they experience in threatening or difficult situations, as well as their level of motivation (Bandura, 1994). Consistent with Bandura's definition, CSE also has been defined as the belief in one's abilities to execute cognitive and behavioral skills to cope with acute negative thoughts (Gyurcsik et al., 2002; Gyurcsik et al., 2004) and "beliefs about one's ability to prevent, control, or cope with potential difficulty" (Williams, 1995). To contrast task self-efficacy and CSE, task self-efficacy refers to people's perceptions that they can complete a task. Whereas CSE refers to people's belief in their ability to manage barriers and challenges that may prevent them from performing the task.

Sources of Coping Efficacy Information

In terms of the sources in information on which coping efficacy beliefs are based, performance accomplishments would include one's past experiences with using coping strategies, such as positive self-talk, relaxation, and distraction strategies. If one has had repeated success in using these strategies, CSE beliefs will increase; if these strategies were viewed as failures, CSE beliefs will decrease.

Coping efficacy information can also be derived through modeling. As Bandura (1997) noted, "Coping modeling is more likely to contribute to resilience in personal efficacy under difficult circumstances where the road to success is long and full of impediments, hardships, and setbacks, and where evidence of progress may be a long time coming" (p. 100). Obtaining coping efficacy information vicariously might involve observing the performance of one or more coping athletes, noting the consequence of their behavior, and then using this information to form judgments about one's own coping use. In fact, the use of coping models to improve performance has been examined within physical activity contexts (McCullagh and Weiss, 2001; Weiss et al., 1998). Coping models demonstrate negative cognitions, affects, and behaviors that may precede or accompany performance on tasks that are perceived as difficult or fearful (Feltz et al., 2008). When used clinically, coping models show a progression from low ability to cope with the demands of the task to exemplary ability to cope with performance stress.

Persuasive techniques as they apply to coping efficacy beliefs include verbal persuasion, evaluative feedback, and expectations by others. These techniques are widely used by coaches, managers, parents, and peers in attempting to influence an athlete's CSE. CSE based on persuasive sources are also likely to be weaker than those based on one's own coping accomplishments, in accord with self-efficacy theory. However, Bandura (1997) has suggested that the debilitating effects of persuasory information are more powerful than the enabling effects. Thus, if an athlete receives evaluative feedback that she does not maintain her focus under pressure situations, it may be harder to persuade her that she can focus under pressure in the future.

As Bandura (1997) has indicated regarding self-efficacy for performance, the extent of the persuasive influence on CSE will also likely depend on the prestige, credibility, expertise, and trustworthiness of the persuader. Coaches, by and large, are credible sources of their athletes' capabilities (Feltz and Lirgg, 2001). In addition to providing inspirational messages, effective coaches also provide messages that convince athletes that they have control over their goals for performance and have the tools to manage the competitive pressure.

Athletes also can obtain coping efficacy information from their physiological or emotional state. Physiological information includes autonomic arousal that is associated with fear and self-doubt or with being psyched-up and ready for performance. As well, positive emotions, such as happiness, exhilaration, and tranquility, are more likely to enhance coping efficacy judgments; whereas, negative emotions, such as sadness, anxiety, and depression are more likely to lower CSE (Maddux and Meier, 1995; Treasure, Monson, and Lox, 1996).

Relationship between Coping Self-Efficacy and Behavior

Self-efficacy theory (Bandura, 1977) hypothesizes that efficacy beliefs are associated with affect, motivation, and behavior. Individuals who lack confidence in their abilities to cope with a demand will dwell on their coping deficiencies and distress over the impending negative impact of the demand (Bandura, 1997). In contrast, efficacious individuals, who hold strong beliefs in their coping abilities, focus their efforts on adopting strategies and effective courses of action in order to overcome the demand. For these latter individuals, worry and distress over the demand is diminished. Preliminary evidence in the general psychological domain supports this relationship between efficacy and affect (Ozer and Bandura, 1990).

CSE, according to Bandura (1994), also regulates avoidance behavior. Those who worry about potential threats are more likely to avoid the situations in which they occur. This often happens with people who have phobias. But athletes who have certain fears about injuries or coping demands may also try to avoid these.

Self-efficacy theory (Bandura, 1997) also states that individuals will exert persistent coping actions only when they have the behavioral and cognitive skills available to them and they believe they are efficacious in those abilities. In an attempt to cope, one must know how to cope with these thoughts (i.e., use a behavioral or cognitive coping strategy) and have confidence in his or her ability to employ the coping strategy. In order to assess whether one has enough confidence in his or her coping ability, good measures must be designed that are tailored to the coping domain of functioning.

MEASUREMENT OF COPING SELF-EFFICACY

The most widely used measure of CSE is the Coping Self-Efficacy Scale (CSES). The CSES focuses on changes in a person's confidence in his or her ability to cope effectively. The CSES scale is not administered with reference to a specific stressful event, but rather addresses generic coping skills. The CSES assesses the person's *confidence* with respect to carrying out coping strategies, so that changes in CSE scores can be attributed to changes in the individual's confidence regarding the ability to cope (Chesney, Neilands, Chambers, Taylor, Folkman, 2006).

The CSES is a 26-item measure of perceived self-efficacy for coping with challenges and threats (Anastasi, 1988). The scale items were developed by creating sample items based upon stress and coping theory and the Ways of Coping Questionnaire with consultation from Dr. Albert Bandura of Stanford University. Respondents are asked, "When things aren't going well for you, or when you're having problems, how confident or certain are you that you can do the following…" Individuals are then asked to rate on an 11-point scale the extent to which they believe they could perform behaviors important to adaptive coping. Anchor points on the scale are 0 ('cannot do at all'), 5 ('moderately certain can do') and 10 ('certain can do'). An overall CSES score is created by summing the item ratings. Chesney et al. reported a mean of 137.4 (SD = 45.6). Exploratory and confirmatory factor analyses performed by Chesney et al. (2006) revealed a 13-item reduced form of the CSES scale with three factors: Use problem-focused coping (6 items, α = .91), stop unpleasant emotions and thoughts (emotion-focused: 4 items, α = .91), and get support from friends and family (social support-focused: 3 items, α = .80). Internal consistency and test–retest reliability are strong for all three factors. Chesney et al. (2006) report that although the scales are moderately correlated, results of the concurrent validity analyses indicate that the scales assess self-efficacy with respect to different types of coping and lend support to using the factors separately. In line with stress and coping theory, predictive validity analyses showed that change in using problem- and emotion-focused coping skills was predictive of reduced psychological distress and increased psychological well-being over time (Chesney et al., 2006).

Although the CSES is the most widely used measure of CSE, some researchers have relied on alternative measures of CSE that are more specific to their context of interest- sport and/or exercise.

For example, Gyurcsik, Brawley, and Langhout, (2002) assessed participants' coping strategies and confidence in their abilities to use the strategies to cope with negative thoughts about planned exercise over the subsequent two weeks. Coping strategies and related self-efficacy were elicited via three steps.

First, participants listed the three most frequent negative thoughts they anticipated experiencing in the subsequent week. Second, they listed the strategies they anticipated using to cope with each thought.

Third, they indicated their confidence in their ability to use each coping strategy to reduce the impact of the listed negative thought. Confidence was assessed on a Likert scale ranging from 0 *(not at all confident)* to 100 *(completely confident)*. For each participant, a mean value was calculated and used in the analyses. The development of this measure was based on one that was used previously in the exercise domain with younger adults that had good predictive validity (e.g., Gyurcsik and Brawley, 2000, 2001).

The Athletic Coping Skills Inventory (ACSI; Smith, Schutz, Smoll, and Ptacek, 1995) has also been used by researchers (e.g., Mummery, Schofield, and Perry, 2004) mainly for determining coping styles. However, because of its inclusion of a confidence subscale, researchers have used this measure when looking at CSE as a moderator (e.g., Smith, Ptacek, and Smoll, 1992). The ACSI contains 28 items describing seven sport-specific subscales: Coping with Adversity, Peaking under Pressure, Goal Setting/Mental Preparation, Concentration, Freedom from Worry, Confidence and Achievement Motivation, and Coachability.

Athletes rate how often they experienced the situations presented in each of the related questions using a 6-point Likert-type scale. The confidence and achievement motivation subscale consists of 4 questions, and confidence is only assessed within this subscale using 2 questions: "I feel confident that I will play well" and "When I fail to reach my goals, it makes me try even harder". However, these two items do not assess CSE. They do not tap beliefs regarding one's ability to cope with perceived threat. Therefore, we do not recommend that it be used as a measure of CSE.

While the CSES (Chesney et al., 2006) has established validity and reliability and has been used in coping self-efficacy research, a sport specific CSE measure is needed. Or, more researchers could use Gyurcsik et al.'s (2002) approach that uses a more context-specific measure of CSE.

COPING SELF-EFFICACY RESEARCH

Research has explored the role of CSE in relation to such things as: stress, anxiety, arousal, fear, judgment of risk, injury and pain, rehabilitation, exercise intention, and acute thoughts. Much of the evidence for the role of CSE as an influential mechanism on coping behavior in sport comes from the sport injury and rehabilitation and stress and coping literatures. While some of the research reviewed is not in the sport context their findings are important in understanding the effects of coping self-efficacy on physiological and psychological responses. The research reviewed in this section explores CSE and its relationship to (a) physiological responses, (b) perceived vulnerability and risk, (c) pain and fatigue management, and (d) negative thoughts and decisional struggle. Finally, some of the research reviewed focuses on enhancing CSE by examining the relationship between Bandura's sources of influence (mastery experiences, vicarious experiences, social persuasion, and emotional arousal) and CSE.

CSE AND ITS RELATIONSHIP TO PHYSIOLOGICAL RESPONSES

The physiological responses that have been studied in relation to CSE include catecholamine secretions (epinephrine, norepinephrine, and dopamine), heart rate, and blood pressure. According to Bandura, Taylor, Williams, Mefford, and Barchas, (1985) perceived coping inefficacy is accompanied not only by high levels of subjective distress but also by autonomic arousal and plasma catecholamine secretion. In their study, the research team examined the physiological mechanism underlying the effects of perceived coping efficacy on stress reactions by linking strength of perceived self-efficacy to catecholamine secretion. Persons with spider phobias observed modeling of coping strategies with periodic self-efficacy probes until self-percepts of efficacy were induced that spanned the entire range of efficacy strength values. Subjects' levels of plasma epinephrine, norepinephrine, and dopac were then measured while they were administered, in counterbalanced order, tasks corresponding to their strong, medium, and weak strengths of perceived self-efficacy. Results showed that high perceived self-efficacy was accompanied by low levels of plasma epinephrine and norepinephrine during interaction with a phobic object, whereas moderate perceived self-inefficacy gave rise to substantial increases in plasma catecholamines. Both catecholamines dropped sharply when phobics declined tasks for which they judged themselves completely inefficacious. In contrast, dopac was released maximally by mere apperception of task demands that phobics regarded as overwhelming their coping capabilities. After perceived self-efficacy was strengthened to the maximal level by participant modeling, all of the tasks were performed without any differential catecholamine responses.

In certain studies, phobics' perceptions of their CSE are raised to differential levels, whereupon their subjective stress and autonomic reactivity were measured (Bandura, 1983; Bandura, Reese, and Adams, 1982). The more efficacious they perceive themselves to be in coping with various threatening tasks, the weaker the stress reactions they experienced while anticipating or performing the activities (Bandura et al.). The generality of the relation between perceived coping inefficacy and stress reactions has been further corroborated using autonomic indexes of stress reactions (Bandura et al.). Phobics in these studies displayed little autonomic reactivity while coping with tasks they regarded with utmost self-efficaciousness. On tasks about which they were moderately insecure about their coping efficacy, however, their heart rate accelerated and their blood pressure rose when anticipating and performing the activities. Phobic subjects rejected tasks in the range of weak perceived self-efficacy as too far beyond their coping capabilities to even attempt them. Their cardiac reactivity subsided, but blood pressure remained elevated. After perceptions of coping efficacy were strengthened to maximal level, everyone performed the previously threatened tasks without autonomic arousal.

CSE AND PERCEIVED VULNERABILITY AND RISK

Perceived CSE has also been shown to affect anxiety arousal and action through its influence on perceived personal vulnerability and judgments of risk. Most risk perception research has been concerned with estimating the likelihood of future environmental events unrelated to the exercise of personal competencies (Ozer and Bandura, 1990). However, to calculate the risk of an action one has to judge the match between his or her coping capabilities and the environmental challenges. Therefore, perceived self-efficacy operates as a key factor in judgments of the riskiness of environmental situations (Ozer and Bandura, 1990). Individuals who perceive themselves as efficacious in their coping abilities will regard a potentially threatening environment, such as a championship competition in an opposing team's hometown, as relatively safe. Conversely, those who lack confidence in their coping capabilities will view potential threats, such as unfriendly sports fans, as dangerous and will perceive themselves as highly vulnerable to such threats.

Additionally, individuals who trust and believe in their coping capabilities might be more likely to seek high sensation-type situations because of their high levels of CSE. Smith et al. (1992) investigated the manner in which high sensation seeking might serve as a protective factor against stressors. Researchers suggested that a possible protective mechanism against stress may be a tendency for high sensation seekers to be more open to a variety of experiences and to thereby acquire a wider range of coping skills and greater flexibility in applying them (Smith et al.). Thus, high sensation seekers may simply cope more effectively than low sensation seekers. Results indicated that high sensation seekers reported generally superior coping skills on the ACSI. High sensation seekers were less likely to be troubled by worrisome thoughts, reported better concentration and better stress management coping skills, and were more likely to appraise pressure situations as positive challenges and to peak under such conditions. Researchers concluded that it is possible that high sensation seekers are less affected by life stress because they have better coping skills or greater CSE, rather than because they are better able to tolerate the emotional arousal produced by negative life changes (Smith et al.). However, Smith et al. did not actually assess CSE in their study.

The importance of CSE in the mediation of negative cognitions and posttraumatic distress was highlighted in a study done by Cieslak et al. (2008). Longitudinal data were collected on survivors of motor vehicle accidents. CSE measured at 1 month after the trauma mediated the effects of 7-day negative cognitions about self and about the world on 3-month posttraumatic distress (Cieslak et al.). The results highlight the potential importance of interventions aimed at enhancing CSE beliefs in controlling distress and negative cognitions. While motor vehicle accidents seem unrelated to sport, the negative cognitions accompanying such an incidence, as well as the pain and rehabilitation challenges that accompany it, can be related to athletes in similar physical and psychological states who suffer an unexpected injury incident.

COPING SELF-EFFICACY AND PAIN AND FATIGUE MANAGEMENT

As the previous example illustrates, CSE has important implications on dealing with pain and fatigue- a stressful situation that many athletes experience. The belief that an athlete has control over his or her pain makes it easier to manage that pain (Bandura, 1997). In addition to pain, CSE plays an important role in the recovery from injury. There is an extensive amount of research that examines the psychological responses and experiences associated with injury and rehabilitation (Bianco, Malo, and Orlick, 1999; Gould, Udry, Bridges, and Beck, 1997). Much of this research has shown that athletes' confidence in their ability to return successfully to their sport decreases in those who are experiencing difficulties dealing with their injury (Smith, Scott, O'Fallon, Young, 1990). Recognizing that a player is having difficulties adjusting to his/her injury is important so that it can be addressed and self-efficacy losses can be avoided. In a study done by Tripp, Stanish, Ebel-Lam, Brewer, and Birchard (2007), fear of reinjury, negative affect, and catastrophizing were examined as determinants of athletes' confidence in their ability to return to sport 1 year after anterior cruciate ligament (ACL) reconstruction. Results indicated that athletes' confidence in returning to their sport was reduced in those with greater negative mood. Greater fear of reinjury was related to a lower return to sport activity. This study highlights the importance of efficacy in coping with the fear and anxiety associated with physical setbacks in sport.

Another study of injured athletes examined CSE more directly as an important predictor of rehabilitation adherence after sport-related injuries (Milne et al., 2005). Results indicated that cognitive imagery significantly predicted task efficacy, task efficacy predicted quality of exercise, and CSE predicted frequency of exercise. Additionally, both task and CSE were predictors of duration of exercise. Researchers concluded that task and CSE appear to be key aspects in rehabilitation adherence (Milne et. al., 2005).

COPING SELF-EFFICACY, NEGATIVE THOUGHTS, AND DECISIONAL STRUGGLE

As the previous studies illustrate, an outcome of stressful situations is often an increase in negative thoughts that can result in decisional struggle. In these cases, efficacious beliefs in the ability to cope should aid in the management of those thoughts. Research has studied the effect of CSE on acute thoughts in exercisers (Gyurcsik and Eastabrooks, 2004; Gyuricsik et al., 2002). Both studies found that confidence in one's ability to use strategies to cope with negative thoughts was predictive of exercise intention and decisional struggle (to exercise). As individuals become more positive in their thinking, decisional struggle is found to decrease.

In another study, Gyurcsik and Brawley (2006) found that healthy younger adults who were enrolled in fitness classes experienced both acute negative thoughts (e.g., muscle soreness, too tired) and acute positive thoughts (e.g., motivated to exercise, weight loss) when making daily exercise decisions. Gyurcsik and Brawley (2006) reported that self-efficacy was associated positively with exercise intention and behavior. Further, acute thoughts were found to be associated positively with scheduling and CSE.

Results from such studies support contentions from self-efficacy theory (Bandura, 1997) that individuals who are efficacious in their ability to cope with negative thoughts should experience less of a struggle when making exercise decisions. Because efficacious individuals are confident that they can overcome their negative thoughts, they are not as bothered by these thoughts and do not struggle as much about whether to exercise as planned (Bandura, 1997).

Raising Coping Self-Efficacy Beliefs

As previously mentioned, according to Bandura (1997), people's beliefs about their efficacy can be enhanced through four main sources of influence: mastery experiences, vicarious experiences, social persuasion, and altercations of stress-reactions and mood interpretations. The most effective way of creating a strong sense of efficacy, be it task or CSE, is through mastery experiences (Bandura). However, creating and strengthening self-beliefs of efficacy through vicarious experiences provided by social models can also be effective (George, Feltz, and Chase, 1992). Consequently, most of the research aimed at raising CSE beliefs use mastery experience and vicarious experience (e.g., participant modeling) interventions.

In one of the earliest studies to use coping modeling to overcome fear in a physical activity, Lewis (1974) examined the influence of a coping model on learning to swim with children who exhibited fear of the water. Children were randomly assigned to one of four experimental conditions: coping model plus participation, coping model only, participation only, and control. The observers viewed a tape of the models mastering three progressive tasks. The first task was simply to put the feet in the water, while the second task involved climbing down a ladder into the water, and the third task involved hanging on to the side of the pool. Results indicated that the combination of a coping model plus participation served as the best model in this case. This study, however, was published prior to Bandura's (1977) seminal paper on self-efficacy theory. Thus, CSE was not measured in her study.

The first study to examine self-efficacy on an anxiety-provoking physical task using participant modeling was conducted by Feltz, Landers, and Raeder (1979). Participants with no diving experience were asked to perform a modified back dive. Their performance and self-efficacy beliefs for the task were compared across three modeling conditions: participant, live, and videotape. Participant modeling involved using physical guidance to help the learners practice the back dive with less fear of hurting their back. Consistent with Bandura's (1977) theory, participants in the participant-modeling condition performed better after the intervention and had higher efficacy ratings than those in the other conditions. However, although a threatening task was used in this study, a coping model was not use and task self-efficacy rather than CSE was measured.

Stidwell (1994) also examined the role of instructional modeling on the treatment of a sport performance phobia in softball. Stidwell's intervention involved demonstrating the feared activity for the participant first and then having the participant perform the feared activity in a specifically designed sequence in order to increase self-efficacy. After the intervention, the participant reported decreased symptoms of her phobia and was less avoidant of the ball in subsequent games, but CSE was not measured specifically.

The only study in the area of sport and physical activity to investigate coping models within a self-efficacy framework was conducted by Weiss, McCullagh, Smith, and Berlant (1998). Weiss et al. (1998) examined the role of peer mastery and coping models on children's swimming skills, fear, and self-efficacy. The students, who were fearful of water, were matched to a control, peer mastery or peer coping model condition. Viewing a model combined with swimming lessons was found to be a more effective behavior change agent for fearful children than swimming lessons alone. In a similar study, Starek and McCullagh (1999) found that adult beginner swimmers reported increased self-efficacy beliefs when they viewed a model. Thus, in these studies, the coping aspect of the model was not important, but the peer aspect was important compared to no model.

As illustrated above, mastery and vicarious experiences are structured in ways to build coping skills and instill beliefs that one can exercise control over potential threats (Bandura, 1994). According to Bandura, it is important to create an environment so that individuals can perform successfully despite themselves. Performing feared activities together with the practitioner (i.e., participant modeling) further enables individuals to do things they would resist doing by themselves (Bandura). Bandura notes that CSE increases with gradual exposure to the feared stimuli. As their coping efficacy increases, the time they perform the activity is extended.

RECOMMENDATIONS FOR PRACTITIONERS

The existing research on CSE has important implications for practitioners. As Bandura (1997) notes, the key to successful coping in sport is to control disruptive thinking, such as dwelling on mistakes and fears of failure. Helping athletes build a strong sense of efficacy to exercise cognitive control will improve their coping skills and sport performance. Feltz et al. (2008) provided a review of how to enhance an athlete's CSE. The strategies described are based on the four major sources of self-efficacy information. Space does not allow for a detailed presentation of these strategies, but brief descriptions are provided here. The interested reader should consult Feltz et al., Chapter 6, further a more indepth review.

Performance-based techniques to enhance CSE include instructional strategies, such as providing a progressive sequence of modified activities, breaking the coping skill into parts, providing performance aids, physical guidance, or a combination of these strategies. The idea is to build success based on relevant and realistic progressions and to remove physical guidance and performance aids as soon as possible to allow athletes to engage in self-directed mastery. Another performance-based technique is to simulate environments that are as realistic as possible where the athlete can practice a coping technique, such as blocking out distractions. Orlick (2000) suggests that athletes think about the things that they are worried about in key competitions (e.g., bad weather, false starts, bad calls from officials, come-from-behind situations) and introduce those things into the practice setting. This helps athletes increase the predictability of the situation and get practice in controlling that situation.

Coping models, as we described previously, are also a powerful way to enhance CSE. This strategy also relies on predictability and controllability. Observing another athlete cope with a threatening situation reduces the uncertainty for the observer and, therefore, increases the predictability and one's preparedness. For example, observing another athlete coping with the discomfort of physical rehabilitation can reduce inhibitions and anxiety in an athlete who is just beginning physical rehabilitation. Feltz et al. (2008) suggest that the athlete model in this situation can describe problems, explain how they were overcome, as well as show that the next stage of the recovery can be reached. Similarity of personal characteristics (e.g., age, race, sex) is important, but similarity of skill sets is the most important factor in modeling (George et al., 1992).

Additionally, imagery (sometimes referred to as cognitive self-modeling, Bandura, 1997) can help improve coping skills. To be effective, the imagery should be structured to be slightly beyond what the athlete can do at that time. For example, if a professional is using imagery in rehabilitation to try to help convince an athlete that she can endure more muscular fatigue or manage pain, the imagery should be structured so that she imagines herself performing just slightly better than what she thinks she can do. The imagery should be challenging but attainable.

Persuasion and communication coping strategies are best used in conjunction with performance-based techniques. Two techniques that are most often described in this category of efficacy enhancement are blocking out distractions and controlling disruptive thinking. Feltz et al. (2008) suggest pre-performance routines help to direct athletes' thoughts and behaviors by concentrating their attention on the task at hand and generating helpful, efficacious thinking. As they state, "When athletes direct their attention toward a consistent pattern of routine tasks and positive thoughts, they are keeping their attention away from thoughts that may create worry or from activities that may be energy draining" (p. 201).

Disruptive thinking (or negative self-talk) can also be distracting. Positive self-talk is the most prescribed antidote for dealing with disruptive thinking. Positive talk or persuasion from trusted others (e.g. a coach or sport psychologist) can help athletes correct their faulty beliefs that lead to an impaired sense of CSE. Encouragement from practitioners, teammates, and friends can also be useful in combination with other techniques. In addition, when setbacks occur, practitioners can highlight the positive aspects of performance while acknowledging the setback, providing instructional feedback, and emphasizing the learnability of the task.

Techniques based on reducing athletes' interpretation of physiological arousal as fear that they can not cope successfully with the task at hand include many of the strategies already mentioned, such as imagery, self-talk, and persuasion. In addition, relaxation techniques, such as deep breathing, controlled breathing, and progressive muscle relaxation, can be used to help athletes regain a sense of control over their physiological arousal levels, which can help them build a sense of coping control.

Consultants working in applied sport settings should measure and monitor CSE among their athletes and devise individual interventions based on these findings. Additionally, because CSE research has important implications regarding the assistance and management of athletes returning to sport after sustaining an injury (e.g., Milne et al., 2005), it is important for practitioners to structure programs for returning athletes in ways that meet their psychological needs for competence, self-efficacy, and control.

CONCLUSION

In this chapter, we provided an overview of CSE and its measurement, along with a review of relevant research conducted in the context of sport and exercise. We also provided some recommendations for practitioners. Athletes' beliefs in their coping capabilities affect how much stress and depression they experience in threatening or difficult situations, as well as their levels of motivation, intention, and decisional struggle. Perceived self-efficacy to exercise control over stressors plays a central role in anxiety arousal. Athletes who believe they can exercise control over threats do not conjure up disturbing thought patterns. But those who believe they cannot manage threats experience high anxiety arousal. According to Bandura (1994, 1997), those who dwell on their coping deficiencies, view many aspects of their environment as fraught with danger and magnify the severity of possible threats and worry about things that rarely happen. Through such inefficacious thinking, they distress themselves and impair their level of functioning. It is critical for researchers to continue to expand the knowledge in the area of CSE in the context of sport in order to enable practitioners in their development of intervention strategies aimed at enhancing CSE in athletes and exercisers.

REFERENCES

Anastasi A. *Psychological testing. 6th ed.* New York: Macmillan Publishing; 1988.

Bandura, A. (1977). Self-efficacy: Toward a unifying theory of behavioral change. *Psychological Review, 84,* 191-215.

Bandura, A. (1983). Self-efficacy determinants of anticipated fears and calamities. *Journal of Personality and Social Psychology 45*, 2, 464-469.

Bandura, A. (1986). *Social foundations of thought and action.* Englewood Cliffs, NJ: Prentice Hall.

Bandura, A. (1994). Self-efficacy. In V. S. Ramachaudran (Ed.), *Encyclopedia of human behavior* (Vol. 4, pp. 71-81). New York: Academic Press. (Reprinted in H. Friedman '[Ed.], *Encyclopedia of mental health.* San Diego: Academic Press, 1998).

Bandura, A. (1997). *Self-efficacy: The exercise of control.* NY: W.H. Freeman.

Bandura, A. (1994). Self-efficacy. In V. S. Ramachaudran (Ed.), Encyclopedia of human behavior (Vol. 4, pp. 71-81). New York: Academic Press. (Reprinted in H. Friedman [Ed.], Encyclopedia of mental health. San Diego: Academic Press, 1998).

Bandura, A., Adams, N. E., and Beyer, J. (1977). Cognitive processes mediating behavioral change. *Journal of Personality and Social Psychology, 1977, 35,* 125-139.

Bandura, A., Reese, L., and Adams, N. E. (1982). Microanalysis of action and fear arousal as a function of differential levels of perceived self-efficacy. *Journal of Personality and Social Psychology, 43,* 5-21.

Bandura, A., Taylor, C.B., Williams, S.L, Mefford, I.N., and Barchas, J.D. (1985). Catecholamine secretion as a function of perceived coping self-efficacy. *Journal of Consulting and Clinical Psychology, 53,* 406-414.

Bianco, T., Malo, S., and Orlick, T. (1999). Sport injury and illness: Elite skiers describe their experiences. *Research Quarterly for Exercise and Sport, 70,* 157–169.

Cieslak, R., Benight C.C, and Lehman, V.C. (2008). Coping self-efficacy mediates the effects of negative cognitions on posttraumatic distress. *Behaviour Research and Therapy 46*, 788–798.

Chesney, M. A., Neilands, T. B., Chambers, D. B., Taylor, J. M., and Folkman, S. (2006). A validity reliability study of coping self-efficacy scale. *British Journal of Health Psychology, 11*, 421-437.

Feltz, D.L., Landers, D.M., and Raeder, U. (1979). Enhancing self-efficacy in high avoidance motor tasks: A comparison of modeling techniques. *Journal of Sport Psychology, 1*, 112-122.

Feltz, D. L., and Lirgg, C. D. (1998). Perceived team and player efficacy in hockey. *Journal of Applied Psychology, 83*, 557–564.

Feltz, D. L., Short, S. E., and Sullivan, P. J. (2008). *Self-efficacy in sport: Research and strategies for working with athletes, teams, and coaches.* Champaign, IL: Human Kinetics.

Gaudreau, P., and Blondin, J. P. (2002). Development of a questionnaire for the assessment of coping strategies employed by athletes in competitive sport settings. *Psychology of Sport and Exercise, 3*, 1-34.

George, T.R., Feltz, D.L., and Chase, M.A. (1992). Effects of model similarity on self-efficacy and muscular endurance: A second look. *Journal of Sport and Exercise Psychology, 14*, 237-248.

Gould, D., Guinan, D., Greenleaf, C., Medberry, R., and Peterson, K. (1999). Factors affecting Olympic performance: Perceptions of athletes and coaches from more and less successful teams. *The Sport Psychologist, 13*, 371-394.

Gould, D., Udry, E., Bridges, D., and Beck, L. (1997). Stress sources encountered when rehabilitating from season-ending ski injuries. *The Sport Psychologist, 11*, 361–378.

Gyurcsik, N.C., Brawley, L.R., and Langhout, N. (2002). Acute thoughts, exercise consistency, and coping self-efficacy. *Journal of Applied Psychology, 32*, 2134-2153.

Gyuricsik, N.C., Bray, S.R., and Brittain, D.R., (2004). Coping with barriers in physical activity during transition to university. *Family Community Health, 27*, 130-142.

Gyurcsik, N.C., and Eastabrooks, P.A. (2004). Acute exercise thoughts, coping, and exercise intention in older adults. *Journal of Applied Social Psychology, 34*, 6, 1 131 -1 146.

Gyurcsik, N.C., Johnson, E.M., and Perrett, J.J. (2006). Prospective and daily measures of acute thoughts, decisional struggle, and coping: Measurement correspondence and the prediction of exercise in young adults. *Journal of Applied Social Psychology, 36*, 1321–1336.

Kirsch, I. (1982). Efficacy expectations or response predictions: The meaning of efficacy ratings as a function of task characteristics. *Journal of Personality and Social Psychology, 42*, 132-136.

Lazarus, R. S., and Folkman, S. (1984). *Stress, appraisal and coping.* New York: Springer.

Lewis, S. (1974). A comparison of behavior therapy techniques in the reduction of fearful avoidance behavior. *Behavior Therapy, 5*, 648-655.

Maddux, J.E., and Meier, L.J. (1995). Self-efficacy and depression. In: J.E. Maddux (Ed.), *Self-efficacy, adaptation, and adjustment: theory, research, and application* (pp. 143-172). *New York: Plenum Press.*

McCullagh, P., and Weiss, M. R. (2001). Modeling: Considerations for motor skill performance and psychological responses. In R.N. Singer, H. A. Hasenblaus, and C. M.

Janelle (Eds.), Handbook of research on sport psychology (pp. 205-238). New York: Wiley and Sons.

Milne, M., Hall, C., and Forwell, L. (2005). Self-efficacy, imagery use, and adherence to Rehabilitation by injured athletes. *Journal of Sport Rehabilitation, 14*, 150-167.

Mummery, K.W., Schofield, G., and Perry, C. (2004). Bouncing back: the role of coping style, social support and self-concept in resilience of sport performance. *Athletic Insight: Online Journal of Sport Psychology, 6, 3.*

Orlick, T. (2000). In Pursuit of Excellence. Champaign, IL: Human Kinetics.

Ozer, E.M., and Bandura, A. (1990). Mechanisms governing empowerment effects: A self-efficacy analysis. *Journal of Personality and Social Psychology. 58*, 472-486.

Smith, R.E., Schutz, R.W., Smoll, F.L., and Ptacek, J.T., (1995). Development and validation of a multidimensional measure of sport-specific psychological skills: the Athletic Coping Skills Inventory-28. *Journal of Sport and Exercise Psychology, 17,* 379 - 415.

Smith, A.M., Scott, S.G., O'Fallon, W.M. and Young, M.L. (1990). Emotional responses of athletes to injury. Mayo Clinic Proceedings, 65, 38-50.

Smith, R.E., Smoll, F.L., and Ptacek, J.T., (1992). Sensation seeking, stress, and adolescent injuries: a test of stress-buffering, risk-taking, and coping skills hypotheses. *Journal of Personality and Social Psychology, 62,* 1016-24.

Starek, J., and McCullagh, P. (1999). The effect of self-modeling on the performance of beginning swimmers. *The Sport Psychologist, 13,* 269-287.

Stidwell (1994). Application of self-efficacy theory: A treatment approach for sport performance phobias. *Journal of Mental Health Counseling, 16,* 196-204.

Treasure, D.C., Monson, J., and Lox, C.L. (1996). Relationship between self-efficacy, wrestling performance, and affect prior to competition. *The Sport Psychologist, 10,* 73-83.

Tripp, D.A., Stanish, W.D., Ebel-Lam, A., Brewer, B. and Birchard, J. (2007). Predicting return to sport activity at one-year ACL post-op for amateur athletes. Rehabilitation Psychology. *Rehabilitation Psychology, 52,* 74-81.

Weiss, M. R. McCullagh, P., Smith, A. L., and Berlant, A.R. (1998). Observational learning and the fearful child: influence of peer models on swimming skill performance and psychological responses. *Research Quarterly for Exercise and Sport.*

Williams, S.L., (1995). Self-efficacy and anxiety and phobic disorders. In J.E Maddux (Ed.), *Self-efficacy, adaptation, and adjustment: Theory, research, and application* (pp. 69-102). New York: Plenum Press.

In: Coping in Sport: Theory, Methods, and Related Constructs   ISBN: 978-1-60876-488-4
Editor: Adam R. Nicholls   © 2010 Nova Science Publishers, Inc.

Chapter 16

FUTURE-ORIENTED APPROACHES TO COPING

Katherine A. Tamminen and Nicholas L. Holt
University of Alberta, Canada

ABSTRACT

Future-oriented coping describes how individuals respond to stressors as well as ways in which they may learn from these experiences and plan to deal with future stressors. Although some aspects of future-oriented coping have been reported in studies of competitive athletes, little research to date has adopted a future-oriented approach to studying coping. We suggest that future-oriented models of coping may offer a fresh perspective for thinking about the ways in which athletes cope with stressors in sport. Using models of coping which captures athletes' preparation, planning, and anticipation of stressors could reveal important insights into coping with stressors before their occurrence. In this chapter we describe two models of future-oriented coping which may be useful within a sport context. By considering coping from a future-oriented perspective, athletes may also learn how to cope more effectively with stressors and achieve better performances.

INTRODUCTION

A bright side to these stressors is, I guess, you kind of know how to deal with the bad. Like if you run like a lot one time [in practice], you're expecting it another time and you're like 'okay, it's coming,' and you know how to deal with it. It's easier after you do it the first couple of times. Instead of like, 'Oh my gosh, it's my first time.'
(High school basketball athlete, post-practice audio diary; Tamminen, 2007).

In sport, coping is usually thought of in terms of how athletes react to and manage stressors that have already occurred. However, as the quote above suggests, coping is more than just reacting to past or present stressors; coping can also be about the future. Future-oriented models of coping describe how individuals respond to stressors as well as ways in which they may learn from these experiences and plan to deal with stressors that may occur in the future. By considering coping from a future-oriented perspective, athletes may learn how to cope more effectively with stressors and achieve better performances. Therefore, the purpose of this chapter is to explore aspects of future-oriented coping – the ways in which athletes plan for and deal with stressors before they occur. We present two models of future-oriented coping from the general psychology literature and provide examples of how they may be relevant to athletic populations. We then we discuss some theoretical, methodological, and applied considerations for adopting a future-oriented approach to coping research in sport contexts.

Some successful athletes appear to use forms of future-oriented coping. Elite Canadian athletes reported using planning to deal with competitions and distractions and they made deliberate efforts to learn "important lessons from every competitive experience ... and direct their focus for subsequent competitions" (Orlick and Partington, 1988, p. 116). Similarly, successful US Olympians planned to deal with 'unexpected' stressors, while other aspects of planning (time management, mental preparation) were also associated with performance successes (Gould, Guinan, Greenleaf, Medbery, and Peterson, 1999). In fact, members of one team in the Gould et al. study described a disappointing finish at the World Championships the previous year, which they used as a source of motivation and created a detailed plan to ensure a successful performance at the Olympics. Other studies have also revealed athletes used planning, mental preparation, and feedback about previous coping attempts to prepare for subsequent performances (e.g., Gould, Finch, and Jackson, 1993; Holt, 2003; Poczwardowski and Conroy, 2002).

Planning and feedback are crucial components of future-oriented coping processes (Aspinwall and Taylor, 1997). Therefore, the findings reported above (i.e., Gould, Finch, and Jackson, 1993; Gould et al., 1999; Holt, 2003; Orlick and Partington, 1988) suggest future-oriented models of coping may be useful for understanding more about coping in sport. However, these studies were not explicitly based on any contemporary frameworks of future-oriented coping. One recent exception was a study by Holt, Berg, and Tamminen (2007) which used a model of proactive coping (Aspinwall and Taylor, 1997) to interpret stressors and coping among 10 female collegiate volleyball players before and after an important tournament. Effective coping strategies reported by the athletes included increasing practice before the tournament, adhering to a pregame routine, and using positive self-talk. Those athletes with more experience coped with stressors better than the less experienced athletes, suggesting that experience may contribute to athletes' preparation to cope with potential stressors. It may be that, with more competitive experience, athletes can learn to cope proactively before stressors occur. This study provides encouraging evidence that future-oriented approaches could be valuable for examining coping in sport.

Future-Oriented Theories of Coping

Future-oriented coping is derived from research on social cognition and social interaction, and is gaining popularity along with the positive psychology movement in the broader field of psychology (Aspinwall and Staudinger, 2003; Folkman, 2008). Future-oriented models of coping are based on the idea that many of the stressors that people encounter can be avoided, but if stressors are unavoidable, the severity of the stressors can at least be decreased by engaging in future-oriented coping strategies. There are two models of future-oriented coping; Schwarzer and Knoll's (2003) model of positive coping and Aspinwall and Taylor's (1997) model of proactive coping.

Schwarzer and Knoll's (2003) Model of Positive Coping. Schwarzer and Knoll (2003), presented a macro-level classification of four different types of future-oriented positive coping; reactive, anticipatory, preventive, and proactive coping (see Figure 1). According to this model individuals appraise stressors according to certainty (how likely the stressor is to occur) and temporal proximity (whether the stressor occurred in the past or present, or whether it will occur in the future). Individuals' appraisals about the timing and certainty of the stressor will then dictate the types of coping responses they deploy.

Schwarzer and Knoll (2003) predicted that when attempting to deal with events which have already occurred, an individual engages in reactive coping. That is, a stressor event has certainly already occurred and people deploy coping strategies in reaction to the event in order to cope with its consequences. This form of coping would typify most sport coping research which asks athletes to report how they coped with events that have already occurred. For example, Holt (2003) described a professional cricketer who used reactive coping strategies such as positive self-talk to 'bounce back' after a poor performance.

Anticipatory coping is different from reactive coping in that the stressor has not yet occurred. This type of coping typically refers to dealing with stressors which are certain or very likely to occur in the near future. In sport, anticipatory coping could be used to deal with an important upcoming game or qualifying trial. The situation may be appraised as potentially harmful or one where some loss may occur, or the situation may also have the potential for gain or benefit (Lazarus, 1999). Within Schwarzer and Knoll's (2003) model, anticipatory coping involves dealing with known risks to either prevent or avoid the stressor, or to maximize the potential for benefit from the situation.

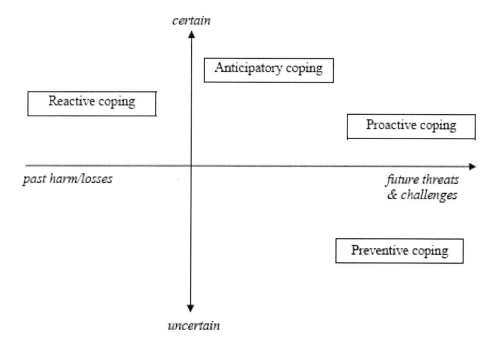

Figure 1. Model of positive coping (adapted from Schwarzer and Knoll, 2003).

Thus, a swimmer facing an important qualifying time trial would not be able to prevent the stressor (since the athlete has to compete in order to qualify). In this case, anticipatory coping strategies might include 'controlling the controllables' (e.g., ensuring optimal rest and nutrition, mental preparation) and choosing not to worry about factors he or she cannot control (e.g., competitors' performances). These strategies would be deployed prior to the occurrence of any stressors and they would be intended to alleviate or reduce the severity of the stressors.

Preventive coping is similar to anticipatory coping in that both approaches deal with stressors which may occur in the future (Aspinwall and Taylor, 1997; Schwarzer and Knoll, 2003). The key distinction between preventative and anticipatory coping is based on the certainty of a stressor occurring. Anticipatory coping refers to efforts undertaken for events that are certain to occur whereas preventive coping refers to efforts undertaken to prepare for events which are uncertain to occur. For preventive coping a person suspects, but is not certain, whether or when the stressor will happen. In sport, an example could be if an athlete is suffering from a minor injury or muscle pain during practice. The athlete has no way of knowing for certain whether he or she will sustain further injury during competition, but preventive coping might be used to reduce the severity of the minor injury, or to reduce the likelihood of the injury becoming worse during competition and impairing performance. For example, the athlete might engage in preventive coping by consulting with an athletic therapist, icing, and stretching to reduce the possibility of the injury worsening and to reduce any anxiety about the injury itself.

The final element of Schwarzer and Knoll's (2003) model is labelled proactive coping, which they described as efforts to build up resources in order to reach a goal or to promote personal growth. In this case, a person is not preparing for potential harm or loss or reacting to past stressors. Instead, individuals who engage in proactive coping are striving toward their goals and seeking to maximize their performance levels. An example would be a high school athlete appraising a tournament as an opportunity to demonstrate his or her skill in front of scouts recruiting for a university team. In this case the event is not viewed as a potential for loss or harm, but rather a situation where there is opportunity to achieve a goal. Of course, another athlete might not appraise the same tournament so favourably, and view it as a situation that would cause feelings of embarrassment if he or she does not perform up to expectations. Thus, whether an individual engages in proactive coping versus anticipatory coping or preventive coping will depend in large part on the type of appraisal made. Generally, appraisals of threat, loss, and harm implicate the use of reactive, anticipatory, and preventive coping, whereas appraisals of challenge refer to proactive coping.

Aspinwall and Taylor's (1997) Model of Proactive Coping. Aspinwall and Taylor's (1997) approach to proactive coping is a process-oriented model describing how individuals deal with future stressors. Emphasis is placed on how individuals accumulate a repertoire of coping resources, identify stressors before they occur, and learn from past coping to inform future coping efforts. The proactive coping model consists of five stages: (a) resource accumulation, (b) recognition of potential stressors, (c) initial appraisal of stressors, (d) preliminary coping efforts, and (e) elicitation and use of feedback about the success of coping efforts (see Figure 2). Although the term 'proactive coping' is used in both models discussed here it has distinct meanings.

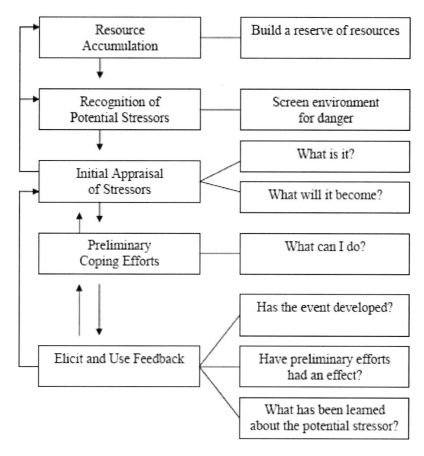

Figure 2. Framework of proactive coping (adapted from Aspinwall and Taylor, 1997).

According to Schwarzer and Knoll (2003), proactive coping refers to efforts to build up resources to reach a goal or promote positive growth. Alternatively Aspinwall and Taylor suggest that proactive coping refers specifically to the efforts undertaken in advance of a potential stressor to prevent or modify it before it occurs.

The first stage of the proactive coping model – resource accumulation – involves gaining coping resources. Coping resources include specific coping skills, organizational skills, time management and planning skills, and establishing a social network of people to help deal with stress when it occurs (Aspinwall and Taylor, 1997). Individuals who build such a 'reservoir' of resources should be better able to cope with a wide variety of stressors in comparison to people who have fewer coping resources. Within sport, these coping resources include things such as sleep patterns, fitness levels, nutrition, time management, and social support (Raedeke and Smith, 2004). In fact, sport psychology researchers have found that athletes who experience a high number of stressors but who have limited resources to cope with these stressors are at a greater risk of injury than athletes with more coping resources (Hanson, McCullagh, and Tonymon, 1992).

The second stage of the proactive coping model – recognition of potential stressors – refers to an individual's ability to detect potential stressors before they happen (Aspinwall and Taylor, 1997). Individuals who are able to plan ahead and think about upcoming events should be able to recognize potential stressors more easily than people who do not plan ahead or think about the future. This ability to think ahead is called 'future temporal orientation.' In sport, future temporal orientation may be linked to an athlete's experience and history of competitive involvement, as he or she may have accumulated knowledge of potential stressors that are likely to repeat themselves in the future. For example, some senior university athletes may predict that trying to manage the demands of practice, games, and exams will be particularly stressful during post-season playoffs because they have experienced these stressors in previous years. By identifying potential stressors ahead of time athletes may be better prepared to deal with them. For example, athletes may complete assignments early or seek to defer exams, thus coping with some anticipated and expected stressors. Research shows that unexpected stressors are considered more threatening than expected stressors, and athletes are more likely to 'hold back' when dealing with unexpected stressors (Dugdale, Eklund, and Gordon, 2002). Thus, by identifying ahead of time which stressors are likely to occur, athletes may be better prepared to deal effectively with the situation.

The third component of the proactive coping framework is the initial appraisal of stressors as they unfold (Aspinwall and Taylor, 1997). This stage first involves defining the problem, where the individual has to make a preliminary appraisal of the nature of the stressor (what is this? Should I be worried about this?) and determine the potential magnitude of the problem (what is likely to happen in this situation?). If a stressor is appraised as a threat (where there is the potential for loss/harm) this might give rise to negative emotional arousal. Thus, the third stage of proactive coping also involves the person regulating his or her negative emotional arousal. Aspinwall and Taylor argued that there is an interaction between defining the problem and regulating negative emotional arousal, which can either facilitate or hinder the coping process. If athletes define a problem as a potential threat and experience an increase in negative emotional arousal, it may reduce their ability to process task-related information (Wilson, Chattington, Marple-Horvat, and Smith, 2007) which can potentially derail performance and any subsequent coping efforts. The appraisal of the stressor and regulation of negative emotional arousal is an important stage in the overall coping process, since the appraisal and the regulation of arousal will influence the choice of coping strategy and perhaps even the outcome of the stressor.

The fourth stage of proactive coping consists of preliminary coping, where a person makes initial attempts to cope with the stressor. The type of coping strategy used to deal with the stressor will necessarily depend on the individual's resources and the type of appraisal made about the stressor. There are also a number of antecedent factors which will likely influence an athlete's resources and stressor appraisals. These include factors such as social support, perceptions of control, and personality characteristics such as competitive trait anxiety (see Hoar, Kowalski, Gaudreau, and Crocker, 2006 for a review).

A critical implication of the fourth stage is that if individuals engage in active coping (e.g., information seeking, problem-solving), they will uncover more information about the stressor than if they engage in avoidant coping (e.g., ignoring the situation, blocking, distraction). For example, a hockey player might be concerned about a lack of playing time during games. By engaging in active coping and approaching the coach about the situation, the athlete might discover the need to improve his or her speed and agility in order to gain more playing time. By avoiding the situation and not approaching the coach, the athlete would not know how to improve his or her performance and increase the playing time. Even if the initial active coping efforts turn out to be ineffective, the athlete will have gained more knowledge about the stressor which can then be used to try and deal with the situation more effectively (Aspinwall and Taylor, 1997).

Finally, the fifth stage of proactive coping involves eliciting and using feedback to modify preliminary coping efforts (Aspinwall and Taylor, 1997). This stage requires that the individual determine whether the stressor has changed, whether coping efforts have been effective or not, and to decide whether or not the event requires further action. For example, if a basketball player is having trouble with free-throws and attempts to cope with this stressor by coming in for extra practice, he or she may find that this coping strategy is effective in improving his or her free-throws. However, if the athlete masters free-throws in practice but does not see similar improvements to free-throws during games, he or she may have to try a different strategy. In this case the athlete must change coping strategies to adapt to the new information gained about the stressor (that performance only suffers in games, not in practices). Thus, proactive coping is a constant loop where feedback can be used to deal with stressors and adapt to changing circumstances. Feedback may come from noticeable changes in performance, but it may also come from coaches or teammates (or other sources of social support), as well as by reflecting on past experiences. In the example of the university athlete who is trying to manage the demands of practice, games, and exams, he or she can think back to the previous year to remember what coping strategies worked (and the ones that did not) and apply those to the upcoming season.

In summary, the model of proactive coping described by Aspinwall and Taylor (1997) is a process-oriented framework which includes the building of resources, the recognition and initial appraisal of stressors, preliminary coping efforts, as well as the elicitation and use of feedback to inform future coping. Although this model has not been specifically tested in a sport context, it holds promise for examining coping among competitive athletes.

To reiterate, there are important differences between the ways in which proactive coping is defined by the two theories reviewed here. Aspinwall and Taylor's (1997) definition of *proactive coping* is most similar to Schwarzer and Knoll's (2003) definition of *preventive coping*. Both involve the perception of uncertain threats and potential stressors and the efforts undertaken to prevent a negative outcome from occurring. The key difference is that Schwarzer and Knoll's definition of *proactive coping* reflects only the individual's appraisals of challenge and opportunities for growth, and does not include appraisals of threat or harm. Aspinwall and Taylor's model of proactive coping deals with appraisals of challenge as well as appraisals of threat or harm. This distinction also reflects the fact that Aspinwall and Taylor's model is a micro-level description of the ways in which individuals build resources, detect potential stressors, and cope with these stressors at the individual level, whereas Schwarzer and Knoll's model provides a macro-level classification of four different types of coping based on the timing and certainty of the potential stressor.

Using Future-Oriented Coping in Sport Psychology Research

We suggest that future-oriented proactive models of coping may offer a fresh perspective for thinking about the ways in which athletes cope with stressors in sport. Using models of coping which captures athletes' preparation, planning, and anticipation of stressors could reveal important insights into coping with stressors before their occurrence. In the following section, we highlight some theoretical, methodological, and applied considerations for using future-oriented coping in sport.

Theoretical Considerations. Competitive sport is a goal-directed activity (Locke and Latham, 1985). Goals provide individuals with a sense of meaning, purpose, and motivation and are central to theories of stress and coping (Folkman, 2008). Indeed, stressors are appraised on the extent to which they may threaten (or potentially threaten) an individual's opportunity to achieve personally meaningful goals (Lazarus, 1999). For example, a veteran athlete competing in a championship game will likely appraise the game as highly stressful if the athlete's goal is to win a championship before retirement. Considering Schwarzer and Knoll's (2003) definition of proactive coping refers specifically to reaching personal goals, future-oriented models of coping appear well suited to examining coping in sport.

Several researchers have demonstrated relationships between athletes' personally valued goals and appraisal or coping responses (Amiot, Gaudreau, and Blanchard, 2004; Crocker and Graham, 1995; Gaudreau, Blondin, and Lapierre, 2002; Holt et al., 2007). For example, reaching one's goals in sport has been associated with positive emotions, while failing to attain one's goals is associated with negative emotions (Gaudreau et al., 2002). Reaching one's goals is also related to the use of particular e.g., active coping and planning) was positively associated with achieving one's goals in sport, whereas disengagement coping (e.g., physically withdrawing from the situation) was negatively associated with achieving one's goals. That is, athletes who used task-oriented coping strategies were more likely to achieve their goals compared to athletes who tried to withdraw themselves from the stressful situation. Athletes who achieved their goals also reported increased positive emotions from pre-competition to post-competition. Thus, goals, coping, and positive emotions appear to be interconnected (see Folkman, 2008 for a review). Using models of future-oriented coping, researchers might identify whether proactive or anticipatory forms of coping can help athletes achieve their goals in sport.

Another implication of future-oriented coping is an emphasis on active coping strategies. Aspinwall and Taylor (1997) suggest that active coping strategies are more effective than avoidant coping strategies. This is contrary to the proposition of Folkman and Moskowitz (2004), who argued that coping strategies are neither effective nor ineffective in and of themselves, but rather effective coping depends on selecting the appropriate coping strategy within particular contexts. However, recent sport psychology research provides evidence to the contrary, suggesting that avoidant coping in particular is not an effective coping strategy to deal with performance stressors in sport (Gaudreau et al., 2002; Holt et al., 2007). For example, if an upcoming match or competition is appraised as a stressor, then physically withdrawing oneself from the competition might not be practical or effective in dealing with the stressor. The question of whether avoidant coping is always an ineffective means of coping in sport remains to be answered.

Stressful encounters may offer opportunities for personal growth (Folkman and Moskowitz, 2000; Kesimci, Goral, and Gencoz, 2005; Linley and Joseph, 2004; Park, Cohen, and Murch, 1996). For example, Dworkin and Larson (2007) examined youths' accounts of negative experiences arising from their involvement in activities such as extra-curricular sports and community groups. Participants described a number of stressful experiences which sometimes led to positive development – the adolescents described learning how to cope with negative situations using active coping or learning how to control anger and anxiety. For example, one girl who joined a new dance team reported wanting to quit because she felt she could not learn any of the new moves. However, by using other dancers' criticism and instruction as a source of determination, she stayed with the team and became the 'most improved dancer.' Hence, negative or stressful experiences can lead to positive developmental change and learning for some youth.

Researchers have begun to examine opportunities in which athletes experience positive growth and development in a sport context. For example, in a study of adolescents' experiences in sport, positive experiences included opportunities to overcome stress and develop resilience and perseverance, however some athletes reported negative experiences related to an inability to deal with excessive stress in sport (Fraser-Thomas and Côté, 2009). Thus, not all athletes experiencing stress reported positive growth. Further research is needed to determine the personal and situational factors which influence how and why negative experiences can give rise to positive growth among some athletes. By embracing future-oriented models of coping, researchers might be able to explain some of these processes and describe how athletes can learn from past stressors in order to cope more effectively in the future.

Methodological Considerations. With some recent exceptions (e.g., Gaudreau, Lapierre, and Blondin, 2001; Nicholls, Holt, Polman, and James, 2005), the majority of research designs used to examine coping in sport have been based on retrospective recall of past coping efforts (see Nicholls and Polman, 2007a). Such retrospective approaches limit the extent to which anticipatory, preventive, or proactive coping can be assessed. Thus, there are some important methodological issues researchers must consider when using future-oriented models of coping in a sport context. One difficulty in identifying future-oriented coping is that it may preclude some athletes from retrospective studies of stress and coping altogether. In fact, Aspinwall and Taylor (1997) noted that proactive coping may be difficult to detect due to the fact that it focuses on the activities undertaken before the stressor occurs. Subsequently, successful copers may not experience the stressor at all, and thus be excluded from studies of stress and coping because they appear to be well-adjusted, healthy individuals. For example, in the study of 91 Olympic athletes from a range of sports Dugdale et al. (2002) found that 20 participants reported experiencing no stress before or during the Olympics. These athletes *may* have anticipated the stressors they would encounter and coped proactively in order to avoid the stressors or reduce the severity of the stressful encounter.

One way to use future-oriented approaches to coping is by adopting longitudinal and process-oriented research designs including measures of coping at several points in time. Schwarzer and Knoll (2003) recognized that studying positive coping is complicated because it is difficult to know when individuals are engaging in anticipatory, preventive, or proactive coping, or when individuals change their approach to coping with stressors. Measurement of coping using daily process approaches (Tennen, Affleck, Armeli, and Carney, 2000) could be useful for capturing athletes' future-oriented coping. For example, Tamminen (2007) examined patterns of stress and coping among high school basketball players over the course of an entire season and provided profiles of the athletes' proactive and reactive coping efforts. In this study, the athletes completed audio diaries (similar to a tape-recorded journal) following games and practices to record stressors and coping strategies over the entire competitive season. Holt and Dunn (2004) also used audio diaries to record stressors and coping strategies among high-performance female soccer players, and Nicholls (2007; Nicholls et al., 2005; Nicholls and Polman, 2007b) used a combination of daily checklists and open-ended responses to record stressors and coping among golfers and rugby players.

Measuring coping over several phases of a competition or over an entire season is becoming more prevalent among qualitative and quantitative sport coping researchers (e.g., Gaudreau et al., 2001; Holt and Dunn, 2004; Louvet, Gaudreau, Menaut, Genty, and Deneuve, 2007; Nicholls, 2007) and is well-suited to identifying instances of proactive coping among athletes. By examining what athletes do before, during, and after a stressor occurs, researchers may be able to examine more closely how athletes learn from their past experiences to cope more effectively with stressors in the future.

It is also important to identify a possible limitation of adopting a purely future-oriented view of coping. Aspinwall (2005) remarked that there may be some contexts in which planning and proactive coping have negative outcomes. For example, an athlete cannot plan ahead for every stressor that will ever occur in his or her sport. By emphasizing the appraisal and recognition of stressors before they occur, athletes may engage in hypervigilance. Hypervigilance occurs when a person attends to a number of real or imagined potential stressors without coping effectively with any of them (Aspinwall and Taylor, 1997; see also Eubank, Collins, and Smith, 2000). This sort of emphasis on recognition and appraisal of stressors may reduce an athlete's ability to engage in reactive coping when it is necessary to cope with unexpected or unforeseen stressors. Aspinwall and Taylor acknowledged this potential liability and recommended further research into how individuals allocate attention to multiple potential threats.

Applied Considerations. Based on theories and evidence from social psychology and supportive research in sport psychology, we tentatively forward some suggestions for sport psychology practitioners. We suggest that it would be wise to inform athletes of the need to develop a balanced array of both proactive skills (e.g., recognition and appraisal) and reactive coping skills (e.g., cognitive restructuring) in order to deal with a wide range of stressors in sport. This position is supported by Nicholls (2007, 2009), who suggested that practitioners should teach athletes a number of different strategies for coping with stressors, rather than teaching a package of 'one-size-fits-all' coping strategies. Thus, it would appear that having an array of proactive and reactive coping strategies in your athlete's arsenal is a sensible approach to dealing with both expected and unexpected stressors.

CONCLUSION

Elements of future-oriented coping have been described in previous studies of competitive athletes (e.g., Gould et al., 1993; Gould et al., 1999; Orlick and Partington, 1988), and some researchers have examined aspects of future-oriented coping in sport (e.g., Holt et al., 2007; Tamminen, 2007). In this chapter, we presented two models of future-oriented coping which may be useful for examining coping in a sport context. We also presented theoretical, methodological, and applied considerations when using a future-oriented model of coping in sport. These frameworks hold promise for capturing the ways in which athletes respond to stressors, learn about coping, and plan ahead for the future.

ACKNOWLEDGMENTS

During the writing of this chapter the first author was supported by a Doctoral Fellowship from the Social Sciences and Humanities Research Council of Canada, and the second author was supported by the Alberta Heritage Foundation for Medical Research as Population Health Investigator.

REFERENCES

Amiot, C. E., Gaudreau, P., and Blanchard, C. M. (2004). Self-determination, coping, and goal attainment in sport. *Journal of Sport and Exercise Psychology, 26*, 396-411.

Aspinwall, L. G., and Staudinger, U. M. (2003). *A psychology of human strengths: Fundamental questions and future directions for a positive psychology.* Washington: American Psychological Association.

Aspinwall, L. G., and Taylor, S. E. (1997). A stitch in time: Self-regulation and proactive coping. *Psychological Bulletin, 121*, 417-436.

Crocker, P. R., and Graham, T. R. (1995). Coping by competitive athletes with performance stress: Gender differences and relationships with affect. *The Sport Psychologist, 9*, 325-338.

Dugdale, J. R., Eklund, R. C., and Gordon, S. (2002). Expected and unexpected stressors in major international competition: Appraisal, coping and performance. *The Sport Psychologist, 16*, 20-33.

Dworkin, J. B., and Larson, R. (2007). Adolescents' negative experiences in organized youth activities. *Journal of Youth Development, 1*(3). Retrieved March 17, 2009 from http://www.nae4ha.org/directory/jyd/jyd_article.aspx

Eubank, M., Collins, D., and Smith, N. (2000). The influence of anxiety direction on processing bias. *Journal of Sport and Exercise Psychology, 22*, 292-306.

Folkman, S. (2008). The case for positive emotions in the stress process. *Anxiety, Stress and Coping: An International Journal, 21*, 3-14.

Folkman, S., and Moskowitz, J. T. (2000). Positive affect and the other side of coping. *American Psychologist, 55*, 647-654.

Folkman, S., and Moskowitz, J. T. (2004). Coping: Pitfalls and promise. *Annual Review of Psychology, 55*, 745-774.

Fraser-Thomas, J., and Côté, J. (2009). Understanding adolescents' positive and negative developmental experiences in sport. *The Sport Psychologist, 23*, 3-23.

Gaudreau, P., Blondin, J. P., and Lapierre, A. M. (2002). Athletes' coping during a competition: relationship of coping strategies with positive affect, negative affect, and performance-goal discrepancy. *Psychology of Sport and Exercise, 3*, 125-150.

Gaudreau, P., Lapierre, A.-M., and Blondin, J. P. (2001). Coping at three phases of a competition: Comparison between pre-competitive, competitive, and post-competitive utilization of the same strategy. *International Journal of Sport Psychology, 32*, 369-385.

Gould, D., Finch, L. M., and Jackson, S. A. (1993). Coping strategies used by national champion figure skaters. *Research Quarterly for Exercise and Sport, 64*, 453-468.

Gould, D., Guinan, D., Greenleaf, C., Medbery, R., and Peterson, K. (1999). Factors affecting Olympic performance: Perceptions of athletes and coaches from more and less successful teams. *The Sport Psychologist, 13*, 371-394.

Hanson, S. J., McCullagh, P., and Tonymon, P. (1992). The relationship of personality characteristics, life stress, and coping resources to athletic injury. *Journal of Sport and Exercise Psychology, 14*, 262-272.

Hoar, S., Kowalski, K. C., Gaudreau, P., and Crocker, P. R. (2006). A review of coping in sport. In S. Hanton and S. D. Mellalieu (Eds.), *Literature reviews in sport psychology* (pp. 47-90). New York: Nova Science Publishers.

Holt, N. L. (2003). Coping in professional sport: A case study of an experienced cricket player. *Athletic Insight, 5*(1). Retrieved March 20 2006 from http://www.athleticinsight.com/Vol5Iss1/CricketPlayerCoping.htm

Holt, N. L., Berg, K.-J., and Tamminen, K. (2007). Tales of the unexpected: Coping among female collegiate volleyball players. *Research Quarterly for Exercise and Sport, 78*, 117-132.

Holt, N. L., and Dunn, J. G. H. (2004). Longitudinal idiographic analyses of appraisal and coping responses in sport. *Psychology of Sport and Exercise, 5*, 213-222.

Kesimci, A., Goral, F. S., and Gencoz, T. (2005). Determinants of stress-related growth: Gender, stressfulness of event, and coping strategies. *Current Psychology, 24*, 68-75.

Lazarus, R. S. (1999). *Stress and emotion: A new synthesis.* New York: Springer.

Linley, P. A., and Joseph, S. (2004). Positive change following trauma and adversity: a review. *Journal of Traumatic Stress, 17*, 11-21.

Locke, E. A., and Latham, G. P. (1985). The application of goal setting to sports. *Journal of Sport and Exercise Psychology, 7*, 205-222.

Louvet, B., Gaudreau, P., Menaut, A., Genty, J., and Deneuve, P. (2007). Longitudinal patterns of stability and change in coping across three competitions: A latent class growth analysis. *Journal of Sport and Exercise Psychology, 29*, 100-117.

Nicholls, A. (2007). A longitudinal phenomenological analysis of coping effectiveness among Scottish international adolescent golfers. *European Journal of Sport Science, 7*, 169-178.

Nicholls, A. (2009). Stressors and coping strategies among early and middle adolescent premier league academy soccer players: Differences according to age. *Journal of Applied Sport Psychology, 21*, 31-48.

Nicholls, A., Holt, N. L., Polman, R. C. J., and James, D. W. G. (2005). Stress and coping among international adolescent golfers. *Journal of Applied Sport Psychology, 17*, 333-340.

Nicholls, A., and Polman, R. C. J. (2007a). Coping in sport: A systematic review. *Journal of Sports Sciences, 25*, 11-31.

Nicholls, A., and Polman, R. C. J. (2007b). Stressors, coping, and coping effectiveness among players from the England under-18 rugby union team. *Journal of Sport Behavior, 30*(2), 199-218.

Orlick, T., and Partington, J. (1988). Mental links to excellence. *The Sport Psychologist, 2*, 105-130.

Park, C. L., Cohen, L. H., and Murch, R. L. (1996). Assessment and prediction of stress-related growth. *Journal of Personality, 64*, 71-105.

Poczwardowski, A., and Conroy, D. E. (2002). Coping responses to failure and success among elite athletes and performing artists. *Journal of Applied Sport Psychology, 14*, 313-329.

Raedeke, T. D., and Smith, A. L. (2004). Coping resources and athlete burnout: An examination of stress mediated and moderation hypotheses. *Journal of Sport and Exercise Psychology, 26*, 525-541.

Schwarzer, R., and Knoll, N. (2003). Positive coping: Mastering demands and searching for meaning. In S. J. Lopez and C. R. Snyder (Eds.), *Positive psychological assessment: A handbook of models and measures* (pp. 393-409). Washington: American Psychological Association.

Tamminen, K. (2007). *Proactive coping among female adolescent athletes.* Unpublished doctoral dissertation, University of Alberta.

Tennen, H., Affleck, G., Armeli, S., and Carney, M. A. (2000). A daily process approach to coping: Linking theory, research, and practice. *American Psychologist, 55*, 626-636.

Wilson, M., Chattington, M., Marple-Horvat, D. E., and Smith, N. C. (2007). A comparison of self-focus versus attentional explanations of choking. *Journal of Sport and Exercise Psychology, 29*, 439-456.

INDEX

motion, 206
motivation, x, 14, 25, 32, 38, 53, 55, 58, 62, 63,
    73, 74, 99, 107, 115, 124, 136, 143, 149, 164,
    170, 172, 177, 179, 180, 181, 182, 183, 184,
    185, 186, 188, 189, 190, 191, 192, 193, 195,
    196, 199, 203, 208, 209, 210, 211, 212, 213,
    214, 219, 222, 225, 232, 233, 236, 246, 257,
    258, 280, 282, 283, 290, 294, 300
motives, x, 148, 177, 204, 219, 224
motor task, 168, 241, 291
motor vehicle accident, 285
movement, 167, 168, 169, 170, 259, 294
MS, 191
MTI, 149
multicultural, 135, 136, 137
multidimensional, 49, 93, 119, 136, 218, 233,
    235, 292
multiple regression, 59, 60, 205
multiple regression analysis, 60
multivariate, 27, 31, 206
multivariate modeling, 27
muscle, 287, 289, 296
muscle relaxation, 289
muscles, 231
music, 7, 97

N

NA, 85
naming, 146
narcissism, 245
narratives, 66, 68
National Football League, 246
National Football League (NFL), 246
nationality, 58, 62
natural, 17, 28, 65, 169, 252
NBA, 253
Nebraska, 190, 192
neck, 168
negative affectivity, 143, 147
negative consequences, 3, 226
negative coping, 209
negative emotions, 4, 143, 181, 223, 235, 264,
    281, 300
negative experiences, 172, 227, 300, 301, 303
negative mood, 146, 286
negative outcomes, 302
negative relation, 63
negative valence, 246, 249
negativity, 172
neglect, 124
negotiating, 182
negotiation, 182, 236

nervousness, 103, 162
Netherlands, 157, 249, 256, 258
network, 297
neuroendocrine, 80, 235
neurotic, ix, 141, 145, 153, 157
neuroticism, ix, 87, 92, 141, 143, 144, 145, 146,
    147, 153, 155
New Jersey, 92, 93
New York, 11, 12, 13, 30, 31, 32, 48, 49, 50, 71,
    72, 73, 74, 75, 90, 91, 92, 112, 113, 115, 134,
    135, 136, 137, 138, 153, 154, 155, 156, 172,
    173, 174, 188, 189, 190, 191, 192, 193, 213,
    230, 231, 232, 233, 234, 235, 236, 237, 243,
    254, 255, 256, 257, 259, 275, 290, 291, 292,
    304
Newton, 203, 213, 246, 258
NFL, 246, 247
nomothetic approach, 20, 22, 23
nonparametric, 59
norepinephrine, 284
normal, 130, 149, 168, 254
norms, 64, 99, 116, 123, 133, 147, 185
North America, 55, 56
Norway, 255
novelty, 109
nuclear power, 251
nuclear power plant, 251
nurses, 157
nutrition, 296, 297

O

objectivity, 68
obligation, 132
observations, 40, 56, 107, 161, 206
occupational, 150, 157
old age, 5
older adults, 108, 291
Olympic Games, 16, 40
olympics, 112
oncology, 14
one dimension, 10
onion, 154
openness, ix, 141, 146, 147
openness to experience, ix, 141, 146
opposition, 101
optimal performance, 131, 166, 167, 168, 169,
    170
optimism, 29, 36, 50, 113, 124, 126, 127, 132,
    133, 151, 156, 237
optimization, 160
organism, 122, 162, 181
organizational stress, 47, 212

Q